PRAISE FOR
THE DEAD AND THOSE ABOUT TO DIE

"John C. McManus's brilliant chronicle of the Big Red One's experience on bloody Omaha captures the grit, pathos, and valor of the battle like no other book that I have read. This is gripping history—beautifully and masterfully told by one of America's premier historians."
　　—Patrick K. O'Donnell, national bestselling author of *Dog Company*

"Magnificent! I could not put this book down. John C. McManus has expanded our knowledge of D-Day history by a considerable factor. It is a great read and will appeal to both devoted students of World War II as well as those with a more casual interest. Don't miss it!"
　　—Joseph Balkoski, author of *Omaha Beach* and *Utah Beach*

"At first I thought I would draw the reader's attention to the simply magnificent narrative of one of the most famous and gripping events of modern military history, the nineteen-hours epic of the First Division's landing, purgatory, and then near-exhausted triumph at Omaha Beach on June 6, 1944. Then I thought I would draw the attention of my professional fellow historians to the outstanding set of notes and oral histories, so neatly tucked away at the end, superb scholarship but worn so lightly. But finally I had to choose its ending, the chapter called Meaning, on the thoughts, emotions, and later lives of this remarkable group of warriors. I closed this book with the deepest respect."
　　—Paul Kennedy, *New York Times* bestselling author of *Engineers of Victory*
and *The Rise and Fall of Great Powers*

"With painstaking research, military historian John C. McManus delves behind the broader canvas of Omaha Beach to capture the courage, grit, and sacrifice of the 1st Division's D-Day landing. This is as real as it gets without having been there."
　　—Walter R. Borneman, national bestselling author of *The Admirals*

continued . . .

"*The Dead and Those About to Die* is a gripping account of the desperate battle for Omaha Beach on D-Day by the legendary 1st Infantry Division, the Big Red One. On the seventieth anniversary of that momentous event, John C. McManus's tale of courage under fire is a vivid reminder that freedom isn't free and that when the chips are down stalwart American soldiers will always answer the call of duty."
—Carlo D'Este, author of *Patton: A Genius for War* and *Warlord: A Life of Churchill at War, 1874–1945*

"A skilled and highly talented author, John McManus has delivered another first-rate piece of scholarship. *The Dead and Those About to Die* is a tour de force of historical writing."
—Robert von Maier, editor-in-chief of *Global War Studies*

"In vivid and chilling detail, this brilliantly organized battle narrative immortalizes the 1st Division's assault on Omaha Beach. Having unearthed eyewitness accounts of courage, carnage, fear, and leadership never told before, McManus's masterful work deserves a place alongside those of Cornelius Ryan, Stephen Ambrose, and Rick Atkinson."
—David L. Roll, author of *The Hopkins Touch*

"John C. McManus has created a portrait with words as Spielberg did with images in *Saving Private Ryan*. Of course, creating such a vivid picture with words is, for my money, far more difficult."
—Paul Reid, coauthor of *The Last Lion: Winston Spencer Churchill, Defender of the Realm, 1940–1965*

"McManus elicits moving details of courage and hardship . . . an exciting account from the personable point of view of the soldier." —*Kirkus Reviews*

"[A] powerful book." —*St. Louis Post-Dispatch*

ALSO BY JOHN C. MCMANUS

Fire and Fortitude:
The US Army in the Pacific War, 1941–1943

Hell Before Their Very Eyes:
American Soldiers Liberate Concentration Camps
in Germany, April 1945

September Hope:
The American Side of a Bridge Too Far

Grunts:
Inside the American Infantry Combat Experience,
World War II Through Iraq

American Courage, American Carnage:
The 7th Infantry Regiment's Combat Experience,
1812 Through World War II

The 7th Infantry Regiment:
Combat in an Age of Terror, the Korean War Through the Present

U.S. Military History for Dummies

Alamo in the Ardennes:
The Untold Story of the American Soldiers
Who Made the Defense of Bastogne Possible

The Americans at Normandy:
The Summer of 1944—The American War from
the Normandy Beaches to Falaise

The Americans at D-Day:
The American Experience at the Normandy Invasion

Deadly Sky:
The American Combat Airman in World War II

The Deadly Brotherhood:
The American Combat Soldier in World War II

THE DEAD
AND THOSE ABOUT
TO DIE

D-Day: The Big Red One at Omaha Beach

John C. McManus

CALIBER

Dutton Caliber
An imprint of Penguin Random House LLC
penguinrandomhouse.com

Previously published as an NAL Caliber hardcover and trade paperback edition
First Dutton Caliber edition: June 2019

Copyright © 2014 by John C. McManus
Maps illustrated by Rick Britton. Copyright © by 2014 Rick Britton
For insert photo credits, see pages 357–58.

THE LIBRARY OF CONGRESS HAS CATALOGUED THE HARDCOVER EDITION AS FOLLOWS:
McManus, John C., 1965–
The dead and those about to die: D-Day:
the Big Red One at Omaha Beach/John C. McManus.
p.   cm.
Includes bibliographical references and index.
1. World War, 1939–1945—Campaigns—France—Normandy.
2. United States. Army. Infantry Division, lst—History—20th century.
3. World War, 1939–1945—Regimental histories—United States. I. Title.
D756.5.N6M37   2014
940.54'21422—dc23   2013044309

Dutton Caliber ISBN: 9781524745509

Printed in the United States of America
10   9   8   7   6   5   4   3   2   1

Set in Adobe Caslon

CONTENTS

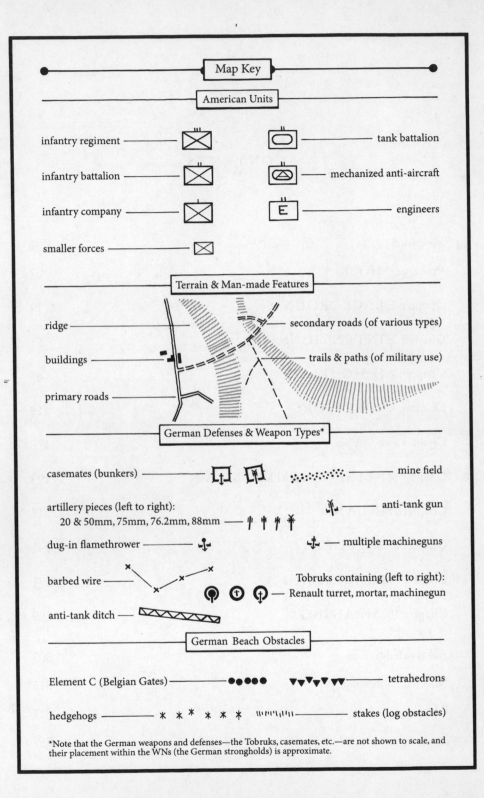

Map Key

American Units

infantry regiment

tank battalion

infantry battalion

mechanized anti-aircraft

infantry company

engineers

smaller forces

Terrain & Man-made Features

ridge

secondary roads (of various types)

buildings

trails & paths (of military use)

primary roads

German Defenses & Weapon Types*

casemates (bunkers)

mine field

artillery pieces (left to right):
20 & 50mm, 75mm, 76.2mm, 88mm

anti-tank gun

dug-in flamethrower

multiple machineguns

barbed wire

Tobruks containing (left to right):
Renault turret, mortar, machinegun

anti-tank ditch

German Beach Obstacles

Element C (Belgian Gates)

tetrahedrons

hedgehogs

stakes (log obstacles)

*Note that the German weapons and defenses—the Tobruks, casemates, etc.—are not shown to scale, and their placement within the WNs (the German strongholds) is approximate.

MAPS

"The First Division from top to bottom believed it was the best infantry division in the United States Army—and conducted itself accordingly. In all its battles in Africa, Sicily, France, Belgium and Germany, there never was one quite like the battle of Omaha Beach. In that battle alone the Fighting First won a niche among the immortals of American history."

—Don Whitehead

To the soldiers of the Big Red One,
no matter the generation

To my family:
Big Mama, Pops, Mike, and Nancy

*In grateful appreciation for the substantial
support provided by the First Division Museum at Cantigny.*

FOREWORD

Desperate. Hellish. Disastrous. Catastrophic. Traumatic. Shocking. Bloody.

Anyone who was at Omaha beach on June 6, 1944—especially in the morning or early afternoon of that momentous day—is likely to have used one or more of those powerful words to describe it. At Omaha beach, the stakes were so high, and the fighting so bitter, that the very name evokes something legendary, even iconic. Originally dubbed "Beach 46" by Allied planners in the spring of 1944, this four-and-a-half-mile strip of rocky Norman coastline is now hallowed ground, as is the sprawling cliffside military cemetery that broods over it like a melancholy sentinel. The battle fought at Omaha beach is among the most famous in American history, occupying a solid niche in the cultural memory alongside such iconic bloodlettings as Bunker Hill, Antietam, Gettysburg, the Bulge, and Iwo Jima. Omaha beach is a symbol, a powerful tale of extreme adversity and ultimate victory.

Amid the sand and stone of this troubled, fire-swept beach, a drama played out that helped decide the future of humanity. Indeed there is something so compelling, so *significant*, about Omaha beach that all my life I have been irresistibly drawn to it, like the proverbial moth to a flame. I have spent a quarter century studying it intently, first as a young tourist, later as a Normandy scholar, eventually as a battlefield historian and author of a book on the Normandy invasion. And I have come to believe that Omaha beach is better known than it is understood; that in spite of several outstanding works by excellent historians, and at least one brilliant film portraying the fighting, there is actually more to the story. The battle for Omaha—not to mention the Normandy invasion of which it was just one part—was such a vast, complicated, multilayered saga that it is still possible to gain new insights about it. I think the key to these new insights centers around the 1st Infantry Division and the ferocious battle it fought to secure the eastern section of the beach. By the spring of 1944, the Big Red One was arguably the most combat-experienced, and certainly the most cocksure, division in the Army. Only the equally accomplished 3rd Infantry Division could match—or exceed, in the view of that division's self-proclaimed dogface soldiers— the combat record of the 1st Infantry Division. Though the Big Red One had suffered heavy casualties in North Africa and Sicily, plenty of veterans remained to lead the way at Omaha, along with a vast array of combat-tested leaders, staff officers, and specialists. As a result, the division carried with it a distinct identity as rebellious and resentful (even mischievous in garrison) but extremely reliable and effective in combat. The division could fight and it could produce results. It was perceived by the American high command as the first string, tempestuous perhaps, but talented and dedicated, a go-to outfit. Twenty years after D-Day, General Omar Bradley, in retirement, would write, "Thank God for the First Division. Any inexperienced division might not have made it that day."[1]

Yet, curiously, the 1st Division's critical role at Omaha beach has tended to be overshadowed—at least in historical memory—by the equally serious fight of the 29th Infantry Division and U.S. Army Rangers elsewhere at Omaha. The most famous example is Steven

Spielberg's masterful, searing portrayal of the fighting at Dog Green beach, located in the heart of the 29th Division sector, in his enormously influential film *Saving Private Ryan*. This inclination toward the 29th's side of the beach actually began with the first chroniclers of D-Day, the Army combat historians who conducted after-action interviews with survivors. They produced 372 pages of interviews and reports on the 29th, and 300 more on the Rangers, as opposed to 83 pages on the Big Red One. This set the tone for the many fine works historians have written on D-Day over the subsequent decades, from Cornelius Ryan's *The Longest Day* to Stephen Ambrose's *D-Day*. Indeed, my own book *The Americans at D-Day* includes only 8 pages on the 1st. Even the great Joseph Balkoski, in his seminal work *Omaha Beach*, leaned toward the 29th for the perfectly logical reason that he is the historian of that division and knows more about it than any other human being on the planet (he has since written a multivolume history of the 29th). Only Flint Whitlock, in his splendidly written volume *The Fighting First*, has specifically focused on the Big Red One. My hope is to build upon the foundation that he and the other accomplished historians have established, not out of some esoteric, misguided, and ultimately useless desire to prove the superiority of the 1st over the 29th, but with the goal of improving upon our knowledge and understanding of the battle for Omaha beach.

For this purpose, I have drawn upon what I believe is a strikingly rich blend of sources. This book is based on every relevant contemporary and postwar source, including after-action reports, combat interviews, historical narratives, historical studies, unit journals, unit critiques, letters, diaries, unpublished memoirs, oral histories, personal interviews, staff rides, articles, analytical papers, photographs, diagrams, books, Internet sources, as well as my own multiple surveys of the battlefield and a nice cache of veterans' accounts, interviews and correspondence with veterans that I have collected over many years of studying the invasion. Needless to say, D-Day was a heavily documented event and there is thus no shortage of good source material for historians, enough to penetrate many layers of legend and get to the heart of what actually happened at Omaha and what it was like. My hope is to produce a fair and compelling portrait of the stark and mortal drama that unfolded along that beach all those years ago. Moreover, I believe the details of this story can yield answers to many questions still unanswered about Omaha beach: Why did the 1st Division succeed amid such horrendous circumstances? How did the division train for the invasion and was that training useful on D-Day? What sort of personalities tended to triumph over this kind of adversity? Did veterans fight better than replacements or vice versa? Who were the real leaders on that bloody beach? How much effect did senior officers have, if any, on the actual fighting? What kind of decisions led to success and what kind led to failure? What impact did the Big Red One's battle at Omaha have on the Normandy invasion as a whole?

At the height of the fighting, when utter disaster at Omaha seemed a real possibility to nearly everyone who was there, Colonel George Taylor, the commander of the division's lead assault regiment on D-Day, strode along the beach—risking death and dismemberment with every confident step—and uttered the day's most famous words: "Only two kinds of people are going to be on this beach, the dead and those who are going to die. Now get moving!" He knew that he had to lead by personal example, with clear orders, conveyed with the most inspiring demeanor he could conjure up in spite of his acute fear. In fact, the phrase had been bouncing around in his mind for many months; he did not make it up on the spot. But it did yield some insight into this man and perhaps even the division as a whole. Taylor inherently understood that in war the human factor was paramount. "Personality is the most important element in the conduct of war," he once wrote; "it may be said that it affects almost everything."[2]

Omaha beach was a prime example of this truth and also of a recurring pattern in American military history—the tendency to place

too much confidence in technology, firepower, and matériel for the ful-
fillment of important objectives. At Omaha, practically all of the preparatory firepower failed miserably, as did some of the top secret
inventions designed to assist the assault troops. The battle came down
to individuals carrying out extremely valorous acts of the sort that were
useful for the success of the mission. Taylor and many thousands of
other soldiers on the beach that day came to know this, not out of any
keen historical insight, but because their very lives depended upon it.
This is their story.

Prologue

SHOCK

All the beauty of the world was gone. Nothing mattered now except this brutal moment, and survival. It was almost as if everything that came before—home, childhood, family, maybe even previous battle experiences—had never really happened. Or perhaps all of that simply no longer had any significance. The same could be said of the future—if indeed there was to be a future for any of them. Actually, to some, the very idea that there could even be a future seemed absurd in the extreme. Instead, there was only the ugly, overwhelming, drab, miserable here and now, and it was stunning beyond imagination. Death lurked everywhere—in the rough waters, on the ramps of wobbly landing craft, in every wet grain of sand, behind every log or steel obstacle, alongside every mine, buried or unburied, near the blanket of smooth stones that composed a bizarre-looking shingle. There was nowhere to hide, at least not for any real safety, and certainly there was nowhere to escape. They were trapped, quite possibly even doomed.

Such moments of extreme, imminent physical danger produce a distinct set of physiological symptoms, generally known as Condition Black, in human beings. The heart rate shoots up dramatically. Stress hormones surge through the bloodstream. The intense fear constricts blood vessels, diminishes hearing, narrows vision, even paralyzes the nervous system, leading to loss of motor skills. Faces turn white. Hands shake. Eyes blink uncontrollably. Voices quaver. Bowels empty or constrict painfully. The ability to reason and think critically is gone. The terror produces a state of physical shock, reducing the person to little more than a panicked animal, desperately trying to survive yet capable only of cowering or hiding.[1]

Few, if any, of the leading assault troops at the Easy Red and Fox Green sectors of Omaha beach on D-Day morning thought in such terms, though most of them experienced the symptoms to some degree. These men knew only that they were in real trouble. The volume of German fire on the beach and at the waterline was staggering— 50-millimeter mortars, machine guns, uncannily accurate rifles, artillery, including at least one 88-millimeter gun, antitank guns, and plenty of mines. "The situation on the beach was critical, and at times looked very black," one company after-action report related. Another spoke of men who "waded and struggled ashore by crossing two hundred yards of open beach under intense enemy fire. Many men were hit and injured while still in the water." To Lieutenant John Spalding, a platoon leader in E Company, 16th Infantry Regiment, "it looked as if they were walking in the face of a real strong wind."

The "wind" in this case consisted literally of bullets and fragments in such volume as to physically hinder normal movement. All along the haphazard landing spots where soldiers struggled ashore, German fire laced into and around them. "Men . . . could be seen wading ashore into the face of intense fire," Captain Edward Wozenski, the commander of E Company, wrote in an after-action report. "Due to the heavy sea, the strong cross current and the loads that the men were carrying, no one could run. It was just a slow, methodical march with absolutely no cover." He watched helplessly as a couple of his men set off underwater mines that blew them out of the sea, into the air, only to splash back down into the waves. "You're up and down, you're in water and then you're ducking," he added years later in an interview. "Small arms and everything's flying all around so you duck down. You're terrified as anyone could be. It was bloody awful."

Nearby, one of his sergeants, Lawrence Fitzsimmons, saw two men in his squad, Privates Peter Walsh and Robert Spencer, run past the waterline, flop down into the sand and "then be blown bodily into the air by mines buried on the beach." Both were killed instantly. Lieutenant Rob Huch was scrambling mightily just to make it out of the water. "The machine gun fire was intense—it came from so many different directions and places, it's unbelievable. The water was deep—the only thing to do was go in. All the way in through the water, the bullets were splashing right in front of my nose, on both sides and everywhere." He made it to the beach—praying fervently every step of the way—only to come under even more accurate fire as he weaved his way around clusters of obstacles, stopping and starting every few yards. "At one point when I hit the sand, a burst went through my pack, radio and canteen. At another point a mortar hit about ten feet away—the concussion knocked me out for a few seconds."

Elsewhere, Private Frank King, a radio operator, started moving deliberately across the beach, only to enter right into the sights of an unseen German machine gunner. "You could see . . . those machine gun bullets hitting in that . . . wet sand. You couldn't hear it, you could see the sand flop up." Somehow the enemy gunner did not hit him. Many others were not as fortunate. As Staff Sergeant Donald Wilson of F Company thrashed through chin-high water, he looked back and asked Private First Class Peter Loney, a machine gunner in his unit, if he was okay. "No sooner had he said that he was, when he seemed to be driven backward by some unseen blow, slowly sinking under water"

(Loney was wounded but survived). Wilson kept going and stumbled onto the sand only to witness something detonate a TNT satchel charge on the back of Private First Class Norman Spechler, obliterating him in an instant. "The burlap, used to strap the TNT blocks together, fluttered down and lay smoldering on the sand." Small pieces of Spechler lay in every direction for ten feet. "The biggest was as big as my fist and just as white as snow," Private William Funkhouser, a mortarman who was pinned down nearby, recalled. Funkhouser was transfixed and terrified by the gory remnants of Spechler in front of him. "I can't crawl through that," he thought. He tried to get up and run, but he was so frightened that his legs gave out and he fell down. "You can't imagine how scared I was," he later said. He threw away his mortar tube, closed his eyes, and crawled over the body parts.

At nearly the same instant, Lieutenant Howard Pearre, the company executive officer, took a direct hit from an antitank gun. "Most of his torso lay just where it happened, but his helmet sailed upward, almost in slow motion, finally landing," Staff Sergeant Wilson said. Staff Sergeant Ben Telinda watched in horror as one of his good friends, Technical Sergeant John Plichta, got blown apart by yet another direct hit from an antitank shell. Earlier that morning Plichta had brashly told Telinda and several other buddies: "The Germans haven't made the bullet yet that would get me."

Looking for any surcease from the overwhelming firepower that was sweeping the expanse of the beach, some men sought the dubious cover afforded by obstacles. Private First Class Onda Murphy, a Browning Automatic Rifleman (or BAR man), settled alongside an upright log obstacle—designed to impede or destroy landing craft, they looked like horizontal telephone poles to the Americans—and began unleashing bursts at the unseen Germans on the high ground that loomed over the beach. "All at once, he practically disappeared with the post," Private First Class Paul McCormick recalled. "A German mine was on top of the post and exploded" when a bullet struck the mine. Private Clarence Cox clustered alongside a couple of other soldiers behind a steel tetrahedron, but soon noticed two disquieting things: the obstacle was mined and German gunners were using it as an aiming point. "Another buddy beside me raised his head up, and a bullet entered the side of his steel helmet and traveled around and got the tip of his ear on the other side as it came out." The close call had the effect of enraging the stunned man. "He got up on his knees and started giving the enemy a stern lecture. I shouted for him to get down; to lay still before he got us both killed."

The bodies of men who had been hit in the water or at the waterline of the beach began washing ashore with the rising tide. Some were dead. Others were wounded. In some places they lay two and three deep, rolling and ebbing with the surf. Merciless strands of machine-gun bullets stitched the sand and fizzed the water into and alongside them. Staff Sergeant Wilson saw one of the bodies thrashing in the water, desperately trying to get ashore. He recognized the wet lump as a BAR man from his outfit and ran to the water to drag him onto the beach. "He must have been weakening fast because, as I got there, he sort of collapsed on me." Wilson was overwhelmed by the task of dragging the big man, plus the twenty-pound automatic rifle strapped to his back, out of the sea. They bobbed in and out of the waves and washed ashore because of the tide more than anything else. "I pulled him up on the bank as far as I could. He seemed conscious, eyes open and moving." Then Wilson rolled him over onto his back and saw a gaping wound in the man's abdomen. He emitted a loud sigh and died. Wilson managed to unstrap his BAR, grab a few cartridges, and crawl several yards up the beach. "I came upon Lt. [Glendon] Seifert, flat on his back, just staring blankly, shot through the throat, just below the Adam's apple. His chest was covered with blood, which was continuing to pump slowly from the wound." He knew there was nothing he could do for the lieutenant. He died in a matter of moments.

In another spot, Private Clayton "Ray" Voight, a BAR man, came upon his friend Private Eddie Saucier, a flamethrower man, lying behind a log obstacle. Saucier was wearing two sets of clothes to ward off the wet and cold (a fairly common practice on D-Day). Like many other men that terrible morning, Saucier needed to empty his bowels—immediately. Yet he could not free himself of his heavy clothes and equipment. "He wanted me to cut his pants open so he could relieve himself," Voight said. He promptly retrieved his knife and cut open the seat of Saucier's trousers, something that the young BAR man thought back on later as a surreal example of the stupor permeating him and so many others. "Yet they say I wasn't in shock," he said of doubters whom he had encountered in his life. "I had to be in *something*." After cutting open Saucier's trousers, Voight advanced a few yards up the beach, only to look back and watch as the flamethrower man took a fatal hit. "He put up his arms sideways, and then just went in a round circle and slowly just went right on down . . . and that was where he stayed." Voight had promised Saucier that if he got killed, he would retrieve his wallet and send it, along with a consolation letter, to Saucier's fiancée in Harper, Connecticut. But Voight could not bring himself to go back into the killing zone where Saucier had been hit.

Medics had no choice but to circulate into the worst places, right within the most devastating cones of fire, especially near the waterline, where so many wounded men lay writhing and flailing for life. Some had already weakened and drowned. Others were half dead. "The tide was rising and many of them were doomed to drown if nobody came to their help," Private First Class Charles Shay, one of the F Company medics, later wrote. "I left what I was doing and returned to the sea which was red with the blood of the dead and wounded. I began pulling the wounded up beyond the waterline by grabbing them under their armpits." He successfully extracted several stricken men and administered first aid, sprinkling sulfa powder onto wounds, bandaging them up, often injecting delirious men with syrettes of morphine. "I do not know where my strength came from." Most likely, adrenaline accounted for his enhanced muscle power and resolve. "I cannot really describe the horror and words cannot do justice to the suffering, the heroism, the chaos on that beach."[2]

The ferocious enemy opposition was bad enough, but the assault troops were dealing with other serious problems as well. Most were carrying onerously heavy loads of equipment, seventy to eighty pounds on average. In many cases, this was equivalent to half or more of a man's body weight. A few were even lugging two-thirds of their own weight. Some units had been issued special olive-drab-colored amphibious assault vests (generally called invasion vests), a load-bearing garment similar in appearance to a hunting vest. "The staggering loads of equipment and ammunition would be almost impossible to carry with our conventional straps and bags," Lieutenant William Joseph wrote. As a communications specialist, he lugged 130 pounds of gear.

The average man carried extra shoes, extra clothing, rations, a haversack, a web waist belt, blankets, tent equipment, an entrenching tool, and such personal items as books, cigarettes, cameras, and the like. Private First Class John MacPhee was a telling example. The young rifleman/demolitions man weighed all of 125 pounds, yet he was hauling about 85 pounds of kit. "I always felt we were burdened down with too much weight," he said. "We became pack mules on the first wave. Our life expectancy was zero."

To some extent, this considerable burden was a necessary evil because the assault troops needed heavy weapons such as bazookas, flamethrowers, Bangalore torpedoes, TNT, and mortars to fight and survive once ashore. They also needed ammo and lots of it. More than that, though, the unreasonably heavy loads stemmed from the flawed notion that once the troops got ashore, it might be difficult to resupply them during the fight to secure a beachhead in Normandy. This was in spite of the fact that the Allies enjoyed complete mastery of the sea and air, with a fleet of more than five thousand ships and ten thousand airplanes, not to mention a logistical buildup of matériel in England unsurpassed in world history. This concern over supply during the early stages of the invasion was really a hangover from the failed Dieppe raid of two years earlier when the Allies enjoyed none of these advantages and a Canadian raiding force was more or less annihilated. These concerns no longer applied in the summer of 1944, yet the planners acted as if they did. The Allies intended to land so many troops and vehicles under such a relentless timetable, and with so much shipping available, that men on the beach—even those who were pinned down—would not be likely to run out of supplies. Even if they did run low on food or water, this paucity of provisions was unlikely to last for long under such circumstances. It really only made sense to load up on ammunition. All other needs were ancillary. Nonetheless, the assault troops paid the price for this flawed planning. "Soldiers were having a difficult time trying to wade ashore burdened with their equipment, which consisted of weapons, extra ammunition, packs, rations and gas masks, while being subjected to small arms and artillery and mortar fire," Captain Fred Hall, the operations officer (S3) of 2nd Battalion, 16th Infantry explained. Thus, at the very moment when the troops most needed agility and quickness, they could hardly move, especially since they were soaked to the skin and covered with sand.

Moreover, most had become very seasick during the two-hour ride into the beach aboard their bobbing and bucking Higgins boats. The experience was absolutely miserable. Waves of nausea engulfed them. Many vomited in their relief bags or onto the deck of their boat or even onto one another. They felt weak and shaky, with spaghetti legs and chalky faces. In one landing craft, a soldier lay immobilized with seasickness, impervious to any command to get out of the boat. A fellow soldier promptly picked him up and hurled him over the side, into the chest-high water.

The seasickness and the dread of combat weakened their bowels, too. "It was far more than just sickness," Captain Wozenski said. "Men loaded their pants and everything else." The stench of diesel fumes, feces, and vomit was disgusting. The men were wearing specially impregnated amphibious uniforms to protect their skin in the event that the Germans used poison gas against them. The protective chemicals made the uniforms look and feel slick and shiny. They also made them stink like sour milk, thus earning the nickname skunk suits, and this only added to the soldiers' nausea. Nor did the sickness abate once they reached the beach—if anything, it grew worse as it evolved from seasickness to the gut-stabbing cramps of primal fear. "Some of the men froze on the beach," Sergeant Fitzsimmons said, "wretched with seasickness and fear, refusing to move." Lieutenant Joseph was deeply struck by "the apathy of the men toward death. As we lay on the beach, shoulder to shoulder, with our feet in the water, the tide kept rising . . . and I saw men watch their comrades die and not reach out a hand to pull them up. They had a dazed and unreal look. In all our combat operations . . . I never saw the shocked condition repeated."

Private First Class MacPhee, like so many of his comrades, was young and in excellent physical condition, yet it hardly mattered under these woeful circumstances. "I could walk for miles, could endure a great deal of physical hardship . . . but I was so seasick that I thought I would die. In fact, I wished I had. I didn't care if Adolf Hitler was waiting for me. I was scared to death." Like so many hundreds of other men who were flailing around in the water or along the beach, he was completely exhausted, in nearly the worst possible condition to fight. Quite a few were so sick and so spent that they hardly cared if they lived or died. They crawled forward or simply lay still, hoping just to feel better, even if that meant death. Those who were able to keep moving and shoot back often found their weapons fouled or inoperable from sand or seawater. In many cases, they huddled behind obstacles, stripped their weapons down and, usually with shaky hands, cleaned them as best they could. Sometimes waterlogged or sand-choked radios failed, hindering communications. The men needed all their strength, physical and otherwise, to fight against a well-fortified enemy now, but instead they were at their lowest ebb, in their worst fighting trim.

Perhaps the greatest shock was the abject and total failure of the supporting preparatory fire. The Air Force had dropped its bombs too far inland. The naval bombardment had damaged some of the German pillboxes and frightened many of the enemy soldiers, but it had done little else. Rocket-bearing ships had unloosed their loads either short of the beach or in scattered, useless patterns. Most of the supporting duplex-drive amphibious tanks had sunk in the rough seas. In total, the pre-invasion bombardment in the 1st Division sector had slightly wounded one German soldier, probably caused a few others to flee, and wrecked two of their automatic flamethrowers; otherwise the effect was next to nil. "Supporting fires were of absolutely no consequence on Omaha [Easy] Red beach," Lieutenant Colonel Herbert Hicks, commander of the 2nd Battalion, 16th Infantry wrote in an after-action critique. "The Air Corps might just as well have stayed home in bed for all the good that their bombing concentration did."

Yet the troops had been briefed to expect great results from all the pyrotechnics, prompting hopes of an open, undefended beach, or at least a beach honeycombed with craters that could be utilized for cover. "As the men came onto the beach the greatest disappointment to them was discovery that it had not been touched," Major Edwin Elder, the operations officer of the 3rd Battalion, 16th Infantry later wrote. "Finding no craters, those men who lived to reach the beach started desperately to dig holes in the sand, but the high waves filled them with water." For those who were new to combat, this divergence between theory and reality was stunning and demoralizing, only adding to their terror. Cynical, skeptical veterans, like Brooklyn-born Sergeant Vincent Michael McKinney, who had fought in North Africa and Sicily, felt nothing but resentment when they emerged from the water and realized the truth of the situation. "They [briefers] told us [we'd] probably be able to walk in there unmolested. There wasn't a hole on that beach. Not one did I see. Not a bomb. [The] barbed wire was still there. Everything was still there." He shook his head angrily and thought to himself, "You sons of bitches!"

Captain Wozenski, pinned down on the beach, watching his men die all around him, wondered bitterly what exactly had happened to the 186 tons of "pinpoint" bombs the Air Force was supposed to provide for his E Company objective alone, along with nine thousand rockets that were supposed to have saturated his section of the beach. Nothing of the kind had materialized. "The prime lesson . . . was that the theorists still give undue weight to the actual effects of supporting weapons—Army, Navy, and Air," he later summed up perfectly.

At Omaha beach, the American planners fell prey to a long-standing pattern in their history—the tendency to overestimate the effectiveness of firepower and technological savvy. In reality, on D-Day morning, the preparatory bombardment failed miserably. Instead of walking over the wrecked remnants of enemy beach defenses and policing up the stunned survivors, the soldiers of the Big Red One found themselves involved in a death struggle with profound implications for the outcome of World War II and, in a larger sense, for the future course of world history. "To cross 400 yards of low water beach and climb a formidable bluff to the enemy's main defenses was little short of murder," Wozenski opined. Maybe so, but it was the brutal reality at the Easy Red and Fox Green sectors of Omaha beach. Wozenski and the others would either succeed or die. There was, for most, nowhere to retreat, nowhere to hide. The beach offered two main outcomes—death or victory. No one in the 1st Infantry Division was truly prepared to deal with this nightmare, but they were trained for it, and that was about to make all the difference.[3]

Chapter 1

BACKGROUND

Seven months earlier, almost to the day, a gloomy autumn mist blanketed the docks of Liverpool. The early November air was chilly but crisp and invigorating. By the thousands, soldiers of the 1st Infantry Division, many of whom were hard-core survivors of bitter fighting in North Africa and Sicily, descended wooden gangways and set foot upon the venerable soil of England. A band played "Dixie," followed by "The Sidewalks of New York." As the soldiers made their way to troop trains, a bevy of sharply contrasting emotions pervaded their ranks. Some were just happy to be out of combat. Many daydreamed about the pleasures Britain offered—pubs, beer, liquor, sightseeing, shelter, running water, but most of all, women. Some of those who had been with the division during its pre-combat training in Britain the year before looked forward to renewing acquaintances with British friends. In several instances, men were so excited that they let out spontaneous whoops of joy. "You can imagine the crescendo that crushed the ears of all within miles," Captain Joe Dawson, a company commander, wrote to his family in an attempt to describe the exaltation of his men.

But there was an undercurrent of tension and gloom, too. The return to England could only mean one thing: the Big Red One was returning to combat, probably in the forthcoming invasion of Hitler's Europe. After nearly a year of fighting, and a slew of victories in the Mediterranean theater, many of the soldiers felt they had earned the right to go home. Already fiercely proud of their outfit, and resentful of most outside authority, they had developed a cynical world-weariness that, for some, bordered on self-pity. After the Sicily campaign, hopeful rumors had spread that the division would be rotated back to the States to train new recruits. When the men boarded ships and found out they were heading to England, and thus eventually back to action, "it caused," in the recollection of one rifleman, "a lot of trouble among the soldiers, a lot of unrest and anger." For Lieutenant John Downing and his men, "the hope of going to the States . . . died hard. We could be sure . . . if we didn't go home this time, we wouldn't go home until the end of the war."

Many of the veterans felt this was unfair and unnecessary. They complained bitterly about the idea of going back into combat. After all, they had been fortunate enough to survive to this point; more prolonged action almost certainly meant that their chances of survival would be diminished. A man could evade the law of averages only so long before his luck ran out. "Their feeling was there must be other infantry units in the United States Army that could be utilized in the assault on Western Europe," Private Steve Kellman explained. There were, of course, other units, but none quite like the Big Red One. The division's experience in amphibious assaults made it indispensable to invasion planners (not to mention its familiarity in the very sort of town fighting, river crossings, mountain fighting, and combined arms maneuver warfare that would follow in the months after the invasion).

Among the American infantry divisions available for the coming invasion of Omaha beach, none had actually assaulted a hostile shore. Lieutenant General Omar Bradley, commander of the First Army, with control over all U.S. ground forces in the coming invasion, knew this all too well. "Although I disliked subjecting the 1st to still another major landing," he wrote, "I felt that as commander I had no other choice. My job was to get ashore, establish a lodgment, and destroy the German. In the accomplishment of that mission, there was little room for the niceties of justice. I felt compelled to employ the best troops I had. As a result the division that deserved compassion as a reward for its previous ordeals now became the inevitable choice for our most difficult job." In essence, they could not be spared. The task ahead was far too important and far too challenging.

At Liverpool, the troops boarded trains that took them to southern England, where they would settle in and begin a new round of training. Many were miffed at the standing order to remove, for reasons of secrecy, shoulder patches and all other indicators of their unit affiliation. The lack of identifying unit insignia made them look like newly arrived stateside replacements instead of proud combat veterans. It seemed a direct affront to their pride and status. Lieutenant Colonel Jimmy Wright, the division quartermaster, was so incensed at the order that he simply refused to follow it. Military police caught him, wrote him up, and referred his case to the First Army Provost Marshal. His defiance eventually evaporated, but only after the threat of a court-martial. He and thousands of other like-minded veterans grumbled, but swallowed their pride and complied with the order.[1]

Even worse, in the view of many Big Red One soldiers, was something else that had happened near the end of the Sicily campaign. Bradley had decided to relieve Major General Terry de la Mesa Allen, the 1st Division's popular and colorful commanding officer. Allen was a soldier's soldier, a down-to-earth cavalryman who loved polo, whiskey, and earthy language. The son of a West Point graduate and the grandson of a Civil War officer, he was born to be a soldier. As a young man, Allen had washed out of West Point because of his independent nature and maverick tendencies, a dismissal that must have smarted for the scion of such a distinguished military family. True to his resilient nature, though, he rebounded from the setback to earn a degree from the Catholic University of America and a subsequent Regular Army commission. Allen's personality meshed perfectly with the independent professionalism of the 1st Infantry Division.

In combat, he was the embodiment of an inspirational commander—courageous, relentless, and energetic—the sort of general who circulated easily among subordinates from the lowest-ranking private to staff officers. On the Tunisian front, he had made a point of regularly visiting the forward positions and speaking to each man personally. "There is nothing that is more inspiring than to have a general walking about the front lines when the bullets are flying, talking with the men," one of his aides wrote about him in a letter home. "He doesn't know what the word fear is and he is just like a hypodermic to the men of his command."

He had little patience for niceties. In action, he dressed in a simple, rumpled olive-drab uniform, helmet often askew or at his side, smoking cigarettes, grinning, tossing around one-liners. He was a natural backslapper and storyteller. He enjoyed an easy familiarity with his men, yet he managed to maintain a strong command presence. Almost everyone who served in the 1st had encountered him firsthand and had come to love him, in part because of his magnetic personality, in part because of his competence, but mostly because of his obvious concern for their welfare. "Do your job," he once told his division. "We don't want . . . dead heroes. We're not out for glory. We're here to do a dirty, stinking job." Over the many months of combat in North Africa and Sicily, he had inculcated an aggressive spirit in his division. True to his cavalry roots, he believed in swift maneuvers, slash and dash, night attacks and esprit de corps.

He cared little for his own promotion or his postwar military career. Command of the unit was the limit of his ambition. The men sensed that they were his first priority, and they loved him for it. "General Allen was loved by his soldiers because he really cared about them," Corporal Sam Fuller once wrote. "He didn't give a damn about playing politics or being famous." Allen had no tolerance for anyone who messed with his boys, whether that meant the Germans or higher command. In combat, this attitude contributed to success, but when the unit was off the line, it sometimes led to disciplinary problems. In the Mediterranean, the 1st earned a reputation as a hard-fighting outfit on the line, but a hard-drinking, rebellious, troublemaking group away from combat, contemptuous of rear-echelon troops, higher authority, and, for that matter, anyone who wasn't affiliated with the division. Allen seemed not only to tolerate this attitude but to encourage it, at least in the view of Bradley, George Patton, Dwight Eisenhower, and other senior officers in the theater. The most notorious example occurred in the spring of 1943, after the Tunisia campaign. The combat-weary men of the division yearned to visit the bars and brothels of Oran, a city they had actually captured during the initial invasion of North Africa back in the fall of 1942. However, only soldiers in rear-echelon-style khaki uniforms were allowed into the city. The Big Red One soldiers were still clothed in the same filthy olive-drab wool uniforms they had worn all winter during the hard fighting among the hills of Tunisia. The combat men felt that if anyone should enjoy the pleasures of Oran, it should be the front-line soldiers who routinely risked their lives. Therefore, they deeply resented being excluded from the city at the expense of the "typewriter commandos," as they often referred to the service troops.

Allen was clearly sympathetic to the views of his men. He defied the off-limits order and issued passes for his soldiers to enjoy some R&R in the city. A substantial amount of brawling, drinking, and mayhem ensued, involving both officers and enlisted men. "I can still remember the feeling I had when I landed a punch to some fat major's belly," Captain Edward Kuehn said. "We had taken Oran before, and we had lost a lot of good men doing it. Rearguard troops were not going to keep us from taking it this time, either." When Patton complained to Allen about the behavior of his soldiers, and demanded that he rein them in, Allen backed them to the hilt. "The troops have been in the line for six goddamned months," he exclaimed. "Let them celebrate getting back alive. It will stop soon." This was a revealing reaction and decision on Allen's part. A more career-conscious officer would have been eager to do the bidding of his superiors, regardless of what his men might have thought about that. Allen was different. Certainly his soldiers came first on his list of priorities, but perhaps he was also eager to remain popular among them even if that meant alienating the higher-ups.

In the view of senior officers, the Oran clashes represented more than just the usual tension between combat soldiers and rear-echelon types. Bradley, for instance, came to believe that a distinct whiff of parochialism, self-pity, and disregard for discipline and the chain of command emanated from the Big Red One. The soldiers had become a little *too* loyal to Allen and his equally charismatic assistant division commander, Ted Roosevelt, son of the former president. "Roosevelt was too much like Allen," Bradley wrote. "They looked upon discipline as an unwelcome crutch to be used by less able and personable commanders." The intense loyalty the troops held for these two generals was, in Bradley's estimation, coming at the expense of the greater loyalty soldiers owed to the Army as a whole. "Under Allen the 1st Division had become increasingly temperamental, disdainful of both regulations and senior commands," Bradley wrote. "It thought itself exempt from the need for discipline by virtue of its months on the line. And it believed itself the only division carrying its fair share of the war. Allen had become too much of an individualist to submerge himself without friction in the group undertakings of war." For the low-key Bradley, a duty-first man who disdained talented mavericks and nonconformity as a whole, the only sensible course of action was to remove Allen. In August 1943, near the end of the Sicily campaign, he fired him. Roosevelt also got the ax, in part because Bradley felt that he, too, had failed to enforce proper discipline and also because "Allen . . . would feel deeply hurt if he were to leave the division and Roosevelt were to remain." Both Patton and Eisenhower concurred with the decision.

Word of the firings hit the division like a sledgehammer. It was hard for the men to understand why such a successful commander had been cashiered. Some were resentful over Allen's relief; their bitterness hardened into anger at the brass and, ironically, an even more insular attitude about their division's greatness and the uselessness of all outsiders. Those who were a bit more even-tempered, like Lieutenant John Downing, simply thought of it as "a bad omen. If a new general took command, we could be sure we would continue on somewhere in combat." These suppositions were, of course, absolutely correct. Other men were simply mystified or sad. "He was the best liked commander that we ever had," Captain Charles Murphy, a company commander, told an interviewer decades later. On the evening Allen left to go home, Captain Dawson, who had worked closely with him, wrote to his family about the melancholy mood that pervaded the ranks: "Terry left tonight, and with him went a record unequaled by any general officer in the divisions of the U.S. Army. We've been through a lot and we all feel keenly sad about his going."[2]

Under these circumstances, a lot was riding on Bradley's selection of a replacement for Allen. Fortunately, he made a very wise choice in Major General Clarence Huebner, a man whose personality could hardly have been more different from Allen's, but whose competence and courage were every bit his equal. Whereas Allen was born to soldiering, Huebner was drawn to it. While Allen's success was a testament to resilience and charisma, Huebner's was a testament to the

Army's culture of meritocracy (at least for white men). Born to a non-military Kansas wheat-farming family, Huebner was educated in a one-room school of the sort that pervaded frontier lore. Hardened by an outdoor life of farm chores, he was an athletic youth, though he was only of medium build and height. He played football, baseball, and basketball in high school. During track season, he was a pole-vaulter. At the age of twenty, with a high school diploma to his credit, he went to work as a railroad secretary. He had no desire to spend his life as a clerk, though. In 1910 he left the job and decided to join the Army, enlisting as a cook in the 18th Infantry Regiment, a unit that became part of the 1st Division seven years later. Huebner discovered that he was a natural soldier. Over the next seven years, he rocketed from private to master sergeant. In 1916, he passed a competitive examination to become an officer and was commissioned as a second lieutenant in November of that year. By the time the division deployed to France in the spring of 1917, he was a first lieutenant. His combat record in World War I was one of the finest of that or any other war. In eighteen months of frontline leadership, he rose from a first lieutenant, leading a platoon, to a lieutenant colonel, leading a regiment at the tender age of thirty. He earned the Distinguished Service Cross, the nation's second-highest award for valor, as well as the Distinguished Service Medal, for outstanding service. He also received a Silver Star, the Purple Heart (for a bad shrapnel wound above his right eye during the Battle of Soissons) and numerous French decorations. Huebner's success as a commander came from personal bravery, his calm demeanor, and a keen intelligence. After the war he served in a variety of battalion and regimental commands, within the 1st Division and other outfits. He also attended numerous Army training schools including the Command and General Staff School and the Army War College. By the summer of 1943, the fifty-five-year-old Huebner was a two-star general serving on British Field Marshal Harold Alexander's Fifteenth Army Group staff in the Mediterranean theater. His hair had thinned out and gone gray, but his square jaw and bright blue eyes hinted at a remnant of youth.

Huebner, of course, had a tough act to follow in succeeding Allen, especially under the circumstances. "Anyone who replaced the Allen-Roosevelt team was sure to incur the wrath and disdain of the entire Division," one veteran wrote years later. In the estimation of Lieutenant Colonel Robert York, a battalion commander in the 18th Infantry, "Huebner seemed old and bland" compared to the colorful Allen. Huebner never made the mistake of denigrating Allen, for he held him in very high regard and respected the record he and his division had attained. He simply felt the division had gotten away from certain fundamentals of soldiering and must now relearn them. Likewise, Allen made sure not to poison the well for Huebner. He actually met one-on-one with Huebner, gave him a tour of the division, and introduced him to every battalion commander. The new commander never forgot the simple decency and professionalism of that gesture.

In the aftermath of the change of command, ignorant rumors soon spread among the resentful ranks that Huebner was merely a desk officer, a "stateside johnny," an outsider with no real battle experience. The rumormongers obviously had no idea of Huebner's brilliant combat record, nor of the ironic fact that he had actually logged more time with the division over the years than the beloved Allen. Huebner was far too understated, mild-mannered, and self-effacing to defuse such falsehoods by bragging about his background or his accomplishments. Rather, he sought to earn the respect of his soldiers through his actions in combat, not by making a speech or issuing a press release touting his résumé.

In truth, Huebner cared less about his own reputation than about the discipline, health, and preparation of his troops for battle. Upon taking command near the end of the Sicily campaign in August 1943, he implemented a regimen of strict, by-the-book discipline. He mandated proper dress and military comportment. No one was exempt, as

Lieutenant Colonel George Pickett, the division signal officer, found out one day when the general noticed he was unshaven. "Anybody in my outfit shaves every day!" Huebner barked. "Yes, damn it, I mean you, too, Colonel!" He routinely chewed out colonels and privates alike for the slightest infractions. "I got the reputation of being an unreasonable and mean old bastard," Huebner later told an interviewer. The general mandated close-order drill, physical training, and regular inspections. The proud veterans felt terribly disrespected, as if the general were treating them like nothing more than raw recruits. "Everybody hated him! Absolutely hated him!" Captain Dawson later said. Huebner was perceptive enough to understand and accept that the notion of him as a mean, loathsome taskmaster was the price to be paid for good leadership (or what a later generation would call tough love). He actually did not have a mean bone in his body. He was a martinet, not out of any sadistic impulse to bully or dominate subordinates, but because he knew this was the best way to save lives and succeed in battle. "When you take over a command, you can start off being an SOB and later become a good guy," he liked to say, "but you can never start off being a good guy and later become an SOB!"[3]

Huebner was a special stickler for saluting. Shortly after assuming command, he ate lunch individually with key commanders and members of his staff. When the meal was finished, he would have a military policeman demonstrate a proper salute to each officer and then order that officer to teach his troops to do the same within twenty-four hours. "I saw officers of all grades going through the hand-salute routine sometimes once, sometimes three or more times with a giant MP stationed at the entrance of the Headquarters," Edwin Sutherland, a staff officer, recalled. Because saluting in combat was a true no-no (for the obvious reason that snipers looked to kill leaders), most of the division's battle-hardened troops thought the order amounted to little more than stateside chickenshit. "We all felt like we were being harassed over something that was of no consequence at all," Colonel Stanhope Mason, the division chief of staff, wrote. Mason and the other soldiers quickly realized that Huebner was dead serious about it and intended to make sure everyone complied. The general soon made a habit of turning up anywhere and everywhere asking men for a salute. One hot afternoon he caught Lieutenant Franklyn Johnson and his antitank platoon lounging in a field during a break in their firing practice. Huebner ordered them to get up. He turned to Johnson and asked him to demonstrate how well his platoon could salute. The result was a ragged blend of eyebrow touching and loose fingers. "Terrible!" General Huebner shouted. "Johnson, how long will it take you to teach these men how to salute?"

"Twenty-four hours," Johnson replied.

"I'll give you three minutes," the general said curtly. He turned on his heel and walked away, leaving Johnson to make it happen.

Huebner's fixation with saluting was not so much about military courtesy as it was about two things he considered of paramount importance in combat: attention to detail and compliance with orders. "No order is ever complete until it is finished," he told his commanders in a conference soon after assuming command. "Therefore, it is incumbent on the officers who issue the orders to check to see that the orders themselves are completed." If they failed to do that, then it would be the same "as if you had issued no order at all." In Huebner's view, good teaching was vital to all effective leadership. "The only way you can get someone to do what you want them to do," he told his commanders, "is to teach them how to do it." Of course this meant that leaders had to know what they were talking about—a teacher must be well ahead of his students in competence. Any officer or noncommissioned officer (NCO) who did not know his stuff risked relief on the spot. This emphasis on teaching, in tandem with his high regard for athletics, had earned Huebner the nickname "Coach" throughout the Army.

The moniker described him perfectly. He understood that his greatest impact on the division would be in its preparation for landing on Omaha beach, not necessarily in leading the way himself. Like a coach, he set about the task of teaching his men and preparing them for the dangers they would soon face, all the while knowing when to chew people out and when to instruct them. By the end of the Sicily campaign, he had come to believe that the infantrymen were overrelying on their artillery support, at the expense of individual marksmanship. The Coach was not the type to take action simply on the basis of a gut feeling. He ordered his G3 (operations) and G4 (supply) staff officers to check on rifle ammunition expenditure levels during the last phase at Sicily. Sure enough, they reported surpluses. Huebner was an expert rifleman with a true passion for marksmanship. He believed the men were not shooting enough because they lacked confidence in their own abilities. When he checked the division personnel records, he found that more than two thousand soldiers—many of whom were actually veterans of both major campaigns—had never even qualified with their rifles. No wonder they lacked confidence! He set about correcting this appalling deficiency in their basic training by ordering the entire division to learn proper shooting techniques. Firing ranges and field target combat courses were built. Anyone who did not qualify as an expert on the range would not serve as a rifleman. The general himself routinely circulated during the training, offering advice on proper body position and firing techniques. "When he made corrections, General Huebner never raised his voice," one soldier later wrote. "He made it plain that there was nothing personal in his criticism of a man's firing technique, but it was just a job that had to be done." Sometimes when he noticed something wrong with a rifleman's shooting, he would ask his squad leader to identify the problem. If he did not know, then Huebner would consult the platoon leader and then the company commander. Eventually these leaders—knowing they might be quizzed at any time in front of their men—began to take a keen interest in learning proper techniques.

Often Huebner shouldered a rifle and showed off his own impressive shooting skills. One day, in the aftermath of bitter fighting at Troina, he collared an entire battalion and demonstrated a unique squatting marksmanship position that he had personally invented. "Then and there across a nearby ravine . . . the battalion had rifle marksmanship practice in the 'squatting' position . . . demonstrated for us by the General himself," Lieutenant Colonel Joseph Sisson, the battalion commander, recalled. Many times Huebner went through the combat firing course with individual rifle squads. Seldom did he miss his targets. He demonstrated proficiency with all infantry weapons and training, the same as any private. This did not escape the notice of the men. One day, after watching Huebner crouch in a foxhole and remain there stoically while a tank ran right over it, an infantryman sidled up to Brigadier General Clift Andrus, the division artillery commander, and said, "The 'Old Man' surely knows his business."

He also possessed a sly, good-natured sense of humor that revealed his essential decency. When he complained one day to Andrus that one of his artillery majors saluted crookedly, Andrus laughed and told him that the man had a broken hand. Huebner grinned, joined in the laughter, and shook his head at his own ignorance. On another occasion, he entered a command post and picked up the phone to listen in on a conversation between the commander and his supply officer. The commander wanted to know when his unit would receive new coats and shoes. The supply officer assured him that General Huebner had already made the necessary arrangements. "Well," the CO replied, "it's about time the old SOB did something for us fighting soldiers." Huebner put the phone down, grinned, and said, "Well, eavesdroppers never hear anything good of themselves." Beneath his gruff exterior was "a soft general who talked gently," recalled Captain Daniel Lyons, his aide-de-camp. Lyons, who spent much time at the general's elbow, came to think of him as a kind and thoughtful man.

Nor did Huebner take himself too seriously. He knew he could err just like anyone else in the outfit. After the division had left Sicily and boarded ships bound for England, Lieutenant General George Patton told Huebner that he was going to board a launch and personally see them off. Huebner told Colonel Mason, his chief of staff, to issue orders for the troops to line the rails of their ships and cheer Patton as he sailed past them. Mason had been with the division since the beginning of the war, so he knew firsthand how much the Big Red One soldiers disliked Patton. Part of the animosity stemmed from their belief that Patton favored armored units; part of it came from disparaging comments about the 1st that they attributed to Patton; the rest came from the relief of Allen, which many Big Red One soldiers blamed on the flamboyant army commander. Basically, there was no way the men were going to greet Patton nicely, especially since they were no longer under his command and would thus fear no reprisal from him. Mason knew trouble when he saw it, so he asked Huebner to reconsider. "I recommended that he not have the troops line the rails—and I filled in all the background which led me to believe the troops would neither applaud nor cheer." Mason felt that their hostility would reflect poorly on Huebner. The Coach heard him out, but told him to go ahead with the order. At the appointed time, Patton appeared on his boat in a resplendent dress uniform adorned with his many ribbons and medals. As the boat cruised around with Patton prominently displayed, the Big Red One soldiers simply stood and stared at him. "Silence was total," Mason recalled. "Every ship had its rails solidly lined with soldiers as deep as space permitted. But not a cheer was heard. No applause. Nothing but sepulchral silence." Huebner was embarrassed and disappointed. Instead of blaming his soldiers for Patton's frosty reception, and punishing them accordingly, he blamed himself for not listening to Mason.

If there was one thing Huebner detested, it was the improper care of weapons. He understood that in combat, a man's weapon was equivalent to his life. A soldier with no workable weapon was little more than a useless burden, incapable of accomplishing any mission, a danger to his own life and the lives of others around him. "I have found many weapons in this division in a bad state of cleanliness," he told his commanders in 1943, "plain neglect on the part of some lieutenant. Weapons can't get in very bad shape if they are inspected every day." Huebner stressed that all squad and platoon leaders should ensure proper cleaning of weapons. Further, they should know the strengths and weaknesses of their men: "who needs training, who has careless habits . . . they must learn their men and learn them thoroughly. Those who are slow should be given extra work." He was so serious about clean weapons that he fined any lieutenant whose men did not properly maintain their rifles and machine guns. "A number of lieutenants 'bought' pretty good fines till they learned that the Old Man meant real business," Sutherland recalled.[4]

1

Once in England, the 1st Infantry Division settled into the various small towns of Dorsetshire, not far from the southern coast. The troops lived in Nissen huts, barracks, and even requisitioned private homes. Huebner soon found out from Bradley about the outfit's mission to assault Omaha beach. The Coach began training the soldiers in earnest, often amid rainy, cold, windy, raw, dismal weather conditions. The pace of the training was unrelenting and quite demanding. "All types of weapons . . . were fired and excellent results were achieved," an 18th Infantry Regiment historical report explained. "Steady improvement was noted in all units in individual proficiency and the tactical employment of weapons and units. Field exercises, night problems and conditioning marches, including a twenty-five mile road march in ten hours with combat equipment was completed by all units." Gradually, as the men ate better in garrison, and spent an increasing amount of time exercising, their physical condition improved. "The companies conducted a progressive series of hardening marches, each week increasing the pace and length of the march," one operations officer wrote in the spring of

1944. Eventually each company was able to march sixteen miles in four hours and seven miles in an hour and a half without halting.

The troops learned to find and disarm mines. They perfected first-aid techniques. They stripped and cleaned their rifles and machine guns so often that they could do it blindfolded in the dark. Huebner also continued to emphasize the basics of soldiering. An April 1944 division training memo mandated that all companies conduct at least thirty minutes of close-order drill per day. Every rifleman had to show proficiency with his weapon, fire it regularly, and demonstrate proper soldierly bearing at all times. Officers had to be schooled in signal communications, chemical weapons, and coordination with supporting arms such as artillery and engineers. Every man learned to use his gas mask in the event the Germans used poison gas on the invasion beaches. Antitank gunners spent half of each week on the range, siting and firing their 57-millimeter guns. The general required each unit, down to the company level, to submit its weekly training schedule for his personal approval. At the Coach's insistence, soldiers were cross-trained to do other jobs. Thus riflemen could take over as machine gunners. Machine gunners could become mortarmen. Each executive officer prepared himself to take command should his boss get wounded or killed. Sergeants learned to take over platoons from lieutenants. Veteran soldiers were groomed to take over squads in the rather likely event that their leaders got hit. Engineers and artillerymen learned to become infantrymen. "Men worked as they had never worked before," a 16th Infantry Regiment history reported. "They trained as an army had never trained for any other war. It was tough, grueling work—work that tasked minds and muscles almost as they would be tasked in the real thing that was to follow."

In addition to this sort of realism, Huebner sought to forge group cohesion and teamwork, a vision that Colonel George Taylor, commander of the 16th Infantry Regiment—the division's leading assault force at Omaha beach—enthusiastically shared. "Team work is one of the most important items to be gained if success in combat is desired," Taylor wrote in a wide-ranging memo several months before the invasion. "It is based on acquaintance, confidence, and association. In order to get it, officers and men must eat, sleep and work together." This meant that leaders had to share the hardships of those they led. Private Frank Beetle, a replacement in the regiment's Cannon Company, vividly recalled that his commander, Captain Thomas O'Brien, and every company officer participated fully in every bit of training, no matter how difficult. "They were all there. I think [there was] this whole sense of comradeship . . . [and] at the same time understanding that he was the boss. You have confidence . . . that he knows what he's doing and that he is fair and that he serves with you."

As someone who had logged a great deal of front-line combat experience, Taylor was also a big believer in practical, simplified training. He taught his men only tactics he felt they would actually use in combat. "Our biggest failure," he wrote, "is that we have too much, and too many ways of doing everything. It all should be simplified." To Taylor, what mattered most was aggressiveness—the will to keep fighting regardless of the situation. He believed this would happen if his soldiers knew their jobs and each other well enough. He worried only about results, so he gave his subordinates plenty of leeway to prepare their troops for the invasion in their own particular way. "[He] gave us freelance in training," Captain Ed Wozenski, his E Company commander, said. "I had the liberty of training my people in any way I wanted to. I knew the job that had to be done and if I wanted to train three days continuously, day and night, that was my option. And then I could knock off for three or four days. When we worked, we worked hard, and when we played, we just did it all the way."[5]

Beginning in February, the training began to focus specifically on amphibious assault skills. At various times, the men were trucked from their bases in Dorsetshire to the U.S. Assault Center in Braunton on the southwestern coast and Slapton Sands on the southern coast for invasion exercises. "Actual landings were made from the type of craft to be used in the projected invasion," a soldier-historian from the 16th Infantry later wrote. "Vessels ran inshore under simulated fire, men charged into the water and up the beaches, across obstacles similar to what they expected to encounter in France, and worked their way inland." The assault units ran so many practice landings that the men soon grew accustomed to the routine. "We spent a lot of time on ships and sometimes I wasn't sure if I was in the Army or the Navy," Corporal Edward Steeg, a mortar gunner, quipped. "For weeks at a time we would live aboard ship and practice climbing down the rope ladder . . . simulating realistic conditions."

He and the other troops got used to the process of boarding the ships, securing their weapons and equipment, eating Navy chow, descending rope ladders into bobbing Higgins boats (officially known as Landing Craft Vehicles, Personnel or LCVPs), staving off seasickness, huddling together to stay warm amid the rough sea spray and the cold bulkheads of the craft, and moving quickly to secure a beach. In many cases, they worked with the same naval crewmen—British and American—and became good friends with them. Often they did not know beforehand if they were about to carry out a real invasion or just a practice one. While aboard ship, it was not unusual for men to make bets with one another on whether the next landing would be the real thing or only another rehearsal. In one instance, Private Howard Johnson, a bazookaman who had just joined his platoon as a replacement, boarded his landing craft without even knowing if he and his new buddies were headed toward a hostile shore. "We hit the beach prepared for battle, armed to the teeth," he said, "no shells coming our way. No bullets flying at us. Then someone told us it was just a training exercise, a dry run." The weather was often foggy, rainy, and cold. Even when it was clear, a cold sea wind blew in their faces, and since they were usually soaked by the time they hit the beach, they were often chilled to the bone. "If hell is any worse than this, I don't want to go there," a sergeant joked one day during a particularly wet and miserable landing. After carrying out the mock assault, they would hike to an encampment, where mud-caked tents had been set up, and sometimes the men would warm up with a hot meal.

The Higgins boats that were so necessary to landing the assault companies could accommodate, at most, thirty-two soldiers. Yet a full-strength rifle platoon generally consisted of forty-one soldiers. This discrepancy meant that invasion planners had to divide rifle companies into thirty-man assault boat teams or sections, usually six boats per company, including a command boat carrying the headquarters group. Weapons companies, armed with heavy machine guns and mortars, were broken down into support boat teams. Each member of a boat team (also commonly called an assault section) had a specific job and a precise spot where he was supposed to stand aboard the landing craft. Indeed, commanders spent considerable time at the assault center instructing their men on proper positioning and conducting literal dry runs on land. To do this, they measured out the size of a Higgins boat in the sand, bunched their men inside and then choreographed an assault from this mock "landing craft." "We would draw a line on the ground with stakes and ribbons the same size of our landing craft, and huddle together inside," Staff Sergeant Harley Reynolds of B Company, 16th Infantry Regiment, wrote. "On command we would rush out of the 'craft,' those on the sides fanning out to thier [sic] side and setting up machine guns."

Once aboard the real boats, each man knew exactly where he was supposed to go. This avoided the chaos that naturally would have ensued from thirty heavily laden men trying to find some personal space. The boat teams represented an ingenious blend of combined small arms, explosives, and crew-served weapons. "The boat groups were so organized that heavy and light supporting weapons were divided throughout every group, thus making each boat self-sustaining," Captain Edward McGregor, the S3 of the 1st Battalion, 18th Infantry Regiment, explained in a February 1944 training memo. On each assault boat, for instance, the leader, usually an officer, stood to the front left. He was surrounded by five riflemen armed with grenades and a Bangalore torpedo (a long pipe filled with explosives designed to blow barbed wire and mines). Behind this group stood four more riflemen armed with two more Bangalores and special wire cutters. Some of these men were equipped with aluminum ladders to breach tank trap ditches. Adjacent to these riflemen, on either side of the craft, were two bazooka teams totaling four men. A 60-millimeter mortar team of four men stood in the exact middle of the boat. Right behind them were a two-man flamethrower team and four BAR men. In the rear of the boat a special demolition team armed with blocks of TNT, detonators, pole charges (designed to take out pillboxes at a distance), and rifles huddled just under the engine and the seat where the coxswain guided the craft. At the extreme left rear, the highest-ranking NCO functioned as the amphibious equivalent of a push man.

In terms of leadership, the setup was similar to the manner in which airborne sticks loaded onto a plane. The officer led the way out the door. His highest-ranking NCO stood at the rear, making sure that everyone jumped, hence the term "push man." So, too, on the boats, the sergeant's task was to make sure that no one froze up or refused to make the assault. This reflected a proper view of the differing shades of leadership offered by commissioned officers and their sergeants. The officer's job was to lead, motivate, think, and inspire. The sergeant's job was to enforce orders and lead by example; whether that entailed coercion, intimidation, or inspiration hardly mattered as long as it happened.

The support boat teams, carrying the heavier weapons, were set up in similar fashion. The platoon leader stood at the left front; his sergeant stood at the left rear. As with the assault boats, a group of five riflemen stood near the front ramp, next to the officer, while a wire-cutting team of four soldiers was positioned right behind them. The five-man demolition group was also in the rear of the boat next to the sergeant. The difference was in the middle of the boat, which consisted of a heavy 81-millimeter mortar team of eight soldiers and a six-man heavy-machine-gun team armed with the Browning M-1917A1 water-cooled gun, a powerful but heavy and awkward weapon.

Beyond the task of learning how to function as members of a boat team rather than a platoon, the troops spent much of their time learning how to attack and destroy coastal defenses. They studied photos of pillboxes and bunkers, listened to lectures from intelligence officers about the thickness of the concrete, the blind spots, and what sort of weapons the bunkers were likely to contain. "Much preparation time was . . . devoted to organizing and exercising assault teams for specific attacks on pillboxes," Lieutenant Charles Ryan, a platoon leader, later said. Through sheer repetition, the troops learned how to move onto and along a heavily defended beach, how to employ a blend of weaponry and how to destroy the German "Atlantic Wall" fortifications. "The men . . . were given special training in the use of Bangalore torpedoes, wire cutters, flame throwers, rockets [bazookas], pole charges, and a variety of smoke, fragmentation hand and rifle grenades," Captain McGregor wrote. Indeed, riflemen learned how to work with explosives—especially Bangalores—but they also focused on providing cover fire for pillbox-busting bazooka teams, flamethrower men, and TNT-wielding demolition teams.

The main goal was for the assault men to work their way close enough to apertures where they could then be in range to employ their devastating weapons. After all, the German defenders in their concrete pillboxes would inevitably enjoy an advantage over troops moving on the open sands of Omaha. For the invaders, the equalizer might well be a jet of flame or a bazooka shell through a pillbox opening, or a pack charge tossed down a ventilator shaft. Every member of a boat team was supposed to be familiar with all the weapons on his boat. At the assault center, riflemen learned how to arm half-pound blocks of TNT with pull ignitors and fuses and then protect them from water corrosion by wrapping them in condoms. The soldiers also practiced with TNT pole charges and built pack charges (often dubbed "satchel charges") by taping together thirty-two of the half-pound TNT blocks, attaching a handle, and packing it all into a sandbag or a satchel. The training was so intensive and so repetitive that it became almost mind-numbing. "We were overtrained," Captain Wozenski even opined. "We had number one man in number two boat team going for aperture number three in pillbox number seventeen." He wondered what might happen if his company landed in the wrong spot on the beach (a valid concern, as it turned out). However, in the bigger picture, the training provided a muscle memory of sorts. Each man had practiced amphibious beach assaults so much and so often that he was likely to carry out a landing almost automatically—especially with good leadership—even under the worst of circumstances when his natural inclination might otherwise be to cower or give up.[6]

As intensely as the troops were training, General Huebner was working even harder, almost round the clock. His daily diary from the spring months chronicled a dizzying series of meetings, conferences, speeches, inspection trips, and, of course, visits to units in the field. The April 11 entry, for instance, detailed a long, but fairly typical day—morning planning meetings with his staff and then the V Corps staff—the 1st Infantry Division was part of this corps during the invasion—a shipboard conference with Admiral John Hall, the commander of naval forces for the Omaha beach landings, more meetings in the afternoon to prepare the invasion field order, followed by a private consultation with Major General Leonard Gerow, his superior at V Corps, and Major General Everett Hughes, a special assistant to Eisenhower. After a short dinner in the town of Beaminster, he returned to his headquarters at Blandford and began planning the next day's round of activities. Nor was his day over just yet. Later that same evening, he entertained General Roosevelt, who was now serving as assistant division commander of the 4th Infantry Division. Roosevelt's son Quentin, a captain in the Big Red One, was scheduled to be married the next day.

Eventually, after enough days like this one, the fifty-five-year-old Huebner's health started to deteriorate. He began to suffer severe abdominal cramps. The pain got so bad it was almost debilitating. Huebner consulted division doctors and charged them with finding a cure, almost as if he could order them to make the pain go away. The cramps persisted until they were so bad that the doctors worried Huebner might have abdominal cancer. They advised him to visit an Army hospital in Salisbury for a series of tests. The general was reluctant to go because he was worried that if his superiors found out about his condition they would relieve him for health reasons. But the possibility of cancer persuaded him to go to Salisbury, where the doctors put him through an exhaustive battery of invasive tests. At last, the hospital commander, a colonel, told Huebner there was nothing wrong with him that a little rest would not alleviate. He diagnosed him with a nervous stomach caused by intense worry and overwork. With eyes sparkling, the Coach leapt out of bed, grabbed the colonel by his tunic, and said, "You know what those damned doctors told me in the First Division? They told me I had *cancer*! Thank you, Colonel, and when I get back to that division this afternoon I'm going to have a little talk with those surgeons of mine. In fact, I'm going to order the whole damn bunch up here to your hospital so you can put them through the same tests they made me take." He was joking, of course, but he did try to find some time to rest.[7]

The same was true for the division as a whole. In spite of the hectic training schedule, the soldiers were able to enjoy some much-needed downtime in England. The recreation contributed to the maintenance of good morale, and the commanders readily understood that this was a crucial ingredient in preparing their troops for the daunting job ahead of them. The division's Special Services section organized a broad range of activities. There were dances with local women, live USO shows, visits to Red Cross clubs, and movie nights. The men got to see a nice array of first-run films including *Flying Tigers*, *The Man Who Wouldn't Die*, *My Heart Belongs to Daddy*, *His Butler's Sister*, *The Vanishing Virginian*, and *Tornado*. In late March, Jimmy Cagney visited the division and appeared in a USO show called "Keep 'Em Rolling." The division boxing championships were decided by an elimination tournament among varying weight classes and levels of proficiency. The culminating matches were staged in front of crowds as large as 1,500 men. The 16th Infantry won team championships in both boxing and basketball. Other men played baseball and softball when weather permitted and equipment was available. In addition to athletics, Special Services disseminated morale items among the various units. In January alone, they dispensed fifty-one cartons of books, fifty-seven dozen decks of playing cards, three Italian record sets, three Spanish record sets, three French record sets, three German record sets, two sets of Chinese checkers, and three sets of dominoes, along with jigsaw puzzles, pinochle, Parcheesi, checkers, darts, and cribbage.

Furloughs were common. Off-duty soldiers had the opportunity to travel to London and other spots throughout Britain. For those who were interested in culture, there was of course plenty to see in a country with such a rich history. For the larger majority who were more interested in liquor and women than erudition—the Big Red One's reputation as a hard-partying unit was, after all, well deserved—England offered a nice bounty in that regard. Wartime rationing restricted how much beer and whiskey the local pubs could serve on any given evening, but anyone with a heavy thirst could usually find a way to drink to excess. Beyond simple hoarding or bingeing, the best way to get drunk was to hop from pub to pub, drinking one establishment after another dry. One night a soldier in Private Howard Johnson's platoon migrated around the Dorchester pubs until he got stinking drunk. He staggered into the barracks, climbed into his top bunk, and fell asleep. The man was so intoxicated that he wet his bed. The noxious urine seeped through his straw mattress and poured onto a good friend named Vigue, alongside whom the drinker had fought in both North Africa and Sicily. Horrified and nauseated, Vigue leapt out of his bunk and screamed at his friend to wake up. "He was dancing around, wiping his face, and watching the drops still falling on his formerly clean and neat bed," Johnson recalled. The offender awoke briefly and looked around but was otherwise unfazed. Vigue cleaned up as best he could. Johnson and the rest of the platoon members laughed "until we were weak." Vigue eventually forgave his old buddy, but it took several weeks.

In numerous instances, the Americans drank up a pub's ration before the locals could complete their workday and stop by for their usual pint of ale, glass of whiskey, and game of darts. The British often muttered the well-worn phrase about "overpaid, oversexed, and over here" Yanks, but tolerated this intrusion with remarkable good cheer. "I know if the American civilian had to contend with a likewise situation," William Faust asserted, "there would have been more serious reactions than we encountered." Instead the British practically went out of their way to befriend the 1st Division soldiers, especially in the pubs, where they swapped yarns and played darts with them. Faust and the members of his unit even organized dart teams to compete in friendly tournaments against teams of civilians. By spending their evenings and off-duty hours in the pubs, Faust and thousands of other young Americans grew accustomed to British culture and society. "Our favorite pub was a small establishment called the Old Borough Arms, on the outskirts of Weymouth," Lieutenant John Downing wrote. "The proprietor was an elderly, white-haired gentleman, who had a son in the RAF." The man made sure to set aside a bottle of whiskey for Downing and his friends. At times, he even invited them to share a few drinks in his private living quarters above the pub. As such friendships developed, many Britons invited Big Red One soldiers into their homes for meals. "They cheerfully shared their meager rations with us," Private First Class Pete

Lypka wrote. When the Americans found out just how sparse those rations truly were, they often reciprocated with gifts of chocolate, cigarettes, oranges, and food from their more plentiful mess halls. In the main, they comported themselves with generosity, decency, and respect.

Even more than liquor and friendship, the soldiers were interested in women. The troops wasted little time in seeking out and finding the local ladies, whether at dances, at parties, in pubs, in restaurants, through chance encounters, or anywhere young couples happened to meet. One night when Sergeant Faust and his comrades were hanging out at a pub, they struck up a conversation with several members of a local Women's Land Army outfit who happened to live at a nearby hostel. In spite of its name, the Women's Land Army (or WLA) was not actually a military organization. It consisted of young women who worked on farms in order to maximize Britain's food production while most of the male-dominated agricultural labor force was serving in the armed forces. "We spent many, many nights at the hostel recreation room," Faust wrote. "The girls were all single and most of us were." The hostel was closely chaperoned but not so much as to prevent several relationships from developing over the months that Faust's unit was stationed nearby.

There is, of course, no way to quantify how many 1st Division men, single or otherwise, had local girlfriends, but the number had to have been substantial. Twenty-nine-year-old Lieutenant John Spalding, a Kentuckian who had been married since 1939, met and soon began dating a local woman named Pauline Shortland. "She is a telephone operator and 19 years old and really sweet," Spalding wrote to his brother. "If you ever get an opportunity to get me some silk or rayon hose—size 9—do so and send them to me. I want them for Pauline. So try hard." Private Lypka was waiting for a truck to take him home from a dance one night when he noticed an attractive blond woman on a bicycle pedaling away from the dance hall. He struck up a conversation with her and learned she was in the Women's Land Army. Thus began a whirlwind courtship in which they spent every moment they could together. Eventually they decided to get married. "Alice's father was not sure he wanted her to marry me because he knew that soon I'd be back in combat and might not survive or come back badly wounded," Lypka wrote. "So he had a lawyer contact my company commander and see if there was a way to keep us from marrying." There were indeed many bureaucratic obstacles (such as paperwork, counseling sessions with chaplains, and permission from commanders) to prevent such marriages, but not enough to deter a determined couple. Lypka got married, as did scores of others. In more than a few cases, pregnancy led to nuptials. This was common enough that when any man in Captain Rafael Uffner's company requested permission to marry, the captain immediately inquired as to the reproductive status of the prospective bride. "Pregnancy was one big gate opener," he said. "I made it short and sweet. First, I asked the pregnancy question. Then I set up a session with our emminant [sic] obstetrician, Dr. Nate Sperling."

Competition for the affection of British women, and the inherent racist mores of mid-twentieth-century America, led to serious tension between a few of the white Big Red One soldiers and nearby black support troops. The animosity was serious enough that it led to occasional violence, such as a shooting incident involving Captain Uffner's M Company, 26th Infantry Regiment. "Two of five black soldiers [were] killed, three others wounded. Civilian witnesses saw white soldiers fleeing." The Criminal Investigation Division restricted both groups to camp while it probed for more information on the murders. But the perpetrators were never found. Finally, after enough tension (and possible injustice) of this sort, the senior officers wisely decided to move the entire battalion to Swanage, away from the black units.

Nor were the division's men always well behaved toward the locals. Private Charles Dye remembered a deeply troubling incident involving the rape of a child in Swanage. "We had a little girl that was a paper carrier," he said. "She was about fourteen, fifteen years old." One day, when most of the company was out training, the girl stopped by to deliver the papers. A new replacement "enticed her to come in and talk," Dye recalled, "and she did. He raped her while she was there." After she left, she reported the crime to her father, who in turn reported it to the town mayor. Eventually the mayor informed Captain John Semanchyk, the company commander. The captain was determined to press charges. However, the father soon informed the Americans that he wished to have those charges dropped rather than subject his daughter to the embarrassment of a trial. Thus the crime went unpunished, effectively swept under the rug (one can only imagine what sort of traumatic impact this had on the girl). The perpetrator's fellow soldiers were so incensed that they ostracized him. No one would even speak to the man. "We completely ignored him and would have nothing to do with him. Of course we had to sleep with him, drill with him, train with him but anything out of the ordinary we just pretended that he didn't exist."[8]

1

Starting in late February, aerial reconnaissance photographs revealed a disquieting reality about Omaha beach. In addition to the fixed concrete fortifications that defended the beach exits, the Germans were saturating the beach itself with belts of obstacles, all of which were of course designed to wreck boats and restrict the mobility of assault troops. The experts identified three distinct types of prefabricated iron or steel obstacles. Element C—often referred to as "Belgian gates" because the Germans had captured thousands of them when they captured Belgium in 1940—stood about ten feet high and were very sturdy. "They were built of reinforced iron frames 7 feet 7 inches high," a combat engineer's report later stated. "These gates were held upright by reinforced iron supports extending to the rear between 8 and 10 feet." The device looked like nothing more menacing than a drawbridge gate, but it could impede boats and vehicles alike. The iron girders could inflict major damage, too. Tetrahedrons were pyramid-shaped obstacles, about four feet tall, constructed of steel rails. The top of the tetrahedron consisted of a sharp point intended to tear open the bottom of a landing craft. Hedgehogs were made of sharply curved steel rails welded together in a crisscross pattern, almost resembling the toy jacks that were so popular with children at the time. These obviously were not toys, though. The hedgehogs were often anchored in a firm base of concrete, and they, too, could rip open the bottom of a boat or hold it in place as a perfect target for enemy gunners. In addition to these ominous impediments, the Germans, with extensive assistance from reasonably well-compensated local laborers, were cutting down trees in local forests, hauling them to the coast, and using them to build stakes and log ramp obstacles (the latter always pointed shoreward).

What's more, the Germans were liberally sowing the obstacles with mines. Allied intelligence analysts confirmed the menacing presence of these mines one day in early April when a bomber returning from a mission to a nearby target jettisoned its bombs over Omaha beach and touched off a series of sympathetic detonations. A subsequent mission elsewhere on the French coast by specially trained members of a British Combined Operations Pilotage Party—who actually swam to shore—conclusively proved the presence of large numbers of Teller mines affixed to obstacles. The Teller mine was designed primarily as an antitank weapon but, provided it did not corrode from exposure to seawater and sand, it could prove quite lethal to boats and amphibious invaders alike. One Teller mine could blow the ramp off a boat, tear a hole in it, or set the fuel tank on fire. The blast effect of the mine could literally blow a man apart. The Germans had tied the mines to wooden stakes and Belgian gates. At high tide the mines would not be seen by landing craft crews until it was too late to avoid catastrophe. "The stakes were heavy logs driven into the ground at an angle," a post-battle analysis stated. "About every third stake had a teller mine attached to it. In some sectors the stakes were also placed between other obstacles in the first and third bands." The Germans burrowed holes in the beach, inserted high-pressure water hoses, pumped out the sand, and then fixed the stakes and logs in place. Three solid belts of mine-laced obstacles coated Omaha beach. "There are approximately 1000 steel hedgehogs in a single broken line," Colonel Benjamin "Monk" Dickson, General Bradley's intelligence chief, wrote in a remarkably detailed description on April 24. "There are 43 single row segments, each comprised of 22–29 hedgehogs. The hedgehogs are 10–15 feet apart . . . segments are staggered approximately 25–50 feet and overlap approximately one hedgehog. They lie from 160 to 400 feet from the back of the beach. Sand has begun collecting around the legs of some of the hedgehogs." With every subsequent day that passed, the Germans only added to this formidable belt of obstacles.

The growing presence of such mines and obstacles reflected the impact of Nazi Germany's most famous soldier, Field Marshal Erwin Rommel. Known as the "Desert Fox" for his exploits in North Africa, Rommel was responsible for defense of the northern coast of France. He strongly believed that the invasion must be stopped at the waterline, where the Allies were most vulnerable. If the Allies carved out a lodgement in France, then their superior manpower, airpower, firepower, and resources would eventually seal Germany's doom, at least in Rommel's opinion. Therefore, they had to be stopped right at the waterline, on the day of the invasion (famously dubbed "the longest day" by the field marshal) before this could happen. "I must restrain myself and try to beat the enemy with small means," he confided to his diary in April, "for he must be beaten, if we do not want Bolshevism to triumph." Rommel felt that only by decisively defeating the Allied invasion could Germany hope to stave off the threat in the east and perhaps even coax the Anglo-Americans to make common cause against the Soviet Union. "Rommel's plan was to make himself as strong as possible near the shore," Admiral Friedrich Ruge, his naval commander, later wrote.

"Numerous measures were taken to execute this plan," one of which was to construct an impenetrable barrier of mines, obstacles, barbed wire, and tank traps. Indeed, in an April training memo meant for circulation among his commanders, Rommel wrote that the Allies would undoubtedly "employ hundreds of boats and ships unloading amphibious vehicles, waterproofed and submergeable [sic] tanks. We must stop him in the water, not only delaying him but destroy all enemy equipment while still afloat." He spent much of the spring visiting coastal defense units, making sure that commanders carried out his vision of defending at the waterline. This accounted for the dramatic acceleration in mining and obstacle construction by the end of April.[9]

Rommel's coastal defense measures presented the very real possibility that the infantrymen of the Big Red One would hit the beach and find themselves trapped in a kill zone, shredded by mines, pinned in place by obstacles and barbed wire, totally vulnerable to German firepower emanating from the pillboxes in the draws and the high ground overlooking the beach. This new threat called for new tactics. Originally, General Bradley had hoped that the combination of air strikes, naval bombardment, bulldozer tanks, and engineers from the assault divisions would neutralize the threat of mines. By April, though, he understood that this would not be sufficient (as did General Gerow, who had already been thinking along these lines for several weeks). The only way to make absolutely sure that the obstacles were cleared and the mines defused was to send in specially trained engineer teams with the leading assault infantrymen. This led to the creation of Gap Assault Teams, consisting of sailors from Naval Combat Demolition Units and Army engineers, primarily from the 146th and 299th Engineer Combat Battalions. The latter unit was composed mainly of men from upstate New York. The Navy's job was to deal with everything under the water. The Army was supposed to handle threats above the waterline. Because commanders understood that mines were easier to spot and obstacles easier to clear when they were not underwater, they

decided that Omaha must be assaulted at low tide. The proper tidal conditions would occur only on June 5, 6, or 7, and this, as much as any other factor, led to Eisenhower's choice of an invasion date, as well as the hour for the amphibious assaults.

In all, sixteen Gap Assault Teams were assigned to Omaha beach, half in the 1st Division sector (teams 9 through 16 comprising primarily the sailors and men from the 299th) and half in the 29th sector (teams 1 through 8). Each team was composed of nine sailors and twenty-seven soldiers, including one medic. The Navy component included one officer, as did the Army contingent; the latter had priority of command. The sailors wore Army-style gear, but to a close observer, they were identifiable as Navy men. Their M1 helmets were painted with a horizontal gray line and were stenciled with "USN" near the front rim. They wore green herringbone twill uniforms, as opposed to wools or ODs, and on their feet, they wore Corcoran jump boots designed for the airborne (one can only imagine the reaction of any paratrooper who might have beheld the sight of such sanctified items on the feet of nautical non-jumpers). One Sherman tank equipped with a bulldozer blade—generally known as a tank dozer—was slated to support each team. Not only would the tank dozers provide fire support, but their blades could sweep aside unfastened obstacles. Every team would hit the beach in a Landing Craft, Mechanized (LCM), which was basically a modified Higgins boat that allowed the teams to carry extra explosives and equipment. The supporting tank dozers would hit the beach from a Landing Craft, Tank (LCT). In addition to their heavy personal load of C-2 explosives, Primacord, blasting caps, fuse ignitors, and other gear, the men would carry extra explosives ashore in rubber boats. "The boys went into the beaches carrying forty pounds of specially prepared explosives," Lieutenant Commander Joseph Gibbons, the senior naval commander, said a few months after D-Day. In his recollection, each rubber boat carried another three hundred pounds of explosives.

Every team was supposed to blow a fifty-yard gap in the enemy obstacle line (totaling sixteen gaps across the expanse of Omaha beach) to clear the way for infantrymen, tanks, and other vehicles to get off the beach. With this accomplished, the engineers would stay behind and dispose of any remaining obstacles and mines. A subsequent support wave of eight more Gap Assault Teams, split evenly between the two divisional sectors, was supposed to land eleven minutes after the initial assault teams, at about 0645, and augment the efforts of their first-wave comrades. At most, they would have about sixty minutes to accomplish their mission before the incoming tide began to engulf many of the obstacles. Over the course of two hectic weeks, the soldiers and sailors trained together for this vital and daunting mission. Obviously this was nowhere near an adequate amount of preparation time for such an important task. Nonetheless, the two groups got along reasonably well and forged a bond of sorts. They did not, however, have the opportunity to work in any substantive way with the 1st Infantry Division prior to the Omaha landings. Their first experience with the Big Red One would be on the sands of Omaha.[10]

1

By the middle of May, when the division was sequestered in marshaling areas, waiting for the word to board ships, the troops had a rich array of intelligence information at their fingertips. "Special devices used in the dissemination of intelligence included . . . scale models, sand tables, low oblique photographs, vectographs, aerial mosaics and scale diagrams of enemy beach obstacles, pill-boxes and emplacements," a division intelligence (G2) report stated. "A set of low oblique photographs, taken from an altitude of 20 feet showing in detail the beach obstacles, was distributed to every company commander." Intelligence specialists set up heavily guarded secret rooms packed with photographs, easels, sand tables, reports, and the like. Once the troops were sealed inside their marshaling areas and thus could not divulge the secrets of the invasion, they were allowed into the previously restricted rooms. "The Secret Room's walls are hung with maps, charts and sketches of Omaha beach," Lieutenant Franklyn Johnson wrote in a present-tense account. "Recent photos outline the steep and bare cliffs along our sector of Omaha. The pictures of known and suspected underwater and beach obstacles which will aid an eighteen-foot tide in hampering us, the intricate machine-gun positions, artillery emplacements, ammo dumps, O.P.'s [observation posts], and bristling concrete pillboxes. Tables along the wall hold the latest G-2 and daily enemy situation reports, and the attack orders emanating so far from higher Allied headquarters." In the center of the room a ten-foot-long scale model of Omaha beach practically enthralled Johnson and his platoon. The detail was almost uncanny, right down to individual trees and fences. The maps of Saint-Laurent-sur-Mer and Colleville-sur-Mer— the two main towns just inland from Omaha beach—were so thorough that they portrayed the exact location and composition of each building. In general, the troops were free to study all of this information as much as they liked. One man in the 16th Infantry, for instance, became so familiar with the beach and its environs that when he landed on D-Day, he felt, according to the regimental history, as if he was "coming back to a countryside with which he had been familiar since boyhood."

For all the wealth of information, there was one major oversight. The small-unit commanders who were charged with the vital task of leading the assault troops ashore on D-Day morning did not possess accurate, up-to-date information about the German order of battle. Allied intelligence officers, from Bradley's First Army on down to the 1st Infantry Division, believed that Omaha beach was defended only by a reinforced battalion of about 1,000 soldiers from the inferior 716th Infantry Division, a static unit composed of overaged men and conscripted Eastern Europeans. In reality, the equivalent of another battalion from the 916th Grenadier Regiment, 352nd Infantry Division, was also in place at Omaha beach. Allied intelligence rated the 352nd as a quality formation, composed mostly of young German replacement soldiers, eastern-front veterans, and a sprinkling of Eastern Europeans.

On the eve of D-Day, Generals Gerow and Huebner, plus their respective staffs, believed that the 352nd was in the Saint-Lô Caumont area, more than twenty miles away from Omaha beach. The planners expected to fight the 352nd inland, not at the waterline. Because the 352nd contained few vehicles, planners estimated that the leading elements of the division would not arrive in the Omaha beach area until, at the earliest, D-Day afternoon or, more likely, the morning of D+1. "During the night," Lieutenant Colonel Robert Evans, the G2 of the 1st Division, wrote in a pre-invasion estimate of German capabilities, "the enemy may employ elements of one regiment of the 352nd Infantry Division to infiltrate our positions." Instead those "elements" were already in position, overlooking the beach. Contrary to popular myth, this was not because they just happened to be in the area conducting anti-invasion exercises. In truth, they were there as a result of Rommel's defend-at-the-waterline strategy, and they had been at Omaha since March. The fallacy of the quixotic anti-invasion exercises grew out of initial—and rather confused—D-Day interrogations with some of the first German prisoners and subsequently showed up as an article of faith in many post-D-Day after-action reports. Later, the story probably took hold in the popular imagination because such a random fortune-of-war tale appealed to the D-Day legend more than did the uncomfortable reality of two failures. First, Allied intelligence failed over the course of more than two months to detect the movement of the 352nd to the coast. Second, even if the 352nd had remained at Saint-Lô, the very real possibility existed, according to the planners' own estimates, that the assault troops would have to fight elements of the 352nd at or near Omaha beach within hours of the invasion. Yet the generals did not adequately plan for this eventuality; nor did they properly alert their subordinate commanders to the likelihood of what they were about to face. Hence, after months of elaborate planning, thinking, training, and rehearsals, all designed to maximize every possible chance of success and minimize losses in anticipation of the greatest invasion in human history and, in spite of the most herculean preparation for any military operation in modern history, the Big Red One was about to head into a death trap.[11]

Chapter 2

INTENTIONS

The sea pounded relentlessly against the stones and shale of Omaha beach. The smell of sea salt, sand, and hydrated vegetation permeated the air. To the German garrison, the rhythmic sound of the tides had become so familiar that they scarcely noticed it anymore. The same was true of the seagulls that soared majestically along the coast, diving at their prey, splashing into the water, then zooming away into the air. Their screeching cries had become part of the ambience of this windswept, moist, misty, cloudy stretch of coastline, just as much as the hard-packed clay soil, the grassy meadows, the whiff of rich dairy products, and the quaint little towns of solid stone houses and steepled churches. The Germans had added their own unique contribution to this sliver of Normandy, though. Through strenuous, backbreaking toil—to the point that the men came to feel more like construction laborers than soldiers—they had built a formidable series of fortifications to defend this section of the Calvados coast. The defenses were

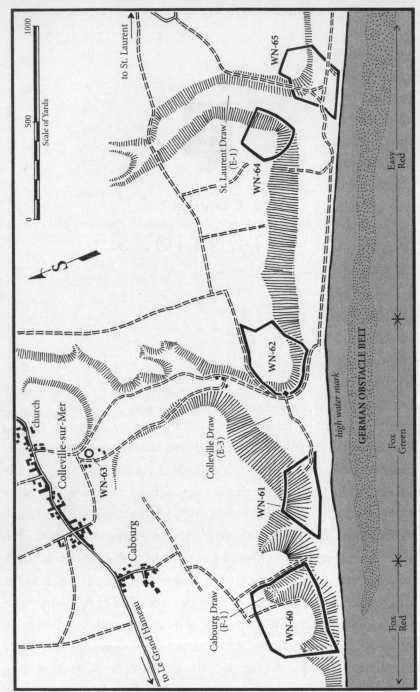

1ST INFANTRY DIVISION LANDING BEACHES

Protected by six distinct German resistance nests (WN-60 through WN-65) and a thick belt of obstacles, the beaches, code-named Fox Red, Fox Green and Easy Red, comprised the eastern half of Omaha beach. The three draws were the vital objectives. Only by controlling the draws could the Big Red One move troops, supplies, and vehicles off the beach and inland.

designed around strong points dubbed *Widerstandsnest* or just "WN" by the Germans; they were sometimes called "resistance nests" by the Allies. The WNs were generally sited along the five natural beach exits, each of which had been created in the valleys between slopes by thousands of years of wind, rain, and erosion. Each of the three exits in the 1st Infantry Division sector, from east to west identified as F-1, E-3, and E-1, contained a small road, but none of the three was paved well enough or was large enough to support armor or other heavy vehicles. Both the Americans and the Germans understood that these exits, or draws, offered the only sustainable way to get off the beach. The infantry would have to take the draws; the engineers would then follow up and pave them into real roads capable of handling large volumes of vehicle and troop traffic.

Omaha was a crescent-shaped, almost concave beach, nestled between cliffs at either end (Rommel once commented that it reminded him of Salerno, in Italy, which the Allies had invaded the year before). The beach sloped several feet in elevation from the waterline to a narrow, rocky shingle composed of a blanket of fist-sized stones that jutted upward at about a forty-five-degree angle. Beyond the shingle were the bluffs and valleys. "Bluffs 100 to 170 feet in height rise sharply from the flat and dominate the whole beach area," an Army official historian wrote. "The slopes are generally steep, but in varying degree. The grass covered slopes are more uneven than they appear when viewed from only a short distance. From Exit E-1 and eastward [the 1st Division sector], the bluff sides are partly covered with low scrub and brush. Along most of the stretch, the bluff ends in a clear-cut crest line as it reaches the edge of the inland plateau; toward the eastern end, where the slopes are longer and more gradual, the edge is not sharply defined." Basically, a pair of prominent ridges overlooked the beach—it was ideal defensive ground, affording the Germans nice fields of fire and observation. Beyond the beach lay rolling plains, the small towns of Cabourg,

Colleville-sur-Mer, and Saint-Laurent-sur-Mer, and hedgerow-enclosed fields.

Along the eastern half of Omaha beach, some 3,500 yards of coastline where the 1st Division was scheduled to land, the German soldiers had prepared six distinct strong points, numbered from WN-60 at the eastern edge of Omaha to WN-65 at Exit E-1, a few thousand yards to the west. Each of the WNs was ringed by mines, barbed wire, and antitank ditches. All contained numerous fortifications commonly and interchangeably referred to as pillboxes, bunkers, and dugouts by American soldiers. In general, they were constructed of ferroconcrete, of almost stony rather than smooth consistency, and reinforced with steel rods. WN-60 was sited on a cliff more than one hundred feet above the beach and contained several concrete emplacements, all of which were linked together by zigzagging trenches. The southeast part of WN-60 was anchored by a "Tobruk" (so named for Italian positions in North Africa). A Tobruk was basically a dugout ring of reinforced concrete that could mount mortars, machine guns, or, as was the case here, a Renault tank turret. Another Tobruk in the center of the strong point contained a mortar. Nearby was a 20-millimeter flak gun with a commanding view of the entire beach. Two more mortar Tobruks were sited at the western flank, another to the rear or landward side. The centerpiece of WN-60 was a dugout with a 75-millimeter antitank gun facing west, right over the beach. There was also a concrete observation post and concrete shelters for the troops. A platoon-sized group of forty soldiers under the command of a Sergeant Eberhardt manned WN-60. They had a breathtaking view of the entire expanse of Omaha beach.

Slightly to the west, on the other side of the valley known to the Americans as the Cabourg draw or Exit F-1, WN-61 was sited directly overlooking the sea and a rocky, flat beach that now rambled out westward from the cliff. WN-61 contained three Tobruks, one with a Renault tank turret and two for machine guns and flamethrowers. A 50-millimeter antitank gun, in a dugout pit, faced westward. By far the most powerful weapon at WN-61 was an 88-millimeter Pak gun ensconced in a concrete casemate that afforded nearly complete protection for the crew and only a small embrasure through which the gun's menacing barrel protruded. The casemate was designed to shield the gun crew from naval and tank fire. Their field of fire commanded all of Omaha beach. The gun could savage tanks, landing craft, and soldiers alike. In fact, this 88, in combination with another one at WN-71, guarding the Vierville-sur-Mer draw on the western edge of Omaha, in the 29th Division sector, bracketed the whole beach. Twelve German soldiers, under the command of a Sergeant Major Schnuell, constituted the garrison of WN-61.

A couple hundred yards to the west, where the ground gently sloped about seventy yards downward from a valley (Exit E-3 or Colleville draw) and onto the now wide-open beach, the Germans had sited formidable WN-62. Because of its ideal location and variety of weaponry, WN-62 was one of the most daunting of all the strong points, not just at Omaha but in all of Normandy. From here, the German garrison, comprising a mixed group of about thirty-five soldiers from both the 716th and the 352nd Infantry Divisions, could scorch every inch of the beach with gunfire. WN-62 was a concentric ring of concrete fortifications, about five hundred yards in circumference, within a belt of mines, barbed wire, and an antitank ditch. The strong point was honeycombed with a disquieting array of death-dealing devices: a trio of 50-millimeter mortar Tobruks, though one of the Tobruks contained a pair of infantrymen rather than a mortar, a dug-in, camouflaged 50-millimeter antitank gun, an antiaircraft bunker mounting twin machine guns, a beautifully sited artillery observation bunker (known to the Germans as B-Stelle) built into the ground from which Lieutenant Bernhard Frerking could call down accurate fire from an inland battery of four 105-millimeter guns from the 1st Battery, 352nd Artillery Regiment a pair of flamethrowers overlooking the draw another 50-millimeter antitank gun facing the draw itself, three machine-gun bunkers sited to saturate the beach, plus a pair of heavily reinforced casemates housing 75-millimeter Czech-made antitank guns, both of which were sited in such a way as to command the beach but shield themselves from naval fire. At the rear of WN-62, an underground two-room bunker provided living quarters, complete with double-decker wooden bunks, for the troops. Each room could house eight men, who slept on thin, straw-filled mattresses. Zigzag trenches connected many of the positions, although they had not been completely finished by June 6. The Germans razed most of the buildings along Omaha beach. However, at the eastern edge of WN-62 they left an old villa standing so they could use it as a headquarters and canteen. Soldiers from both WN-62 and WN-61 ate their meals in this building. Initially, a man who was a pastry chef in civilian life served as the cook. But he got fired when Senior Corporal Valentine Lehrmann found a pair of rats in his soup one day. The replacement cook was so poor, though, that eventually the pastry chef, at the behest of his comrades, resumed his duties.

WN-63 was located inland at the edge of Colleville and was really little more than an underground concrete command bunker. Two resistance nests, WN-64 and WN-65, covered the Ruquet Valley, known to the Americans as the Saint-Laurent draw or Exit E-1. WN-64 overlooked the eastern edge of the draw, at roughly the same spot where the American cemetery is located today. The defenses here were oriented westward, straight into the valley. They included a pair of mortar Tobruks, a 20-millimeter antiaircraft gun, and a 76.2-millimeter Soviet-made field gun situated alongside an unfinished casemate, along with the usual zigzag trenches and dugouts. On the other side of the draw was WN-65. Here the fortifications were oriented eastward to cover the valley and the beach. The anchor of the strong point was a brand-new casemate sheltering a 50-millimeter antitank gun sited to savage any vehicle that tried to enter the draw. In front of the casemate were a pair of mortar Tobruks whose guns could rake the beach with fire.

Nearby, a 50-millimeter field gun was dug into a pit, camouflaged and reinforced with earth. Farther inland, another 75-millimeter gun, sheltered only with wooden beams, protected the draw. Fortunately for the Americans, neither WN-64 nor WN-65 was completed by D-Day, though both were obviously still quite potent even in this unfinished state.

So, in addition to a beach laced with obstacles and mines, draws sown liberally with more mines, antitank ditches and marshes, barbed wire and formidable terrain, the 1st Infantry Division was faced with a troubling array of enemy weaponry—at least thirteen fortified, well-sited antitank or field guns, two Tobruk tank turrets, a pair of 20-millimeter antitank guns, a couple of automatic flamethrowers, a dozen or perhaps even a dozen and a half mortars (each of which could fire fifteen to twenty-five shells per minute), and more than forty machine guns, many of which were protected by concrete emplacements—plus innumerable riflemen. The equivalent of four German companies, tantamount to an understrength battalion of about four hundred to five hundred soldiers from both the 716th and the 352nd, defended the 1st Division sector (not to mention reserve companies from the 352nd that were stationed inland, positioned to counterattack). Moreover, the beach was well covered by inland artillery. In addition to Nebelwerfer rocket batteries at Saint-Laurent, twenty-four 105-millimeter field guns were in position to shell the Big Red One's landing spots. Fortunately, the Germans had almost no air or sea assets to defend the beach. Even so, the defenses, when combined with such forbidding terrain, were of sufficient strength to inflict massive casualties and foil the landing itself, particularly if the Germans could reinforce the relatively small number of soldiers at the beach positions. Rommel intended for this very outcome, though as of early June, he still felt that Omaha's defenses were not yet strong enough to realize his vision.[1]

Meanwhile, the 1st Division's plan of assault represented a convergence of intense training, combined arms coordination, interservice cooperation, firepower, and innovation. The divisional beaches were divided roughly equally between the Fox Green sector in the east, abutting the cliffs defended by WN-60, and the Easy Red sector, whose westernmost sands bordered the E-3 draw and thus WN-64 and WN-65. Following the naval and aerial bombardment (about forty minutes in duration), the landings on these two beaches were to take place on a very precise timetable. At 0625, five minutes before H-Hour, two companies of specially designed amphibious duplex drive, or DD, tanks, after swimming some five thousand yards to shore, would hit Fox Green and Easy Red, respectively. Company B, 741st Tank Battalion, was assigned to Easy Red, and Company C of the same battalion to Fox Green. Each company consisted of sixteen DD tanks. Their job was to spread out just above the waterline and lay down a heavy blanket of covering fire from their 75-millimeter main guns against the German fortifications. They would be followed five minutes later, at the stroke of 0630, or H-Hour, by A Company of the 741st Tank Battalion, a non-amphibious outfit equipped with waterproofed but otherwise standard M4 Sherman tanks and Sherman tank dozers ideally suited to clear obstacles. They would be deposited on both Fox Green and Easy Red by eight amphibious assault ships known as Landing Craft, Tanks, or LCTs. Like their comrades in B and C Companies, the tank crewmen of A Company were to lay down supporting fire. The same was true for self-propelled howitzers aboard landing craft offshore. As they waited to land, they would fire at targets along the coastline. One minute later, at 0631, four infantry companies from the 2nd and 3rd Battalions, 16th Infantry Regiment, would arrive by Higgins boats and carry out the main assault—I and L Companies at Fox Green, E and F Companies at Easy Red. Two minutes later, the Gap Assault Teams would come ashore to deal with the obstacles and mines. This sequence would constitute the entirety of the first wave, although there were some advance parties of divisional engineers, artillery observers, reconnaissance troops, and the like.

The second wave, consisting of K and G Companies, would not land until H+30, at 0700. They would be supported by machine-gun-toting M16 halftracks from the 397th Antiaircraft Artillery Battalion. Ten minutes later, M and H Companies, with heavy machine guns and mortars, were to land at Fox Green and Easy Red, respectively. At H+50, A and C Companies, 81st Chemical Mortar Battalion, would land and provide even more mortar fire to the riflemen, machine gunners, and bazookamen who planners expected would be fighting their way up and along the draws by now. Just over an hour after the initial landings, at H+70, the 1st Battalion, 16th Infantry would beach, with A and C Companies leading the way. Company B would follow ten minutes later. At H+90, D Company, the battalion's heavy weapons company, would hit the beach, as would the 62nd Field Artillery Battalion.

From H+105 through H+130, the headquarters detachments, Cannon Company, rear echelon elements and vehicles of the rifle companies, and more supporting halftracks from the 197th Antiaircraft Artillery Battalion in addition to three batteries from the 7th Field Artillery Battalion were to land, plus division engineers and medics. At that point, most of Colonel George Taylor's 16th Infantry Regiment (often termed "regimental combat team" because of its combined arms nature for the invasion) would be ashore. His mission was to secure the beach, the draws, the high ground overlooking Omaha beach, and to patrol inland. In addition, the 16th Infantry soldiers were to cover the subsequent landings of the division's two other infantry regiments.

Colonel George Smith's 18th Infantry Regiment (or regimental combat team) was scheduled to come ashore at Easy Red beginning at three hours after H-Hour. Its mission was to link up with the 16th and then, according to the unit's pre-invasion orders, "move with greatest possible speed to its assigned sector, capture objectives, prepare the high ground east of Trevieres for all-around defense." Basically, that meant the 18th was to forge inland, while maintaining contact with the rest of the division, and gradually push eastward to link up with the British 50th Infantry Division coming from Gold beach. The 26th Infantry Regiment (again, it can also be referred to as a regimental combat team) would function as V Corps reserve and go ashore at Fox Green and Easy Red whenever General Gerow or General Huebner dictated.

The plan was, of course, more detailed, more minute, more synchronized than this mere summary might indicate. There were many smaller specialty units involved. There were intricate instructions for communications, medics, and follow-on engineers to organize the beach and begin the road building in the draws. There were plans for liaisons between units, plans for the landing throughout the day of V Corps troops, military police, follow-on supplies, vehicles, and communications gear, not to mention intricate plans for the loading and unloading of troops, vehicles, and matériel. In essence, though, this was the blueprint for the assault on Omaha, and it represented the best and the worst of the U.S. Army's mind-set at the time. Its success depended on fast action, a lethal mixture of firepower, an exacting—and almost exasperating—multiplicity of specialized jobs on the part of the assault troops, and, more than anything else, good small-unit leadership and valor. All of this was present in substantial quantities in the assaulting units, especially in the 1st Division.

However, the plan also revealed an American tendency to overestimate the capabilities of heavy bombers, warships, and, in general, supporting firepower to neutralize enemy resistance. Moreover, the plan relied too heavily on matériel and vehicles, rather than an abundance of assault infantry, which was what the mission would ultimately demand. This meant that the average soldier was going into the fight of his life overloaded with too much gear and restricted in his mobility by too many vehicles and too much equipment, all of which presented the Germans with ideal targets. In addition, the plan underestimated the German commitment to defend Omaha at the waterline with a vexing array of quality troops, fortifications, and firepower. Regardless, even a perfect plan could not have thoroughly prepared the soldiers for what was to come or, for that matter, guaranteed their success. Only the troops themselves could make that happen. "Suddenly and for the first time, I began to realize the magnitude of invasion and its relentless force," Don Whitehead, an esteemed war correspondent who was scheduled to land with the 16th Infantry, wrote in wonderment. "It was as though man for centuries had lived, begotten offspring and labored toward this moment which would shape the world's history for all time to come. I wondered how easy it would be and how red the sand before another sundown. I wondered how many thousands of those battle-tough, homesick youths bobbing around us in assault craft would get beyond the beach." As those landing craft began to head for the Fox Green and Easy Red sections of Omaha beach, many others were contemplating the same thing. After so many months of preparation, deliberation, and planning—filled with times of soul-searching, camaraderie, hard work, joy, and anticipation—the moment of decision was finally at hand.[2]

Chapter 3

H-HOUR

From nearly the first moment, disaster lurked like an assassin in the shadows. The sky was overcast. A bone-chilling wind blew relentlessly. The sea was angry. Heavy waves lapped at the prows of tank-bearing LCTs as they plowed toward Omaha beach, as yet unseen beyond layers of sea mist, clouds, and smoke some six thousand yards away. Aboard LCT-537, Captain James Thornton, a short, muscular North Carolinian and 1940 graduate of the Citadel, surveyed the ocean with his penetrating blue eyes. As commander of B Company, 741st Tank Battalion, he had trained his men to launch their amphibious "duplex drive" (DD) Sherman tanks into less-than-tranquil seas, but never in waters this rough. The twenty-six-year-old company commander contemplated whether to order his ship's crew to raise a yellow flag, the prearranged signal to launch his company's tanks. He radioed Captain Charles Young, commander of C Company, who was aboard LCT-598, elsewhere in the column of eight LCTs carrying their two companies. According to the 741st's after-action report, the two officers conversed briefly and agreed that "the advantage to be gained by the launching of the tanks justified the risk of launching [them] in the heavy sea." Moreover, they both felt duty-bound to proceed with their mission as planned. As the senior of the two, the ultimate decision belonged to Thornton. Without consulting Lieutenant (j.g.) J. E. Barry, the senior naval officer of the group, who was aboard LCT-549 somewhere at the head of the column, Thornton gave the order to launch. This was a shame because, in Barry's estimation, "it was obvious even before launching that the sea at that distance was too choppy for the tanks." In fact, the first Barry learned of the order was when he saw LCT-537 come to a halt and lower its ramp.

The DD tanks were equipped with an inflatable canvas skirt for flotation and dual propellers in the rear to power them once they were in the water. They were ingenious devices, but suitable only for calm waters and good weather. Even in ideal conditions, they could be vulnerable to the wake of landing craft and ships, as well as the concussion from exploding shells. Nor was it a good idea to disgorge them at distances farther than four thousand yards away from the beach, for the obvious reason that the longer they were in the water, the better chance they would swamp and sink. Their purpose—beyond just fire support for the infantry—was to surprise and shock the Germans. From previous Allied invasions, the Germans were well used to seeing LCTs beach and land armor, but they had never seen swimming tanks. Captain Thornton believed that the chance to stun the enemy defenders, combined with the many months he and his troops had trained to become amphibious tankers, justified the risk of braving the poor conditions. He made the wrong call. The yellow flag went up and the amphibious tankers of the 741st sprang into action.

Within minutes of his launch order, as the DD tanks gingerly edged their way off LCT ramps and into the water, a tragic debacle ensued. "In most cases," the after-action report stated, "the sea was so rough that the DDs were damaged after proceeding a short distance toward shore. This damage consisted mostly of broken struts, torn canvasses, and improperly functioning engines which had been clogged with sea water which had flooded the engine compartments." The unruly sea began to overwhelm and collapse the canvas skirts. Tanks lost their buoyancy. As they took on water and lost their stability, engines failed and the thirty-ton steel monsters began to slip under the waves and sink like stones. The skipper of LCT-602, Ensign R. L. Harkey, watched helplessly as four tanks from C Company left his craft and soon ran into trouble. He saw one of them drop into the ocean, "turn right, past the forecastle. It bobbed for a moment, then suddenly sank. The soldiers in it promptly inflated a rubber life raft. The third and fourth tanks were launched and when both were in the water, one sank." The fourth tank soon sank as well, much to Harkey's dismay. "Needless to say, I am not proud of the fact nor will I ever cease regretting that I did not take the tanks all the way to the beach." The same was true for the other skippers.

The tank crewmen were equipped with Mae West life vests and, as Harkey indicated, life rafts. Each man also carried the Davis Breathing Apparatus (sometimes called the "Davis Lung" by the crewmen) to sustain life in the event they could not immediately escape the sunken tank. This contraption pinched off the man's nose and fitted a rubber breathing hose over his mouth. The hose was connected to an oxygen bag. The gadget was awkward and difficult to use. For one thing, it was hard to fit through the hatch of a tank. For another, the pieces were hard to fit snugly onto a man's mouth and nose under good conditions on dry land, much less within the chaotic confines of a sinking tank. Thus, most of the tankers did not even mess with it. Instead they invested their hopes of survival in escaping the tank, inflating their vests, and finding a raft. Indeed, many of them sat atop the turrets of their tanks after launching; this made it easier to escape in case they swamped.

Sitting on the turret of one B Company Sherman, Staff Sergeant Millard Case heard the ugly sound of his tank's canvas skirt tearing. He looked around, saw water lapping over the canvas, and knew exactly what that meant. "I knew damn well [the tank] was going down. And that life raft we had, I had it arranged so that when I pulled the string . . . it would inflate." He pulled the string, but the raft inflated only halfway. The massive suction created by the sinking tank plunged him downward. Somehow, he managed to hang on to the raft. When he surfaced, he and another crewman piled into the raft. The other three men in his crew drowned.

Elsewhere, Private First Class Ralph Woodward was sitting in the assistant driver's seat of Captain Young's tank when the waves began crashing over the canvas cover. "We were lucky we didn't wash back against the ramp. I don't think we went one hundred feet, pretty soon the pipes started kinking, the struts started snapping back in center, the canvas started tearing." They were sinking, and the captain gave the order to abandon the tank. Woodward inflated his life vest. He got partially through his hatch, wrenching his left arm out of the socket, but then he got caught on the tank's .50-caliber machine gun. With terrifying alacrity, the Sherman plunged beneath the waves and down to the seabed, all the while dragging Woodward with it. "When we hit bottom, sand came up in my face. The first thing that came to my mind was my folks will never know where the hell I'm at." He was so convinced he was about to die that he did not even bother fastening his Davis Lung. "I thought no use setting down there, laying down there, thinking for ten minutes— just that quick you think of things. So I started drinking water." Somehow, though, he got loose of the .50-caliber, and the flotation of his life vest propelled him upward. The water grew lighter until he finally came to the surface. A small rocket boat picked him up, and Captain Young as well. Woodward coughed up water and blood, and he had to have his arm maneuvered back into place, but he was otherwise okay. The driver of the tank never got out of his seat, and drowned at the bottom.

Sergeant Phil Fitts's tank had made it about halfway to the beach when the engine died from water intake and the waves began to swamp the turret. The tank commander ordered the crew to inflate the life raft and abandon the tank. "I was the last one to step off of the tank rail and into the raft," Fitts later said. "The tank disappeared from under my foot into a swirl of water, gone." In some instances, the suction caused by the sinking tanks capsized rafts or sucked unfortunate crewmen under the waves, but not in this case. Fitts and his comrades bobbed around in the water for more than half an hour until a patrol boat took them aboard. Many others did the same. There were so many in the water that the assault troops could not help but notice them as their Higgins boats headed for the coast. At first, the infantrymen thought the men in the water were downed fliers, but eventually the truth sank in. Needless to say, the realization that their DD tanks were at the bottom of the Channel rather than about to land on Omaha beach was not a morale booster for those about to go in with the first wave.

In total, twenty-nine tanks from B and C Companies were launched into the inhospitable waters. Only a pair, under the command of Sergeants George Geddes and Turner Sheppard of B Company, managed to swim to shore. Three more made it, ironically, because of a mishap aboard LCT-600 when the tanks collided and damaged their canvas frames. Ensign Henry Sullivan, the skipper of the boat, decided to abort, pull the ramp up, and carry them into the beach. So, a total of only five out of thirty-two DD tanks were of any use to the leading assault troops. Among those that sank, most of the crewmen survived. Nonetheless, Lieutenant Colonel Robert Skaggs, commander of the 741st, later estimated that an average of one man per tank drowned.[1]

As the tank crewmen struggled with Poseidon, a couple dozen landing craft, bearing the assault companies of the 2nd and 3rd Battalions, bucked and smashed their way through the tumultuous waters, toward the Normandy shoreline. The men were already soaking wet from sea spray and miserable with seasickness. In many cases, they had difficulty maintaining their footing aboard the jostling boats. Both battalions were struggling to stay on course and on time and both were failing, especially the 3rd Battalion. The 3rd had been transported from England by HMS *Empire Anvil*, a British vessel. This meant that the infantry companies rode in an LCA (Landing Craft, Assault), the British version of the Higgins boat, piloted by Royal Navy coxswains. The LCA was equipped with armor on the sides and partially over the main compartment, where the troops were seated on three rows of crude benches. In the middle row, they sat face forward with their knees dug into the next man's side or back. Along the two end rows, they sat facing the opposite side of the landing craft, looking directly at the men in the middle row, their knees often bumping against the equipment, weapons, or bodies of those in the middle row. The taller men on the end rows had to bend their necks to keep from bumping their helmets against the overhanging armored bulkhead. "It felt like we were squeezed tighter than sardines in a can," Corporal Albert Mominee, a runner in I Company, said.

The LCA was more maneuverable than the American-made LCVP, but it was also lower to the water, making it vulnerable to flooding. "They were easily 'swamped' in the water," Major Edwin Elder, the battalion operations officer, asserted. This was especially true in heavy seas of the sort that raged right now off Omaha beach; several of the boats were already taking on dangerous amounts of water. Men removed their helmets and frantically bailed seawater to keep from sinking. Moreover, the sea mist, combined with the cloudy conditions and the plumes of smoke from the bombardment, reduced visibility substantially. The coxswains had great difficulty seeing where they were going. What's more, the tide was flowing steadily to the east, so the tendency for all the landing craft was to veer off course in that direction.

The poor conditions and the confusion wrecked the carefully planned landing timetable. As H-Hour approached, the 3rd Battalion LCAs were floundering in confusion, nowhere near in position to land. Captain Kimball Richmond's I Company was in the worst spot of all. The coxswains attempted to land the company on a small beach at Port-en-Bessin, some six thousand yards east of Fox Green, the company's actual target. Richmond was a combat-wise officer with a regiment-wide reputation for valor and competence. He immediately picked up on the mistake and ordered the sailors to put their ramps back up, take the company back out to sea and head for the proper landing spot at Fox Green. With more than a little disgust, Richmond radioed his battalion commander, Lieutenant Colonel Charles Horner, informed him of the mishap, and told him that there was no way I Company would land on time. Horner radioed Captain Anthony Prucnal, commander of K Company, and told him to take Richmond's place. Prucnal would try, but his outfit was running late too, as was Captain John Armellino's L Company. Basically, the battalion was going to land late and in piecemeal fashion, and there was very little the commanders could do about it now.[2]

▼1

In the strong points overlooking Omaha beach, the German defenders were groggy from lack of sleep. Most had been up since 0100, on alert status, in response to the reports of airborne landings on the Cotentin Peninsula and multiple bombing raids around Normandy. Their ears were still ringing from the noise of the pre-invasion bombardment, and their eyes stung from the dust and dirt kicked up by so many explosions. Now, as they gazed seaward, through layers of fog, mist, and smoke, they could just begin to make out the sight of the vast Allied armada and the approaching landing craft. At WN-62, overlooking the E-3 draw, Lieutenant Bernhard Frerking, an artillery observer from the 1st Battalion, 352nd Artillery Regiment, was standing outside his observation bunker and peering through binoculars at the horizon when the full immensity of the sight began to dawn on him. He lowered the binoculars and muttered, "But that's not possible, that's not possible." He thrust the binoculars into the hands of his orderly, Private First Class Hein Severloh, and raced into the bunker to prepare for a fire mission. Severloh ran around warning the other soldiers to be ready at their posts. Frerking entered the bunker, picked up the phone to his battery of 105-millimeter guns located a couple of kilometers away at Houtteville, and was pleasantly surprised to find that it was working in spite of the massive bombardment. He was also amazed to realize that all of the battalion's batteries were still intact, ready to fire. "Target Dora, all guns, range four-eight-five-zero, basic direction twenty plus, impact fuse," he told the gun position officer. "Wait for the order to fire!" The standing order from regiment was to hold fire until the landing craft reached the waterline.

Several yards away, in a hexagonal concrete shelter overlooking the draw, Corporal Franz Gockel, an eighteen-year-old recruit with less than a year of service time in the army, hunched over his Polish-made 7.9-millimeter SMG 248 water-cooled machine gun. His position was protected by a full meter of dirt and wooden planks, but he felt anything but safe. He glanced at the approaching craft and repeatedly checked his machine gun to make sure it was ready to fire. Terror crept up his spine. He came from a devout Catholic family. During bombing raids back home in Hamm, the family had often clustered into a shelter and prayed to Jesus, Mary, and Joseph. As Gockel inspected his gun and watched the boats grow closer, he murmured his Catholic prayers to himself, repeating them over and over, soothing his taut nerves. In retrospect, he felt almost as if he were "kind of getting myself into a trance." Senior Corporal Siegfried Kuska, who was crawling past

Gockel's position on his way to man a 50-millimeter antitank gun in a camouflaged hole closer to the draw, paused a moment, looked at Gockel, and yelled, "Watch out, Franz, they're coming!" Gockel's gaze shifted from his comrade to the beach. The boats were almost at the waterline. Gockel leaned into his weapon and opened fire. At WN-62 and elsewhere, many other Germans did the same.[3]

In those boats, confusion reigned. Just as with 3rd Battalion, the twelve LCVPs carrying E and F Companies had lost all semblance of organization. They were supposed to touch ground simultaneously in the middle of Easy Red, between Exits E-3 and E-1. Instead most were bearing too far left, in the direction of Fox Green, WN-62, and the eastern side of Exit E-3. Aboard the heavily rolling LCVPs, miserable, seasick soldiers struggled to keep their footing on decks wet with seawater and vomit. Half-nauseated, sea-soaked leaders peered intently over the ramps and sides of their Higgins boats, catching misty glimpses of the approaching beach. Their ears were assaulted by so many sounds—the roar of the engines, the splashing of the sea, the yelling of men—that they only gradually became aware of the unnatural splashes of water, pings, and muffled explosions that indicated the presence of German fire. Many of the boat section leaders and their NCOs were well aware that they were off course. Aboard E Company's command boat, First Sergeant Lawrence Fitzsimmons and several other soldiers yelled at the coxswain, "You're going left!" Much to their chagrin, the sailor ignored their warnings and kept heading in the wrong direction. At the front of the boat, Captain Edward Wozenski, the company commander, could only shake his head in exasperation. "How anyone who had been briefed could make such an error, I will never know," he later said, "for the one house which so prominently marked Exit #E3 was in flames, and clearly showed its distinctive outline." This was the

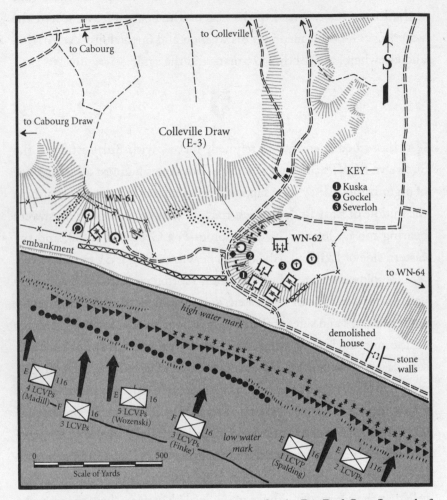

The worst moment of the Normandy invasion for the Big Red One. Instead of landing west of WN-62, in a comparatively safe spot where Lieutenant Spalding's boat section came ashore, almost all boat sections from E and F Companies, 16th Infantry, plus several wayward boats from the 29th Infantry Division's 116th Infantry landed too far east, at the Colleville draw. This placed them in a terrible kill zone between WN-61 and WN-62. Mines and obstacles only added to the carnage.

same house where Corporal Franz Gockel and the other defenders of WN-62 had eaten their meals. Wozenski ordered the LCVP crewmen to lay down some fire with the machine guns that were mounted on the stern of the boat. "The naval man on one gun fired a burst straight up into the air as he hid his head below the deck—a disgusting performance if I ever saw one. No one would man the second gun."

On a neighboring boat, an LCVP crewman yelled to the commanding officer, "They're shooting at us!" The lieutenant turned back and hollered, "Well, shoot back!" Lieutenant John Kersey, a platoon leader in E Company, was concerned that the meandering direction of his LCVP might tempt the crew into simply dumping his men into deep water and leaving. He told the coxswain, "Listen, you hit bottom or I'm going to leave a grenade for you." Aboard another E Company boat, the coxswain was so confused that he asked Technical Sergeant Calvin Ellis, "What is the objective?" Ellis pointed in the direction of Easy Red beach, but this information did not seem to sink in. Ellis then "told the coxswain he was bearing too far left, but the man kept on the same course." Captain John Finke, the commander of F Company, was also frustrated to realize that his boat was heading too far to the left. He relayed corrective instructions to the stern of the boat, where the coxswain sat guiding the craft, but to no avail. In the boat carrying the company's second assault section, Lieutenant Bernard Rush attempted to do the same. "The coxswain refused to follow these directions until too late," the boat section survivors later said in a post-combat interview. Aboard the boat carrying the company's fourth assault section, Lieutenant Glendon Siefert and his coxswain were equally confused. The sailor thought they were off course; Siefert thought they were on track. By the time they sorted this out, they were eleven hundred yards left of their proper landing spot.

The errors in placement may well have been largely due to coxswain errors, as the soldiers indicated—of course only the soldiers' perspective remains for posterity, not the sailors'—or the problems might simply have been inevitable given the circumstances. Regardless, there is no doubt that the divergence from the original landing plan was an ominous harbinger. The boats were supposed to touch down together at the exact same moment in the least-defended portion of the beach, so as to take advantage of any dead spots in the German fields of fire and present the enemy with more targets than they could shoot at. All of that careful choreography and preparation was out the window now (it was something of a metaphor for the failure of the Omaha beach assault plan as a whole). With the exception of one boat, they landed haphazardly between ten and fifteen minutes late, from 0640 to 0645, an average of about a thousand yards too far to the left, at Fox Green, right in the kill zone between WN-62 and WN-61. More specifically, three boats from F Company landed on the eastern edge of Fox Green, three others at the western edge, right where it intersected with Easy Red, under the very nose of WN-62. Five E Company boats touched down in the middle of Fox Green, in the shadow of the E-3 draw. Indeed, as a group, they could scarcely have landed at a worse spot or in a more vulnerable posture.[4]

Pandemonium and tragedy soon ensued for the two unfortunate companies. The boat carrying the first section of F Company, under Lieutenant Aaron Dennstedt, Jr., got hung up on an obstacle about thirty yards from the beach and the coxswain could not free the craft. Machine-gun bullets began to plink off the sides and the ramp. Feeling like sitting ducks, the men roared at the crew to lower the ramp and they obliged. As the ramp fell, and the men began to pile out and into water up to their chin, a lethal wave of machine-gun fire from the left front (possibly from WN-61) swept through and around the LCVP. A couple of soldiers were hit on the ramp and went down. Others were hit in the water and slipped beneath the waves. Desperately, the survivors sloshed and swam toward the beach, an onerous task under the weight of so much equipment and hindered as many of them were by acute seasickness. Lieutenant Dennstedt, a college kid who had once attended UCLA, was new to combat. Back in England, during training, he had earned a reputation among his NCOs as remarkably humble and soft-spoken for an officer. "He would say, 'You know what to do, I'll just watch and if you need something I'll get it for you,'" Staff Sergeant Andrew Nesevitch, his combat-experienced platoon guide, said of him. Nesevitch came to like him very much and appreciate that "he would never try to pull that rank." The men affectionately referred to him as "Denny" or "Lieutenant Denny."

Amid the accurate fire, Nesevitch and his lieutenant instinctively led just by wading as fast as they could to the water's edge, where they plopped down exhausted and eyed the shingle bank. The beach was, of course, a maze of obstacles, some of which were tipped with mines. As the soldiers lay there and pondered what to do, Sergeant Nesevitch suggested that the lieutenant should veer to the left while he went right. "The men will disperse and we'll get up under that bank," Nesevitch said. Lieutenant Dennstedt agreed. As they got up, the machine gun began to chatter again. Dennstedt turned to urge his men forward. A bullet smashed right through his helmet and hit him right between the eyes. "He went down with his behind up in the air," Nesevitch recalled, "and his head down." He collapsed immediately into an unnatural bent-over position in which his head rested against his knees. Blood poured from the side of his shattered helmet. Nesevitch ran to him but soon realized that the lieutenant had been killed instantly. "He's done," the young sergeant whispered softly to himself.

The platoon sergeant, Tech Sergeant Edward Zukowski, had been the last man out of the LCVP, making sure everyone left the boat. He worked his way through the water and plopped down next to Nesevitch. The latter pointed at the lieutenant's body. "Zuk," he said, "you better take over because Dennstedt got it between the eyes." Zukowski attempted to organize a small group and lead a push up the beach toward coils of barbed wire near the draw. "I set off one of the anti-personnel mines and it really blew," Zukowski recalled. "Both my arms and legs almost went. My left leg was hanging—compound fracture. [The] right one was full of shrapnel." More fragments tore into one of his arms, breaking it. His rifle was totaled. He lay still, bleeding and hoping a medic might reach him, but he was isolated in a kill zone. Only fourteen of the thirty-two men in Dennstedt's boat even made it to the shingle. The rest were killed in the water, drowned, or lay wounded at the waterline.

Immediately adjacent to Dennstedt's boat section, the second section touched down in knee-high water, a rather shallow depth by the standards of the first wave. The men poured out of the LCVP and splashed their way onto the sand (the location of the waterline varied according to tides and sandbars). They ran into a storm of mortar and machine-gun fire. "Both BAR gunners were hit almost immediately," a post-combat company interview with the survivors stated. "The man on the right, PFC Frank DeBellis, was killed and the gunner to the left, PFC George Bert, lost his leg from a shell fragment." The mortar squad was led by Sergeant Joe Zukowski, the younger brother of wounded Tech Sergeant Ed Zukowski. The brothers were close, and their bond had only strengthened in combat during the Mediterranean battles. Back in England, Joe had confided to his older brother that he did not think he would survive Omaha beach. Sure enough, a shower of mortar shells engulfed Joe Zukowski and his squad as they struggled up the beach, probably setting off sympathetic mine detonations as well. The younger Zukowski went down face-first with fragments in the chest. He got up and tried to keep going. Another shell exploded nearby, wounding him again. He tried to get up once more, but was too weak. Three of his men, Private First Class Reuben Schatz and Privates Goza Fazekas and P. L. Wells, lay dead nearby. Zukowski was bleeding profusely from multiple wounds, the life pouring out of him. "Sgt Zukowski's last act was to pass the mortar sight to Sgt [George] Hammond," one survivor recalled. Zukowski crumpled over and died. Hammond looked at the sight—it was shattered, useless. He tossed it rocky beach and jagged cliff just ahead. Several men piled onto the boat, adding to Hurlbut's considerable burden. All at once, a mortar round scored a direct hit on the boat. "It hit all our demolition stuff. I was knocked head over heels. I guess I blacked out. When I came to, I was on my hands and knees. I was spitting blood. And I had the worst headache you can imagine." The explosion killed three men—most likely the men on the raft were blown to bits—and wounded several others.

Amid the carnage, Hurlbut kept moving, darting for cover behind several obstacles, until he came across his friend Private Joe Nokovic lying wounded and moaning in the water. Nokovic was hit badly, weakening him to the point where his body washed back and forth with the incoming tide. Hurlbut got to him and took a look at his wounds. "His legs had really got it," Hurlbut said. "I could see the raw bone through the flesh." Hurlbut knew that if he left Nokovic, he would drown. The problem was that Private Nokovic was considerably bigger than the diminutive Hurlbut. The latter knew he could never lift Nokovic and carry him, especially soaking wet and laden with equipment. So Hurlbut sat down, grabbed Nokovic by the armpits, planted his feet in the sand and shoved off "with my feet and pulled him with my arms. It was slow, tortuous, but we were making progress, very, very slowly and I was exhausted." Hurlbut only hoped that the Germans would notice his mission of mercy and take pity on him. Whether they did or not was, of course, unknowable, but no one shot at him for the few moments it took for him to find a medic for his buddy. As he did so, other team members were also under fire, attempting to place their charges on the Belgian gates located farthest from shore. "Enemy fire cut away fuses as rapidly as the engineers could rig them," a post-battle report said. "A burst of fragments carried away a fuseman's carefully set mechanism, along with all of his fingers. The heavy fire left the team no choice but to run for the protective low shingle bank on shore." All but four members of the team were killed or wounded.

aside and moved on. About twenty men from this boat team made it to the shingle bank. Half of these were already wounded. The rest lay dead or wounded closer to the waterline, with the cold water of the incoming tide lapping at their bodies, lolling them back and forth.

Elsewhere, the fourth boat section of F Company, under Lieutenant Siefert, landed in water nearly over their heads, all the while under heavy machine-gun, rifle, and mortar fire. The LCVP crewmen covered them with machine-gun fire as they left their boat, but in the recollection of one soldier, "the fire was extremely inaccurate." Staff Sergeant Donald Wilson yelled at his men to spread out and move as fast as they could. The water was so deep that he had to inflate his life belt or risk going under and drowning. The vests were inflated by squeezing a pair of CO_2 tubes on the belt. Because the assault troops were hauling such heavy loads, they tended to wear their belts not at the waist but at the breast, fairly close to the chin. This was not good because the higher up the vests were on the body when they were inflated, the less buoyancy they provided. Plus they could clamp around a man's throat; in some instances, they nearly choked men to death. Fortunately for Wilson, his belt was in good position and it popped him above the water from the waist up. With his head bobbing just above the waves, he forged ahead as best he could. Machine-gun bullets snapped around him, and he could hear fragments from mortar-shell explosions splashing in the water. In his peripheral vision, he could see other men getting hit and pitching downward into the water. "To reduce my exposure," he said, "I used my trench knife to puncture the life belt, and somehow I found sand under my feet." He staggered ashore, took cover behind a hedgehog obstacle, aimed at the unseen Germans on the bluff overlooking the beach, and managed to squeeze off several ineffective shots. All around him, other men from his boat were braving the withering fire, trying to cross the beach. "Several riflemen moved forward, trying to zig ten yards, hit the sand, and then zag ten yards, but the machine guns were on them by the second stop."

Several dozen yards to the left of where Wilson lay behind an obstacle, the members of the headquarters section were still thrashing in the water, trying to get to the beach. The ramp of their LCVP was slow in lowering, accounting for a slight delay. When the ramp finally did go down, they poured into the water, led by Captain Finke, the commander, who stepped into a particularly deep spot where the water went nearly over his head. Back in the marshaling area in England, Finke had badly sprained his left ankle, which was now heavily taped but still rather unsteady. Instead of carrying a rifle, the captain was clutching a cane. He and the other men from his boat made it through the water, but ran into a wall of machine-gun and mortar fire near the waterline. "I was lucky I could get that far because we were running and I wasn't in very good shape for running," Finke said. The heavily laden men were already exhausted, and of course rather seasick from their miserable ride in the landing craft (for most every boat section, the ride lasted more than two hours). As was natural, the fire dispersed the soldiers and destroyed any semblance of an organized assault. "The fellow right next to me, our company clerk [Private First Class] Ed Cox, yelled to me that he was hit and he fell down and rolled over on his back," Tech 5 James Thomson, the captain's radioman, recalled. Thomson and the other survivors kept lumbering up the beach as best they could, bullets spackling off the stones under their boots. Fragments whizzed by menacingly. Thompson noticed Lieutenant Howard Pearre, the company executive officer, running ahead and then, after a couple of explosions, he seemed to just disappear. "I looked up and he was no longer living." Pearre had absorbed a direct hit from one of the 50-millimeter antitank guns. A pair of F Company machine-gun teams set up their weapons at the water's edge and opened up on the German-controlled bluffs. After only a few moments, accurate, lethal bursts of enemy machine-gun fire tore through the two teams, killing or wounding everyone.

In the face of such withering fire, the men sought cover wherever they could find it, and the only alternative on this forlorn beach was the obstacles. The hedgehogs and tetrahedrons were the safest alternative, but they were small and provided little protection. The Belgian gates and log ramps thus became more attractive options to the frightened troops. "Any port in a storm," Finke explained, "people would just try to take cover behind one of those poles. They were about the size of a ten or twelve foot telephone pole with a Teller mine on the top of it. Not a very healthy place to be." Finke knew that this was a recipe for disaster. Bad as the fire was, and vulnerable as the men were when they were on the move, it would be even worse if they simply cowered in place as stationary targets in a pre-sighted kill zone, especially in the shadow of Teller mines. He walked around wielding his cane as a veritable whip. "I used it to good effect to just whack people until they moved." Several times he rapped prone forms only to discover that they were dead. Other times, he smacked men with the cane several times, got no reaction, and assumed they were dead, only to see their petrified faces and understand that they were too frightened to move. "Come on! Get up! Go on!" he yelled, while whacking them with the cane. Finke reasoned that if he only yelled without wielding the cane, then each man could pretend that he was talking to someone else. But if he hit a man personally with the cane, there would then be no ambiguity—get moving or else—and he was right. In this fashion, he mercilessly got many of them up and running several hundred yards toward the comparative safety of the shingle bank. By the time he made it there himself, he estimated that he had lost more than 25 percent of his command.[5]

The losses were even worse for E Company. The five errant boat sections landed in the worst of the kill zone, right at the foot of the E-3 draw, on an open beach, under the angry muzzles of nearly every German weapon at WN-62 and WN-61. "The boats were hurriedly emptied—the men jumping into water shoulder high," an after-action report chronicled, "under intense MG [machine-gun] and AT [anti-tank] fire." Private First Class Earl Chellis, a BAR man, watched in horror as the three men in front of him all got hit even before leaving the ramp of their Higgins boat. "I jumped off the landing craft and into the water. I went right to the bottom. It must've been maybe eight, nine feet deep . . . and here I've got all this weight on me. I just sunk right to the bottom." The tide washed him toward the beach and he managed to gulp enough air to stay alive. Even if Chellis and the others had been able to sprint onto the beach like rabbits, they would have been in serious trouble; instead they came ashore at a turtlelike pace. Half-drowned, soaked, seasick, heavily encumbered, they made perfect targets as they walked unsteadily forward, bent over, often wobbling as if drunk or concussed. Interlocking belts of machine-gun fire laced through them (in the recollection of one man, they sounded "like a bunch of bees"). Mortar shells exploded almost at their feet or alongside their torsos. Antitank shells, probably intended for the landing craft, sailed nearby and exploded above the water or along the beach. "Many fell left and right, and the water reddened with their blood," the after-action report said. "A few hit on under water mines of some sort and were blown out of the sea. The others staggered on to the obstacle covered, yet completely exposed beach. Men were falling on all sides but the survivors still moved forward."

The very idea of negotiating four hundred yards of obstacles and open beach to the shingle seemed an utter impossibility. To Lieutenant Rob Huch, it appeared so insurmountable that "right then and there I thought of every sin I committed and never prayed so hard in my life. I'd advance about 30 yds and then hit the dirt, bullets going everywhere." Like Huch, most of the men moved in short rushes, dove for cover, composed themselves, and then tried their luck again. According to survivors, the veterans tended to have a better feel for how to do this than the replacements. This, of course, meant that the rookies were initially more likely to get hit until they got the hang of what to do. Huch made it to the shingle bank, caught his breath, and took a look back to see how many men in his boat section were on the way. "It was awful," he wrote, "people lying all over the place—the wounded unable to move and being drowned by the incoming tide. At least 80% of our weapons wouldn't work (my own included) because of the sand and salt water. Needless to say, I lost many good men and friends." Some men were so frustrated with their jammed rifles that they pulled out their pistols and fired ineffectually at the unseen enemy.

A couple hundred yards up the beach, Captain Wozenski was negotiating his way to the shingle bank. "Every time I got up, I thought that it was pure terror that was making my knees buckle until I finally hit the shale and realized I had about one hundred pounds of sand in [my] pockets that had accumulated on top of the maybe fifty or sixty pounds that we were all carrying." At the bank, the fire did not slacken at all. "I just was pinned down. Everybody around me was being shot. You'd stick your head up and they would just hose you right down."

As other men joined him, they formed what one report called "a 7 yard beachhead" on the stones of the shingle. The few with working weapons fired back. Some stripped their rifles down and cleaned them. Some simply lay still, collecting themselves or watching machine-gun fire cut down their buddies who were closer to the waterline. First Lieutenant Edmund Duckworth, the company executive officer, had recently married a British woman named Audrey Travers. The new bridegroom pulled out a bottle of Scotch and shared a drink with Staff Sergeant Benjamin Telinda and another man. "Five minutes later the lt. raised his head over the bank," Telinda recalled, "[a] sniper got him in the temple scattering his brains on the other fellow and me. Naturally he died instantly."[6]

It was difficult for the Germans to miss any target they shot at, and no one realized this more than Private First Class Hein Severloh, who was pouring down relentless sheets of deadly machine-gun fire from his concrete position in the middle of WN-62, about seventy-five feet above the beach. The fields of fire were nearly perfect. In spite of the tufts of smoke floating over Easy Red from explosions, gunpowder and grass fires, he had no trouble spotting the desperate Americans. "I could see the water spouts where my machine gun bursts were hitting, and when the little fountains got close to the G.I.'s, they threw themselves down." Severloh was all of twenty-one years old, with much more interest in farming than soldiering. He held no particular grudge against the Americans, yet he knew that did not matter now. Like it or not, he was in a fight to the death and his fondest wish was to make it out of this hellish situation alive. "I didn't want to be in this war. I didn't want to shoot a machine-gun at young fellows my age. But there we were. I was a soldier . . . who was going to be attacked and as such I now had to defend myself. What could I do? Them or me—that's what I thought." His technique was to spray groups of men with machine-gun fire and then, when they were pinned down, pick up his rifle and kill them individually. "I shot at anything that moved in the water and on the beach." At one point, his eyes were drawn to one particular man stumbling through the water. Severloh grabbed his rifle and took aim. "He was looking for somewhere to hide. I shot him in the head. I saw his steel helmet roll into the sea. Then he dropped. I knew he was dead. After only a few seconds panic broke out among the Americans. They all lay in the shallow, cold water; many tried to get to the most forward beach obstacles to find some cover behind them."

Severloh was almost mesmerized by the sheer power and noise of his MG-42 machine gun. He watched with almost morbid fascination as corpses rolled and swayed with the steadily incoming tide, about three hundred meters away. Near the corpses, he saw many other dark forms in the water, moving ever so slightly, crawling out of the sea. He shouldered the gun back and forth, back and forth, spraying them with controlled bursts. "There was blood everywhere, screams, dead and dying. Wounded moved around in the bloody, watery slime, mostly creeping, trying to get to the upper beach to get some cover behind its embankment about one-and-a-half meters high [the shingle bank]." The 75-millimeter guns and other, heavier weapons were pummeling the vulnerable landing craft. "We took [them] under direct fire with our gun and we could see very precisely when it hit," Corporal Han Selbach, a crewman on one of the 75-millimeter pieces, recalled. "It was terrible."

Other Germans around WN-62 were equally fascinated and horrified by the slaughter. Lieutenant Frerking could not help but feel some pity for his enemies. "Poor swine," he whispered in awe. Corporal Franz Gockel could hardly believe his eyes, though he had little time to reflect on the carnage unfolding before him. "My main thought . . . was that I had to fight to survive. I wanted to get back home to my six brothers and sisters." He felt some level of satisfaction at being able to fight back against those who had bombed his hometown, but otherwise held little animosity toward the dying men on the beach. "They had a long way to go up the sand and hardly any cover. You could see when the tide rose some would move, crawling up the beach to get out of the water." He fired short bursts for fear of jamming his machine gun; he focused at first on the ramps of landing craft and then on the attacking soldiers, whether crawling, walking, or running. Unlike Severloh, he was taking quite a bit of return fire, spraying dust and dirt in every direction but otherwise leaving him unscathed. Gockel was keenly aware of the fire emanating from neighboring spots around WN-62. A few yards downward and to the left, Corporal Kuska was blazing away with his 50-millimeter antitank gun (possibly this weapon killed Lieutenant Pearre). To his left, Corporals Faust and Kwiatkowsky were firing steady bursts with their MG-42. Gockel assumed that others beyond his line of sight were doing the same, and he was right. Most were orienting their fire to the right (east) at the hapless E and F Company boat sections landing at or near the draw.

This actually worked to the advantage of the one boat section from the two companies that landed in some rough proximity to the intended landing spot at Easy Red beach. They came in about five hundred yards west of the E-3 draw (though about fifteen minutes late), in what amounted to a weak spot in the German defenses, where they were partially covered from the worst cones of fire emanating from WN-62 and WN-64. The original plan called for F Company to land here. At this particular moment, this boat section comprised the western (right) front of the whole 1st Infantry Division. It was led by twenty-nine-year-old Lieutenant John Spalding, a new platoon leader from Owensboro, Kentucky, who had joined the Army voluntarily in 1941, served a couple of years as an enlisted soldier, and then earned a commission through Officer Candidate School. Spalding had once worked as a sportswriter for his hometown newspaper, authoring a popular column entitled "Sports Sparks." He had a wife and a young son back home in Owensboro.

When the boat was about two hundred yards from the beach, and taking inaccurate machine-gun fire, the coxswain halted the LCVP and ordered the soldiers to lower the ramp. Spalding and Staff Sergeant Fred Bisco kicked the ramp downward until it splashed into the water. At the rear of the LCVP, the other crewman sprayed return fire at the folds of high ground looming over Easy Red beach. Lieutenant Spalding peered beyond the ramp and the water at his feet and saw many obstacles protruding out of the wet beach at low tide. He noticed that Teller mines topped several of the obstacles. None of them had been touched. The beach, in fact, looked pristine, and it dawned on him that the pre-invasion bombardment had done nothing. Back in England, while briefing his men in the marshaling area, the rookie officer had naively told them that the Navy and Air Force would pummel the enemy so badly that all the platoon would have to do was form a line and walk inland. It now occurred to him how credulous he had been. "How little we knew," he said later. "How great our faith!"

Spalding looked down at the water but could not gauge how deep it was. He told his men to hold fast while he checked. "I jumped out of the boat slightly to the left of the ramp, into water about waist deep," he said. Seeing that the water level was tolerable, the men piled out of the LCVP and splashed into the surf. They spread out into a V forma-

tion about fifty yards in length and began wading into the beach, all
the while dodging the obstacles. As was common that day, especially
at low tide, the depth of the water varied from step to step. Soon the
water got deeper and men began struggling to stay afloat. "We began
to swim when it was over our heads," Spalding said. "There was a strong
undercurrent carrying us to the left." Spalding inflated his life belt and
lost his M1 carbine. "I swallowed so much salt water trying to get
ashore. I came so near drowning I shudder to think about it." In his
peripheral vision he noticed Private George Bowen, his medic, and
Tech Sergeant Philip Streczyk, his platoon sergeant, struggling with an
eighteen-foot ladder they were carrying to help them cross an antitank
ditch on the beach. Spalding grabbed for the ladder in an attempt to
use it for flotation. "Lieutenant, we don't need help!" the sergeant said.
Spalding did not have the heart to tell them what he was really trying
to do. He ordered them to abandon the ladder. At last, his foot touched
the bottom. He and Streczyk pulled Sergeant Edwin Piasecki from
underneath the waves, saving him from drowning.

Nearby, Private First Class Stanley Dzierga, a rifleman/grenadier,
also slipped under the water and feared he was about to drown. Then
he felt a hand on his collar. "Get up! Come on!" Tech Sergeant Philip
Streczyk said to him. Dzierga took a breath and kept moving. Streczyk
withdrew his hand from the rifleman's collar. "I'm gonna let you go
now." Several yards away, Private Vincent DiGaetano was attempting
to carry his seventy-two-pound flamethrower and keep his nose above
the water. He bounced along for several strides but feared he might not
be able to stay afloat. He inflated his life vest. Ironically this sent him
facedown into the water, so he cut himself free of the straps and used
his flamethrower as an ad hoc raft. Private Fred Reese had stuffed a
large roll of toilet paper in his helmet. As the waves sloshed over and
around him, the paper unraveled and got wet. Gobs of it draped over
his glasses and down his face until he could hardly see, but he managed
to keep going. Lieutenant Spalding called out to his overloaded men,

ordering them to get rid of anything that was too heavy to carry into the beach. "We lost our mortar, most of the mortar ammunition, one of our two bazookas, and much of the bazooka ammunition."

All thirty-two members of the section made it to the beach, although many, including Spalding, were drenched, shocked, and exhausted from their watery ordeal. Several had lost their personal weapons, too. "I was considerably shaken up," Spalding wrote a couple of weeks later in a letter to his mother. "Completely soaked, my equipment, heavy when dry, seemed to weigh a ton when I came out of the water." They began taking machine-gun and rifle fire from the right, probably from the trenches adjacent to WN-64. Staff Sergeant Curt Colwell blew a hole with a Bangalore torpedo through a strand of barbed wire near the waterline. As best they could, the men filtered through the gap and began to make their way across the rocky beach in the direction of clumps of brush and a slight ravine that led steadily upward in the direction of the ridge that paralleled the beach. Spalding did not have to tell them to do this; they had trained so often for just this sort of situation that they knew instinctively that they must keep moving. "They were too waterlogged to run," Spalding commented, "but they went as fast as they could."

The enemy fire worsened. Several soldiers were hit and wounded. Private William Roper caught a round in the foot. He sat down, rolled over, and attempted to administer first aid on himself. But he could not seem to reach the laces of his leggings. Spalding paused, undid the laces, took off Roper's brogan-style combat boot, and then moved on. The section medic, Private George Bowen, administered first aid to the injured soldier. Meanwhile, the lieutenant heard mines exploding on the beach and mortar rounds bursting somewhere nearby. All around him the men kept pressing inland, off the beach. It occurred to Spalding that he ought to report his situation to Captain Wozenski. He halted, squatted down, grabbed his SCR-536 walkie-talkie radio and extended the antenna. "Copper One to Copper Six," he said. For a few seconds, he listened for a reply from Wozenski. Nothing. "Copper One to Copper Six. This is One. Come in Copper Six." Still nothing. Spalding glanced down and only then noticed that the mouthpiece of the radio had been shot away. "Instead of discarding the useless radio, I folded the antenna and slung the 536 over my shoulder, proof that the habits you learn in training can often stay with you even when you are scared."

After a few minutes, the platoon made it off the beach shingle and reached the partial cover of demolished stone buildings, which the Americans came to call "the Roman ruins." At least three men had been hit on the beach (and possibly more, since accounts vary), leaving Spalding with probably twenty-seven unscathed soldiers to continue this assault. The ground around the ruins consisted mainly of thick scrub brush, muddy marshes, and the aforementioned ravine. Several hundred yards to their left, they could hear fire spewing from one of the fortifications of WN-62 in the direction of Fox Green beach, and could even catch glimpses of that fire lacing into soldiers from F Company. "There was nothing we could do to help them," Spalding lamented. Besides, his group had problems of its own. A German machine-gun crew firing from somewhere along the ridge locked in on them and began pouring accurate fire into their midst. They were also taking rifle fire. Sergeant Louis Ramundo, a Philadelphian, decided to go and make contact with the rest of the company. He got up to run but was hit and killed, probably by a rifleman. The Americans returned fire as best they could while Spalding and Sergeant Streczyk considered what to do next. They had no idea what had become of the rest of their company. They had landed about a thousand yards from their intended spot; they did not know any detailed information about the German defenses in this area. They had almost no heavy weapons. They figured that the marshy ground ahead was probably mined. Even so, they just knew they had to keep moving inland and destroy any German positions they encountered. The only advantage the Spalding group enjoyed was the cover of the little ravine and the fact that they had blundered into a dead spot in the German strong points.

Spalding and Streczyk decided to recon the ground ahead of them. Streczyk was the sort to do a job himself. The East Brunswick, New Jersey, native was a classic child of the Depression. As one of ten children, he had quit school after eighth grade to help support his family. He had worked as a truck driver until, at age twenty-one, he was drafted. "He was fearless," Private Dzierga asserted. "I never saw a man like that in my life. He wasn't that big of a guy. He just went, did everything and it just seems he was immune to the fire." Streczyk took Private First Class Richard Gallagher and carefully began to check out the marshy ground. Sure enough, it was mined, so they changed direction and set off through the thick brush. Several minutes passed before Gallagher returned and urged everyone to follow him up a defilade in the ravine located to the right of the emplacement that was still raking the F Company men with deadly fire. "I called my men forward," Spalding recalled, "and we cautiously moved along the defile, keeping our eyes open for the little box mines the Germans had planted throughout the area. We made it through without mishap. The Lord was with us on that one." In fact, the ground was mined. Spalding's group missed them either out of sheer luck or, more likely, because Sergeant Streczyk had carefully sniffed out a way around or past them. They were off the beach and, as far as they knew, they were the first.[7]

1

The German defenses were designed not just to kill the invaders but to pin them down, impede their movements, hold them in place, destroy any semblance of unit integrity, disrupt their common sense of purpose, and sever soldiers from their leaders so that they would be reduced to little more than an aimless, isolated mob with no chain of command, lying inert on the wet sand or in the surf as passive, con-

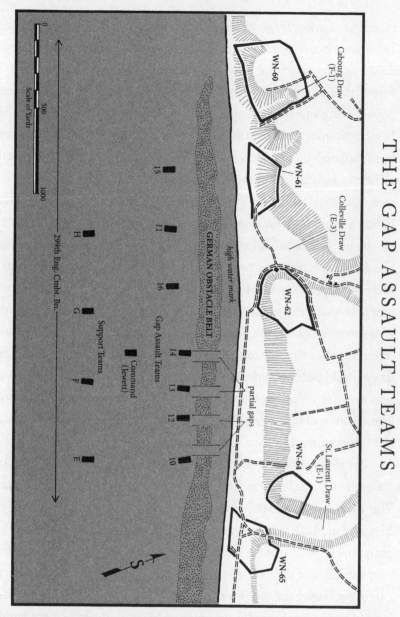

THE GAP ASSAULT TEAMS

In the months leading up to D-Day, the invasion planners grew so concerned about German mines and obstacles at Omaha beach that they created joint teams of Army and Navy engineers whose job was to blow gaps through the obstacle belt. The sailors were responsible for everything under the water, the soldiers everything on the beach. Landed in tandem with the lead assault troops, the teams were soon enmeshed in the carnage and made little headway. Between 40 and 50 percent of them became casualties.

fused, stationary targets. The number one way that this grisly set of circumstances might come to fruition was not necessarily the formidable firepower of the strong points; even deadly accurate fire can sometimes be evaded by luck, accident, heroism, or the vagaries of physics. The mined obstacles were, quite literally, the Germans' first line of defense. As such, they constituted the defenders' best chance of immobilizing the invaders and slaughtering them in place. All tactical military assaults—or at least the successful ones—depend to some extent upon having the ability and the space to maneuver on an enemy, perhaps avoid his deadliest cones of fire and hit him where he is weakest. If the Americans failed to destroy the blanket of obstacles at Omaha beach, they would have no ability to maneuver soldiers, tanks, and vehicles effectively enough to outflank the strong points, get off the beach where they were so vulnerable, and overwhelm the Germans with their superior numbers. If the obstacles pinned them in place, it hardly mattered that they could throw throngs of men and vehicles onto the beach. They would only present the Germans with more targets and pile atop one another in an overcrowded mess, probably saved from complete annihilation only by the protective fire of friendly naval destroyers and the limits of the German ammo supply.

For this reason, no one at Omaha beach, except for the assaulting infantrymen, had a more important job than the Gap Assault Teams. The carefully calibrated plan to land the teams three minutes after H-Hour unraveled in the face of the conditions and the ferocious German opposition. As with the rifle companies, the strong eastward current led many of the Gap Assault Team LCMs to run off course in that direction. Thus, the eight teams supporting the 1st Infantry Division landed just as haphazardly, and precariously, as their infantry buddies. Few, if any, landed in sequence with their supporting tank dozers, which came in on LCTs. The average team member carried seventy-five pounds of explosives, Bangalore torpedoes, Primacord rolls (used to wire up an obstacle and spread a detonation), wire cutters, fuses, detonators, personal weaponry, and the like. Each of their LCMs contained a pair of rubber boats, one for the naval combat demolition group and the other for the army engineer group. Each rubber boat contained supplemental supplies including five hundred extra pounds of explosives, mine detectors, and mine gap markers. No matter where they landed, the beach they found was, of course, untouched. "The first line of obstacles were Element C's," Lieutenant Colonel John O'Neill, the commander of the Special Engineer Task Force, later said. "These were spaced approximately forty to fifty yards apart and had mines attached to them. There were roughly three of these to each fifty yard gap that was to be cleared. Second row of obstacles consisted of saw-horse ramps with the nose toward shore made of timbers, with mines attached, spaced thirty to forty yards apart. Third line of obstacles consisted of piles mostly of timber twelve to fourteen inches diameter sloped seaward some with mines attached. In between were cross channel . . . hedgehogs . . . about fifteen or sixteen obstacles to the fifty yard gap."

During training back in England, Lieutenant (j.g.) Carl Hagensen, an imaginative naval officer, had designed an ingenious way to take out the Element C or Belgian gate obstacles. He had placed two-and-a-quarter-pound C-2 explosive blocks in sealed canvas bags, tied fourteen of them to the joints of the Belgian gate, connected them together with Primacord, and then detonated them, causing the gate to collapse onto itself into nothing more than a pile of junk. The trouble was that now, on D-Day morning, these so-called "Hagensen Packs" were in scarce supply. As an alternative, many of the engineers placed their C-2 blocks in GI socks, stabilized the explosives with rocks, ran Primacord from inside the socks, and then sealed them with twine or bailing wire. They planned to tape or tie the explosives-laden socks to the obstacles. The Primacord looked no more threatening than yellow-colored clothesline, but it could actually be quite combustible. The men did not—contrary to popular mythology—wrap it around their helmets, for the obvious reason that none of them wanted to blow off their own heads.

Time was not on their side. With every minute that passed, the tide grew higher. Roughly speaking, the Omaha beach tide on D-Day morning rose one foot every ten minutes. If the engineers failed to clear gaps quickly enough, probably within an hour, the incoming high tide would overtake the obstacles and hide them, posing a deadly menace for follow-on boats, soldiers, and vehicles. Moreover, underwater obstacles and mines were more difficult to destroy than otherwise.

Team 14, under Lieutenant Phil Wood, hit the eastern edge of Easy Red, in the shadow of WN-62, actually ahead of the infantry. For some reason, Wood was under the impression that H-Hour was 0620. The LCM carrying the team landed five minutes later, isolated and profiled perfectly for the German gunners. A hail of machine-gun bullets clanked off the boat. An LCM crewman got on his boat's gun and returned fire. In the process, he also tried unsuccessfully to shoot Teller mines attached to stakes on the beach. The ramp went down. Wood and the other soldiers disembarked first, hauled their rubber boat into waist-high water, and headed, under the weight of their crushing loads, for the nearest belt of obstacles. The lieutenant looked back at the LCM and saw an artillery shell—possibly originating from the 88-millimeter gun at WN-61—tear into the LCM, where the sailors were struggling to manhandle their own rubber boat to the beach. "The ammunition in the rubber boat was detonated," he recalled a few weeks after D-Day, "and the fire enveloped the LCM. The coxswain was blasted off the vessel." Most of the naval combat demolition men were killed. As the boat burned and men died, other survivors from the team piled onto the beach as best they could and tried to wire up obstacles for demolition. The assistant boat team leader, Sergeant Harrison Marble, remembered that for him and the others, there were "only basic thoughts of self-preservation . . . and praying."

The other teams in the 1st Division sector all landed within the next fifteen to twenty minutes, in random spots along Easy Red and Fox Green beaches, often alongside or intermixed with the infantry

LCVPs, amid nearly total chaos. "I was the first in line to get off our boat," Private David Snoke, a member of Team 16, wrote to his parents, "and just as the ramp was going down, 3 shells . . . hit on our port side about 10 ft. out." His team landed nearly right in front of the E-3 draw, though the shells almost certainly originated from WN-60 or WN-61. Snoke was hauling forty pounds of explosives, twenty pounds of mine-clearing equipment, and an M1 carbine strapped to his back. He fell into the water and began laboriously wading ashore. "I glanced behind me in time to see the lieutenant [Grover M. Hobson] get hit in the head with an 88. That was when I first started to get scared. He was only 5 ft. behind me. A couple seconds after that, a mortar hit about 7 ft. to the left & behind me." He caught fragments in the hand, the arm, and the side, but fortunately none of the wounds were serious. Behind him he could see the sailors on his team struggling to exit the LCM. They were instantly recognizable by the gray stripes and the stenciled USN letters painted on their helmets along with the jump boots they were wearing. As Snoke watched, the sailors laboriously lugged the rubber boat off the LCM just in the nick of time before an 88-millimeter shell smashed through the engine room, exploded, and set the craft on fire. Chief Electrician's Mate Alfred Sears was as heavily laden with explosives and gear as Snoke. "All hell poured loose on us," he said. "I went under. I inflated my life belt and it caught on the gas mask. I went under again, head-first. I was top heavy. Finally I got the life belt up under my arms." A shell exploded nearby, but still he kept going. He managed to get his head back above the water only to hear his team leader, Ensign H. G. Stocking, call out, "I'm hit!" He had taken a round through the shoulder. Sears kept moving toward his leader. Another sailor from the team, new to combat and in shock, asked Sears, "What will I do? I'm scared!"

"Help me with Ensign Stocking," Sears replied decisively.

This gave the man a task to focus on, rather than his fear, and snapped him out of his shock. The two sailors reached Ensign Stocking.

By now the officer had been hit again, this time in the leg. "I stripped off his gear, inflated his life jacket and towed him in to the beach." They were completely pinned down, essentially immobilized. Sears subsequently discovered that he had been wounded by a fragment in his right knee.

Not far away, Private Snoke watched as Corporal Jay Armstrong got hit in the head and shoulder by machine-gun bullets. Snoke's fear gave way to anger. He abandoned his mine-clearing equipment, lay down on the beach, and fired two full clips at "some Jerries I saw running around beyond the beach." The shooting sated his rage somewhat. He heard Armstrong crying for help. "[He] was calling for a medic, but none was around, so I went over to cut his equipment off him." There was little else Private Snoke could do besides that (Armstrong was badly wounded, but he lived). Snoke took cover behind a nearby obstacle, glanced back at the water, and saw that his team's LCM was burning fiercely. "I noticed the Jerries were starting to shell the obstacles with our men behind them." Snoke crawled back about five feet and began frantically digging a hole in the sand with a hunting knife he was carrying. A pair of infantrymen, probably from F Company, 16th Infantry, took cover behind the obstacle Snoke had just vacated. "A mortar hit in front of them and blew their heads clean off." Horror-struck, Private Snoke began crawling up the beach, almost washing upward with the incoming tide. He watched as yet another mortar shell exploded near an obstacle, killing four men from his boat, including his friend Private First Class Steve Gordon. Exhausted and separated from the rest of his team, Snoke managed to make it to the shingle bank.[8]

The Germans seemed to instinctively understand the importance of the Gap Assault Team mission and zero their most effective artillery, mortar, and machine-gun fire on the arriving boats. Team 15 landed at Fox Green, just underneath WN-61, taking machine-gun fire all the way in. Private Chuck Hurlbut grabbed the tow rope of his team's rubber boat and began arduously dragging it through the water, toward the

Team 13 landed on Easy Red just west of Private Snoke's Team 16. The Army members of the team exited first. Then the sailors pulled their rubber boat off the LCM. An artillery shell scored a direct hit on the rubber boat, touching off the Primacord into a catastrophic explosion. Three of the sailors were killed, and probably more wounded, by the blast. The survivors made it ashore and set their charges, but could not get their faulty fuse to work. Immediately adjacent to this section of the beach, Private First Class Michael Accordino and his comrades from Team 12 were standing on the ramp of their LCM, pushing, pulling, and prodding their rubber boat in a vain effort to haul it off the LCM. "All this time the Germans were trying to put a shell in our boat," Accordino recalled. Knowing it was just a matter of time before the Germans succeeded, they abandoned the boat and jumped into the deep water. They swam to shore and began dealing with the belt of obstacles. Infantrymen from E and F Companies were also landing. Not far away, Accordino noticed a cluster of engineers around Sergeant Billy Scanlon, a fellow native of Buffalo, New York. "I knew that was a bad situation because that would draw fire." Accordino was correct. As Scanlon's group worked on a line of obstacles, an enemy mortar shell exploded near the Primacord they had strung between the obstacles and set off a premature explosion. Ten team members were killed (Scanlon was among the dead), and nine were wounded. Several nearby infantry soldiers were killed or wounded as well. The only good news was that the explosion created a thirty-yard gap in the obstacle line.

Sergeant Barton Davis came in a few minutes later with one of the support teams and immediately got pinned down by accurate machine-gun fire. Seasick, frightened, and miserable, he clutched his rifle and tried to crawl for the closest obstacle. He saw a dead body float past him on the incoming tide and recognized it as a man who had told him, on the way in (with eerie accuracy, as it turned out) that he would not survive. Davis's team and several others had been augmented back in England with a sprinkling of soldiers from the 2nd Infantry Division.

Not all of these men were thrilled to become demolition engineers. One of them had told Sergeant Davis that when he hit Omaha beach, he would ditch his onerous sixty-pound load of explosives and Bangalore torpedoes. "I told him that if I saw him on the beach without his explosives that I'd [shoot] him," Davis said. Sure enough, as the sergeant looked around and took in the horrifying scene unfolding in front of him, he spotted the recalcitrant 2nd Division man about twenty-five feet away, pinned down, cowering, with no rifle, no explosives, and no helmet. "I lay there with my rifle in my hand and our eyes met. He turned just as white as [a] sheet of paper, until I smiled. A look of relief came over his face." Like many other engineers, Davis was absorbed mainly with personal survival. As he kept crawling ahead, he came upon a group of 1st Division infantrymen clustered around one of their friends who had been hit in the jugular vein. "He was propped up by his buddies who were frantically trying to stop the bleeding. The man apparently knew it was no use. They were stuffing towels in his neck and trying pressure points to no avail. The man smiled at his buddies, waved his hand in a gesture of 'so long', and died so fast it was as tho a hand passed over his face." His friends laid him down gently and, with tears in their eyes, moved away.

Only Teams 9 and 10, both of which landed on Easy Red, had much luck clearing gaps in spite of considerable enemy resistance. "Floundering & swimming I made it to wading distance & struggled toward the seaward obstacles," Seaman 2nd Class John Talton of Team 9 later wrote. "The machine gun fire at this time resembled rain drops on a mill pond." He saw that Warrant Officer William H. Reymer, his team leader, and Chief Mitchner, the boat chief, were wounded and in danger of drowning. Talton went back and helped them ashore. The warrant officer had "a triangular hole in his helmet and was bleeding down the front of his face. Mitchner's right eye was hanging [out of] his socket & he was addled." Talton got them to the rocks of the shingle bank, went searching for a weapon, and then subsequently fought as a veritable infantryman. Other team members set charges and managed to blow a gap on the beach. His Team 9 eventually blew two gaps—one of ten yards' width and the other fifty yards across.

In many instances, the engineers had to climb the log ramps and greatly expose themselves to the attention of the Germans on the higher ground above the beach. "Men shinnied up the stakes and stood on each other's shoulders all in the face of heavy enemy gunfire," Lieutenant Commander Joseph Gibbons, commander of the naval component of the Gap Assault Teams, told an interviewer three months after D-Day. The price of their success was considerable. Both teams were decimated by casualties. Talton opined that the only way to truly describe the scene would require "three essential ingredients, noise, color & the smell. All of these combined with the proximity of dead, wounded & body parts creates a mixture that defies a verbal or pictorial description." As Talton looked around, he saw a headless tank dozer driver with shoulders protruding through his hatch, an infantry soldier who had lost his face from nose to chin, a man with the top of his head gone, "as neatly as if it had been removed surgically," and a pair of legs sticking out of the water, feet pointed toward the sky, in a grotesque position reminiscent of a ghoulish "V for Victory" sign.

The intense, accurate fire impeded all of the teams from carrying out their missions with any semblance of order. The invasion planners obviously knew that the job of placing explosives on the obstacles, wiring them up, disarming mines, and clearing the beach by touching off major explosions was a complicated task that required the total, unharassed absorption of the engineers. In theory, the infantry, the DD tanks, and the landing boats were supposed to provide enough fire support to win some breathing space for the teams. However, the failure of the pre-invasion bombardment, the sinking of the tanks, the chaotic landings, the blown schedule, and the strident German resistance all eliminated any possibility that the teams could proceed with their work unmolested. Instead they had to carry out their challenging job *and* fight for their lives at the very same time. Many were either killed or wounded within minutes of landing or trying to land; many others were engrossed completely in self-preservation, either by fighting back or by cowering in fear. This probably absorbed the majority of the manpower of the eight teams.

Even for those who could do their jobs under such horrible circumstances, there was another factor that conspired to keep them from carrying out their vital mission. Because they generally landed alongside the infantrymen, and more or less at the same time, a crowding effect soon ensued. As engineers set their charges, strung Primacord, and prepared to blow obstacles, they had trouble clearing enough space to detonate safely. In many instances, they simply could not persuade the infantry soldiers to abandon the dubious cover of the obstacles. Lieutenant Wood and the survivors of Team 14 tried several times to chase wounded and huddling soldiers away from the obstacles they had prepared for detonation, but to no avail. They eventually gave up in exasperation and simply joined a line of men taking cover at the shingle bank along Easy Red beach. Private First Class Carroll Guidry and another engineer set up charges on a Belgian gate and other obstacles amid a chaotic crowd of soldiers. "There was approximately a company of infantrymen in the vicinity," he said. The other man activated the fuse and three times called "Fire in the hole!"—a common signal to get away and take cover. "Nobody moved," Guidry recalled. "We were trapped within the perimeter of the explosive charge . . . we were all going to be blown up. I clasped my hands and prayed very hard. After sweating it out for a few minutes which seemed to be a lifetime, the charge did not go off." Guidry suspected that the other man had purposely deactivated the fuse, but he never knew for sure.

Only six out of sixteen tank dozers made it ashore to support the teams. In some instances soldiers tried to take cover behind the dozers as the vehicles were attempting to clear obstacles. Corporal Gerald Burt, fresh from seeing two of his buddies killed right next to him, then watched in horror as several soldiers attempted to escape heavy machine-gun fire by crouching behind a tank dozer. "The tank driver couldn't see them and he backed right over them killing them instantly. I can still hear their screams." Accurate fire from the antitank guns soon destroyed five of the six dozers.

The crowding problem reflected yet another flaw in the Omaha beach assault plan. Since the Gap Assault Teams and the rifle companies were scheduled to land at nearly the same time, they were bound to work at cross-purposes. In fact, surviving engineers later urged that in future invasions they be landed at least half an hour after the assault companies. At Omaha, the infantry soldiers were trained to get off the beach, but obviously the obstacles and mines (not to mention the heavy fire and terrain) made that very difficult, if not quite impossible. This practically guaranteed that the dogfaces would cluster near those obstacles, right in the kill zone of any engineer detonations, yet no one at the high-command level seemed to have anticipated this. Nor were the infantrymen prepared to back off and lay down fire support for the engineers. Instead they did what nearly all reasonable men would do in the midst of such mortal danger—they sought protection any way and anywhere they could get it. Even under ideal circumstances, it would have been difficult for the rifle company officers and NCOs to herd their men away from the detonations as the teams set their charges and cleared gaps. Amid the furious violence of Omaha beach on D-Day morning, with squads and platoons fractured, decimated, isolated, and at times leaderless, it became an utter impossibility. This issue, as much as any other, prevented the engineers from clearing more than a few small gaps in the 1st Division sector.

The heavy loads only made this problem worse. "Most of the equipment the LCM's carried [was] useless or worse," the Army's engineer branch historian wrote cuttingly. "The rubber boats with their explosives [drew] heavy fire, and the engineers . . . abandoned them as quickly as possible. The mine detectors were useless since the enemy had buried no mines in the flat, and German snipers made special targets of any men carrying them. With no barbed wire strung among the obstacles, the bangalore torpedoes . . . were only an extra burden. Overloaded and dressed in impregnated coveralls, the engineers found their movement impeded, and wounded and uninjured men alike drowned under the weight of their packs."

Among the teams, the naval component reported 42 percent casualties, including twenty-four killed, thirty-two wounded, and fifteen missing, nearly all of whom were dead. A subsequent accounting raised the losses among the sailors to 52 percent. The Army losses were almost as bad. The 299th Engineer Combat Battalion lost 41 percent of its men who served on the teams. These figures did not include those who were wounded on the beach but were never medically evacuated. Seven of the sailors earned Navy Crosses. Their outfit earned a Presidential Unit Citation. The Army decorated fifteen of the soldiers with Distinguished Service Crosses.[9]

The carnage would have been even worse if not for the support—sometimes unseen by engineers and infantrymen—of the tanks that did make it ashore. Generals Gerow and Huebner were skeptical enough about the viability of the DD tanks to hedge their bets and assign a company of standard Sherman tanks to support the first wave. These deep-wading Shermans, hailing from A Company, 741st Tank Battalion, were waterproofed and, to keep water out of their engines, were equipped with a pair of sheet metal intake and exhaust shrouds, located right behind the turret. The tanks could move and shoot in turret-high water. They had performed quite successfully in all three amphibious invasions in Italy, thus earning the confidence of the V Corps and 1st Division commanders. On D-Day, they were ferried to the landing beaches aboard LCTs, one of which sank. This subtracted two wading Shermans and a tank dozer from the landing force. By 0640, eleven tanks from A Company (the records conflict as to the exact number) had made it to various landing spots along Fox Green and Easy Red.

Six of them were waders; five were dozers. Several even fired on the way in to the beach. These waterproofed Shermans, in tandem with the five DD tanks that made it to the beach, brought the total number of tanks available at H-Hour to sixteen out of an original complement of fifty-six. Though they were small in number, they provided a base of supporting fire—albeit far short of what the planners envisioned—for the hard-pressed assault troops.

The mobility of the tanks was severely restricted by the obstacles, the crowds of soldiers, the limited visibility on the hazy, smoky beach, and, of course, German antitank fire. They also dealt with a far grislier impediment to movement. "Smooth operation was hampered by the dead bodies which lay about all over the beach," the 741st Tank Battalion history commented sadly. "Frequently the crews had to pull a few bodies from their path, and proceed." To a tank in combat, mobility sustains life; a stationary tank is an ideal target. Many of the tanks were actually towing ammunition trailers in case they needed emergency resupply (the armored equivalent of the oversized loads carried by the troops). Hence, the crewmen immediately found themselves in a vicious fight to the death, with little room to maneuver. Three tanks were hit and destroyed almost immediately by frighteningly accurate fire from the 88-millimeter gun and the 75-millimeter guns. Others could do little else besides lurk in the water while gunners frantically spotted targets through the smoke and traded shots with the Germans. Fortunately for the tankers, the Germans were dealing with more targets— between the landing craft, the tanks, the Gap Assault Teams, and the assault troops—than they could effectively engage. This gave the Sherman crews a fighting chance. "We became an automatic weapons group to support the infantry," Lieutenant Edward Sledge, one of the platoon leaders, later wrote. A native of Mobile, Alabama, Sledge had a kid brother named Eugene serving with the Marines in the Pacific who later became famous for writing one of the great war memoirs of all time. The elder Sledge landed in the vicinity of Exit E-1 and began firing on the 75-millimeter guns of WN-62. One of the tanks in his platoon was hit right at the waterline and caught fire. Sledge and his crew focused on firing their main gun in support of "infantry pinned down by enemy machine gun and sniper fire."

Farther down the beach to Sledge's left, Corporal Jack Boardman, a gunner, was peering through his narrow slits in an attempt to spot anything to shoot at through the smoke. His commander, Staff Sergeant Dick Maddock, kept pounding him on the shoulder, telling him to open fire. "It was completely murky," Boardman recalled. "There was this dust and I guess smoke pall all over the beach. And I'm wondering what to shoot at because all I can see here is this soup." As the smoke shifted, Boardman spotted a concrete emplacement, probably in WN-62, and opened fire. He saw puffs of dust rise from the rear of the pillbox but could not tell if he had hit or killed anyone.

Staff Sergeant Thomas Fair's tank landed to the west, almost right in front of Exit E-1, and took shelter in turret-high water. His bow gunner sprayed the bluffs ahead with machine-gun fire while Fair searched for specific targets. After a few moments, he saw a machine-gun emplacement and ordered his gunner to pound it with 75-millimeter shells. "His first shots went low but after the correction was made the next shots entered straight through the opening and put it out of action." A German shell exploded nearby, touching off a sympathetic detonation from a Teller mine; fortunately it did not damage Fair's tank. He knew, though, that he could not remain in place indefinitely. Even if the next enemy round did not tear through his Sherman, the incoming tides would drown his engine and swamp his tank (the same was true, of course, for every other Sherman at the waterline). He ordered his driver to start rolling down the beach while he searched for Lieutenant Gaetera Barcelona, his platoon leader, whose tank was painted with the recognizable moniker "Always in My Heart." Fair's tank emerged from the waves and warily rumbled along the sand at a snail's pace. Another tank, under the command of Sergeant James Larsen, followed. With agonizing slowness and with the threat of being torn apart by German antitank or artillery shells looming as a possibility at every moment, Fair's tank led. "The going was slow for we had to weave in and out among bodies, sometimes stop till the medics cleared them from our path." He found his platoon but, in the process, one of the German 50-millimeter guns scored a hit on Larsen's tank. His gunner was wounded and his own face suffered powder burns. Larsen gave the order to abandon the tank. Fair attempted to maneuver but was hindered by the ammo trailer he was towing. "It was in our way all the time. If I had known what an obstacle it was in the first place I would have left it on the LCT." As it was, Fair had to dismount and unhook the trailer. On the bright side, though, the extra ammo allowed him to fire about four hundred fifty high-explosive shells in the course of the day.

Perhaps the most significant contribution from the armor came from the only two DD tanks that succeeded in swimming to the beach. These two tanks, one of which was commanded by Staff Sergeant Turner Sheppard, the other by Sergeant George Geddes, landed independently of each other on Easy Red beach. Both came from B Company. Both unleashed heavy volumes of 75-millimeter fire on the enemy 88-millimeter gun at WN-61 and the 75-millimeter guns at WN-62. "My gunner Corporal [Corlin] Legler started firing immediately at targets I designated," Staff Sergeant Sheppard said. He watched as one of the shots touched off a large explosion. "I believe it was the ammunition supply for an 88 that was working nearby." His tank also managed to batter the pillboxes shielding both 75-millimeter guns at WN-62, silencing them at least for the time being.

Nearby, Sergeant Geddes's gunner scored a direct hit on the narrow embrasure of the 88-millimeter casemate, a truly world-class shot. The ensuing explosion disabled the gun, depriving the Germans, as early as 0710, of their most powerful weapon among the six strong points defending the 1st Division sector of Omaha. The handful of Shermans continued to pump shells and spray machine-gun bullets at whatever targets they could identify and, as the achievements of Geddes and Sheppard demonstrated, they were scoring many hits and silencing enemy guns as German soldiers were stunned, frightened into inaction, concussed, or forced to take cover. However, they could not, and did not, destroy the concrete fortifications. Thus, unless the enemy's heavy weapons were wrecked, as with the 88-millimeter gun, the Germans could, and did, simply set up shop again and resume their firing. The tanks were doing great work—but only the infantry could silence the fortifications for good.[10]

1

The timetable was wrecked, shattered like a prized picture window, but the consequence was not mere shards of glass but the destruction of many lives, all of them precious to someone. For the soldiers of the first wave, tardy landings meant isolation from supporting units and firepower. This, in turn, meant death, for the rather simple reason that the Germans could more easily concentrate their fire against a small, isolated group of invaders than a numerous, continuous host. The invasion planners had hoped to overwhelm the enemy defenders with perfectly synchronized landings, mutually supporting firepower, and the sheer weight of numbers. Those hopes were now dashed.

At 0700, a full thirty minutes behind schedule, five LCAs carrying assault troops from Captain John Armellino's L Company, 16th Infantry approached Fox Red beach just to the east of Fox Green. The boat carrying Armellino's fourth section had capsized in the heavy seas about two miles offshore. Eight men drowned; the others were fished out of the cold waters by rescue boats. The five remaining LCAs beached just shy of several rows of Belgian gates, hedgehogs, tetrahedrons, and Teller-mine-laced poles, in varying depths of water. Aboard one of the boats, Private First Class Giles Lee Hamlett, a proud South-

LATE LANDINGS AT THE CABOURG DRAW

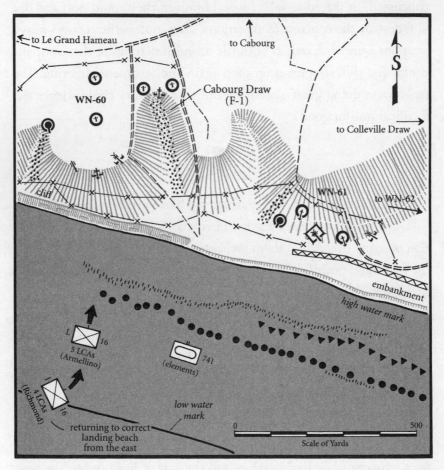

With the timetable blown, the assault companies of the 3rd Battalion, 16th Infantry landed more than half an hour late, right in the crosshairs of German defenders at WN-60 and into a thick belt of mine-laced obstacles

erner from Danville, Virginia, peered over the side in an effort to get a better look at the beach. Hamlett was new to his platoon, and it seemed to him that everyone else was a Northerner. Back in England, his sergeant had hung the derisive nickname "General Lee" on him. Now, as Hamlett strained his eyes for a look at Fox Red beach, the sergeant snapped stiffly into a posture of mock attention, saluted, and asked, "And what do you see, General Lee?" Hamlett did not like being the butt of a joke, but he was actually more worried that the Germans would see the sergeant saluting, figure Hamlett was someone important and shoot him first. Hamlett jumped the sergeant and began fighting him until other soldiers interceded, broke it up, and separated them.

The first section boat, under Lieutenant Kenneth Klenk, was actually on the verge of swamping, so the coast was a welcome sight for these men. "There was no supporting fire on the beach defenses at all when the company landed," L Company's morning report for June 6 chronicled. As the ramps lowered and the men prepared to debark, those looking beyond the obstacles could see about two hundred yards of beach ahead of them. The open, rocky beach gave way to cliffs, varying in height from twelve to fifteen feet. Above those cliffs were the fortifications of WN-60. Immediately they began taking fire from the strong point's 75-millimeter antitank gun and its mortars. Two shells from the 75 smashed into Lieutenant Klenk's flooding LCA, one in the rear and one under the ramp. The explosion killed and wounded several men. The survivors scrambled madly to exit the dying boat. "I had to climb over several bodies that were just laying there, floating in the water," Staff Sergeant Vincent "Mike" McKinney, the section sergeant, recalled. He splashed into the water and began wading ashore. Several soldiers climbed over the sides or followed McKinney off the ramp. From the back of the boat, Private First Class James Jordan stepped over the dead bodies of several friends and made it to the ramp. "As I got close to the ramp I was hit by a large wave that knocked me all the way to the back of the boat. Again, I made my way to the front and managed to leave the boat just as it was sinking behind me. I was the last man off." Another wave swept him off the ramp and under the waves. Because of the heavy load he was carrying, he sank like a stone. Fortunately, he managed to cut himself free of his pack, resurface, and begin wading ashore. Of the thirty-one men who were riding on the first section LCA, thirteen either did not make it off the boat or already lay wounded on the beach.

The Germans narrowly missed hitting at least two of the other boats, wounding several men but killing no one. Machine-gun, mortar, and rifle fire soon rose to a terrifying volume. The machine guns stitched Fox Green and Fox Red laterally from left and right. Mortar shells exploded on or over the fist-sized rocks that dotted the beach. The rifle bullets tended to be aimed at vital areas such as the head, the heart, or the throat. As quickly as the troops could, they poured out of their LCAs, waded sluggishly through the chilly water, and tried to make it across Fox Red beach to the comparative shelter of the cliff. For most, the two-hundred-yard journey seemed interminable. Under the weight of their crushing loads, many of the machine gunners, BAR men, mortarmen, bazookamen, and demolitionists could do no more than walk. The riflemen, especially those who had lost gear in the surf, could move faster. Private First Class John Sweeney was focused on following his boat section leader, Lieutenant Jimmie Monteith, a good-humored, self-effacing kid from Richmond, Virginia, who had once attended Virginia Tech. "All of a sudden I got hit by machine gun fire coming from the left-front," Sweeney later wrote. "I was turned completely around, the bazooka I was carrying was full of holes, the life belt I was wearing was taken right off me." Sweeney had been hit in the arm and the leg. He fell down and lay still for a few moments, but found the strength to get up and stagger to the cliff.

Elsewhere, Staff Sergeant McKinney could see no one ahead of him or around him. He almost felt as if he were invading France all by himself. "I didn't see a soul. I thought how eerie this was. I could see little puffs coming out of the sand where they were shooting machine gun fire." In his peripheral vision, McKinney finally saw other men, some of whom came from his boat section, similarly struggling, almost as if running in place. At least two got hit and fell backward as if dragged that way by the weight of their packs. They lay numb with dazed looks on their faces, their eyes glazing over with shock. He glanced around and took in the sight of "men all around, falling—some out of breath, some out of life." McKinney made it to the cliff and flopped down to rest.

The men had been trained by their commanders, from General Huebner on down, to zigzag and advance by rushes in order to present the smallest, most elusive target. "Our training served us in good stead," Private Steve Kellman later said. Under the incredible stress and excitement of the moment, the veterans seemed to zigzag better than the replacements. "I lost many of those young soldiers who joined my company right before the invasion in England," Captain Armellino said. "They had no fear and failed to hit the ground after every few yards. The more seasoned men hit the ground very often [and] as a result avoided being hit by enemy fire" (though it should be noted that Kellman was a replacement, as were many other survivors). Private First Class Jordan, a veteran of the Sicily campaign, employed a different trick to stay alive. "The entire beach was a killing field," he recalled. "[A]rtillery and machine gun fire were exploding all around me. Men were lying dead and wounded on the beach. As I was running across the beach, machine gun bullets began whizzing past me and hitting the ground just inches from my feet. Thinking that a German machine gunner had me as a target, I hit the ground. I laid there motionless, hoping the German machine gunner would think he had killed me and stop firing in my direction." It must have worked, because the machine-gun fire soon stopped. Jordan then got up, bolted for the cliff, and made it.

The company medics, Tech 5 Louis Iorio, Private First Class John Ryan, and Private First Class John Williford, did not have the luxury of simply running for cover. As wounded men fell, they ran right where the enemy fire was heaviest, feverishly trying to save lives. "The aid men were treating right at the edge of the water," the survivors reported in a post-invasion interview with the Army's historical section. "They worked back and forth from the water dragging those back to the cliff who could not move under their own power." Huddling against the rocky cliffside, Staff Sergeant McKinney was filled with admiration as he watched these courageous men disregard their own safety to save others, often in vain. "I can see men swathed in bandages," he later wrote in a letter to his mother. "God only knows how they were bandaged, fighting to keep the life in their bodies, and failing." In the recollection of Tech Sergeant John Worozbyt, "the sand . . . was almost covered with dead and wounded. German fire was so heavy we couldn't even drag some of the wounded ashore. They drowned when the tide came in."

Captain Armellino estimated that, out of his original complement of about 200 men, 125 made it to the cliff (regimental records put the estimate at 123 men). He also had some refugees from E Company, 116th Infantry Regiment of the 29th Infantry Division. Four boat sections from this company had been mistakenly landed along Fox Green, two others at the western end of Easy Red, literally miles away from their intended landing spots on the western edges of Omaha beach. Small groups from these wayward boat sections simply attached themselves to the 16th Infantry soldiers and fought alongside them. Armellino and the other leaders began to reorganize the company as best they could.

In the meantime, the six LCAs carrying Captain Anthony Prucnal's K Company arrived at Fox Red. Prucnal's company was filling in for I Company, which was still on the water, working its way from Port-en-Bessin to Fox Red. The LCAs disgorged the K Company soldiers, though two of the boats subsequently struck submerged mines and blew. Prucnal's people ran into the same wall of fire that had plagued L Company only a few minutes earlier. "Machine guns were constantly chattering and the cross fire was sweeping up and down the beach," the company history recorded. Mortar and artillery shells only added to the danger. As the K Company soldiers zigzagged for the cliffs, they sometimes had to jump over the dead bodies of men from L Company. For Private First Class Roger Brugger, a nineteen-year-old rifleman seeing his first combat, the scene was almost surreal, more typical of Hollywood than real life (modern American soldiers have a strong tendency to compare the overwhelming experience of combat to films). "I remember thinking as I ran from the boat and seeing the bullets tearing up the sand on either side of me, this is like a war movie," Brugger said. He reached the cliff, looked back, and watched as an antitank shell blew up his landing craft and then a mortar shell scored a direct hit on another K Company soldier. "All I could see of him were three hunks of his body flying through the air." Back on the beach, Lieutenant Leo Stumbaugh was running as fast as he could for the cliff when he saw "a man running across the beach hit a mine and was blown to bits right in front of me." Undeterred, and resigned to the inevitability of his own death, Stumbaugh continued in the same direction. "I felt that I would surely die on the beach because of the heavy shelling and direct fire." As this nearness to death set in, he experienced something remarkable, almost spiritual. "I could see my wife's and mother's faces crystal clear all of a sudden." He followed the sight of their faces until he got up the beach and took shelter underneath the cliff.

The lee of the cliff represented a dead spot in WN-60's field of fire, and thus it offered some protection from enemy machine guns and rifles. Mortar shells were another matter. Sergeant Eberhardt's defenders of WN-60 had pre-sighted this narrow strip of cliffside coastline, and they continued to drop deadly accurate mortar fire among the frightened, wet, and nauseated Americans. The shells exploded among the stones on the beach, against the rocky soil of the cliff's embankment, and in air bursts anywhere and everywhere. One shell badly wounded

Lieutenant Frederick Brandt, K Company's executive officer. He lay in a heap. Captain Prucnal rushed to him, grabbed him, and tried to pull him to the cliff. Another shell sailed in and exploded close to the two officers. Brandt was killed immediately. Prucnal was hit badly in the left leg. The fragments severed an artery. Prucnal's blood surged through his trousers. A medic tried desperately to stanch the flow of blood, but to no avail. Captain Prucnal bled to death in a matter of minutes. Elsewhere, as Captain Armellino moved about, reorganizing his company from the chaotic landing, a shell exploded near him. Fragments tore into his right leg, cutting an artery. "[It] was gushing blood," he later said. "A medic came to my assistance quickly. He applied a tourniquet to stop the bleeding, treated the wound with penicillin [actually probably with sulfanilamide powder] and wrapped it with a bandage." Armellino lay wounded, clinging to life. Command of L Company passed to Lieutenant Robert Cutler.

There were also spots along the shaky cliffside enclave where men were still in danger from small-arms fire, especially well-aimed rifle shots. Death could come swiftly and anonymously. Staff Sergeant Al Townsend knelt down alongside Staff Sergeant McKinney to discuss what to do next. McKinney, who was lying down, turned around to face Townsend. "He wanted to say something . . . and he just keeled over," McKinney recalled, "got shot in the head." Townsend collapsed in a dead heap. To McKinney's left along the cliff, Lieutenant James Robinson had assumed de facto command of K Company after the deaths of Captain Prucnal and Lieutenant Brandt. Robinson was walking around, trying to round up men and organize them into cohesive assault groups, when an unseen enemy rifleman spotted him, opened fire, and killed him, all in an instant.

Clearly the cliff offered only temporary shelter. Moreover, the tide was coming in rapidly, limiting the amount of space in the lee of the cliff. The longer the men stayed in this spot, the sooner the sea would reach them. They knew they had to get off this beach, but the question was how. They could not climb straight up the cliff. That was an utter impossibility, plus it would lead them right into the muzzles of WN-60. The left was a dead end, too; the cliff simply extended more steeply in that direction with no visible beach exit. Only the right, where the cliff gave way to an embankment, incremental bluffs, and a small draw known as Exit F-1, offered any hope. This route would place them directly in the line of fire from WN-60, but there was no other way forward. The surviving sergeants and lieutenants prepared to lead the way. It was time to get the hell off this beach.[11]

Chapter 4

SURVIVORS

Captain Joe Dawson hoped he would measure up. To a certain extent, he had lived for thirty years with that challenge never far from his mind. His parents had set the standard, and he strove to maintain it. Dad was one of the most prominent Baptist ministers in the country, practically a legend to his congregation at First Baptist Church in Waco, Texas. Mom was the consummate preacher's wife—kind, compassionate, dignified, pious. The Dawsons were, according to one of Joe's children, "a family of over-achievers." Lanky and self-assured, with deep-set eyes and a prominent, almost sloped nose, Joe was the third of five children. Raised in a deeply religious, stable environment, surrounded by love and expectations, he evolved into a focused, deep-thinking young man with definite ambitions. In 1933, he had graduated from Baylor University—following in the footsteps of his father and grandfather—at age nineteen with a degree in business administration. Like so many other Texans, he was drawn to the oil business. In the late

1930s he worked for Humble Oil Corporation and the Renwar Oil Corporation. To enhance his knowledge of oil drilling, he educated himself in geology and soon became one of the most widely respected experts in the state. In 1941, with his country on the verge of war, and a peacetime draft in effect, he decided to join the military and become an officer before Uncle Sam nabbed him as a draftee. He settled on the Army because it had so many posts within close range of his hometown and family.

By June 6, 1944, he had been with the 1st Division for two years, mainly as a staff officer, and he had seen plenty of action but, until this momentous morning, he had never commanded troops in combat. He had taken command of G Company, 16th Infantry in the aftermath of the Sicily campaign from his good friend Edward Wozenski, who had been reassigned to command E Company. The men of G Company revered Wozenski, even idolized him. They did not like the idea of an untested staff officer supplanting a man who had led them through so much heavy combat (and had earned a Distinguished Service Cross for his valor in Sicily). Dawson knew he could never hope to eclipse Wozenski's popularity or make the men forget him. He determined to lead the only way he knew how—up front, by example, with concern only for the mission and the welfare of his soldiers. His main goal was winning respect, not popularity. During the long months in England, he had prepared his troops for the invasion with the toughest, most realistic training imaginable. "I tried to make my men into a fighting force, physically and mentally, and I didn't spare the horses," he later said. They hiked and patrolled endlessly; they rehearsed amphibious exercises until they knew every man's job by heart; they maintained and fired their weapons to the point of overkill. While other units rested in their quarters or went out on the town, Dawson's people were often training.

He was brutally honest with his men about what to expect on the beaches of France. When Private Frank Mutter asked him one day what G Company's role would be in the coming invasion, Dawson replied forthrightly, "We will have a one shilling seat." The term referred to the cheap front-row seats in the cinemas of England that spring. Anyone with a one-shilling seat was up front, in the lead. That theme of leading the way in the face of terrible danger reverberated in Dawson's fertile mind, appealing to his deep sense of service, obligation, and personal honor. "I tried to instill . . . an understanding and awareness of the gravity of the situation and the necessity for total teamwork," he said. "It didn't necessarily endear me to my men. And I could not do anything about that except to covenant with God and my own self that I was going to be the one that would lead them when the time came."

He knew that could mean death or, perhaps even worse, failure. Back in England, as the company sat in a marshaling area waiting for the order to board ship, he had written to his mother, "I shall never be able to measure up to you and Dad, but in my humble prayer, I hope that God will somehow find my destiny a reflection of credit to you both. I am truly conscious of the responsibility that rests upon all my men and me. In your prayers and communions with God, I beg of you to remember each of my men and officers to Him that they may have His living care and protection." The night before the invasion, he had made a point of visiting each man in the company, wishing him luck and explaining that he expected the best out of them. Even then, in such a personal and emotional setting, he was still not sure that they truly accepted him as their leader. "To be perfectly honest," he later asserted, "I didn't know when I landed whether I was going to get shot from the back or the front." So, in a most immediate sense, on D-Day morning, as Captain Dawson stood near the ramp of his LCVP, he wondered if he would measure up to the expectations of his men. The secret, he reminded himself yet again, was to lead from the front, come what may.

At 0705, pretty much on time, the six LCVPs carrying G Company approached Easy Red beach, at nearly the same place where Lieutenant Spalding's boat section had landed about twenty minutes earlier in a relative dead spot in the German fields of fire. In later years, Dawson would modestly claim that this occurred through sheer luck. In reality, it was no accident. Dawson specifically directed his boat's coxswain here. He had studied the terrain intently, and if there was one thing he had learned in the oil business, it was how to remember terrain features. The beach exits were imprinted on his memory, so he knew exactly where to go. The other five LCVPs carrying G Company followed suit. By this time, one of the boats was taking on water due to a defective ramp, so the soldiers had to clamber over the sides. The other five beached without mishap, though one initially got hung up on a sandbar before it was piloted expertly to the waterline by a courageous coxswain.

Enemy fire had been desultory during the run into the beach, but it picked up in tempo and accuracy once the troops began to debark into waist-deep water. Machine-gun bullets stitched the sand and water; mortar shells burst within yards of the landing craft. For many the journey was sheer misery. Aboard Sergeant Joe Pilck's LCVP, the soldiers were passing around a vomit bucket. One man had a different, and arguably more wretched, problem than nausea. "Hurry up," he said, "pass the bucket. I have to shit." The task of dropping one's trousers and answering this call of nature was nearly impossible in the crowded, rocking boat. Another man turned to him and said, "Just do as I did. Shit in your pants." By the time the ramps dropped, many of the troops were racked with exhaustion. "Some of the men couldn't move ashore," Lieutenant Marvin Stine, a boat section leader, said. "They had become so cramped because of crowding that their muscles could not respond. They lay in the water for a few minutes, rubbing their legs, then they crawled ashore." The majority, who could run, seemed, in the view of one sergeant, as if they "were glad of the chance to assault, so miserable had they felt on the in-journey."

1

Under the intense machine-gun and mortar fire, the men made for the shingle some two hundred yards distant, where they saw a long line of inert men "pinned down, mentally if not physically," in Captain Dawson's estimation. These troops probably came from E Company of both the 16th and the 116th Infantry Regiments, plus the engineers. Some were wounded. Along the beach, men from the Gap Assault Teams were working on obstacles. Dawson had no sooner left his landing craft than a mortar shell scored a direct hit on it, inflicting several casualties, including his naval forward observer. He later described the company's landing and the situation in front of them as "total chaos." With his radioman and communications sergeant in tow, he made it quickly across the beach and paused at the shingle. Ever the geologist, he glanced at the sandy rocks beneath him and identified them as "arkosic sand which is a very sharp granitic sand . . . pebbly granular material."

All around him, soldiers from G Company awkwardly zigzagged, under the crushing weight of their heavy loads, across the deadly beach, bound for the shingle. Private First Class Carl Atwell stumbled and fell next to an obstacle. "I looked up and I saw a big mine up there," he recalled. "I got up and scampered [up] the beach." Sergeant Pilck took cover behind a tank until he realized that it was a prime target for German antitank shells and machine-gun fire. He jumped up and ran as hard as he could—not particularly fast because he was hauling a bazooka and three rockets in addition to all his other equipment—for the shingle. "A machine gunner started to shoot at me. [My] buddies told me later that they saw tracer bullets go between my legs as I was running." He was lucky. He made it to the shingle unscathed. He turned around and watched in horror as the tank backed up, ran right over two of his buddies who had taken cover behind it, and crushed them to death. Pilck turned away, grabbed his rosary and began to pray the Hail Mary as his fingers unconsciously ran along the smooth beads. Dozens of other G Company men got hit and went down. The air was full of cries for medics. The ocean waves, crashing relentlessly against the brittle sand, ran red with the blood of the dead and wounded. First Sergeant Bill Lambert got hit badly in the upper right arm and right thigh. He lay on the sand, critically wounded, vulnerable to the withering fire. He needed to be evacuated immediately, but that was impossible under the circumstances, so his soldiers helped him the only way they could. "We piled dead bodies around his so he would be protected from enemy fire," Tech 5 Larry Krumanocker, the company clerk, said.

It took the company between ten and fifteen minutes to make it across the beach, at the cost of sixty-three casualties, most of whom were felled by mortar and machine-gun fire. "It was the feeling of the men that their losses would have been cut in half had their loads been cut likewise," an Army historian related on the basis of a post-combat interview with the survivors. As Captain Dawson took stock of the situation and began to organize the men lying along the shingle into coherent assault teams, he was almost amazed that anyone had made it across the deadly, wide-open beach. He attributed this primarily to poor German marksmanship and the relative cohesiveness of his command. Already his mortar crews and machine gunners were in place, unleashing suppressive fire at the unseen enemy soldiers up the bluff. The Germans responded in kind. "Mortar shells were bursting in the shingle, sending shrapnel and rock flying over the crowds of men," one of the engineers who was with them later wrote. This pointed out a real peril at Omaha. The fist-sized rocks of the shingle and along the expanse of the beach served as ready-made fragments. The enemy had only to explode mortar or artillery shells within a few feet of the ground and the fragmentation effect of the blasts was substantially multiplied.

Dawson looked over the shingle and surveyed the terrain. About five yards beyond this spot lay double apron strands of barbed wire, augmented by a line of concertina wire, all coiled together in large loops, some ten feet high, with strands curled and intermixed into almost incomprehensible circles. To the right was a marshy swamp; to the left an embankment and upward slope of scrubby grass that he supposed must be chock-full of mines. A small dirt path knifed through the grass on a gentle upward slope, to unseen points beyond. Dawson figured the path too was probably mined, but it was the only viable route off the beach. As he formulated a plan of action—he felt remarkably calm, given the situation—his battalion commander, Lieutenant Colonel Herbert Hicks, arrived and lay down next to him. In a brief meeting, Hicks ordered Dawson to advance inland, something the young Texan already planned to do. "There was nothing I could do on the beach except die," Dawson later said. "I felt the only way I could move was forward . . . off the beach. I felt the obligation to lead my men off, because I felt the only way they were going to get off was to follow me. They wouldn't get off by themselves."

The Bangalore torpedo was designed for just this kind of situation. The five-foot-long Bangalore pipes were small enough to fit under the barbed wire strands, and the TNT inside the pipes was powerful enough to blow gaps in the wire. Dawson told his men to assemble their Bangalores and deal with the wire. The men had done this so many times in training that it was practically second nature. Each individual soldier carried one section of tube, which he then attached to a section carried by another soldier. In practice, only about three or four sections could be connected and manipulated into position. Two soldiers, Lieutenant John Burbridge and Private First Class Henry Peszyk, constituted one Bangalore team. They hugged the ground and began crawling under the coils of wire, all the while under small-arms fire. They had made it halfway through when Burbridge's pack caught on the wire. As the lieutenant struggled to free himself, Peszyk yelled, "Keep going! I'm going back for the Bangalores!" Peszyk hurriedly placed the pipes in position while Burbridge finally got loose of the wire. Then they touched off two explosions, while lying only six feet away from the blasts. A bullet creased Peszyk's arm. Nonetheless, he and Lieutenant Burbridge got the job done. The two explosions tore a sizable opening in the wire. "This was the best placed and cut lane along the beach," one company history said. "Through it most of the men of 'G' passed, and the [battalions] which came after them took the same route."

True to form, the first man through was Captain Dawson, acting as a veritable scout. Accompanied by Private First Class Frank Baldridge, he crawled through the gap in the wire and to the path. He saw two dead Americans sprawled on the path and assumed that they had been killed by mines (this may or may not have been true, since the identity of these men and their unit remains a mystery). Dawson slithered over their bodies and followed the little dirt track. With every forward movement, he watched carefully, and fearfully, for mines. He and Baldridge continued past the stone ruins of three small houses and into a draw. These were the same ruins where Lieutenant Spalding's boat section from E Company had taken cover about twenty minutes earlier, though Dawson had no way of knowing that. At last, as the ground rose, Captain Dawson and Private First Class Baldridge arrived at a spot where they could see more than a few feet into the distance. "Suddenly I saw what was ahead," Dawson later recalled. "From the beach flat to the top of the bluffs was a little over two hundred fifty feet, and it was almost sheer." He could tell, though, that the path went all the way to the top. The sloping ground that led to the bluff formed a shallow valley or draw, roughly in the shape of a V. Enemy machine-gun fire was coming from somewhere atop the heights. From behind them, G Company's covering fire was whizzing overhead, uncomfortably close. Dawson and Baldridge found a sheltered spot next to a log and took cover. "Leave your equipment here," he said to Baldridge. "Go back and get the rest of the company. They've got to get off the beach."

Baldridge scrambled away, in the direction of the beach, careful to retrace the exact route he and the captain had traversed.

Dawson studied the bluff (roughly where the U.S. cemetery is located today) and immediately recognized that this was the surest way off Easy Red, not straight through the heavily defended beach exits. At a promontory atop the bluff, he caught a glimpse of the German machine-gun position and decided to act. He crawled forward about seventy-five yards, from covered spot to covered spot, shielding himself from the gaze of the German gunners. In all likelihood, their view of the beach itself was panoramic, but their field of vision of the brush-and-mine-covered valley just beneath their noses was more limited. As the captain worked his way nearer to the machine-gun nest, he lost sight of it until he reached a vertical crest underneath it and heard voices. "I looked up and, sure enough, just above me was [the] machine gun." He looked in the direction of the beach and saw some of his men walking single file through the gap in the barbed wire back on the beach. The gun opened fire, about ten feet above his head. He armed a pair of grenades and threw them into the machine-gun nest. The Germans saw him at the last minute and attempted to swing their gun around at him, but it was too late. The grenades exploded right between the pair of machine gunners, killing them and thus creating the first major breach in the enemy defenses and the first real avenue off the beach for the Americans. "It was a miracle," he later claimed. "It doesn't mean anything on my part. It was just one of those wacky things that happen, that I was on the right spot." While it is true that Dawson was fortunate to find himself in the right place at the right time, this did not happen out of sheer randomness or freak luck. The situation could have played out many other ways—he could have frozen up on the beach, he could have hung back and ordered someone else forward with no results, he could have blundered into the minefield, he could have been too frightened or confused or cautious to deal with the machine-

INLAND FROM EASY RED

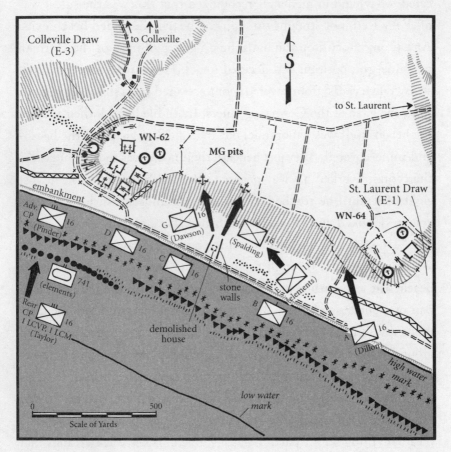

Throughout the morning, small groups of soldiers found weak spots in the German defenses and advanced inland, up the bluffs between WN-62 and WN-64. Two of the first groups to make it off Easy Red were led by Captain Dawson and Lieutenant Spalding; others from the 1st Battalion, 16th Infantry soon followed. In the meantime, follow-up waves landed and either became pinned down or ever so carefully fought their way off the beach.

gun nest. The list of possibilities is nearly endless. What Dawson accomplished was the product of not just good fortune but also courage, know-how, and resolve.

At nearly the same time, a couple hundred yards to the west, Lieutenant John Spalding, the Kentuckian, and his stalwarts from E Company clashed with another enemy machine-gun emplacement on the same ridgeline or bluff. Since tiptoeing past the stone ruins and the mines on the path that led off Easy Red, they had carefully ascended a small ravine that led west in the direction of WN-64 (roughly along the path that leads today from the beach to the cemetery). The machine gun they encountered was an outwork of the trenches that guarded the approaches to WN-64. The enemy gunner caught sight of the Americans as they worked their way up the ravine, and he opened fire. Sergeant Hubert Blades fired at the gun with a bazooka but missed and, in return, took a bullet through his left arm just above the wrist. Private First Class Raymond Curley also got hit, as did Sergeant Joe Slaydon. Blades was not in too much pain. As a veteran of three invasions, he was convinced that the new wound would probably earn him a ticket off the front line. He rushed over to Spalding, showed him the wound, and said, "Gee, Lieutenant, ain't it a beauty?" Spalding noticed an envious look on the faces of several of the other men.

Led by Staff Sergeant Grant Phelps, who sprayed the bluff with BAR fire, Spalding and several other soldiers got up, rushed the enemy nest, and overran the lone gunner. The man's hands shot into the air and, terrified, he pleaded, *"Kamerad!"* (the German word for surrender). "We could have easily killed him," Spalding said, "but since we needed prisoners for interrogation I ordered the men not to shoot him." The prisoner claimed to be an ethnic Pole, probably from the 716th Infantry Division. Spalding's platoon sergeant, Phil Streczyk, was a Polish American, and among his many skills was an ability to speak the language of his ancestral land. For several moments, he interrogated the hapless man. The Pole claimed that there were sixteen soldiers behind him whose job it was to defend the flank of the strong point. They were somewhere in the trench system, beyond the group's line of vision (actually Sergeant Clarence Colson and a few others from the Spalding group had, at that very moment, overrun at least one of their positions). These enemy soldiers had apparently taken a vote that morning on whether to fight and decided not to, but they were forced by their ethnic German NCOs to stay put and resist. Streczyk was not in a forgiving mood. He hit the prisoner in the head and asked, "So why are you shooting at us now?" The terrified soldier only cowered. Spalding was equally dubious. "He also said . . . he had not fired on any Americans, although I had seen him hit three," the lieutenant related with skepticism. Spalding detailed the wounded Sergeant Blades to escort the prisoner back to the beach with only a trench knife (the group, now numbering about twenty men, needed his rifle and ammo). Contrary to Blades's expectations, his wound was not of the million-dollar variety. He returned to the platoon a few weeks later. "He was asked if he got the prisoner back ok," Spalding later wrote. Blades's response was chilling. "He replied that the prisoner tried to escape. No further questions asked."

In the aftermath of the fight at the machine-gun position, Spalding's group made their first contact with soldiers from G Company. Lieutenant Kenneth "Den" Bleau, one of Captain Dawson's platoon leaders, had already begun leading men through the gap in the wire and up the path, even before Private First Class Baldridge, the captain's messenger, reached the company with orders to get moving inland. Although the wire had been breached, the tendency for many of the soldiers was to lie low and do nothing, especially if their leaders were not in sight. Before the war, Bleau had been a star swimmer and he still had the muscular physique to prove it. He simply pointed the men in the right direction and told them to get going. To Staff Sergeant Vincent Kachnik, one of Bleau's squad leaders, "it seemed that the new men came along quite as well as the old men, and in some cases, with more dash." A few minutes after Bleau met up with Spalding, Captain Dawson appeared and spoke with the lieutenant. After conversing for a short time about the whereabouts of E Company—which neither of them knew—they decided to proceed in different directions. Dawson and his men would go straight over the destroyed machine-gun nest on the bluff and head for Colleville-sur-Mer. Spalding was to bear right (west) in the direction of WN-64 and Exit E-1, clear the trenches he had found, and destroy any fortifications he encountered. Bleau agreed to cover Spalding's men as they spread out and advanced in the direction of the trenches. Dawson returned to the task of gathering his company and pushing over the bluff and inland, toward Colleville. He was in his element, making decisions, using his brain, *leading*. He and Spalding both knew that the penetrations they had made were shaky, vulnerable to formidable enemy counterattacks, especially since most of the invaders were still pinned down on the beaches. Even so, they represented a mortal threat to the Germans—an American on the beach was generally a target; an American roaming around inland was a hunter. So, like knives probing the vitals of the Germans, the two distinct groups resumed their relentless advance.[1]

1

Back on Easy Red beach, the follow-on waves were arriving with the rapidly incoming tides. The beach was already littered with dead and wounded men, scattered weapons and equipment, obstacles, wrecked tanks and bloody bandages. The surviving Germans at WN-62 reacted to the sight of new targets and shifted their fire from the decimated remnants of E and F Companies at the mouth of the E-3 draw to the arriving boats at Easy Red. Colonel George Taylor, commander of the 16th Infantry Regiment, believed it was foolhardy to cluster his entire command group together and land at the same time in the same spot. A few accurate shots, or even a single direct hit, could take out the proverbial brains of the regiment in an instant. So, beginning with the Sicily invasion, he had employed the practice of dividing his headquarters element into two sections, an advance command post and a rear command post; they even sailed aboard different troopships. The advance CP, coming from the USS *Henrico*, was scheduled to hit the beach at 0720. The rear CP, sallying forth from the USS *Samuel Chase*, would arrive about an hour later.

Taylor placed himself in the rear group and his highly competent executive officer, Lieutenant Colonel John H. Mathews, in charge of the advance group (in the twenty-first-century U.S. Army, the roles almost certainly would have been reversed, with the commander in the lead, but the custom of the World War II army was often otherwise). Taylor had nothing but the highest confidence in the thirty-six-year-old Mathews—and with good reason, since the young West Pointer was one of the finest professional officers in the division. Mathews had served as a battalion commander in North Africa, earning a promotion to executive officer. During the bitter fight for Sicily, he had been pressed into temporary command of the 2nd Battalion when the commander became a casualty. His valor and inspirational leadership had earned him the Distinguished Service Cross.

Known as "Huey" to his many friends, Mathews was the sort of officer who led by personal example and the natural warmth of his personality. Though his personal life was in tatters—his wife had divorced him just before the war and he had not seen his seven-year-old daughter, Marianne, in several years—his dedication to the division and its soldiers was near total. His advance CP numbered 102 soldiers, consisting mainly of the intelligence and reconnaissance (I&R) platoon, the communications section, liaison officers, and assorted headquarters troops. Mathews's job was to lead them ashore, find a good spot for the regimental headquarters, and set it up so that it was fully functional by the time Taylor came ashore.

The soldiers of the advance CP landed in waist-deep water about one hundred fifty yards from the beach. From the first, they were under intense machine-gun and mortar fire. A shell smashed into the back of the landing craft, wrecking the controls. Many of the soldiers had filled their vomit bags on the way in; they were woozy and unsteady, but now they had to pull themselves together well enough to make it through the water, across a sandbar, and to the shingle. "It looked like Easy Red was a mile away," Corporal Sam Fuller later wrote. Lieutenant Kenneth Hill, in charge of the I&R platoon, led the way into the veritable wall of fire. Men stumbled and thrashed at the ramp or over the sides and into the water. Lieutenant Colonel Mathews turned to Sergeant Raymond Briel and said, "This is it! Good luck." Mathews lunged forward and stepped off the ramp into the water. Master Sergeant Frank Carpino was right at his side. A machine-gun bullet tore through Carpino's gas mask (carried in a black rubber pouch just under his throat) and smashed into the colonel's head. In the flick of an instant, Mathews was dead. He slumped forward and fell into the water. Carpino was unscathed. "Not knowing he was dead, Sgt Carpino with much difficulty got his body to shore only to learn that he had been killed instantly," the regiment's morning report said. All told, the advance CP suffered thirty-five casualties just moving from boat to beach. "There was indescribable confusion," the survivors later told an Army historian. "The beach was crowded. There was no exit off the beach that was open. There were dead and wounded all over, on the beach and in the water." With Mathews dead, and his group devastated by casualties and confusion, there was now no question of setting up an advance CP. The surviving members of the group simply spread out, took cover, and added to the throngs already clinging to the shingle. The destruction of the advance CP guaranteed continued confusion and disarray at Easy Red, at least for the time being.

Every minute on that hellish beach felt like an hour. For every shivering and disoriented soldier, each instant presented a range of possibilities and choices, often centered around whether to move, to do something or to just lie still. Any movement or action could bring swift death; a soldier could of course just as easily get killed or wounded as a stationary target huddling uselessly under the dubious "cover" of the shingle. It is fair to say that any act, especially those that required movement, took courage or resolve or discipline or perhaps just a sense of not caring anymore about what might happen next. In most instances, acts of cowardice and heroism (and there were many more of the latter) took place anonymously, undocumented by any observers or official records. This was especially true for medics, who circulated unglamorously near the waterline, where the fire was heaviest, trying to save badly wounded men before the advancing tides engulfed them. According to the I&R platoon diary, "the medics were everywhere dressing wounds and rescuing men" from the water.

In a few cases, soldiers were so brave that their actions were impossible to miss. Tech 5 John Joseph Pinder, a radioman with Mathews's command group, fully understood the vital importance of his radio equipment. The radio was the key to the unit's communication, and communication was central to command and control, resupply, and fire support, as well as myriad other details. Indeed, the dearth of functioning radios was a major reason why the initial waves at Omaha beach were so badly bogged down—commanders were out of communication and this created confusion, ignorance, and inertia. Witness, for instance, the inability of Lieutenant Spalding to contact Captain Wozenski, some fifteen hundred yards away, and inform him of his whereabouts, thus marginalizing Wozenski's company command group and the remnants of E Company for much of D-Day morning. Even the intrepid Captain Dawson had been forced to gather his company for an inland move by runner, which cost a great deal of time and initiative. Just as General Huebner had trained riflemen and machine gunners to always care for their weapons, he had taught his radiomen to do the same with their equipment.

Hence, Pinder understood full well that without the radios of his section, Lieutenant Colonel Mathews and the other officers could not set up a proper headquarters, contact Colonel Taylor before he landed with the rear CP or, really, do much of anything. Pinder, who went by his middle name, Joe, was actually celebrating his thirty-second birthday that morning. The eldest son of a Pennsylvania steelworker, he was a talented athlete who had pitched in the minor leagues during the latter half of the 1930s before joining the Army in early 1942. He once retired the great Josh Gibson twice in an exhibition game against the Pittsburgh Crawfords. Pinder earned a reputation as a gentleman off the field and a bulldog on it. One former teammate remembered him as "a real competitor with a live fastball and a good curve." As a member of the 16th Infantry Regiment's communications section, he was thought of as a reliable, courageous soldier.

Soon after Pinder left the landing craft and hit the water, a mortar shell exploded, showering the left side of his face with hot fragments. "The side of his face was left hanging and he could see only from one eye," recalled Sergeant Robert Michaud, who was only a few yards away. "He held his hanging flesh with one hand and gripped the radio and dragged it to shore." The radio was the ungainly SCR-284, an awkward, forty-five-pound set, "roughly the weight, size and shape of a modern window air conditioner," one officer quipped. For Tech 5 Pinder, the job of dragging the radio and holding his wounded face in place was arduous, but he made it to the beach. At this stage, the rational—and not to mention most common—thing to do would have been to lie low and wait for a medic. Instead, to the astonishment of his exhausted comrades, he plunged back into the surf, right into the worst of the incoming fire and began to salvage more floating radio equipment that had been dropped by other wounded soldiers. He plowed through the waves, manhandling the equipment as best he could. He made at least three trips into the water, including one for another SCR-284. On one of his trips, a burst of machine-gun fire caught him in both legs, but he hardly wavered. "He continued ashore with the load he was carrying, although by this time he was greatly weakened by loss of blood," Sergeant Leeward Stockwell, a member of the I&R platoon, later said.

Despite his wounds, Pinder insisted on helping his comrades set up the equipment. "He would not stop for rest or medical attention," Captain Stephen Ralph, his company commander, said. At this point, Pinder's luck ran out. He got hit again and died on the beach. If not for him, the communications section probably would have lost all of its radios. According to Stockwell, the sets "were the only means of communication that the Regimental Command Post had at the time." The Army later awarded Pinder a posthumous Medal of Honor. When his grief-stricken family found out the details of what he had done, they were not surprised. "He was the type of guy who always seemed to do things a little better than others . . . a very competitive person," his brother Harold, a combat aviator, explained.

Not far from Pinder, another soldier was also on the move, constantly risking his life. Private Carlton Barrett was part of a three-man liaison team from the 18th Infantry Regiment's I&R platoon, which was commanded by Lieutenant Cecil Fitzpatrick. The team's job was to land with the 16th Infantry's advance CP, size up the situation on the beach, reconnoiter enemy dispositions, and then guide the landing of their own units later in the morning. In other words, they were supposed to be the eyes and ears of the 18th. Instead, they were enmeshed in a fight for survival alongside their 16th Infantry buddies. The twenty-four-year-old Barrett hailed from Fulton, New York. He was anything but a Hollywood version of a hero. Diminutive at five feet four and 125 pounds soaking wet, the diametric opposite of the athletic Pinder, Barrett had served courageously with his outfit since North Africa. "[He] reminded me a bantam rooster, short, stocky and not afraid of anything," Sergeant Thomas McCann, who served with him in the I&R platoon, said. "He was a happy go lucky young man who enjoyed life." Barrett had a rebellious streak, too. Back in England, when his outfit was sealed into a marshaling area prior to boarding a ship for the invasion, he had snuck out to see his girlfriend and had gotten caught. Lieutenant Fitzpatrick had him placed under twenty-four-hour guard. In McCann's recollection, Barrett "was very mad at the lieutenant," yet the young New Yorker gave his guards no trouble.

Barrett, Lieutenant John Foley, and Private William Carter comprised the small advance team. They quickly realized that their mission was no longer feasible amid the chaos and death on Easy Red. "It was apparent that the mission could not be accomplished for some time," Foley later wrote. Instead of simply taking cover and waiting for the situation to improve, Barrett sprang into action. At the waterline, exactly where the enemy fire was deadliest and at its most accurate, he began to grab wounded men and drag them up the beach to the comparative safety of the shingle. "He rendered first aid to the wounded, quieted the hysterical, and found them what little shelter was available," Foley said. He also acted as an informal runner, carrying messages for Foley to other spots along the beach. He braved so much withering fire that, many who saw him wondered how he did not get hit and killed (though he did eventually catch some fragments in the legs and buttocks). "You only had to be lucky," he cheerfully opined. At one point, after Barrett returned to the lieutenant's side from one such errand, a mortar shell exploded near Foley. Fragments tore into the lieutenant's head just above his left eye, and blood began pouring from his scalp, down into his eye. Barrett bandaged Foley's head and prevented him from losing consciousness; Foley believed that he otherwise would have bled to death.

The shell that felled Foley had also wounded several other men. Barrett dragged them to cover and attended to their wounds. He was like a man possessed, seemingly bereft of fear, though, like any other man, he must have been frightened. When he came upon a small group of men who were too scared to cross an antitank ditch filled with water, he simply walked across the ditch in order to show them that it could be done. They quickly calmed down and followed suit. He was everywhere—helping wounded men, carrying messages, directing boats into open spots on the beach, carrying stretchers for the wounded. More than anything, his presence was calming amid the most terrifying of circumstances, a sort of inspiration by example for those who so badly needed it. There is no telling how many lives he saved or how many soldiers he inspired or shamed into productive action, but the number was probably considerable. "[He] moved around as if nothing were going on," Captain John Brownlee, his company commander, wrote in wonderment, "moving in and out from one place to another with utter disregard for the shells that were falling around him and the bullets passing by him. He acted as calmly and collectively as if he were enjoying a Sunday afternoon at the beach. Everyone else was pinned down. The calm, collected, efficient figure Pvt Barrett presented—so out of keeping with the bursting shells, smashed equipment, and wounded and dead men—had an inestimable effect on all those around him, both the unharmed and the wounded." That effect made such a powerful impression on those who saw him that he received the Medal of Honor.[2]

1

Some of the boats that Barrett guided in to the beach were from Colonel Taylor's reserve outfit, the 1st Battalion of the 16th Infantry. From 0740 to 0750 the battalion's three rifle companies all made their runs in to the crowded beach, as did soldiers from the 37th Engineer Combat Battalion, a supporting unit whose mission was to clear mines from the beach exits and build roads. The infantry companies were spread out over a six-hundred-yard expanse of Easy Red, with C Company on the left (east) flank quite close to where Captain Dawson's company had landed earlier; B Company was in the middle and A Company on the right (west) flank quite near the mouth of WN-64 at Exit E-1. Besides the fire, coxswains struggled with sandbars, the swift tides, and obstacles that had not been cleared, above and below the water. In the recollection of one Coast Guard coxswain, the water was "like a mud puddle in a hailstorm. It seemed impossible that we could make it in without being riddled."

By most accounts, they did an excellent job and demonstrated great courage in spite of these issues. Staff Sergeant Harley Reynolds, a thoughtful native of St. Charles, Virginia, who spoke with a hint of a Southern accent, led a machine-gun section in B Company. He studied his boat's coxswain and was impressed with his cool, calm resolve. "It gave me confidence in him," Reynolds commented. Aboard another B Company LCVP, just as the ramp was about to drop, a private poked Sergeant John Ellery in the ribs and wisecracked, "Hey, Sarge, how about putting me in for a three day pass starting right now?" Like the units that had preceded them, the 1st Battalion soldiers generally landed in waist- or chest-high water. In a now familiar routine, the men concentrated on making it to the crowded shingle bank. Most were wearing invasion vests and lugging about seventy to eighty pounds of gear. This, of course, slowed them down considerably. "I think we would have had much better luck . . . if we hadn't been loaded down with so much junk," Ellery, who was making his third invasion, opined. Private First Class Harold Saylor had such difficulty running that "I thought that somebody was holding me back." Only when water and sand began to drain from his vest did he pick up any speed.

The German opposition intensified. The beach was raked by artillery shells (probably from inland batteries), antitank gunfire from WN-62, and machine-gun, rifle, and mortar fire from that strong point and probably WN-64 and WN-65 as well. In all likelihood, other enemy soldiers in the zigzag trench systems overlooking portions of Easy Red added to that fire. One artillery shell scored a direct hit on the LCVP carrying the second section of C Company, inflicting several casualties. Most of the other boats disgorged their troops without getting hit. "All I can remember is that the ground was shaking with all the shells going off," Corporal John Weaver of C Company wrote.

The smooth stones of the shingle and along the beach of course added that much more to the fragmentation effect of the exploding shells and the ricocheting bullets. "These stones burst like grenades . . . and we had to keep our faces protected from the rock fragments," one soldier said. Sergeant Ellery felt it was "the greatest concentration of mortar, machine gun, and artillery fire that I have ever seen. Direct fire, plunging and grazing, and flanking fire." For Private First Class Art Schintzel, a member of a machine-gun team, the job of crossing the beach was "a little bit like I've always imagined Pickett's Charge would have been like in Gettysburg." As Private First Class Niles Knauss hurried across the beach, he glimpsed "a guy with half his head shot away sitting by a tank trap talking to himself." Captain James Pence, the commander of A Company, had inflated his life preserver as he jumped into the water. It encumbered him so much as he moved onto the beach that he could hardly breathe. He lay down and curled up in an indentation that had been made by a mortar shell. "I was unable to get out of the life preserver because it was so tight and I was so cold and numb I could not unbuckle it," he said. "I could see machine gun bullets tracing a pattern all around me in the sand." Fortunately, a soldier from his light-machine-gun section happened along and punctured the preserver with a trench knife.

Robert Capa, an experienced combat photographer who had covered the Spanish Civil War and the 1st Division in the Mediterranean, was lying among the obstacles, taking shelter, snapping pictures. *"Es una cosa muy seria,"* he kept repeating to himself. Translated, that meant, "This is a very serious business." In a postwar memoir, Capa wrote that he landed in the first wave with E Company, but given his ship of origination and the camera angle of his famous photos, he probably hit the beach in the second wave, with either the regimental headquarters group or the 1st Battalion. Regardless, he was in the thick of the Easy Red meat grinder, in mortal fear for his life like all the soldiers around him.

The tide kept washing in relentlessly over Capa, thoroughly soaking his trousers. A lieutenant with whom he had played poker the night before took cover alongside him, so close that the two men were nose to nose. "You know what I see?" the lieutenant asked.

"No, I don't think you can see much beyond my head," Capa replied.

"I'll tell you what I see," the officer deadpanned. "I see my ma on the front porch, waving my insurance policy."

Sergeant Reynolds, the machine-gun section leader from B Company, bolted for the cover of a hedgehog. The shape and design of the obstacle reminded him of the jacks he used to play with as a kid. He could hardly believe he had not already been hit. He could hear the hissing sound made by near misses from machine-gun bullets. "I could see bullets hitting the sand in bursts and ricocheting in front and to the sides of me." He spotted the shingle, took off, and made it, though he felt several tugs at his pant legs that must have been near misses (he ended up a few hundred yards east of Exit E-1). Somehow he did not get hit. Ahead lay marshland with a flooded, canal-sized antitank ditch—Reynolds thought of it as a pond—plus coils of barbed wire and mines. Even at the shingle, men were getting hit with alarming frequency. One bullet tore into the helmet of a man lying next to Private Charles Thomas. "It went through a pair of socks . . . inside his helmet but it didn't hit his head, so he was lucky." Another adjacent soldier was not so fortunate. "[He] had a large chunk of his buttocks blown away, so we poured sulfa powder on it. He was laughing. I guess he was numb from shock." Boat sections were scattered and shattered. Unit integrity was completely wrecked. As Captain Albert Smith, the battalion executive officer, looked around and took in the sight of many inert bodies lying dead in the sand and in the water, he thought, "How are we gonna get off this beach?"

Many others were wondering the same thing. They did not know quite how they could exit this deadly morass, but they realized they had to do it, regardless of how much improvising that might require. In spite of the danger of continued movement off the beach, Reynolds and scores of other exhausted men from the follow-on waves who managed to make it to the shingle bank knew that they must keep going. Most did not know of the openings in the wire blown earlier by the Dawson and Spalding groups. A man was lucky to see more than a few feet in any direction, especially because it could be fatal just to raise one's head a foot or two. When Private Thomas had to urinate he opened his fly and lay on his side rather than chance standing or kneeling. "I was soaking wet anyway! I guess I was just being neat or something." Anyone who wanted to move had to stay low and crawl on his belly or his side. Even if they had known of the fledgling gaps, it would have been impossible, and almost suicidal, for hundreds of men to funnel through those small openings. So these men thought in terms of creating their own gaps in the coils of barbed wire. Moreover, with the passage of every inevitable minute, the tides behind them grew nearer until, in the recollection of one man, they were "almost lapping at our feet." Clearly, the troops could not stay here indefinitely. Captain Victor Briggs, the commander of C Company, bellowed, "Stay here and die or go ahead and die!" Captain Pence, who already had blood dripping down his arm from a bullet wound, stood up, gestured with his good arm, and roared, "Come on, you bastards, let's go! If we're gonna die, we might as well die a little farther inland!"[3]

The statement was less an order than a confirmation of what so many other men at the shingle bank were thinking. Along the expanse of Easy Red, several Bangalore teams began to deal with the barbed wire. Some of the teams were impromptu—the chaotic landing had hopelessly disorganized and intermixed boat sections and thus Bangalore teams. Under the ultimate pressure of life and death, they could function because they had trained so well and so repeatedly or, in the case of many, because they had performed in the terrible stress of combat before. They also had leaders, not always in the sense of rank but by example. "Let's get that barbed wire blown and get the heck off this beach," Private First Class Edward Foley called out to Sergeant Reynolds. The young machine-gun section leader heartily agreed. He chanced a look over the shingle and spotted a lone man "small in size, pushing a long bangalore torpedo under the wire. I don't know where he came from. Suddenly he was there within a few feet on my right." Reynolds called out to Sergeant Jim Haughey and another man in his section and told them to get ready to go through the wire. The intrepid Bangalore man, whose name is unfortunately lost to history, carefully inserted the fuse lighter into the torpedo, pulled the string to activate the fuse, pushed the Bangalore, and propelled himself backward under cover. A few seconds passed and nothing happened. The fuse had not lit. Undaunted, the man crawled over the shingle and replaced the bad fuse lighter with a new one. "He turned his head in my direction, looked back, pulled the string and made only one or two movements backward when he flinched, looked in my direction and closed his eyes looking into mine," Reynolds said. "Death was so fast for him. His eyes seemed to have a question or pleading look in them." The Bangalore exploded with a mighty *crump!* and tore a sizable gap in the wire. The dead man's head was only a few feet away from the explosion, but it wasn't damaged. Dirt flew in every direction. With hardly a pause, Sergeant Reynolds and his men rushed through the gap. Behind them, another group led by Private Frank Ciarpelli threw a smoke grenade to cover them and then followed in their footsteps.

A different Bangalore group, under the leadership of Tech Sergeant Richard Swanger, blew a separate hole in the wire, as did at least three, and possibly four, more from A Company. "Our one bangalore wouldn't go through," First Lieutenant William Dillon, who supervised this particular team, later wrote. "Soon some more men came up and we got two more torpedoes from them. We slid all 3 under the barbed wire and pulled the fuse and jumped behind a sand dune. It went off and made a hole big enough to drive a truck through." Captain Pence was gratified to see how well his men worked together under such trying conditions. "The thing that struck me was that strangely and amazingly, all . . . bangalores went off at exactly the same time—just one explosion. It had never been done so perfectly during training."

Under fire all the way, men began to run through the openings and plunge into the flooded antitank ditch. Many had to inflate their life preservers to keep afloat in the nose-high water. Wet and coughing, they emerged from the ditch and began to ascend the steep embankments, dunes, and rolling ground that led upward to the ridge overlooking Easy Red beach. This area, with its humble dirt pathways, was of course heavily mined, as both the Spalding and the Dawson groups had discovered an hour or so earlier. In many spots, the Germans had placed signs depicting a skull and crossbones and the warning *"Achtung! Minen!"* Some of the signs were decoys; some were not. Because Spalding and Dawson were leading relatively small and manageable numbers of men, and because they were not under the same kind of heavy fire as they ascended, the mines did not cause them much trouble. It was a far different story for the larger formations of 1st Battalion infantrymen. Their greater numbers almost guaranteed more difficulties, as did the fact that the Germans were better alerted to their presence than they had been to the earlier infiltrators.

In general, they had to watch out for two types of mines here—the S Mine or "Bouncing Betty," and the Schu mine. The S Mine was typically buried, with only its three prongs protruding from the ground. When a man tripped the prongs, the mine popped out of the dirt to a spot about waist high and exploded, spraying hundreds of steel balls in every direction, with a kill radius of twenty-five to thirty yards. The S2 officer of the 37th Engineer Combat Battalion called it "one of the most deadly and ingenious devices to be used in modern warfare." The Schu mine was a small box made almost entirely of wood and plastic. With a mere six pounds of pressure, the lid would pop open and the mine would detonate. The Schu was designed to wound, not kill. The explosion would most likely blow a man's foot off or maybe part of his leg. Some of the GIs referred to them as "toe poppers." Since the only metal part of the mine was its striker, American mine detectors were of no use in finding it.

For all the expansive training the infantry soldiers of the 1st Division had received back in England, few of them were well schooled in how to spot and disarm these mines. The planners assigned Lieutenant Colonel Lionel Smith's 37th Engineer Combat Battalion the task of clearing and marking a path through the minefields. Within minutes of landing, Smith was killed at the shingle bank by a mortar shell as he peered through a pair of binoculars. "Even though he had a steel helmet on," one of his men recalled, "I could see the blood gush from his head and just down he went . . . killed almost instantly." Fractured groups of engineers followed the infantrymen through the openings and began to deal with the mines. Sergeant Zolton Simon led one small team, with mine detectors in hand, through a gap and partway up the bluffs, under heavy German fire. "They worked slowly through the minefield," the battalion history chronicled, "clearing and marking the path while the enemy concentrated their efforts to stop them." The 50-millimeter mortar fire was especially accurate and worrisome. The fragmentation effect of each explosion was bad enough, but even worse, every shell might conceivably touch off a sympathetic detonation among the hidden mines. "They would drop one mortar and we'd know three would follow," Sergeant Frank Chesney, a member of the team, recalled, "so every time you heard that first one come in, we hit the ground." They would yell, "Hit it!" and then dive to the ground, hoping each time that they did not happen to land on a mine. Both Simon and Chesney were wounded by fragments. "He had a more severe wound than I had," Chesney said of Simon. "He had a bad leg wound and was hemorrhaging and there was a tourniquet on it." All but one of the men eventually got wounded, but they continued their mission. They managed to clear a small mine-free path about two feet in width, marked it with white engineer tape, and told any soldier they saw not to stray from the path. Private Thomas, after seeing several nearby soldiers wounded by a mine, saw the path and used it.

In the confusion and chaos of the action, though, most of the 1st Battalion soldiers did not enjoy the luxury of using Sergeant Simon's cleared pathway. They either scouted ahead on their own while enjoying the cover afforded by many dips and swales, or they were under such deadly plunging fire from the Germans in their elevated positions that they simply kept moving and took their chances on setting off a mine. Staff Sergeant Reynolds was leading one such force, approaching a small fence, when a man he did not know dashed ahead of him. "He got maybe fifteen feet when he tripped a mine hanging about waist high on a fence post. It blew him in half and splattered me. I was sick every time I thought of it for days." They kept going and a short time later, another soldier stepped on a Schu mine and blew off his heel. Nor were the attackers impervious to small-arms fire. Private First Class Foley was trailing behind Reynolds, dropping every fifty feet or so, hitting the ground and then taking off, but to no avail. He "got shot in the left leg between the thigh and knee." He lay there for several hours until medics found him.

Several hundred yards behind the Reynolds group—closer to the beach—Private First Class Knauss and his buddy Private First Class Walter Orlowski of C Company made it through a gap in the wire and kept running, with Orlowski in the lead. The latter made it to the demolished homes (called the "Roman ruins" by the Americans) where Spalding and Dawson had taken shelter earlier in the morning. Orlowski stopped and yelled something at Knauss, but the latter could not understand him. When Knauss finally made it alongside Orlowski, he asked him, "What did you say?"

"I was trying to tell you to watch out for the mines," Orlowski replied.

Knauss looked back and saw several S mines, each about a foot apart, in the very ground he had just traversed. Only by blind luck had he missed them. "I felt my heart in my throat," he later commented.

Closer to WN-64, where members of A Company had breached the wire and the antitank ditch, Lieutenant Dillon was moving up the draw with a group of soldiers from the company, dodging mines with practically every step. "I looked at the ground and could see both types of foot mines," he said, referring to S mines and Schu mines. In some cases, the location of the mines was obvious because the grass around them had dried out or burned out as a result of shells or tracer rounds (other mines had been degraded over time by the elements into duds). Most in this spot, though, were still quite potent. A pair of machine guns atop the ridgeline spewed bullets at the Americans, stitching the ground from both flanks. Private Albert Papi hit the ground and attempted to find some cover. Near-miss bullets buzzed angrily over his head. He soon heard the sickening thud of bullet impacts (almost like a baseball bat striking a watermelon). One of the bullets struck Tech Sergeant Ray Derry in the neck. Another hit Sergeant William Christiano in the back of one leg. Private Papi crawled over to help Christiano. In Papi's recollection, "the bullet went clean through, a little hole in the back and a big hole out the front. I tore open his trouser leg and poured some sulfa powder into the wound." In hopes of examining the large exit wound, Papi began to turn Sergeant Christiano over, but the wounded man yelled, "Stop, Pap, stop!" A few inches away, the prongs of a Bouncing Betty mine pointed menacingly out of the sandy soil. "If he had not stopped me," Papi commented, "I would have rolled him over right on top of [it]."

Private First Class LeRoy Herman could not see the machine guns that were pouring out so much fire, but he fitted his rifle with a grenade launcher and sent several grenades up the hill. Still the fire kept up unabated. At that point, Private First Class Manuel Otero told Herman to hold his fire while Otero crept forward to act as a spotter. "He crawled on ahead to the next knoll and laid his hands on a mine and it hit him right in the face," Herman remembered. "There was nothing I could do for him."

In the meantime, Lieutenant Dillon, Private First Class Harold Saylor, and several other men were still moving despite the heavy fire. "As the machine guns opened fire, we hit the ground," Saylor said. To his right, Staff Sergeant John "Pat" Forde jumped into a shell crater, right on top of a Schu mine. "It blew Ford's [*sic*] leg off," Dillon recalled, "threw him into the air and he came down on his shoulder on another one that tore up his arm and threw him onto a 3rd mine." A medic, Private First Class James Babcock, got to him, but there was little he could do except try to quell Forde's terrible pain. Babcock gave the sergeant three syrettes of morphine (the kind of dosage given only to the dying). Forde did not make it. Lieutenant Dillon and the other unscathed soldiers had to shake off their horror and keep going. For one thing, a runner reached him and told him that Captain Pence was wounded back on the beach and required evacuation—Dillon was now in command of A Company. For another, the company's orders were to keep moving inland. "I knew that the Germans had to have a path up the hill," Lieutenant Dillon said. As a boy, he had been a good rabbit hunter, so he had an eye for trails. He studied the ground ahead and, sure enough, "saw a faint path zig zagging to the left up the hill so I walked the path very carefully." Behind him a mine detonated, blowing off the lower leg of a soldier who had not followed exactly in the lieutenant's footsteps. Even so, the trail was largely clear. Dillon went back, organized his men, and led them up the small trail.[4]

Similar to Dillon, other groups of fortunate or intrepid soldiers, nearly always prompted by lieutenants or sergeants, were skirting the mines and engaging in close-quarters fighting with enemy defenders along the ridge. Like Dawson and Spalding, they had found the weaknesses, or dead spots, in the German defense of Easy Red. "I think that the Germans had located their weapons so as to cover every inch of the beach, but didn't have any weapons in depth that would get us as we came up the ridges," Captain Smith later commented. Staff Sergeant Al Nendza, a C Company NCO who had earned the Distinguished Service Cross for his valor in the invasion of North Africa, led a three-man team up the bluffs, along the western edges of WN-62. Back on the beach, just beyond the shingle, Nendza had blown a thirty-foot gap in the wire and then cut away several pesky strands of it. The two men with him, Privates Fred Erben and Buddy Mazzara, were unusual in one significant sense—they had managed to hang on to their heavy weapons in spite of the wet landing and heavy fire on the beach. Erben carried a twenty-pound TNT pole charge. Mazzara lugged an eighty-two-pound flamethrower. Led by Sergeant Nendza, they came upon the unfinished bunker at WN-64 containing the captured Soviet 76.2-millimeter gun. While Mazzara covered the opening with his flamethrower, Erben stuck his pole charge through it. This prompted the two soldiers inside to throw their hands in the air, emerge rapidly from the bunker, and shout, "No shoot! Me Pole!" The two Polish conscripts were named Wisniewski and Boleslaw. In a classic case of "it's a small world," Nendza actually knew Wisniewski because the latter had gone to school with Nendza's stepbrother.

At another spot to the west, Lieutenant Lawrence Beach led a ten-man force whose ranks included Sergeant John Ellery through the wire and upward along the high ground, where they ran into individual German defenders (probably in the valley just below the present-day American cemetery). "We didn't meet any *friends* up there when we arrived," Ellery deadpanned. Indeed they did not. At one point, a machine gun opened up to their right front. Everyone hit the dirt and found cover. "I scurried and scratched along until I got within ten meters of the gun position," Ellery recalled. "[T]hen I unloaded four of my fragmentation grenades, and when the last one went off, I made a dash for the top. Those other kids were right behind me, and we all made it." The gun crew was gone. Ellery did not know if he had hurt any of them or if they had just retreated. The Americans kept moving in a westerly direction in hopes of linking up with other men from B Company. As he led the squad-sized force past a hedgerow, he came face-to-face with an enemy soldier. The German pointed his rifle at Ellery but did not fire. "I was carrying a 'Beretta' pistol I had liberated from an Italian officer in Sicily. I dropped down and cut loose with the pistol, killing him." Ellery searched the dead man's body for loot and noticed that his rifle was not loaded. "I must have jumped him before he had a chance to reload."

The incident, though tragic, spoke volumes about the importance of good training, combat experience, and a willingness to kill face-to-face. Either the enemy soldier did not know that he should never leave cover with an unloaded weapon or he was too careless or he could not bring himself to shoot another person (an unloaded rifle was a perfect subconscious way to express that unwillingness). Ellery had seen a great deal of combat in the Mediterranean. Fighting for his life was nothing new to him. His training had prepared him to carry multiple loaded weapons, especially when on the move. In a crisis moment, he grabbed the most appropriate weapon for such a close encounter and, without a second's hesitation, gunned down a fellow human being from an intimate distance. He even had the presence of mind—or perhaps the callousness—to search the dead soldier's body for anything of value or interest.

At nearly the same time, farther to the west, Sergeant Reynolds was leading another impromptu squad of soldiers in a southwesterly direction along a path with fresh footprints. The young Virginian reasoned that if someone had recently trod along the path, then it must not be mined, and he was right. They skirted south, unconsciously bypassing WN-64. They came to a line of empty trenches overlooking the E-1 draw (also sometimes called the Ruquet Valley). These trenches were undoubtedly part of the defense network that led to WN-64. From this spot, Reynolds and the others could see across the draw to another series of trenches dug into the bluff above WN-65, as well as the reinforced concrete casemate or pillbox housing the potent 50-millimeter gun. Reynolds and the others spotted movement in the trenches across the draw. "Germans were carrying what appeared to be cases and satchels from a dug out type shelter on the edge of the cliff overlooking the big pillbox." The enemy soldiers were carrying this material away in trenches that led inland out of sight and then they were returning with other boxes that they placed in the dugout. The Americans set up a machine gun and opened up on the enemy soldiers. Reynolds added his own rifle fire. "I saw several . . . go down," Reynolds wrote. "It caught them by complete surprise, and the ones standing ran back into the shelter." A moment later, Reynolds saw an American soldier whom he recognized as "one of our own" stand up just beyond the trenches and hurl a grenade at the dugout shelter. Several other soldiers who were with him did the same. The enemy soldiers emerged from the shelter waving a white flag. As the Americans moved to take them prisoner, Sergeant Reynolds, who was watching from the vantage point of a spot overlooking the draw, noticed another group of Germans sneaking up on them. "I started firing at them and they jumped up, raised their hands and moved very fast towards the men cleaning up the trenches. These men didn't know the Germans were there."

A few hundred yards to the north, Lieutenant John Spalding's group was fighting to subdue the actual fortifications of WN-64. Amazingly, the men in these two American units seemed to have no idea of the near presence of the other unit. Their ignorance says much about the myopic nature of modern infantry combat. As had been the case for much of the morning, two of Spalding's bravest soldiers, Tech Sergeant Philip Streczyk and Private First Class Richard Gallagher, were in the lead. Behind them everyone was spread out over a distance of nearly five hundred yards, which made it hard to coordinate their movements (Lieutenant Spalding and many other leaders in command of small units that day found it exceedingly difficult to keep them together amid the terrain and the opposition). They swept through a network of well-camouflaged trenches that protected the eastern approaches to WN-64. Streczyk spotted a three-man machine-gun team. He shot the gunner. The two other soldiers surrendered. The Americans tried to interrogate them, but they would not talk. "We continued to the west with them in tow," Spalding said. They warily crossed an orchard and several hedgerows. They navigated two mine-fields. Sergeant Fred Bisco told everyone to avoid patches of dead grass, since that usually indicated the presence of mines. Fortified with this knowledge and the use of a well-worn trail, they kept going until they saw the trenches and fixtures of WN-64 in the distance. They were taking some inaccurate small-arms fire now, so Spalding and Streczyk spread their people into a defensive semicircle while Sergeant Kenneth Peterson fired a bazooka rocket into a construction shack. Nothing happened. The lieutenant and the sergeant scouted ahead. "We found an underground dugout and an 81mm mortar emplacement, a position for an antitank gun, and construction for a pillbox," Spalding said. The mortar position was unoccupied, but it was equipped with accurate, vivid range cards seemingly depicting every inch of Omaha beach. Streczyk fired a few shots into the dugout, then yelled in Polish and German for the occupants to come out. This rousted seven enemy soldiers, three of whom were wounded.

No sooner had the Americans consolidated their custody of these new captives than they started taking small-arms fire from their right flank. This began a running firefight with another group of enemy soldiers who were occupying communications trenches that led over the bluff and down to the beach, and others who were in the Ruquet Valley, between WN-64 and WN-65. Most likely, they had been flushed out of their positions at WN-64 by the approach of the Spalding force. "The trenches had teller mines, hundreds of grenades, and numerous machine guns," Spalding recalled. The two sides hurled grenades back and forth. In one instance, a German soldier threw three grenades at the Americans before they overran him and forced him to surrender.

"We should have shot him but we didn't," Spalding later wrote to his mother. "He was a young Nazi, the type which is crazy about Hitler."

The lieutenant had lost his carbine during the landing. He had subsequently picked up a discarded German Mauser 98K rifle, only to trade it later for another carbine. He never checked to see if the safety lever was off and this could have cost him his life. At one point during the firefight in the communication trenches, he encountered an armed German. Spalding tried to open fire, but since the safety was deployed, the carbine would not shoot. "I reached for the safety catch and hit the clip release instead, so my clip hit the ground." Fortunately for him, Sergeant Peterson had the German covered and he surrendered. Elsewhere, Private DiGaetano was hauling the same flamethrower that he had earlier used to keep from drowning. Covered by Sergeant Streczyk, he pointed the nozzle of the flamethrower at a dugout aperture and unleashed a stream of fire. "[Germans] were hiding in the back or something. If you get them, they know about it. Had to be like napalm. In thirty seconds, or a minute, all gone. The tank was empty." Several smoldering enemy soldiers popped out and surrendered. Streczyk clapped the flamethrower man on the back and exclaimed, "Good going, Dig!"

By the time the small battle was over, the Americans had captured the only antitank gun at WN-64 in addition to the mortar emplacements, several concrete dugouts, and an unfinished casemate that would have housed the gun if the Germans had enjoyed more time to complete construction of the strong point. To a great extent, this neutralized the weakest spot in the German defense of Omaha beach and slackened the amount of fire directed at Easy Red. None of Spalding's men were hurt. Maybe two or three Germans had lost their lives. At least seventeen others were prisoners. Many of them were actually ethnic Poles who volunteered or were pressed into German Army service. Sergeant Streczyk, a Polish American, had no sympathy for these kinsmen in enemy garb. "He was kicking them in the ass and talking to them in Polack and he wanted to know why they fought so hard," Private First Class Bruce Buck later recalled with a chuckle. "He was really raising hell with them." Spalding had nothing but contempt for all these prisoners, whether German or Polish. He derisively referred to them all as "Hermans." In his recollection, "some of the prisoners we took were scared as hell, others extremely arrogant." The arrogant prisoners were the ethnic Germans from the 352nd, and the frightened ones were of course the Poles from the 716th or the ethnically mixed units of the 352nd. Spalding seemed to recognize no such distinction. They were all "Hermans" to him.

A steady wind blew in from the sea. As was so typical of the Norman climate, the breeze was moist, heavy with the droplets of a small rain squall. The drizzle splotched their already damp uniforms with new circles of cold water. One of the men smiled and yelled to his comrades, "Everything is okay now. G2 [intelligence] is on the ball again. They said the weather would be fair. . . ." Everybody laughed. The tension of the previous two hours had evaporated. If only they could have said the same about the rain.[5]

1

As always in combat, the most dangerous fire was coming from the flank. The strong points at WN-60 and WN-61, located as they were on the curvature and the cliffs at the eastern edge of Omaha beach, were situated perfectly to rake the open shoreline below with accurate, withering fire. As long as the two strong points remained in operation, the Germans were in a position to slaughter anyone who attempted to land at Fox Green and most of Easy Red. The destruction at 0710 of the 88-millimeter gun at WN-61 by Sergeant George Geddes's tank was a positive development in solving this problem, but only a first step. No one understood this better than the able-bodied survivors of F Company who were strung out at various spots along Fox Green, try-

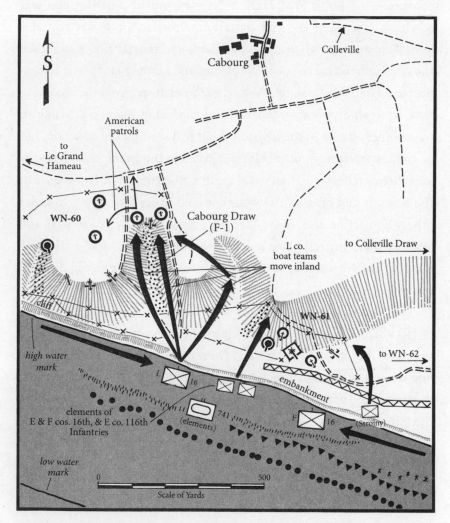

After their tardy landings, troops from the 3rd Battalion, 16th Infantry spent much of the morning pinned down under the cliffs beneath WN-60, until the incoming tides threatened to engulf them. Led by several boat sections from L Company, and supported by at least two Sherman tanks, they laboriously fought their way up the Cabourg draw, through a strongly defended belt of mines and barbed wire. At the same time, other survivors, most notably Staff Sergeant Strojny, destroyed the German defenses at WN-61.

ing to avoid the worst of the kill zones. "The beach was in a state of confusion," Captain Fred Hall, a New Hampshire native who was serving as the S3 of the 2nd Battalion, wrote in a postwar memoir. "We were under small arms and artillery and mortar fire. I could see the tide had reached the beach obstacles and landing craft were letting people off into deeper water. As the beach narrowed from the incoming tide, it became very crowded and the confusion increased." Like so many other officers in the division, Hall had seen plenty of action, but he could scarcely remember being subjected to this much noise—small-arms fire, machine-gun fire, naval gunfire, the engines of landing craft, the screams and cries of the wounded and of leaders trying to order others into action and, of course, the many explosions of mortar and artillery shells (inland batteries were reaping a grisly harvest all along the beach). "No wonder some people couldn't handle it," Hall commented.

The best way to handle it was to focus on accomplishing some sort of task. Sergeant David Radford crawled to a double strand of concertina wire that barred the invaders from exiting the beach. He shoved one section of a Bangalore torpedo under the wire but soon realized that he needed at least one more to destroy the wire. "He returned from the wire to the beach, ran to a wounded man to secure another bangalore, returned to his exposed position at the wire, fastened the torpedoes, and successfully blew a path through the wire," surviving members of the company revealed in a post-D-Day interview. Tech Sergeant Edward Zukowski and Staff Sergeant Andrew Nesevitch had lost eighteen of the thirty-two men in their boat section, including their commander, Lieutenant Aaron Dennstedt, within moments of landing. They rounded up anyone they could find and moved toward the opening in the wire. On the way, Nesevitch encountered Captain Edward Wozenski, the no-nonsense commander of E Company, who was trying to piece together whatever remained of his decimated unit and then figure out what to do next. The captain shook his head and told the young sergeant, "This is one big screw up!" Nesevitch naturally concurred with the colorful officer. "He was that way. He didn't pull any punches," Nesevitch summarized with admiration.

A bit farther down the beach, Nesevitch saw Private First Class Sanford "Sandy" Rosen, a man from the I&R platoon whom he had known for some time. Rosen's left arm was blown off. Someone had tied a tourniquet around the stump. Almost proudly, Rosen held his stump up for Nesevitch to see. "Look what I got," he cried excitedly. "[L]ook what I got!"

"You poor bastard, you're better off dead," Sergeant Nesevitch replied.

Staff Sergeant Henry Krzyzanowski also saw the new amputee and was shocked enough to ask, "Where's your arm, Sandy?" Rosen only waved the stump in reply. Krzyzanowski wrapped the stump in a raincoat, gave Rosen a shot of morphine, and left. Soon after, Sergeant Ted Aufort spotted Rosen and bent over to see how he was doing. "The sad part of it was that he was a trumpet player in the regimental band," Aufort said. The young sergeant took out a pack of cigarettes, lit one, stuck it in Rosen's mouth, and carefully placed the package in the wounded man's shirt pocket. "See ya later, Sandy."

"Thanks, Ted," Rosen replied.

Moments later, an improvised squad under Tech Sergeant Zukowski and Staff Sergeant Nesevitch crawled through the gap in the wire and into a grassy field. Private First Class Homer Richard, a French Canadian with American citizenship who had been drafted into the U.S. Army while on a brief visit to the States, covered them with a BAR. With Zukowski leading the way, they worked their way deeper into the field, seemingly out of the line of German fire for the moment. Zukowski's younger brother, Joseph, a mortarman in the same company, was lying dead on the beach, but Edward did not know that yet.

Crossing the field, the elder Zukowski tripped an anti-personnel mine that wounded him, breaking his left leg and one of his arms. "It threw him up in the air about six to eight feet," Nesevitch said. Zukowski lay stunned and bleeding. Everyone else hit the dirt. Nesevitch and Private First Class James Hamby crawled to their platoon sergeant. Nesevitch took one look at Zukowski and said to Hamby, "He's done for." But Zukowski moaned loudly and they realized he was alive. Nesevitch pulled fragments from Zukowski's wounded hands and gave him a shot of morphine in his right leg, but there was little else he could do. He left Zukowski for the medics (they did not find him until that night, though they did save his life). Nesevitch turned to the other soldiers and said, "Men, we gotta push our way through here. We're either gonna die fighting or we're gonna die here." With Nesevitch now in the lead, they went right, skirted the mines, and kept going until they climbed a steep hill and came under accurate sniper fire that killed Private Richard, the French Canadian BAR man.

Back on Fox Green, another NCO, Staff Sergeant Raymond Strojny, was painfully aware of the same kill-or-be-killed reality that had prompted Nesevitch to keep moving through and beyond the minefield. Even with the 88-millimeter gun out of commission, Sergeant Major Schnuell and the twelve German defenders of WN-61 were creasing the beach with machine-gun bullets and particularly devastating fire from the 50-millimeter cannon (in addition to the heavy volume of accurate artillery fire coming from inland batteries). The fortifications of WN-61 were perched on a knoll only about forty yards away from the high-water mark. The close proximity to Fox Green made the fire of the enemy defenders especially lethal and accurate. However, this was also a disadvantage—WN-61's closeness meant that the Americans could spot it and destroy it more readily than other unseen strong points on the bluffs.

The twenty-five-year-old Strojny was a Taunton, Massachusetts, native who had once worked for Reed and Barton, a manufacturer of fine crystal and flatware. He had fought with his outfit since North Africa. His boat section leader, Lieutenant Otto Clemens, had been killed within a few minutes of landing. Strojny had then gathered up what men he could and dodged the heavy fire. He watched in abject frustration and anger as the 50-millimeter gun destroyed three Sherman tanks along the beach. He raised his rifle and fired several ineffective shots at the gun crew. To have any chance against the 50-millimeter gun, he needed a heavier weapon. He looked around and called for a bazooka crew, but apparently the team from his section was either dead or wounded. "So I went in searching for a bazooka on the beach, knowing that that gun had to be knocked out to make our sector a success," he later wrote. After searching for several minutes, he found an unfamiliar sergeant (probably from the mislanded E Company, 116th Infantry Regiment) who was carrying a bazooka. Strojny instructed the sergeant to fire his bazooka at the 50-millimeter, but the man said he could not see it. Sergeant Strojny pointed it out to him. The other soldier, who did not seem especially eager to comply with Strojny's wishes, told him that he could not shoot because he had no one to load his bazooka. Strojny quickly loaded a rocket into the tube. The man fired and missed badly. Strojny crawled over to him, loaded another rocket, and crawled to a spot about five yards away. The man fired and missed again.

Most likely, these two shots attracted the attention of an enemy mortar crew. A round zipped in and exploded in the five-yard gap between them. The sergeant from the 116th was badly wounded. Strojny was fine. He knew it was time to move. He grabbed the bazooka and took off in search of a better firing spot. The 50-millimeter gun continued spitting out shells at targets on the beach. The monotonous rapidity with which the gun spewed death and destruction infuriated the young sergeant. He glanced at the bazooka and noticed that it had been damaged by the mortar fragments. "But I had to try it," he said. "Maybe it was not damaged enough, I had to take the chance." It was not uncommon for a defective bazooka to explode in the face of a shooter. He loaded a rocket into the tube, no small feat since it required the loader to connect an arming wire to the rear of the bazooka while making sure the rocket did not slide down the tube and out the front, perhaps arming itself in the process. The job of loading and firing was designed for two people, but he was determined to do it himself. He managed to fire a pair of shots, but they had no effect. Bazooka gunners were trained to glance backward before firing and make sure no one was in the line of the weapon's back blast. In the excitement of the moment, Strojny forgot to do that. "When he fired the bazooka, he was not too careful about seeing who was behind him," Tech 5 James Thomson, a radioman in the company who witnessed Strojny's exploits, later said. "The back blast burned one of the wounded men who was lying there on the beach." Fortunately the wound was not serious, "but at least it caught him and he knew something had happened."

Strojny continued his search for the best vantage point from which to attack the 50-millimeter gun. All alone, he dashed beyond the shingle (probably along the same route where Nesevitch and company had exited the beach), and into the grassy minefield where Sergeant Zukowski lay so badly wounded. Somehow Strojny crossed the minefield without touching off any explosions until he found a spot with a good field of fire. He fired several times and scored at least two hits in the vicinity of the 50-millimeter, but still it kept firing. "I ran out of ammunition, then went back to [the] beach, found more ammunition, came back to [the] bazooka, took up firing again." According to a post-action interview, he fired six rounds, each one of which hit the gun or its vicinity. The final rocket detonated a nearby ammunition dump. Flames roared in and around the gun pedestal. The explosion and the fire finally put the gun out of commission and probably killed at least two of Sergeant Major Schnuell's defenders. "A number of dead were observed," the interview claimed, "and only one German was seen to escape." Sergeant Strojny grabbed his M1 Garand and fired at the fleeing soldier. At the same time, an enemy rifleman spotted him and fired. A bullet tore through his helmet just above his left eye. Instead of penetrating his skull, it deflected to the left, circled his head, and exited his helmet near his left ear, leaving the fortunate Strojny with only a superficial flesh wound.

If he was chastened by this close call, it did not show. He tossed the empty bazooka aside, rounded up a mixed group of soldiers from his boat section and the 116th Infantry, and began to lead them through the minefield to attack the remaining machine-gun positions of WN-61. Several times he had to urge men forward, particularly those from the 116th who did not know him. His experience and competence were self-evident, though. The 116th Infantry soldiers, experiencing their first taste of combat, were happy to benefit from this savvy and follow the example of 1st Division men like Strojny. Thus they were eventually inclined to do what Strojny said. Indeed, several survivors from the 116th later told an Army historian that they were "glad to follow soldiers who had combat experience and who seemed to know what they were doing."

One of Strojny's men, Private Charles Rocheford, detonated a mine that blew his hand off. The records of F Company claim that Strojny's group silenced at least two machine-gun posts and killed seven enemy soldiers. One soldier from the 116th was killed, another wounded. The destruction of the 50-millimeter gun and several other emplacements (not just by Strojny but by other F Company soldiers as well) within WN-61 relieved some of the intense pressure the Germans were applying against Fox Green beach. Strojny's elimination of the 50-millimeter gun, in particular, was a crucial accomplishment that saved many American lives. It was the first major step in the vital mission of securing the eastern flank of Omaha beach. Sergeant Strojny inherently understood this. Like any good NCO, he possessed a keenly practical sense of how to get a job done. But his actions also stemmed from a powerful need to set an example for others. "All my superiors were dead or wounded," he later wrote, "some[one] had to take over. I had lots of combat experience. All relied on me." For his actions and his leadership, he received the Distinguished Service Cross.[6]

1

At the jagged edges of the rocky cliff where Fox Red beach gave way to Fox Green, soldiers from L Company huddled for cover. The lee of the cliff presented a scene of horror, anguish, and confusion. The heaped, soaked bodies of dead soldiers floated and bobbed with the rapidly incoming tide. Moment by moment, the onrushing water began to lap at the boots and the butts of the dead, the wounded, and the able-bodied alike. Medics walked the narrow stretch of rocky beach, tending to wounded and crying soldiers. Enemy mortar shells exploded among and above the rocks of the beach, steadily adding to the casualty numbers. The cliff offered only dubious protection from the firepower of WN-60, much the same way a mini-umbrella provides only limited defense against a storm. For the men huddling under cover of the cliff, there was only one way forward, and it was daunting indeed. The cliff petered out and gave way to a raised embankment about six feet high. The embankment led inland up an open draw known to the invasion planners as Exit F-1. Historian Joseph Balkoski aptly described the draw as "a natural amphitheater, through which a rough track ascended to the inland plateau." The exit was sealed off with coils of barbed wire and honeycombed with mines. The German defenders of WN-60 were situated at the top of a steep hill (the zenith of the plateau) and thus enjoyed wonderful lines of sight. In fact, from this strong point they could see along the entire expanse of Omaha beach. Their view of the draw beneath them was of course even better. Any American soldier who attempted to ascend the draw had little chance of escaping their notice, though there were many dips, culverts, and swales to offer some semblance of cover or concealment.

The draw, then, was hardly the perfect place for an inland assault, but it offered the only possible route off the beach for the embattled men of L Company and the rest of the 3rd Battalion, 16th Infantry. The bottom line was that it had to be taken, regardless of the cost, or else the battalion would be inundated by high-tide waters and probably annihilated or marginalized underneath its cliffside fig leaf. The officers and NCOs who had survived the slaughter of the initial landing at Fox Green shortly after H-Hour understood this all too well. They circulated along the cliff, rounding up men for an assault up the draw. At times, it was difficult for them to distinguish the wounded from those who were still unscathed. Private Steve Kellman was sitting with his back to the cliff, attending to a leg wound he had suffered, when a mortar shell blew up about ten yards away, knocking Kellman out. When he came to, he thought a concussion was the extent of the damage inflicted on him by the shell, but he discovered blood soaking through his leggings and realized he could not walk on the damaged leg. As he sat bandaging his wound, First Lieutenant Robert Cutler, who had assumed command of L Company after the wounding of its commander, Captain John Armellino, came along and said, "Come on, we're moving out."

"I can't," Kellman replied.

Lieutenant Cutler stared at the young private. "Kellman, I didn't think I was going to have any trouble with you."

"I can't walk, sir," Kellman said.

"What's the matter?"

Kellman showed him the gaping wound between the ankle and knee on his leg. Cutler promised to send a medic and told him to stay put. The young officer organized his attacking elements by boat sections. The second and third sections would head up the draw first, followed by the fifth section, all more or less in squad columns, roughly analogous to a diamond formation. As they did so, they would provide cover fire for one another, employing the fire-and-maneuver (or bound-

and-overwatch) tactics that were second nature to such an experienced, well-trained unit. A pair of .30-caliber machine guns under the command of Sergeant Glenn Monroe and two Shermans from the 741st Tank Battalion (presumably deep-wading tanks from A Company) provided the only covering fire. The two tanks were perched on the beach, no doubt experiencing the mobility problems that plagued all American armor at Omaha on D-Day.

The volume of fire support for the attack was frighteningly low considering the difficulty of the task at hand. Even worse, the infantrymen had no way of communicating with the tankers. Because of the heavy machine-gun and shell fire sweeping the beach, the Sherman crewmen had buttoned up their hatches, essentially making themselves blind and deaf. Someone from L Company had to let them know what was in the offing and direct their supporting fire. Captain Armellino had actually been wounded while attempting to accomplish this very mission.

First Lieutenant Jimmie Monteith, the leader of the second section, now inherited the dangerous job. The twenty-six-year-old lieutenant embodied the white-collar, educated, middle-class professionals who had risen to prominence in the rapidly modernizing United States of the twentieth century. His father was vice president of the Cabell Coal Company in Virginia. Jimmie was the youngest of three children, every bit the baby of the close-knit family—fun-loving, full of mirth, lovable, and irrepressible. A high school buddy once fondly referred to him as "an unshakeable Rat with a great sense of humor." Another friend said, "I never knew anybody who didn't like Jimmie." Yet another friend once quipped that he "could have sold iceboxes to the Eskimos."

Six feet two, with a full mane of red hair and a wide, friendly face, young Jimmie had played basketball and football in high school. Like his grandfather, father, and older brother, he attended Virginia Polytechnic Institute (now known as Virginia Tech). But he was an undisciplined, indifferent student, bereft of direction and focus. He left school after only two years and went back home to Richmond to work as a field representative for his dad's company. In October 1941, the peacetime draft snared him, and in the harsh world of the Army, he found purpose and maturity, earning a commission as an infantry officer in 1942. "I know you all look upon me as the baby," he wrote in a letter to his mother. "I know my educational failure has always been a big disappointment to [Father] and is one of the things I would change if I had to do it over. But taking all this into consideration, my . . . informal education has been good. I have seen a lot of this thing they call life."

Monteith's parents were major worriers. He once wrote to his mother that "the thought of you worrying frightens me more than the [enemy] ever could." Nonetheless, his dad was consumed with concern over Jimmie and his older brother, Robert, who was serving as a naval officer. The constant worry was probably a factor in Jimmie Senior's death in August 1942. Young Jimmie later joined the 1st Infantry Division in time for the Sicily campaign and quickly earned a reputation as a courageous officer whose pride in the unit was immense. "Every time I look at the shoulder insignia . . . I get a thrill," he wrote. "There is no better fighting unit in the world." His natural friendliness and decency, combined with a reputation for bravery, made him one of the most popular officers in the 16th Infantry, if not the entire division. "He was a man that I had the utmost admiration and respect for," his thirty-one-year-old regular Army platoon sergeant, John Worozbyt, said of him. Decades after the war, Captain Albert Smith—a retired general by then—commented that Monteith's personality was "a lot like Tom Selleck, only Jimmie was red headed. He also had the loyalty of every soldier in L Company."

That loyalty stemmed from the belief on the part of Monteith's men that he cared for them and would know what to do during times of crisis, when lives were on the line. Lieutenant Monteith, like any good junior officer, instinctively understood that if the second section was to make it off this hellish beach, then he himself must lead the way and set an example. He left the cover of the cliff and ran to the tanks. "I saw Lt. Monteith go to the same place where [Captain Armellino] was struck down," Sergeant Hugh Martin, one of his men, later said. "He went right through the thick of the fire to the tanks and got them into action." By banging on the sides of the tanks and yelling to the men inside, he pointed out where he wanted them to lay down fire. With this accomplished, he ran back to his men at the bluff, all the while under fire. Sergeant Monroe's .30-calibers chattered in support. Together, Monteith's section scaled the embankment and pressed forward to the barbed wire. "After selecting a place where it could be blown up," Private First Class Aaron Jones said, "he led men with a Bangalore torpedo in blasting the wire open." Actually the wire was breached by one of Monteith's bravest soldiers, Staff Sergeant James Wells, with the able assistance of Staff Sergeants Frederick Frock, John Griffin, and Norman Holmberg. The NCOs led the way, along with Lieutenant Monteith, through the gap and up the mined draw without touching off explosions. As they carefully advanced, they were basically looking straight upward at the western side of WN-60. "The field was traversed by machine gun fire from . . . two enemy emplacements and from a pillbox," Jones recounted. The "pillbox" might have been a bunker or perhaps one of the mortar Tobruks. Staff Sergeant Wells laid down accurate covering fire with his rifle while everyone else poured through the gap, advanced, and took cover. A full-blown firefight soon raged.

If there was one thing Lieutenant Monteith had learned from his first days in officer candidate school and throughout combat in Sicily, it was that an officer must not only *lead* in combat but *think*. He undoubtedly understood that no weapon was more formidable than a clever and thoughtful human brain. "When the men took cover, he stood studying the situation," Jones recalled. Monteith decided to go back to the beach, braving heavy enemy fire, to retrieve the tanks. He retraced his steps, back through the mined draw, over the embankment, back to chaotic Fox Green. "Completely exposed to the violent fire directed at the tank, Lieutenant Monteith led them on foot through a minefield into firing position," a post-battle citation explained. The danger in this act was considerable. Not only did he present a perfect target walking ahead of the tanks, but he had to keep a careful watch for mines, while also navigating a usable path for the Shermans. The latter was no mean feat because the two tanks were probably the first ones to exit the 1st Division side of the beach on D-Day. Monteith found them a good spot. They unleashed 75-millimeter main gun rounds and machine-gun fire on the enemy machine-gun nests and the pillbox. This put them out of action and reduced the amount of flanking fire that was raking the beach.

As Monteith and his men worked their way up the draw, other sections from L Company were doing the same thing and with similar valor. On the right flank of Monteith's force, Sergeant Frank Cama blew lanes through the wire for the third section. Led by Lieutenant John Williams and Staff Sergeant Bernard Rulong, the third section soldiers sidestepped mines and ascended the bluffs under sniper and machine-gun fire. "Having reached the first high ground," the company history recorded, "Lt. Williams had his section take up a hasty defensive position and made contact by runner with the 2nd section on the left." The two sections coordinated their efforts and slowly continued their advance, supported much of the way by the fifth section and Cutler's company headquarters. In many instances, they could see the Germans moving around atop the hill; BAR men unleashed a steady stream of bullets at them.

As the Americans scaled the draw, sharp and intimate firefights proliferated. The rough terrain and the nature of the German defenses made this diffusion a near certainty. Lieutenant Kenneth Klenk's first section had taken a beating in the water and on the beach, leaving him with only a dozen men by the time the attack began. His remnants were reinforced with mislanded 116th Infantry soldiers. A scout patrol led by

Private First Class Joseph Likevich took the lead and navigated through the mines. "The ground of this incline was furrowed with numerous small circular ditches so that it was almost terrace like," the section's survivors told an Army historian in a post-combat interview. They moved up unscathed, but soon became involved in a close-quarters grenade duel with German soldiers in the barbed wire–protected trench network that snaked around the draw. "Because of the steepness of the hill, most of the grenades the Germans were throwing would roll down the hill past me before exploding," Private James Jordan recalled. Led by Staff Sergeant Paul Mansfield, a squad leader, the Americans responded in kind. "They were throwing grenades at the Germans," Staff Sergeant Mike McKinney, the platoon sergeant, remembered. In a few instances, soldiers grabbed enemy grenades and threw them back. At one point, a German grenade rolled to within ten feet of Private Jordan. "The explosion blew me completely off the ground. I was thrown about five feet in the air and landed hard on my back." He caught some shrapnel in the left leg, but he was too stunned to realize that. The deadly game of catch went on for several minutes until Lieutenant Klenk ordered the section to fix bayonets and overrun the enemy-held trench. "That was a morning when some of us knew in our hearts why they were fighting, and knew we had to go inland off the beach, no matter what it cost," McKinney later wrote in a letter to his mother. They pushed up the hill. The trench led to a grove of trees a couple hundred yards inland. The Germans apparently wanted no part of a hand-to-hand fight with Klenk's men. They fled through the trench all the way to the grove of trees. With fire support from a machine gun, and possibly the destroyer USS *Doyle*, Mansfield's squad went forward into the trees and captured some fifteen prisoners.[7]

The L Company sections accomplished something of substantial significance: they breached the barbed wire and the minefields of the F-1 draw and made it to the top of the bluffs. They were now in a position to take WN-60 as well as the dizzying array of trenches and fighting positions the Germans had dug between the strong point and the village of Cabourg. At the same time, the remainder of the 3rd Battalion, most notably boats from I and M Companies, approached Fox Red and Fox Green beaches. Since the aborted landing at Port-en-Bessin, Captain Kimball Richmond's I Company had spent more than an hour and a half backtracking to Fox Red. On the way, the fourth and fifth section LCAs swamped, leaving Richmond with only four boats, including his own. Most of the stranded soldiers from the two sunken LCAs were picked up by patrol boats.

In spite of L Company's success in advancing up the F-1 draw, the approaches to Fox Red and Fox Green remained under intense fire from WN-60 and inland artillery pieces. Moreover, the rising tide made the uncleared obstacles significantly more dangerous than at low tide for the obvious reason that coxswains could not see them. Captain Richmond's LCA struck a mined obstacle and exploded. Corporal Albert Mominee, one of the captain's runners, remembered seeing "a blinding flash of fire" sweep through the boat. "Flames raced around and over us. It happened so quickly. The first reaction or thought one gets in a situation like that is survival." He managed to hop over the side of the boat and into the deep water, roughly four hundred yards from the waterline. He inflated his life preserver and swam in laboriously, all the while under machine-gun fire. Staff Sergeant Salvatore Albanese was so shocked by the explosion that he had no idea how he ended up in the water. "I was [too] stunned momentarily to realize what happened and didn't know I was burnt until I had swam [sic] ashore and got up against the cliffs." Only then did the pain of facial burns begin to register.

Nearby, the boat carrying the first section also struck a mine and blew up. The third section LCA got hit and sunk by fire from WN-60, quite possibly from the 76-millimeter antitank gun. The second section boat got hung up on a pair of stakes, though it did not trip any mines. After being dumped so unceremoniously into the water, several men drowned. Private First Class Geatino Bracciale had no idea how to swim (surely this represented a training deficiency in the division's otherwise thorough preparation). Wounded and panicked, he succumbed to the waves. Private First Class Eake DeMarco's life preserver did him no good. He went to the bottom and never surfaced. Almost every survivor had to swim to the beach, including Captain Richmond. The same was true for many of the M Company soldiers. Private Joe Argenzio had lied about his age to get into the Army. He was still two days shy of his seventeenth birthday, and had the baby face to prove it. Back in England, only a few days earlier, he had joined M Company as a bewildered replacement shortly after the outfit boarded the *Empire Anvil*. The company's hardened veterans had taken one look at him and razzed, "Hey, kid, the Boy Scouts are down the street. Are you lost?"

As he hit the water, he began to grow up fast. Half drowned, he flailed his way to the stony beach. "There were dead bodies all around so I laid down and grabbed two of them which were right in front of me and I pushed them in and they were taking the fire that was meant for me," he said. "They were mutilated but they saved my life. Finally I made it to a point where I figured I could run and I did. I zigzagged, slipping on the wet stones and tripping and falling. There were guys getting hit all around me and going down and screaming and yelling for medics." He made it to the cliff.

Huddling against that same cliff, Sergeant Albanese watched in abject horror as his buddy Sergeant Robert Johnson fought to stay alive. "His side was ripped open, and some of his organs were sticking out," Albanese wrote. "He smiled when I talked to him, but he never survived." Sergeant Jack Polnoroff, a machine-gun squad leader, was frustrated that he could not move faster through the rushing water. "Boy, it was exciting to walk through the water," he later said. "Your feet were working fast but you were just barely moving and the machine gun and mortar fire was hitting all around." He staggered to the cliff, caught his breath, and immediately whipped out several miniature liquor bottles he was carrying in his pack. "There were two wounded lying there and

I gave them each one and my buddy got one and there was one for me. It tasted good, but you really didn't need it. The adrenaline was pumping through you so fast." The heavy fire claimed the life of Captain Alan Morehouse, the battalion adjutant and personnel officer. A bullet slammed into his leg. He stumbled in to the beach, but then got hit in the head and died. Morehouse had served with the unit since North Africa. "He indicated he never expected to make this trip as he had hoped for a white boat home," Lieutenant Karl Wolf, a newly minted West Point–trained officer who served with him in Headquarters Company, later wrote. Sadly, and presciently, Morehouse had earlier that week written a letter to his wife in which he confided a deep foreboding of impending death. "He said he felt like his luck had run out," his son, Randy, said many decades later.

Corporal Michael Kurtz, a Pennsylvania coal miner turned squad leader, was making his third invasion. On the way in to the beach, Private James Steinberger, a nervous replacement from Wisconsin, looked at Kurtz and said, "Corporal, I'm going to get killed and not even see a German."

"Look where in hell I've been," Kurtz replied confidently. "I've pulled two invasions and they haven't even nicked me."

"Do you think we have a chance?" Steinberger asked almost incredulously.

"Hell, yes, don't never worry about getting killed," Kurtz reassured him.

But when they swam their way to the beach and began running to the cliff, a full burst of machine-gun fire stitched through Steinberger. "He lived about 10 minutes," Kurtz later wrote sadly.

Kurtz and Private First Class Donald Burton, a radioman, sat next to each other along the cliff face. Only five feet away, in the direction of the waterline, Lieutenant Alexander Zbylut, a platoon leader from K Company, lay badly wounded, under withering machine-gun fire. "This Heinie was really chopping him," Kurtz said. "[We] couldn't get to him til this bastard quit choppin'." At Kurtz's prompting, they waited until the enemy machine gunner changed ammo belts. At the right moment, they lunged away from the cliff, grabbed Zbylut, and pulled him to safety. The lieutenant was in bad shape. One of his legs had nearly been shot off, but he did survive, thanks in no small part to Kurtz and Burton.

Soon leaders began to round up groups of men for a new push up the draw to reinforce L Company and consolidate the American toehold atop the bluffs. The most important of these leaders was Captain Kimball Richmond, a man whose charisma and dedication to soldiers was second to none, even in a division blessed with so many talented combat commanders. Small in physical size but combat-tough, with curly black hair and a round face given in equal parts to pensiveness and intensity ("swarthy, svelte good looks" in the estimation of one fellow officer), Richmond was a former Vermont National Guardsman who had earned his commission through Officer Candidate School. His Vermont youth had been a tough one—his father died when he was four years old, thus forcing his Victorian mother to set aside her life as a housewife and support the family by working long hours as a cleaning lady in the local post office. Richmond had been in command of I Company since North Africa and had earned a near legendary reputation in the division. Sergeant Ben Franklin, a machine gunner, once referred to him as "probably the greatest soldier in the American Army, absolutely fearless." One of his commanding officers thought him "probably the best soldier in the battalion." In Lieutenant John Carroll's recollection, Richmond was "'all army' and this title was exhibited time and time again. He long since had reached a position so elevated he was the 'second battalion commander' particularly in all activities carrying heavy responsibilities and dangers." Battalion commanders routinely asked him to look in on their plans and movements just to make sure everything unfolded properly. Sergeant Robert Michaud believed he was "cut from the same cloth as men of George S. Patton's caliber." Along those lines, Richmond liked to challenge each man in his outfit to a special bayonet drill. He promised a London pass to anyone who succeeded in stabbing him with a bayonet. No one ever did. "They always would be flipped over his shoulder onto their backs," Michaud said. Like many outstanding combat officers, Richmond was drawn, like some sort of inexorable magnet, to wherever the action was heaviest. He made a habit of leading from the front. "Kim had extraordinary courage and rare good luck," Albert Smith once said, "a combination that made him a great combat soldier." His soldiers trusted him implicitly. Even more important, they would follow him anywhere.

Captain Richmond understood that organization led to action. Given the chaotic circumstances of the 3rd Battalion's landing, and the perilous situation on the beach, it no longer mattered which company a man came from or where he had landed (Richmond himself could lay hands on no more than about a dozen of his own men). All that mattered was what to do next. From prior experience, Richmond knew that even brave men tended to freeze into inaction amid the bewilderment and horror of close combat. However, they would follow someone who seemed to know what to do. This indeed was an officer's job and it really had nothing to do with rank, better education, more social advantages, living in fancier quarters, or wearing nicer uniforms. It had everything to do with *leading*. And that meant setting an example—demonstrating what must be done. Richmond understood that soldiers in mortal danger followed the *leader*, not necessarily the *rank*. This was the secret to his effectiveness. In this instance, he knew that the best course of action was to organize them into a new team and then personally lead them up the draw, thus making each soldier individually accountable to a flesh-and-blood inspirational, instructional leader. This required courage and know-how, qualities he possessed in abundance. He organized the water-soaked remnants of the three companies into a new ad hoc unit that pushed up the draw. One after-action report recognized that his "aggressive and cool head, under fire, effected much of the reorga-

nization which got the third battalion off the beach and into a semblance of an organized unit." Sergeant Albanese believed that he "used
great ingenuity in reforming not only the Company but what was left
of the Battalion and continuing on to take the objectives."

As their commander he operated in a sort of netherworld between
company and battalion command. Like the L Company soldiers before
them, when Richmond's force climbed the bluffs, they inevitably
clashed with the Germans in the outworks around WN-60. "It was a
little wet, and going up that cliff was slippery," Sergeant Polnoroff said.
In his recollection, they "started taking trenches and bunkers." Mines
caused several casualties. At one point, they got into a close-quarters
firefight. A couple feet away from Polnoroff, his good friend Staff Sergeant Thomas DeNicola shot one of the German soldiers. DeNicola
rose excitedly, either out of exultation or in hopes of getting a look at
his victim, and a burst of enemy fire tore into him. He collapsed in a
dead heap. "We used to talk about going to South America together
when this was all over," Polnoroff said sadly. Elsewhere, Private Argenzio, the underaged soldier, was with a group that snuck right up on a
distracted enemy machine-gun crew. "They were peppering the beach.
They didn't see us, they were so busy shooting. So I started throwing
grenades and I got two of the son-of-a-guns." He followed up his grenade attack by firing an entire clip from his M1 Garand at them and
the survivors ran away.

The intimate firefights raged atop the bluffs, all around WN-60.
Richmond was the glue that held the force together. "It took a special
person to lead men at that time and he was one," Tech 5 Joe Hopta, one
of his medics, said. Richmond eventually made contact with Lieutenant
Cutler and the L Company boat sections that were fighting for the
same terrain. Richmond established a unified command structure with
104 men from the various companies under his control. At the same
time, Richmond's embattled band of assault troops enjoyed some effective fire support from the beach and the sea. Lieutenant John McCar-

thy, the highly experienced leader of M Company's mortar platoon, managed to salvage enough ammo, tubes, and crewmen to get his guns into action. "[He] set up four of his 81MM mortars in battery under the cliff and sent observers with the rifle groups that were working their way to the strong points on top of the ridge," the company history stated. Because they were firing directly over a cliff, at elevated targets less than a couple hundred yards away, the mortarmen had to place their tubes at a perilously high, almost perpendicular angle. "They were elevated at 85 degrees," Corporal Kurtz, who was part of McCarthy's platoon, wrote. "We were hoping that there was no wind blowing, because they would drop on us." McCarthy himself later climbed the draw to act as an observer. In addition, a heavy machine-gun platoon, under the supervision of Lieutenant George Lazo, provided fire support.

The USS *Doyle* was also a key supporter throughout the morning for the 3rd Battalion attack up the F-1 draw. Commander James Marshall, the skipper, ordered his crew to sail the destroyer to within eight hundred yards of the beach, take up station and risk running aground in the shallow water in order to provide the best possible supporting fire. For obvious reasons, running aground was a major no-no in the Navy, but in this instance it could mean not just humiliation but death. If the *Doyle* ran aground, it would become a stationary target for German artillery (and possibly for the naval guns in concrete casemates at Port-en-Bessin to the east). So, Commander Marshall assumed considerable risk in ordering *Doyle* to operate so close to the beach, but it was worth it.

As of 0810, the ship's Combat Information Center had established communication with the shore fire control party, and this of course greatly enhanced the accuracy of the *Doyle*'s salvos against the antitank gun position and several machine-gun emplacements. The attacking soldiers also took to firing tracer rounds at any targets they wanted the *Doyle* to destroy. Private First Class Roger Brugger remembered looking back, from the perspective of the bluff, and seeing the destroyer stop dead in the water and zero in on a nettlesome machine-gun nest. "A sailor came out of the hatch and went forward to the gun turret, turned the gun towards the machine gun emplacement and let go with a couple of rounds. This silenced the machine gun." The naval fire was so accurate and destructive that, in one instance, Lieutenant Monteith's section had to request that the fire be lifted in order for his section to proceed with its attack. The *Doyle*'s effectiveness was instructive. As inaccurate as the pre-invasion bombardment had been against pre-selected targets from a distance, the accuracy of the maneuverable destroyers at close range against sighted or shore-directed targets could be absolutely devastating.

It would be an overstatement to say that the 3rd Battalion attack up the F-1 draw completely captured or negated WN-60 by midmorning. However, the L Company boat sections, along with Captain Richmond's mixed group, did succeed in neutralizing the worst of WN-60's opposition to the ongoing landings. The German defenders of WN-60 arguably enjoyed the finest fields of fire and better observation of Omaha beach than any other strong point garrison. After the 3rd Battalion attack they were now primarily focused on fighting their attackers at close range rather than saturating the landing beaches with machine-gun, mortar, and antitank fire. In pushing up the draw, the Americans also established an inland lodgment from which they could outflank WN-60 and begin pushing for Cabourg and Le Grand Hameau. The survivors were off the beach.[8]

Major General Clarence Huebner, commander of the 1st Infantry Division. Because he took command from the popular Terry Allen, many of the division's veterans did not accept him, at least until D-Day.

Brigadier General Willard Wyman (*left, with arms crossed*), assistant division commander of the 1st Infantry Division, stands with two other officers. He was one of only two senior officers to have any real impact in the 1st Division sector on D-Day. One of his aides later claimed that "the beach would have gone without him."

Colonel George Taylor, commander of the 16th Infantry Regiment, pictured later in his career as a brigadier general. On D-Day, the effect of his leadership was profound. He was responsible for the famous rallying cry "Only two kinds of people are going to be on this beach, the dead and those who are about to die!" The phrase was hardly spontaneous—it had been bouncing around in his mind for many months before the invasion.

(*Left to right*) Captains Kimball Richmond, John Finke, and Edward Wozenski, three of the most important company commanders on D-Day. All three were recipients of the Distinguished Service Cross.

A famous photograph, taken from a Coast Guard Higgins boat, of C Company, 16th Infantry Regiment, landing about sixty minutes after H-Hour at Easy Red beach, under the menacing nose of the prominent ridgeline. Notice the tidal and situational similarity with the Capa photograph.

A waterlogged boat section heads toward Easy Red beach. An officer, presumably the commander, is at the front left, peering over the ramp. This was the position of most boat section commanders on D-Day. Interestingly, another officer (vertical white stripe on helmet) is visible in the back.

A Coast Guard photograph of the grim situation on Easy Red beach about an hour after the first landings. Men wade through the water and take cover on the beach under a pall of smoke.

A grim-faced medic moves along the cliffs at Fox Green beach. In the 1st Division sector on D-Day, the medics faced some of the greatest danger, especially while moving wounded men from the waterline to the shingle bank or the cliffs. Medics were overwhelmed by the number of casualties and the severity of their wounds. Invasion planners erred greatly in earmarking ships and landing craft for useless vehicles and artillery pieces instead of medical evacuation boats.

Photographer Robert Capa's iconic photograph of soldiers pinned down at the waterline, seeking the dubious cover of a hedgehog obstacle. The position of the landing craft and disposition of the tides both indicate that the picture was taken at least a couple hours after H-Hour.

Another classic Capa image, looking straight at Easy Red beach and the prominent ridge-line just inland. A line of men is pinned down at the shingle bank and, in the foreground, a deep-wading tank and what appears to be a duplex-drive Sherman are both stationary. More men are either pinned in the water or taking cover behind obstacles. Most D-Day accounts presume that Capa was with the first wave that hit the beach, but he probably landed about forty-five minutes later with troops from the 1st Battalion, 16th Infantry.

The view looking west on Fox Green beach about midday on June 6, 1944, at high tide. A pair of deep-wading Shermans from the 741st Tank Battalion can clearly be seen, as can the carnage along the beach. Though damaged by a mine, the Coast Guard's LCI-83 is in the process of landing reinforcements, presumably from the 20th Engineer Combat Battalion.

A heavy-machine-gun team moves along the cliffside at the convergence of Fox Red and Fox Green beaches. Teams like this one provided fire support for the push up the easternmost exit of Omaha beach.

Dead soldiers, probably from the 3rd Battalion, 16th Infantry, lie on the hard, round stones of the shingle bank at Fox Green beach. One of the dead soldiers is on his back, and someone has placed a cardboard box over his head, rather than stare at his lifeless face.

The shingle bank, probably looking east, on D-Day. This photo, taken by Lieutenant Robert Riekse, an aide to Brigadier General Wyman, clearly shows the steep angle of the bank and the desperation of the fighting. As a line of men seeks shelter, a deep-wading Sherman tank is working its way to the apex of the shingle. Other vehicles can also be glimpsed in the gloomy mist.

Another Riekse shot of the shingle bank, looking in the opposite direction.

Weary Big Red One soldiers huddle under the temporary cover of the cliffs near Fox Green beach. The man in the middle, with his back to the camera, is probably Private Joe Argenzio, an underaged replacement who had joined M Company, 16th Infantry only a few days before D-Day.

A modern-day view, looking east, of the cliffs overlooking Fox Green and Fox Red beaches. Once upon a time, Big Red One soldiers took cover along these very rocks and cliffs.

The aftermath at Easy Red beach. Dead bodies and wrecked vehicles, including a deep-wading Sherman, are visible. Notice that the log obstacles all point toward the shore, not the sea.

The flooded antitank ditch at Omaha beach. Many infantrymen had to wade across the ditch while under fire. Eventually engineers with bulldozers filled it in.

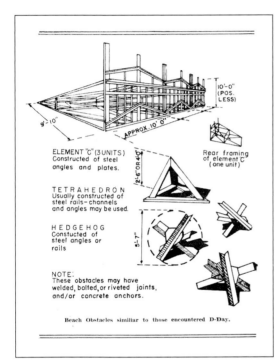

ELEMENT "C" (3 UNITS)
Constructed of steel angles and plates.

TETRAHEDRON
Usually constructed of steel rails-channels and angles may be used.

HEDGEHOG
Constucted of steel angles or rails

NOTE:
These obstacles may have welded, bolted, or riveted joints, and/or concrete anchors.

10'-0" (POS. LESS)

9'-10"

APPROX. 10'-0"

Rear framing of element C (one unit)

2'-6" DIA. 4'-0"

5'-7"

Beach Obstacles similiar to those encountered D-Day.

A descriptive diagram of German obstacles at Omaha beach. Many were laced with mines. The Element C obstacles were generally known as "Belgian gates." The obstacles were such a serious threat to the landings that invasion commanders created special Gap Assault Teams of Army engineers and Navy demolition teams to land alongside the leading assault troops. The mission of the teams was to clear paths along the beach. They suffered heavy casualties.

A fascinating aerial view of the 1st Division side of Omaha beach on D-Day. The antitank ditch is quite visible, as are vehicles and soldiers on the beach.

Lieutenant Jimmie Monteith, one of three Big Red One soldiers to earn the Medal of Honor for bravery on D-Day. He was killed while staving off a German counterattack on the afternoon of June 6.

T/5 John "Joe" Pinder, a member of the 16th Infantry Regiment communications section and a recipient of the Medal of Honor. Pinder braved extremely heavy fire and debilitating wounds to salvage vital radio equipment. He ended up dying of those wounds. In civilian life, he had been a professional baseball player.

Private Joe Argenzio. Still two days short of his seventeenth birthday on D-Day, he found himself in the middle of a grenade duel to the death.

Sergeant Fred Bisco, one of two soldiers from the Spalding-Streczyk boat section to be killed on D-Day.

Lieutenant John Spalding (*second from right*) with three of his brothers, before D-Day.

Spalding shortly after returning home from the war. The strain of combat can clearly be seen on his face. Like so many other soldiers, he came home a changed man.

Tech Sergeant Phil Streczyk, one of the most decorated NCOs in the Army and second in command to John Spalding for their boat section on D-Day. Their group was probably the first one off the beach in the 1st Division sector. Streczyk logged more than four hundred days of frontline combat service.

The E-1 exit overlooking Easy Red beach two days after D-Day. At the lower right, the contentious pillbox of WN-65 can be seen just over the shoulders of the soldiers.

A path through the minefields beyond Easy Red. The Spalding-Streczyk section probably exited the beach on this path.

Soldiers stride past the remnants of the church at Colleville-sur-Mer. Believing that German artillery observers were holed up in the steeple, Navy destroyer crews shelled and demolished the steeple and much of the church on the late afternoon of D-Day. In reality, Captain Joe Dawson's G Company, 16th Infantry held the church and the surrounding area at the time. As a result, at least eighteen men were either killed or wounded in this tragic friendly-fire incident.

After the battle, soldiers from the 5th Engineer Special Brigade use the pillbox at WN-65 as a headquarters and collecting point. The damaged 50-millimeter gun can clearly be seen in the aperture, as can pockmarks along the facing of the pillbox. The tarp covers damage from naval guns.

The pillbox at WN-65 today. A plaque commemorating the exploits of the 467th Antiaircraft AW Battalion is visible above the aperture. The wrecked gun is still inside. Damage from .50-caliber bullets, 37-millimeter shells and, above the aperture, naval shells is all quite evident. Several units claimed credit for the destruction of the pillbox, but it was probably neutralized by a combination of firepower and attackers. Once it fell silent, Exit E-1 was open.

General Dwight Eisenhower and Lieutenant General Omar Bradley decorate several 1st Infantry Division soldiers with the Distinguished Service Cross on July 2, 1944. In a brief speech, Eisenhower referred to the 1st Division as his Praetorian Guard. The bespectacled soldier who is receiving his medal from Ike is Major Charles Tegtmeyer, surgeon of the 16th Infantry Regiment. Standing to Tegtmeyer's left is Captain Joe Dawson, commander of G Company, 16th Infantry and, to Dawson's left, is Captain Kimball Richmond, commander of I Company, 16th Infantry.

Private Carlton Barrett (*center*) receives his Medal of Honor from Lieutenant General J. C. H. Lee (*right*). Barrett was a member of the Intelligence and Reconnaissance section of the 18th Infantry Regiment. He landed early on D-Day with the 16th Infantry Regiment and distinguished himself with remarkable bravery. Like many Medal of Honor recipients, Barrett's postwar life was troubled.

The 88-millimeter gun casemate at WN-61. At 0710 on D-Day, Sergeant George Geddes's Sherman tank knocked out the gun. Today the casemate serves as somebody's home.

The rebuilt church at Colleville-sur-Mer. Captain Joe Dawson and several of his soldiers fought for their lives inside this church. Today it is peaceful.

The farm complex just across the road from the church at Colleville-sur-Mer. Captain Joe Dawson and many soldiers from his G Company, 16th Infantry Regiment took up positions here and fought the Germans for much of the day and night on June 6, 1944.

The view today from Easy Red beach, looking in the direction of the prominent ridgeline, roughly in the spot where the Spalding-Streczyk section exited the beach. The Normandy American cemetery is just beyond the tree line.

Easy Red beach, from the perspective of WN-62, the resistance nest near Exit E-3 that inflicted so much damage on D-Day. One glance at the topography and the wide-open sand is enough to understand why WN-62 was so deadly.

Panoramic view today of Omaha beach from WN-60 at the eastern edge of the beach area. The entire expanse of this hallowed beach is visible, all the way to Point de la Percée in the distance. Upon observing this four-and-a-half-mile crescent (known initially to Allied planners as "Beach 46"), Field Marshal Erwin Rommel remarked that it reminded him of the beach at Salerno, Italy. He predicted that the Allies would land here, and he was obviously right.

Chapter 5

BRASS

Colonel George Taylor knew amphibious warfare. He had helped mastermind the Allied landings in North Africa as a key planner, and he had led the 16th Infantry into Sicily. In that time, he had developed two strong opinions about any invasion: the beach was death and inertia was the mortal enemy of success. "In a landing operation, there are two classes of men that may be found on the beach," he wrote several months before D-Day, "those who are already dead and those who are about to die." This notion of the dead and the soon-to-be-dead was never far from his mind, almost to the point of obsession. On the beach, men were like penned animals, just waiting for the slaughter. Taylor had already seen too much death in this war and he had no wish to see any more. His troops were like family. The idea of a beach choked with their dead, shattered bodies was horrifying. Taylor was an unambiguous, rather clear-thinking man who believed that excellence came through simplicity. In the aftermath of one pre-invasion exercise back in England, General Huebner had huddled with his commanders for a critique. One by one, they spoke glowingly of the training exercise, especially the overall plan. In stark contrast to his colleagues, Taylor said that such a plan would never work. "Why not?" Huebner asked.

"Because it's too damned complicated," Taylor replied curtly.

He was a thinker and a doer, the sort of soldier who felt equally comfortable in a frontline foxhole or a seminar room at an Army staff college. "He was a good officer and really should have been a general by then," Private Pete Lypka, who had served under him since Sicily, said, "but he had a habit of saying what was on his mind in as few words as possible. He was no apple-polisher." Taylor knew that the true antidote for slaughter on Omaha beach was rapid movement, though he admitted that maneuvering against powerful defenses "was almost impossible in modern combat."

The forty-five-year-old West Pointer had spent more than half his life in the Army. Shades of gray crept over his close-cropped hair now, and crow's-feet spidered from the corners of his penetrating blue eyes, though his face retained a boyish sheen. Like many other effective combat leaders in the Army, he was diminutive in height at five feet seven, but somehow large in physical presence. An infantryman to the core, he was steeped in the commonsense world of field soldiering, both peacetime and wartime. "Beneath all the officer veneer," Corporal Sam Fuller wrote, "Colonel Taylor had a heart of gold. I loved the guy." Taylor loved the Army, though his fertile mind had generated several dozen ideas about how it could be, and should be, run much better. One idea stood above the others. Taylor believed that senior officers were too distant from soldiers, too reluctant, or perhaps unable, to teach and show their subordinates what to do, especially in combat. "What we lack, and need more of, is the worm's eye view of leadership," he once wrote. "No one ever tells the junior officer just exactly what he should do, and how he should do it."

As Colonel Taylor approached Easy Red with the rear command post at 0815, he was determined to do just that—in this circumstance, he was certain that this would mean getting them to move, so this notion preoccupied his mind. He knew he would be greeted by sights of carnage, destruction, confusion, and inertia. Indeed, the evening before, aboard the USS *Samuel Chase*, Taylor had told war correspondents Don Whitehead, Robert Capa, and Jack Thompson, "The first six hours will be the toughest. This is the period during which we will be the weakest. But we've got to open the door." His words were prophetic, probably more so than even he himself appreciated. When he and his command group landed, the various inland fights were raging in full force. Thus, much of the beach was still under intense fire from German artillery, machine-gun nests and mortars.

Taylor's rear CP consisted of two boats, an LCM and an LCVP. In stark contrast to the forward CP under Lieutenant Colonel Mathews, the two boats landed without loss, though they were under machine-gun fire. Taylor and the others waded, under fire all the way, about fifty yards through chest-high water to the beach. "It was a helpless feeling wading while shot at," Taylor later said. When he reached the beach, the scene that greeted his eyes was even more grim than what he had expected. Wrecked Higgins boats floated aimlessly on the crashing surf. The water was colored a muddy pink from blood; the sand was dotted and splotched with lines and circles of crimson. Body parts—everything from arms and legs to heads and fingers—littered the sand and stones. Angry-looking obstacles still honeycombed the beach, seemingly oblivious to the prodigious and costly efforts of the Gap Assault Teams to clear them. Blood-soaked bandages, discarded equipment, and sand-choked rifles lay in random clusters. Dead and wounded men—some facedown, some faceup on arched backs—littered the waterline and the sands. Other figures lay huddled at the shingle. Some looked dead. Others howled for medics. Several tanks were burning or immobilized. Mortar and artillery shells exploded—oily puffs of smoke, dust, or sand floated in the wake of the explosions. Bullets snipped against the sand and stones of the beach.

Taylor emerged from the water and, in the recollection of Private Warren Rulien, a member of the I&R platoon, the colonel came under accurate machine-gun fire. "He laid down on his stomach and started crawling towards shore," Rulien said. The young private chuckled at the sight of the mighty colonel crawling ashore. He overheard Taylor say to one of his officers, "If we're going to die, let's die up there," and he pointed at the bluffs. The colonel and the men around him got to their feet and crossed the beach. The natural tendency of nearly every person who was entering this inferno, including many in Taylor's command group, was to gravitate toward the faux safety of the shingle. Not Taylor, though. He remained upright and strode purposefully to the left in the direction of the E-3 draw, where he and Mathews had planned to situate their CP. "It soon became evident that no such command post existed and most elements [were] pinned on the beach," a post-battle report stated.

Taylor was not surprised. All that really mattered now, he knew, was getting his people into motion, off this beach. He was consumed by this idea; he understood what to do and he knew he must tell them in no uncertain terms. He moved west along Easy Red beach and roared at his men to get moving. As he did so, he gathered members of his headquarters into a veritable entourage, following him everywhere he went. Major Charles Tegtmeyer, his regimental surgeon, was lying against the shingle bank, wet and shivering from the landing, catching his breath and gathering his medics, when he spotted Taylor. "He passed us walking erect, followed by his staff and yelled for me to bring my group along," the doctor recalled. Major Tegtmeyer had become very seasick during the ride to shore. The rocking of the boat, combined with the stench of exhaust fumes and the sight of Captain Lawrence Deery, the regimental chaplain, munching contentedly on an apple, had caused Tegtmeyer to throw up the entire contents of his stomach. He was worried that the invasion was a complete failure and that any minute the Germans would come down from the bluffs and overwhelm them. Even in the event of that disaster, the idea of retreating back into the icy sea was repugnant. "I'll be damned if I go back into that water even if Hitler himself should order me," he exclaimed sardonically to the men around him.

The sight of Taylor and his demeanor galvanized the weakened physician into action. He and many of his medics stood up and followed the colonel along the beach. Under heavy fire, Tegtmeyer and the others pulled wounded men from the surf, treated their wounds, and deposited them in open spots along the shingle bank. Major Tegtmeyer bound up more wounds (and probably saved more lives) than he could count; he was dismayed to find, though, that many soldiers were beyond his help. "The number of dead, killed by mines, shell fragments, machine guns and sniper bullets was appalling." The doctor was especially surprised to see that "a great percentage were dead from bullet wounds through the head," since this was unusual in modern war. Father Deery trailed along and kept very busy administering last rites or just comforting the dying. In Tegtmeyer's estimation, "every man who moved along the beach had utter disregard for his own personal safety."

The mere act of movement was exhausting, and not just because of the enemy fire. The sand was wet and sticky. The incoming tide made that problem even worse. It was easy to stumble over the shingle bank's fist-sized stones, as well as the bodies of the living and the dead. At one point, Tegtmeyer tripped and fell over the inert body of an engineer. Tegtmeyer was so tired he needed to rest for several minutes before he could get up and move again. To make matters worse, Nebelwerfer rockets—generally called "Screaming Meemies" by the troops—shrieked overhead and exploded closer to the waterline. The rockets originated from batteries just west of Saint-Laurent and only added to the terror experienced by the men on the beach. Tegtmeyer watched with fascinated admiration as Lieutenant Colonel Robert Skaggs, commander of the 741st Tank Battalion, stood near the waterline, and swung his life preserver in the air, like some sort of magic wand, to gather several of his tankers. He ordered them to get back into any abandoned tanks they found and then resume firing at the Germans. Somehow Skaggs did not get hit.

Colonel Taylor, during his trek, succeeded in gathering three functional radios. Most likely this was the same equipment for which Tech 5 Joe Pinder had sacrificed his life to drag ashore. The raised antennas of the radios and Colonel Taylor's erect posture began to draw heavy small-arms fire. "For Christ's sake, Colonel," Tegtmeyer cried, "get down, you're drawing fire!"

Taylor grinned at the doctor, ordered the radioman to pull the antenna down, and said, "There are only two kinds of men on this beach, those who are dead and those who are about to die. Let's get the hell out of here."

Corporal Sam Fuller, a thirty-two-year-old former newspaper reporter, novelist and Hollywood screenwriter turned combat soldier, flopped down next to Taylor. During the Sicily campaign, the two men had bonded over their mutual love of cigars. Fuller had run through a gauntlet of fire to reach Colonel Taylor. A discarded cigar butt had actually helped him locate his colonel. "Even in the eye of that tornado of bullets and explosions, there was no mistaking a Havana," Fuller wrote. "Taylor smoked them. He had to be somewhere nearby."

The talented writer had been ordered by his lieutenant to tell the colonel about the Spalding group's success in blowing a breach in the wire and getting off the beach. "Who blew it?" Taylor asked.

"Streczyk," Fuller replied.

"All right," Taylor replied with a smile. He reached into a bag, removed a box of cigars and handed it to Fuller. "Enjoy 'em, Sammy. You earned them, running over here."

Fuller barely had time to thank the colonel and register his pleasure at receiving the cigars, when Taylor stood up, amid heavy fire, and shouted to everyone around them. "There are two kinds of men out here! The dead! And those who are about to die! So let's get the hell off this beach and at least die inland."

For Taylor, obsession was now combined with simplicity. Seemingly oblivious to danger, he roamed Easy Red, repeating these words, or some variation of them, to practically anyone he encountered. There is no way to tell how many men saw him, heard him, or were affected by his presence, but the number must have been substantial, probably in the hundreds. Jack Thompson, a correspondent for the *Chicago Tribune* who had parachuted into Sicily the year before, landed with Taylor's command group and followed the colonel as much as the situation permitted. He remembered Taylor saying, "Gentlemen, we are being killed on the beach, let us go inland and get killed." Thompson was struck by the colonel's use of the word "gentlemen" amid such chaotic and deadly circumstances "when the world was exploding around us . . . to say nothing of the machine guns up on the bluff." Captain Thomas Merendino, commander of B Company, was on the receiving end of the same phrase, probably at the same time, and remembered that "men surged forward" as a result of hearing Taylor. In another spot, Private Frank Ciarpelli heard the colonel say, "It's better to be shot to death than drown like rats on the beach." Private First Class Harold Saylor was focusing on staying alive from one moment to the next, when he noticed someone running by and screaming, "Two kinds of people are staying on this beach: the dead and those who are going to die! Now let's get the hell out of here!" Only later did Saylor realize that it was Colonel Taylor. Private First Class John Bistrica, a rifleman in C Company, had gotten separated from his squad. As he pondered what to do, he heard Taylor yell the same phrase. The colonel's words prompted Bistrica to get moving in the direction of a gap he saw in the barbed wire. Private Rulien, who witnessed the colonel's landing, felt that his words had a significant effect on the men around him. "The officers began moving their men along that . . . beach to reach their objective." Taylor passed right by Captain Richard Lindo, an artillery liaison officer. Lindo heard the colonel make his famous statement. One of Taylor's aides was an officer with whom Lindo had competed for the affections of the same barmaid in Weymouth. As the colonel's group passed Lindo, the young aide looked directly at him and said forcefully, "She loves me!"

Naturally the colonel's influence was not limited to his own 16th Infantry soldiers. Tech 5 Albert Sponheimer, a bespectacled medic, landed with the 197th Anti-Aircraft (SP) Battalion, a unit equipped with machine-gun-laden halftracks whose primary job was to ward off German air attacks on the beachhead. Sponheimer was hunched over a wounded man, trying to save his life, when he heard Taylor roaring about the dead and those who were going to die. "I clearly heard the statement," Sponheimer said. "I looked up and saw the officer and went back to work on the wounded. It was an impressive moment." Pharmacist's Mate Richard Borden was an eighteen-year-old corpsman with the recently landed 6th Naval Beach Battalion, an outfit whose mission was to mark safe sea and beach lanes for incoming craft, assist in the removal of mines, and provide medical care. Borden was in a state of shock. The carnage of the beach was overwhelming to such a youngster—so many jagged, bloody wounds, so many cries for medics. A mortar shell exploded nearby, bouncing him in the air but otherwise leaving him unhurt. The same could not be said for his littermate, a young man with a brand-new baby daughter at home. Several times Borden tried to rouse him. Finally he turned him over and was greeted by the sight of "glazed eyes and sandy face in that awesome fixed expression. His helmet . . . rolled upward . . . exposing a handful of gray matter surprisingly clean!" Having never seen death, Borden began to administer a vial of human serum albumen before the terrible truth dawned on him. "Tears gushed. I begged my God with all my heart to allow me to exchange places with [the] youth before me." Angry and devastated, Borden stood up and roared at the unseen Germans on the bluffs, "God-damn you, every-one!" He also raged at God. "What is life about that you should do this to my friend?!" Soon thereafter, he noticed a gray-haired colonel—Taylor, he later realized—walking by and hollering like a madman. "Get off the beach! You are going to be killed here if you stay! Move it on, boys! Let's go!" The words helped him snap out of his grief-stricken trance and begin caring for men he could save. Elsewhere, Private First Class Earl Chellis heard Taylor urging him and several other members of a small pinned-down group to get off the beach. "Then everybody seemed to get up and we all went," Chellis said. Watching Taylor and trailing along behind him, First Sergeant Raymond Briel thought his actions were "as heroic and memorable a sight as any soldier would want to see." Staff Sergeant Kenneth Quinn, another member of his head-quarters group, never forgot "the manner in which Col. Taylor . . . took over the situation on the beach, got the men organized and off the beach."

It is impossible to say with any precision how much impact Taylor's actions had on salvaging a bad situation and turning the momentum of the Omaha beach battle, but they were undoubtedly a significant factor. He was the first senior officer on the 1st Division side of the beach. His presence, his force of personality, and the simplicity of his orders—not to mention the colorful, stark nature of his "dead or going to die" phraseology—stirred many soldiers into positive action. At a time of deep crisis, Taylor made two major contributions: he saved the lives of many men by motivating them to get off the beach where they were vulnerable and nearly helpless, and in so doing he reinforced the groups that were already infiltrating the draws and bluffs even as he stalked Easy Red. Both contributions did much to wrest control of the battle away from the Germans in favor of the invaders. The Army awarded him the Distinguished Service Cross. One of the descriptive docu-ments in his medal file perhaps best summarized the significance of his actions: "He found officers and gathered groups of men together for them to lead. He found, led and drove men into action. Calmly and coolly he assigned objectives to these newly organized groups. He converted a bewildered mob into a co-ordinated fighting force. He cleared an exit from the beach, and moved men through it."[1]

Another senior officer, Brigadier General Willard Wyman, the assistant division commander, also arrived at the right time and place. Wyman's mission was to establish the division's advance command post and act as a high-level point man for General Huebner. The manner in which the two generals divided responsibilities, with Wyman the deputy landing first and Huebner the commander aboard ship during the initial hours of the invasion, mirrored the arrangement between Lieutenant Colonel Mathews and Colonel Taylor. Moreover, the commanders thought it advisable to separate the leaders so that one lucky hit or one sunken ship could not take them both out. The forty-six-year-old Wyman was a good choice for this difficult assignment, for he had already served in multiple theaters in this war and had seen plenty of action. Tall and slim, with narrow, penetrating brown eyes, the West Pointer and Maine native cut an impressive figure. "To me he looked like a Greek god dressed in helmet, jacket and boots," Ensign Ernest Carrere, an officer aboard the boat that ferried him part of the way in to the beach, later recalled. Wyman had served in the China-Burma-India theater as an operations officer under General Joe Stilwell during the chaotic retreat in 1942 (before the war Wyman also logged several years as an attaché and liaison with Chiang Kai-shek's army). Having escaped from the clutches of the Japanese in Burma, he was sent to the Mediterranean theater and was assigned, during the Sicily battle, to the 1st Infantry Division as Huebner's second-in-command. Wyman was the father of three kids. Like so many of his colleagues in the Regular Army, he was totally dedicated to the service, sometimes at the expense of family. He had been away from home so long that the burden of raising the kids and running the family had fallen squarely on his wife, Ethel, who was now on the verge of a nervous breakdown. Nonetheless, he considered himself "lucky as hell" to be serving in the Big Red One under Huebner.

Wyman, a small group of aides, and the war correspondent Don Whitehead landed on Easy Red together at 0839. They hurried across the beach and, for several minutes, huddled together along the shingle bank. The smooth and jagged edges of shingle stones poked against their ribs and thighs. Whitehead was practically in a state of shock at the violence of the fighting going on around him and the carnage he witnessed on the beach. Wet, shivering, and still feeling some seasickness, he formed the opinion that the invasion was a miserable, catastrophic failure. He expected the Germans to pour over the bluffs at any moment and kill or capture everyone on the beach. "They'll come swarming down on us," he thought.

Lying next to Whitehead, the general was studying the situation almost clinically with no trace of fear evident on his lean face. "We've got to get these men off the beach," he said. "This is murder!"

Before Whitehead could digest that statement, General Wyman stood up, heedless of the heavy enemy mortar and machine-gun fire, and began to stalk the beach. "Calmly, he began moving lost units to their proper positions, organizing leadership for leaderless troops," Whitehead wrote. "He began to bring order out of confusion and to give direction to this vast collection of inert manpower waiting only to be told what to do, where to go." Wyman organized runners and sent them in multiple directions with information for battalion and company commanders. The messengers ran, dove to the ground when shells screamed in, got up again and disappeared from sight. The correspondent found it hard to keep up with the general as he stepped over the bodies of the dead and wounded alike. At one point they walked past a wounded young soldier who was moaning deliriously, "Oh, merciful God! Please stop the hurt! Get me out of here!" The group kept moving. Whitehead never knew what happened to the wounded soldier.

Wyman was not as colorful or as charismatic as Taylor. He did not holler inspirational phrases. Nor did he stand out all that much among the crowds of soldiers scurrying to and fro along the beach. Indeed, relatively few soldiers have recollections of any encounter with him. He does not seem to have crossed paths with Taylor, though they must have been close to each other, if only for moments at a time. However, Wyman made a difference at Easy Red through his businesslike courage, his sense of what to do, and his powers of organization. First Lieutenant Robert Riekse, one of his aides, vividly remembered him "moving up and down the beach, talking, moving men, redeploying troops, urging them to use there [sic] equipment . . . meeting the incoming troops and always exposed."

As long as Huebner was still on the water, aboard the USS *Ancon*, Wyman functioned as the de facto division commander. As such, he was empowered to make important decisions. One of the first things he noticed was that Omaha beach was crowded with too many vehicles, too many supporting soldiers, and not enough infantrymen. Mines and obstacles, many of which were submerged now at higher tide, impeded landing craft of all sizes but especially the larger LCTs and Landing Craft, Infantry (LCI) ships, from disgorging cargo and troops. The 16th Infantry Regiment's Cannon Company, for instance, was in complete disarray and not just because of the obstacles. The unit was designed to provide something of the fire support of an artillery battery but with the immediacy and mobility of the infantry. The company was equipped with six M3 105-millimeter howitzers. The crews towed the howitzers with jeeps or halftracks until they were ready to shoot. Their thirty-pound projectiles could wreak great havoc upon a tank, a pillbox, or any clustered group of soldiers. On the face of it, the M3 105s served as a perfect close-support weapon against the German defenses. The problem was getting them ashore. Each gun and its accompanying crewmen were loaded aboard swimming DUKW amphibious trucks and disgorged from Landing Ship, Tanks (LSTs) into the water. "We were supposed to fire our cannon off the trucks as self propelled artillery as we proceeded up the beach, but it didn't quite work out that way," Tech Sergeant William "Happy" Otlowski said. Similar to the DD amphibious tanks, the DUKWs were swamped by the rough seas. Five of the DUKWs sank. Only one of the Cannon Company howitzers made it in to the beach, but it was damaged so badly as to prove useless. Fortunately the crewmen were picked up in patrol boats. Some were taken back to LST-376. Others made it to the beach, where they only added to the crowd of leaderless and weaponless men.[2]

At nearly the same time, A Company of the 1st Medical Battalion and elements of the 6th Naval Beach Battalion were approaching Easy Red beach aboard LCI-85, a Coast Guard vessel with a crew of four officers and thirty enlisted men. An LCI was capable of carrying, quite uncomfortably, a complement of about two hundred men, a force roughly the size of an infantry company. Company A numbered about ninety soldiers, including three doctors; the beach battalion sailors rounded out the rest of the LCI's human cargo. The ship was designed for secure landings against little or no opposition. It was equipped with long ramps, quite similar to gangways, on both sides of the craft. Both gangways had railings to steady the descending troops, who picked their way carefully downward in long single-file lines and into the water. Naturally, this made them and the ship perfect targets.

In the conning tower at the rear of the slender ship, Lieutenant (j.g.) Coit Hendley, a Coast Guard reservist who had worked as a journalist for the *Washington Star* newspaper before the war, found what he thought was a suitable gap in the obstacles. He gave the order to go into the beach and land the troops. Ideally, the LCI needed a fifty-yard gap in the obstacles to make a proper landing. This gap was more like ten yards. LCI-85 eased carefully through the narrow opening and came to a stop on a sandbar. Several hundred yards in the distance, Lieutenant Hendley could see three burning tanks near the waterline. Clouds of smoke drifted from the wrecked vehicles. Another tank still seemed to be in action. At the bow of LCI-85, the crewman lowered the two ramps into the water. Seaman First Class Gene Oxley volunteered to jump into the water first and carry an anchor line (or rope) in to the beach and fasten it in place. The line's purpose was to give the troops something to grab to steady themselves as they exited the ramp and worked their way through the water to the beach. Seaman Oxley jumped off the ramp and into water over his head. At the same time, Hendley realized that the ship was actually hung up on an unseen obstacle. He ordered the crew to haul Oxley in and retract the ramps. As they did so and the ship disengaged from the obstacle and began backing away, German antitank gunners found their range. Three shells tore into one of the troop compartments below the deck. "We could hear the screams of the men through the voice tube," Chief Quartermaster Charge McWhirter recalled.

As medics worked on the wounded men below and LCI-85 retreated, Lieutenant Hendley searched for another landing spot. "We went down the beach about 100 yards and there seemed to be one spot clear of debris," he later wrote. With no subtlety, the LCI rammed through obstacles and ground to a halt. Immediately a Teller mine exploded under the bow, damaging the forward compartment. Heedless of the explosion, crewmen hurriedly dropped the port-side ramp into place. Waterlogged Seaman Oxley leapt into the waves. "The water was chest deep off the end of the ramp," Hendley wrote in a medal citation for Oxley. "He made his way ashore and stood in the sand keeping a strain on the line as the troops began coming to the beach. This was in disregard of fire on the beach." Ashore, soldiers helped Oxley keep the anchor line fastened. Aboard LCI-85, the medical soldiers and the beach battalion sailors laboriously lined up and carefully began to descend the gangway into the water. "They went off as fast as possible but the water was so deep and swift that they had to use the life line all the way and it was slow going," Lieutenant (j.g.) Arthur Farrar, the executive officer, later wrote. Farrar was standing at the ramp supervising the landings, wishing the troops could disembark more quickly.

Once again, the Germans quickly zeroed in on the vulnerable ship and the excruciatingly silhouetted troops who were lined up like proverbial ducks in a row. A torrent of shells battered LCI-85. "I remember waving to two friends, an Army officer and a Navy lieutenant, who were standing on the deck just below the pilot house," Lieutenant Hendley recalled. As the skipper watched in dismay, a shell exploded just below the pilothouse, killed both officers, and wounded several others. From the vantage point of the beach, Staff Sergeant Don Wilson, who had landed a couple hours earlier with F Company of the 16th Infantry, looked back and watched as "an antitank shell struck the hull next to the port gangplank, blowing it away so that it just dangled in the water. The Jerry gunner then raised his barrel and put one right down the deck, followed by a couple more. The explosion sent medics and their gear flying in all directions. I vividly recall seeing a cloud of white bandages floating down into the smoke on deck."

Men fell or dove into the water and waded ashore as best they could. Others hung on to the twisted remnants of the ramp or scrambled for cover along the deck. One of the shells actually grazed Lieutenant Farrar in the left thigh and slammed into the hull. "When I was hit I looked back and saw a hole the size of my head where the shell had gone through the ship without exploding," he recalled. The shell left a large, bloody flesh wound in the lieutenant's thigh, but it did not break any bones or nick any arteries. A different shell tore through the radio shack and exploded, severing Radioman Gordon Arneberg's leg. "The crew dragged him out," Lieutenant Hendley said. "I found his leg lying on the deck and kept walking around it. Finally, one of the crew with more guts than I had kicked it over the side."

Flames swept through the damaged LCI. Smoke billowed out of the holds. Some of the troops, including several wounded men, were still in the holds. Their comrades braved the smoke and fire to drag them up to the crowded deck. As the ship took on water, it began listing badly. The crew feverishly fought the fire and attempted to repair the damage. "By this time the holds and deck were littered with dead and wounded," the survivors of A Company later told an Army historian. Accurate machine-gun fire only added to the horror of the moment. Bullets swept through men on the deck and in the water. Near misses pinged off the metal hull and the superstructure. Seaman Herbert Goodick was in the process of working his way along the rope when bullets began to splash in the water and buzz past him. "While the machine gun fire was going on . . . you wonder if anything is going to hit you." He made it in, but several others around him did not. Quite possibly, the machine-gun fire emanated from Private First Class Hein Severloh's MG-42 in the middle of WN-62. "I emptied the whole ship with my firing," the German gunner later said, probably with a touch of hyperbole.

With the ramps shot away and his vessel on the verge of sinking, Lieutenant Hendley ordered LCI-85 to withdraw. "The skipper backed the ship off the beach as fast as possible and was soon out of the firing sector of the beach defense guns," Lieutenant Farrar said. "The broken ramp was hanging down in the water and three men, all wounded, were still clinging on. I happened to be one of them and can testify to a rough ride with plenty of dunkings." Other crewmen eventually hauled him back aboard. The majority of the troops either escaped from the stricken ship or had already disembarked before the enemy fire intensified. Hendley estimated that, among the troops, fifteen were dead and another thirty wounded. Four of his own men, including, of course, Farrar and Arneberg, were wounded. The intrepid Oxley remained ashore. The troops who were unhurt and still aboard LCI-85 were off-loaded onto a smaller craft and landed late in the day. Damage-control parties tried desperately to save LCI-85, but she sank at 1430, though Hendley and his remaining crewmen were evacuated safely. "I found myself crying and a great feeling of guilt came over me," he admitted. "I felt that I was to blame for the deaths and wounding of all those men. It was several years before those feelings faded."

Back on Easy Red, General Wyman took note of what was happening to vehicles and landing craft. He realized it was time to stop landing more matériel (he did not know then that the beach master on the 29th Infantry Division sector had just decided the same thing and issued the necessary orders). Easy Red was bottlenecked. The draws were not yet completely open. Any new vehicle on the beach—even if it could make it in—would simply add to the crowds and become a prime target. To a great extent, the same was true of supporting troops. The larger landing craft that were needed to land heavy equipment, vehicles, and the like were only going to get hung up, blown up, or shot up before they could even land. Wyman understood that the situation called for more infantry, and not much of anything else. Only infantry could reinforce the hard-pressed groups that were fighting to open the draws and thus provide a decisive push.

During his travels along the beach he managed to find a working radio suitable for communication with the *Ancon*. His first communication to General Huebner, sent at 0907, was laconic yet descriptive: "Beach slow." At 0950 he radioed Huebner again. This time, instead of describing the situation on the beach, he made a request that was tantamount to a decision: "There are too many vehicles on the beach; send combat troops." Twenty minutes later, he followed that message with a plea to "reinforce 2nd Battalion, 16th at once." Again this was really a decision, not a request, and it was the right decision, made by a man with credibility and courage. It was one of the few instances in which a senior officer on the 1st Division side of Omaha beach affected the battle in any substantive way, at least through immediate, on-the-spot actions. Colonel Taylor and General Wyman proved to be perfect partners, albeit not by design. Taylor's leadership was inspirational and motivational. He got people moving off the beach. Wyman's influence was cerebral and logistical. It is true that he, like Taylor, got men off the beach. But more than that, he got the right people moving *to* the beach, and this was every bit as important. Lieutenant Riekse probably best summed up his contributions when he later commented that "the beach would have gone without him."[3]

1

Aboard the *Ancon*, General Huebner was like a caged lion. Surrounded by his staff in a command room, he was desperate for information. Aside from the terse radio messages from Wyman, he was getting most of his other news by eavesdropping on the spotty radio communications of V Corps, the First Army, or the naval task force. "A Division Commander exercises his command functions through the training, deployment and the launching of his troops for combat," Huebner later opined. "I had no control . . . didn't expect any control" of the situation on the beach. Though Huebner intellectually understood the reality of his limited impact on the battle at this stage, it was nonetheless difficult for him to truly accept. He was the type of commander whose instinct was to size up a situation for himself, with his own eyes, probably in the thick of the action. He had always led that way, but it was impossible to do so on this day. The *Ancon* was too far offshore. During multiple forays to the deck, neither the general nor his binocular-wielding staff officers could see well enough through the smoke, haze, and sea mist to glean any sense of what was really going on ashore. The sea winds carried with them the fleeting sounds of shooting, but again, this revealed nothing of the brutal realities on the beach. As a converted passenger liner displacing more than 14,000 tons, *Ancon* was an ideal amphibious command ship. Both Huebner and his immediate superior, Major General Leonard Gerow, had placed their respective headquarters on the ship.

As Huebner paced helplessly in his command post, he took stock of what he did know. "I had not had very many good reports," he said. "Most of these reports were rather fragmentary in character but they informed me that the fighting was heavy and we were still confined to the beach itself." That was pretty much the extent of what he knew. He had no sense of the struggle for the draws or the heavy casualties experienced by the initial waves, nor any inkling of the decimation of the Gap Assault Teams; instead he had only a strong sense that something was not right. If not for Wyman, he would have been almost completely in the dark about the 1st Division side of the beach.

Huebner's chief of staff, Colonel Stanhope Mason, was equally frustrated. His job was to oversee every aspect of the division headquarters and act as a trusted counsel for Huebner. Mason knew that the mother's milk of any decent headquarters was accurate information. A general with no knowledge of a battle situation was obviously in a poor position to make decisions. As chief of staff, Mason knew that communications were the key to the problem, and yet they were practically nonexistent between the division headquarters and the units on the beach. In Mason's opinion, this troubling state of affairs was made worse by Colonel Ben Talley, the commander of a special information team for General Gerow. Talley was a forty-one-year-old Georgia Tech–educated engineer who had served with distinction in the Aleutian Islands–Alaska campaign the year before. His accomplishments had earned him the sobriquet "the father of military construction in Alaska." Upon joining the V Corps staff before the invasion, he had impressed General Gerow as an adept planner, a keen observer, and someone who understood amphibious invasions. On D-Day, Gerow assigned him the rather unique job of heading up an "Information Team" whose mission was to clamber aboard a DUKW, sail around, observe what was happening on Omaha beach and report the details back to Gerow aboard the *Ancon*. In essence, Talley served as Gerow's eyes and ears (the fact that he assigned an engineering officer of Talley's caliber to such a job spoke volumes about the importance of information to a commander).

By D-Day, Colonel Mason and most of the 1st Division officers had come to dislike Talley because of his tendency to lecture to them about amphibious operations and supervise their planning, as if they knew nothing about invasions. "He was fluent, ambitious, glib and opinionated," Mason wrote. The chief of staff thought of Talley as "a thorn in our side . . . we had all had an overdose of the Wizard of Attu [the staff's derisive nickname for Talley]. Lt. Col. Fred Gibb, Division G3, swore that if he had an opportunity en route to the beach to put a .30 caliber bullet into Talley's big head he would certainly do so. And I think he might actually have." Regardless of whether Mason was serious about Gibb's intentions, or was simply engaging in hyperbole, there is no doubt that the 1st Division staff officers were boiling with anger at Talley. "We needed badly all the communications we could get from our assault echelons," Colonel Mason said, "but Talley had so much useless 'bafflegab' blocking *our* communications we were suffering an unnecessary handicap." At one point, Colonel Talley monopolized the radio waves with a vague report that "LST just passed me headed for the beach." Mason and his colleagues shook their heads in complete exasperation. In their view, it was obvious that LSTs were headed for the beaches and there was no need to clog the command net with such trivialities. "Talley's message would have deserved notice *only* if the LST were NOT going toward the beach," Mason opined. In fairness to Colonel Talley, his mandate from Gerow was to report everything he saw, sparing no details. The real problem was that there was such a paucity of news and that it was disseminated along a rather limited command communications network.

By late morning, General Huebner was anxious to get ashore (the same was true of General Gerow elsewhere on the *Ancon* and, to a lesser extent, General Omar Bradley aboard the cruiser USS *Augusta*). Huebner was simply fed up with the news vacuum and his isolation from the battle. "I had a lot of trouble trying to hold General Huebner aboard the command ship," Colonel Mason wrote. Huebner told him it was time to land, but Mason would not hear of it. "I knew that, from the standpoint of psychology, it was good for him to be there but I had to tell him, and rather insist on it, that if we went in there ahead of time before we could get some communications established with wire lines laid and good communication set up, he, as Division Commander, would be just making matters worse as we wouldn't be able to control any farther than he could throw his voice, which with a din was not very far."

And that was just on the beach. Mason argued that Huebner would be even more isolated, and powerless, aboard a small boat or landing craft on the way in to the beach. Plus, it was evident from their limited knowledge of the landings that all craft were having a tough time dodging obstacles, making landfall, and disgorging their troops. Huebner might end up drifting aimlessly aboard a patrol craft boat or a Higgins boat, waiting to land, completely out of touch with the rest of the division. Huebner was a rational man. He knew his chief of staff was right. For now, he had no other choice but to sit tight aboard the *Ancon*. In a way, his nickname, "the Coach," fit him perfectly on this most important of all days. His troops—the players—were the ones actually in the game, experiencing the action, shaping the ultimate outcome. He had prepared them as best he knew how, but that outcome was no longer really in his hands. As a coach, his place was on the sidelines and he knew it. There was, however, one thing he could do to help them. Though Wyman's messages were cryptic, they were clear on one thing. He needed infantry reinforcements as fast as he could get them. Thus, the Coach issued the necessary orders: send in the 18th Infantry Regiment.[4]

Chapter 6

REINFORCEMENTS

Although German resistance had diminished, landing on the beach was still no easy proposition. In fact, by late morning, it was probably even trickier than at H-Hour when the tide was low and coxswains could at least see the obstacles in their way. From late morning until early afternoon on D-Day, roughly 1000 to 1300, the tides were at their highest for the daylight hours. By late morning, the remnants of the Gap Assault Teams, plus other engineers, had cleared some of the obstacles at Easy Red, but nowhere near enough to enable smooth landings. Indeed, the tide was so high that there was hardly even a beach to speak of now, just water, the shingle bank, and the rough terrain beyond. Thus, the biggest problem now for anyone trying to land was submerged obstacles and mines, and secondarily enemy fire.

Lieutenant Colonel John Williamson's 2nd Battalion led the way into Easy Red for the 18th Infantry Regiment. The original schedule called for the battalion to land at 0945. Because of the heavy fighting and the crisis as a whole at Omaha beach, they were nearly an hour late. Williamson's rifle companies were dispersed among eighteen LCVPs from the USS *Anne Arundel*. His headquarters soldiers, plus some rifle-men to act as bodyguards, were aboard LCI-489. For more than three hours, the assault troops, including Williamson himself, had ridden miserably in their LCVPs as coxswains circled and waited for the order to go in. Most were seasick. Almost all of them were soaked by sea spray. Some had headaches from breathing exhaust fumes or perhaps just from the fear of what they might encounter on the beach. They had no idea what was really going on, but their limited glimpses of thick balls of smoke on the horizon and the sound of heavy shooting, along with the blown timetable, made it clear to everyone that the invasion was not unfolding as planned.

Williamson's radio communication with the beach was good enough that he understood two things: his battalion was needed im-mediately, and he was to land a few hundred yards west of Exit E-1 so as to outflank WN-65. After experiencing some reluctance from his naval colleagues to head for the beach—at least according to the 18th Infantry records; the naval records are mute—Williamson made it clear that it was time to land. "We were told that no channels were marked [as free of mines and obstacles] and that it was not safe to go in," the battalion after-action report stated. "The Battalion Commander then told the Navy Officer to take the boats in regardless of channels."

As they sped and bounced over the heavy waves, they began to take enemy artillery and machine-gun fire. When the LCVP skippers dropped their ramps in water ranging from two to five feet in depth, the troops scrambled ashore. The clouds and mist began to clear and the men now saw the terrible reality of Easy Red. "The beach shingle was full of tanks, vehicles, tractors, bulldozers and troops," the same after-action report chronicled. The shingle was also inundated with the bodies of the living and the dead, a shocking scene of carnage for the newcomers to behold. "What I saw gave me a chill," Captain Rob-

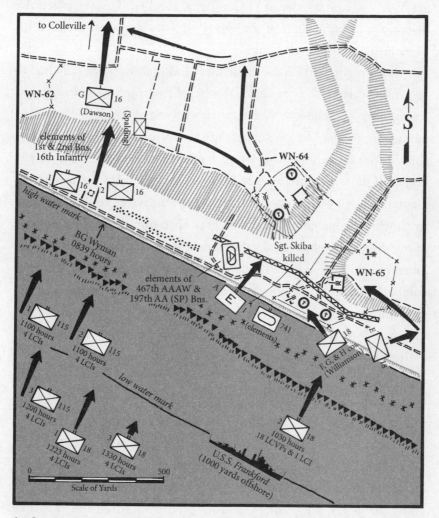

As Captain Dawson led a push for Colleville and Lieutenant Spalding's group neutralized WN-64, reinforcing battalions from the 18th and 115th Infantry Regiments landed around midday. The 115th was part of the 29th Infantry Division and landed in this area by mistake. In order to secure the Saint-Laurent Draw and open up a major route of advance inland, the Americans had to destroy an H677 casemate—or pillbox, in common parlance—located within WN-65 at the foot of the draw. A 50-millimeter gun inside this pillbox wreaked havoc on the invaders. A combination of attackers, including halftracks, tanks, individual soldiers, and, most notably, the USS *Frankford* neutralized the pillbox by about noon.

ert Murphy, commander of H Company, recalled. He was especially discomfited by the sight of stationary vehicles and men huddled for cover against the shingle bank.

Captain Richard Lindo, an artillery liaison officer, literally had to step over a dead body to make the beach, prompting a disengaged feeling that "somehow we weren't there and somehow all this was happening around us." Lindo's experience was a microcosm for Williamson's entire battalion—they were landing and advancing over the bodies of those who had already fought and bled for this hellish beach. Captain Murphy came upon a man lying in the water, rolling back and forth with the incoming surf. "I went over to him to see if he was one of my men," Murphy said. As the captain watched, horrified, the body lolled toward him and "his head was gone." He was not from Murphy's company. Lieutenant Richard Conley, a brand-new platoon leader in E Company, stumbled off the ramp of his Higgins boat and pitched face-first into the water. Soaked to the skin but otherwise okay, he gathered his platoon along the shingle and told them to get rid of their Bangalores and pole charges, since he could see that the 16th Infantry had already blown enough holes in the barbed wire beyond the beach. He happened to glance back in the direction of the waterline and noticed a lone American about a hundred yards away, walking parallel to the sea. "[I] heard an extra loud explosion, and when I turned and looked where he had been, it was nothing but a tall plume of smoke going up in the air." Conley and his soldiers figured the man had touched off a submerged Teller mine, but they never knew for sure.

In spite of a watery, sloppy landing under fire, Williamson's battalion made it onto Easy Red more or less intact, although most of the men came in on the east side of Exit E-1, which exposed them to fire from WN-65 and positions on the bluffs overlooking the draw. Inevitably, there was confusion as boat sections landed separately and commanders lost contact with one another. The shock of seeing the carnage and facing enemy fire only enhanced the sense of discombobulation.

Moreover, the 29th Infantry Division's 115th Infantry Regiment landed almost in its entirety, right in the 2nd Battalion's wake on Easy Red, adding to the disarray of the moment. Williamson spent most of his initial minutes on the beach making contact with his company commanders, organizing units, dispensing orders. His plan was for E Company to hook right and hit WN-65 from the west, while the rest of the battalion attacked up the draw.[1]

At the foot of the draw, a 50-millimeter gun inside a reinforced concrete H677 casemate pillbox continued to fire unabated. The narrow embrasure of the fortification faced east and was angled in such a way as to make it difficult to hit from anywhere but directly to the front. The gun had already destroyed numerous vehicles and inflicted an untold number of casualties upon the invaders of Easy Red, even though the German defenders inside the pillbox were probably now cut off from their comrades farther up the draw (the reader may recall the violent efforts of the Reynolds and Spalding groups to rout some of those other defenders). If the Americans were to take the draw and truly begin an unabated inland advance, the pillbox had to be neutralized. Sure enough, throughout the late morning, it began to attract the fire of nearly every American weapon with a feasible shot. Individual soldiers sprayed the area with rifle grenade, rifle, and machine-gun fire. At least two Shermans from the 741st Tank Battalion peppered the edges of the concrete embrasure. The tanks were vulnerable to return fire, not just from the 50-millimeter, but also from mortars. One shell exploded right next to Staff Sergeant Walter Skiba's tank, killing him instantly. His crewmen dragged his prostrate body out of the commander's hatch and onto the embattled beach, but found that there was nothing they could do for him.

Halftracks from the 197th Anti-Aircraft (SP) Battalion and the

467th Antiaircraft AW Battalion maneuvered into position either in shallow water or at the slope of the shingle bank to unleash a steady cadence of .50-caliber machine-gun bullets and 37-millimeter shells. Sergeant Hyman Haas, who commanded a pair of halftracks from A Battery of the 467th, found a suitable spot at the waterline from which to shoot at the pillbox. As he looked around Easy Red, he was stunned at the carnage. "I saw mutilations that I never expected . . . pieces of bodies, heads loose . . . a bloodied man . . . so bloody that he looked like he was painted." Sergeant Haas was breathing heavily, his eyes darting to and fro. He was dangerously close to Condition Black, the physiological state of shock and paralyzing fear that can lead to panic and incapacitation. Nonetheless, he focused on his job and gave the command to open fire at the pillbox. The adjacent M15 halftrack was equipped with .50-caliber machine guns. Haas could see tracer rounds zipping in every direction as the gunner fired. His own 37-millimeter gun shot several times, but the rounds fell short. He and the crew adjusted the range. "The next ten shots went directly into the port hole of the pillbox. We . . . fired one full clip and part of a second clip . . . and they went directly into the pillbox." Lieutenant Wallace Gibbs, a platoon leader in the same battery, remembered it as "thirty to forty rounds . . . fired into the opening." Puffs of dust, smoke, and concrete billowed from the pillbox as the shells scored hits.

The destroyer USS *Frankford* added to the overwhelming firepower. At 0950 Admiral Carleton Bryant, commander of the Navy's bombardment force, had radioed his destroyer group and ordered them to sail close to the beach and do whatever they could to support the hard-pressed troops; throughout the day, they were to provide crucial assistance. The *Frankford*'s skipper, Lieutenant Commander James L. Semmes, responded to Bryant's order by sailing his vessel straight at the E-1 draw for a point-blank confrontation with the pillbox. Like many other destroyers that day, the *Frankford* was not in touch with its fire control party, probably because that group was pinned down on the beach alongside so many other invaders. In order to get any kind of decent shot, the ship had to get close—very close. "The tide was in our favor at the moment," Lieutenant (j.g.) Owen Keeler, the gunnery officer, wrote. "Navigating by fathometer and seaman's eye, [Commander Semmes] took us in close enough to put our optical rangefinder . . . on the bluff above the beach . . . 300–400 yards away." There was a very real danger the destroyer could run aground and become a stationary target for German artillery, but Semmes was willing to take that risk.

On the beach, Tech Sergeant Jim Knight, a pinned-down member of a Gap Assault Team, watched in fascination as the ship glided inexorably toward the E-1 draw. "Even though she wasn't listing or smoking, my first thought was that she had either struck a mine or taken a torpedo and was damaged badly enough that she was being beached." Instead the sleek ship turned parallel to the beach and prepared to open fire. In the words of Captain Harry Sanders, the destroyer group commander, the ship thus "assumed the role of mobile artillery in direct support of the troops." However, the enemy camouflage, in addition to the smoke and chaos on Easy Red, still made it difficult, even at this incredibly close range, for *Frankford*'s spotters to see their targets. Eventually, Lieutenant Keeler noticed the direction in which one of the tanks was shooting and simply followed suit with a salvo of five-inch shells. "For the next few minutes he was our fire-control party," Keeler said. "Our rangefinder optics could examine the spots where his shells hit." Several of the five-inch naval shells smacked into the top of the pillbox, sending shards of concrete flying in every direction. Tech Sergeant Knight watched in awe as the *Frankford*'s guns blazed away. "I saw smoke leave the gun barrels, shells landed a few yards above my rock cover." The noise and concussion of the naval gunfire and the ensuing explosions were immense. "I remember being just lifted up when some of these shells went over us, and kind of slammed back down in the ground after the shell had gone by and exploded," Sergeant Alan Anderson, a halftrack section commander in the 467th, recalled. "It was an awful experience and the concussion was beyond belief. We were showered with debris, and with sand and smoke." By the time *Frankford* was finished, Anderson's hearing was gone (it would not return for several days).

The German gun crew, of course, was even worse off. Every direct hit from a five-inch shell felt like a combination of an earthquake and an explosion. Their hair was full of dust and concrete chips. Most likely some bled from the nose and ears. Emboldened by the copious supporting fire, groups of American soldiers worked their way close to the pillbox, around it, behind it, and added their own close-range fire. The surviving Germans surrendered. As Tech 5 Sponheimer, the medic from the 197th, saw them emerge from the pillbox with their hands up, he thought to himself, "I hope to hell none of those sons-of-bitches are wounded, because I'll have to work on them!" Some must have been wounded, but Sponheimer still got his wish. He did not have to treat any of them. Tech Sergeant Knight believed that the *Frankford* had saved his life and those of many other soldiers on the beach. "If you had not come in as close as you did," he wrote years later to veterans who had served aboard the destroyer, "exposing yourselves to God only knows how much, than [*sic*] I would not have survived overnight." Colonel Stanhope Mason later wrote to Rear Admiral John Hall, commander of the naval forces at Omaha beach: "Without that gunfire, we positively would not have crossed those beaches."[2]

1

The capture of the pillbox occurred sometime between 1140 and noon. With the objective taken, and the Germans mostly expunged from Exit E-1, General Wyman knew he could now push the newly arriving 18th Infantry soldiers through the draw and inland. What is more, the engineers, many of whom had been pinned down by the pillbox's 50-millimeter fire, could now get to work constructing an exit road at E-1. Wyman ordered Lieutenant Colonel Williamson to take his 2nd Battalion, move up the draw, and reinforce the battered 16th Infantry soldiers who had managed to make it off the beach. Starting at 1223, almost the same time Wyman gave these orders to Williamson, the 1st Battalion of the 18th Infantry, under Lieutenant Colonel Bob York, approached Easy Red. Because of the dangers presented by untrammeled mines and obstacles, York's people had laboriously transferred from LCIs to LCVPs. For these men, and those of the 3rd Battalion who followed the 1st Battalion about an hour later aboard LCIs, the apprehension of what lay ahead was nearly unbearable. They knew enough about the landing timetable to understand that they were several hours behind schedule. In the minds of most, especially the veterans, this meant only one thing—something was wrong. Other than that, their ignorance about what was happening on Omaha beach was near total (compared to them, General Huebner was awash in information). They had spent the morning hours in brooding anticipation, their minds plagued with dreaded thoughts of gruesome worst-case scenarios. It all amounted to a terrible fear of the unknown—possibly the worst, most dreaded form of terror, if for no other reason than the feeling of intense, powerless anticipation.

Lieutenant John Downing, making his third invasion, began to "get a sickening feeling in my stomach." He passed the time pacing back and forth from the deckhouse of LCI-489 to the deck, smoking cigarettes, drinking coffee, muttering worriedly with other officers. "We didn't like the delay in landing plans, but we couldn't appear concerned before the few men who were on duty on the deck." The apprehension was probably the worst for officers like Downing and Lieutenant Charles Ryan, a platoon leader, if only because of their immense responsibilities and the fact that they could not betray their inner fear or misgivings in front of their men. "There were about sixty men looking to me for leadership," Ryan said. "I knew that if I did my job properly, more of these men would survive than if I [failed]. For me it was duty first. I was affected by the spirit of the Big Red One."

The combination of inactivity, nervousness, and the monotonous rocking of the various landing craft produced a sickly feeling in many others, too. One soldier remembered that "most men were half sick and couldn't keep their food down." Such was the case for Staff Sergeant Donald Parker, who had gorged himself the previous evening on candied citrons, a tart, sweet fruit confection. "Never again have I eaten citron except in minute quantities," he wrote drily decades later. As he struggled to keep his stomach in check, a palpable sense of dread permeated the men around him. "Most of the faces were pretty sober. Men would glance at each other and shake their heads. Occasionally someone would try to tell a joke. There would be a few polite chuckles. No one felt like laughing. Some read prayer books, others, their New Testament. Some recited the rosary over and over." The pervasive, and nearly overwhelming, stench of diesel fumes did nothing to help queasy stomachs. In Private First Class Howard Johnson's recollection, the smell was strongest near the heads. "When I smell diesel fuel today, I am immediately transported back in time to the LCI," he said.

Sergeant Dean Weissert, heading into his first invasion, was surprised at the fear he noticed on the faces of the veteran soldiers around him as they talked about wives, sweethearts, and home. "I suddenly found myself living my past life over, starting from the time I started in a little country school in Gosper County, Nebraska. I thought about the many nights my father, my two brothers, and I sat around the kitchen table playing cards using a . . . Kerosine lamp for light. My mother would be sewing or baking something good to eat." Weissert closed his eyes and began praying earnestly. Another rookie, Private First Class Ralph Burnett, also saw his young life flash before him.

"Everything really does fly through your mind . . . everything you've ever done, everything you ever loved, everyone you've ever loved."

The fear was almost a physical presence. It had a smell, almost like sweaty body odor but more pungent. Everyone dealt with it differently—some tried to pretend it wasn't there; some became introspective; some fought the urge to panic; some just tried to think of other, more pleasant things. Few could forget it, though. "There is no way to describe that dreaded feeling of fear that persists," Corporal Edward Steeg, a mortar gunner, said. "It has to be experienced." Private First Class Elmer Seech had been with the outfit since North Africa, and he had seen plenty of intense combat, to the point where he was surprised he had survived this long. A moody fatalism overtook him (and many other veterans that morning). As Seech waited for the order to hit the beach, he turned to a buddy and said, "I'm so disgusted, this is my third invasion already and it's like I'm playing baseball, three strikes and you're out. I just wish they could take my right leg from the knee down, just to send me home."

Over the long months of training, and during previous operations, many of the soldiers had befriended the sailors and coastguardsmen who manned the landing vessels. Aboard LCI-487 one sad-faced veteran who had become friends with eighteen-year-old Seaman First Class Robert St. John offered him a beautifully adorned plate—probably his most cherished possession—that he had been carrying since North Africa. The soldier was convinced he would not survive the invasion and he wanted St. John to keep the plate. St. John refused, but the soldier was so insistent that he finally relented and took it, but only with the assurance that the man would be fine.

In the early afternoon hours, the 1st and 3rd Battalions landed on Easy Red amid largely similar circumstances to their comrades in the 2nd Battalion. "The gaps blown by the engineers in the underwater obstacles were few and narrow and the beach was under heavy concentrated artillery, and some machine gun and scattered sniper fire still fell in the sands," the regimental history chronicled. What is more, mines and enemy shells inflicted significant damage on several of the LCIs carrying the 3rd Battalion. The 3rd suffered eighty casualties just getting ashore (numerous casualties among the LCI crewmen only added to the toll). Among the 3rd Battalion dead was the soldier who had given his plate to Seaman First Class Robert St. John.

Once ashore, the newcomers gravitated toward the recently taken Exit E-1. They were wet, cold, scared, queasy, and exhausted from their many hours of tense waiting as well as their imperfect landing. Many waded through the flooded antitank ditch or the marshes. Commanders moved them along as best they could. Captain William Russell, the CO of K Company, had taken some fragments in the head when his LCI was hit by shell fire, and his face was a bloody mess, but he could not have cared less. He stood in knee-deep water waving his men forward in the direction of the draw. "Blood was all over his face," Private First Class Ralph Burnett recalled, "but he still was worried about his men getting across that beach." In the estimation of another man, Russell led the way "with utter abandon." Leaders like Russell probably saved many lives by promoting such a sense of urgency.[3]

With disorienting rapidity, the troops came face-to-face with the horrors of the beach. "I saw hundreds of dead and dying" along the shingle, Lieutenant George Duguay later wrote. "I saw amphibious tanks, unable to get traction on gravel and rocks, get blown to bits by German artillery." Lieutenant Hyrum Shumway almost stumbled over "a fellow on his hands and knees . . . in a kneeling position looking at me. His face was white and his hair fiery red." Shumway was so stunned at the dead man's lifelike appearance that he jerked backward and nearly stepped on a nearby mine. Private Lewis Smith, a rifleman and demolition man, took cover at the shingle and happened to glance at the men on either side of him. "On my left . . . he had a hole blown out of his back. It looked like he had taken a direct hit from a mortar shell.

On my right . . . the top of his head had been shot off, it looked like by machine gun fire. And this was my first combat." Private First Class James Furey was transfixed by the sight of a foot lying randomly on the beach. With morbid incongruity, he asked the man next to him, "Is that a left foot or a right?" Staff Sergeant Donald Parker, fresh from the nauseating aftermath of his citron feast, was following the rest of his company across Easy Red, stepping over the bodies of dead and wounded men alike. At one point, he came upon a young soldier in his death throes. Parker got down on his hands and knees, and leaned over the man. "Get a chaplain," the soldier said softly.

"I won't be able to find one now," Parker replied. "Our line will move any second."

The dying soldier reached out and grasped Sergeant Parker's arm. "Do something. I'm dying." He paused a few moments and then spoke again. "Let's repeat the Lord's prayer together."

"Our Father, which art in heaven, hallowed be thy name," they said in unison.

A shell screamed in and exploded nearby, prompting Parker to flatten himself on the ground beside the praying soldier. "When I raised up again, the war had ended for him," Parker later said.

The biggest impediment now for anyone trying to exit Easy Red was mines. Because of the tenacious German resistance, engineers had been able to clear only a narrow path, perhaps just a bit wider than a man's shoulders, through the mines along the E-1 draw. The path was marked by strips of glossy white engineer tape. Here and there, outside the cleared trail, among the grassy slopes and bramble, individual soldiers had marked live mines with wisps of olive drab toilet paper. "I've often thought about that white tape the combat engineers laid down before we got there and how many of them died getting the job done," Private First Class Howard Johnson later wrote. "You talk about guts!"

The path itself was the only feasible exit route off the beach for the newly arrived mass of 18th Infantry Regiment reinforcements (not to mention the 115th as well). It was the functional equivalent of pouring a barrel of beer through a funnel. What this meant for Colonel George Smith, the 18th Infantry's commander, was that his battalions had to stretch out in long, single-file columns as they moved up the draw. Moreover, they remained under a steady stream of mortar and artillery fire. Thus, the journey up E-1 was tense in the extreme, an exercise in patience, discipline, and controlled terror. "All infantrymen are taught the necessity for a safe interval (5–10 yards) between men expecting enemy fire and of course survival instinct dictates 'hitting the dirt' when fired upon," Lieutenant Conley wrote.

In this instance, though, the men could do neither. The columns of men were usually closely packed together; nor could they afford the luxury of diving to the ground to avoid shells lest they stray from the swept path and touch off mines. "We were 'bumper to bumper' in our anxiety to get off the beach," Conley explained, "and could only squat in place" to avoid enemy fire. "It was very narrow, and you had to keep your eyes on the man in front of you, and make sure you walked where he walked," Sergeant Frank Murray recalled. As his group steadily progressed up the draw, he noticed a man working his way back in the opposite direction. "There was no such thing as stepping aside and letting him pass, or stepping to the side and walking around us. He'd hug each man he came to, and they'd swing around keeping their feet on the path." When he reached Murray, the two men stood face-to-face, staring blankly for a moment before they realized they knew each other. "He was a friend of mine from the neighborhood where I'd grown up. We said hello to each other, [but] there was no time to talk." They briefly hugged when Murray's old friend sidestepped around him and then continued in this manner to the beach.

Lieutenant Teno Roncalio, leading a platoon from A Company, was in a spot where soldiers from the 115th, who were experiencing their first day of combat, were mixed together with the hardened veterans of his outfit. Artillery shells whistled overhead and exploded in or near the water. To Roncalio and the other Big Red One soldiers, the shells were obviously not meant for them and there was no sense ducking. The new men did not understand this yet; they ducked or squatted whenever they heard a shell. "This I recall as a unique distinction between green troops and case-hardened troops on being able to sense where a round was going to fall," Roncalio wrote. But some of the shells were exploding uncomfortably close. All the men could do was squat, hunch their shoulders, and hope for the best. Inevitably, some got hit. A pair of shells exploded near the leading troops of the 2nd Battalion. Fragments wounded Lieutenant John Genua in the leg. Major Elisha Peckham, the battalion executive officer, was badly hit in the head and neck. "Major Peckham's helmet . . . saved him from being killed," Lieutenant Downing, who saw him in the aftermath of the wounding, later wrote: "The shell fragment . . . penetrated the steel and cut his scalp, but its force had been slowed down by the helmet. Another fragment was imbedded in his neck." Private First Class Elmer Seech happened to come under an especially intense barrage, so much so that he braved mines by hurling himself into a nearby shell crater. "That's when I felt this hot sensation in my leg, a piece of shrapnel went through the back of my knee, up a little above the knee, and down through the calf and tore it all open. But luckily it didn't hit any bones." A medic got to him, bandaged him, and gave him a shot of morphine. Aboard ship, Seech had offered to sacrifice a leg to live through the battle; instead he made it out with only a damaged knee and a lacerated calf muscle.

In many instances, the troops saw the dead, dismembered bodies of 16th Infantry soldiers or engineers who had touched off mines earlier in the day and had paid with their lives. More commonly, they came upon live men who had tripped mines and lost feet or entire limbs. Most of the new amputees lay in place with bandaged or splinted stumps, buzzing on morphine, waiting to be evacuated. Lieutenant Conley observed one such soldier "lying just off the trail with the front half of one foot gone. But he was smiling. He knew he'd be going home." This attitude was not unique. Most of the maimed men seemed upbeat to those who saw them (perhaps their attitude was similar to that of Private First Class Seech—they would trade a leg to live through the war and get home).

Invariably, some of the 18th Infantry soldiers strayed from the path and ran into mines. Lieutenant Downing no sooner saw a heavily bandaged soldier—his face and chest "swathed in bloody bandages"—who warned him not to come close for fear of mines when the young officer heard a nearby explosion and was blown to the ground. "Dirt and pebbles hit my back and rattled on my helmet as I hit the ground," he wrote. The lieutenant was okay, but he could see that one of his men, Private First Class Chester Mayer, was not; he wore a stunned, stupefied expression. "He shot me in the ass and the head," Mayer said, pointing at a new replacement who had joined the unit just before they left England. Downing looked at the replacement. His face was white. He was quivering with tears. "His trouser leg was shredded, scorched and bloody. His foot was an unrecognizable bloody pulp. He had stepped on a mine, and in falling he had pulled the trigger of his rifle and the bullet had grazed Mayer's buttock and the back of his head." Elsewhere, Private Lewis Smith was carefully following in the footsteps of the man in front of him when he saw movement that did not look right. "One of our men had gotten out of the path, and he stepped on a mine and he was blown up immediately."

Progress up the bluff was slow to the point of excruciation. When Captain Frank Fitch's L Company started to come under accurate sniper fire—in addition to dealing with the mines and some incoming mortar shells—he decided to take matters into his own hands. "I saw him jump up from behind my position and run outside the taped area," Private First Class Howard Johnson, a bazookaman in the company, recalled. "A mine blew off a foot, and he fell back on the sand. Seconds later we saw him disappear in a cloud of smoke as a shell hit him direct." Johnson and the other men around him turned away in sorrow and disgust. Moments later, another group from L Company captured the sniper. As they prodded the prisoner in the direction of the beach, the young German pointed at the area off the path, smiled, and said, *"Minen."* Already angry at the death of their captain, the casualties the sniper had inflicted on the company, and the tension of negotiating the minefield, the troops were agitated enough to kill the young German. "Yeah, mines, we know it, you SOB!" many screamed menacingly. The guards hustled the POW away before the situation got out of control.

At last, the leading units made it up the trail, over the bluffs, and into hedgerow-lined fields where they began to assemble for an inland move. As Lieutenant Conley reorganized his platoon, the tension of the landing and the ascent began to take its toll on him. "I was shivering, shaking uncontrollably, and I was ashamed of it, until I noticed that all of the combat veterans of North Africa and Sicily were shaking just as much as I was. And I immediately felt better, to see the evidence that we all shared the same fear." Indeed they did.

It took hours, but the three battalions from the 18th Infantry, plus those of the 115th Infantry, made it up the draw and began the assembly process. This added about five thousand infantrymen to the American effort at Omaha beach. In traversing Exit E-1, the Americans, in essence, exploited a key weak spot—the equivalent of barreling through a slightly open door—in the German defense of the beach. The reinforcements consolidated American control of the draw to the extent that it became the key exit spot for men and vehicles on the 1st Division side of the beach. While the new units did not necessarily coordinate their efforts with the groups of 16th Infantry soldiers, and others, who were already off the beach, they relieved enemy pressure on them since the Germans now had many more invaders to deal with than before. More than anything, the successful landing of the 18th Infantry, and the capture of E-1, signaled that the struggle for the beach itself was ending in favor of a fight to get inland and stay off that beach.[4]

Chapter 7

INLAND

At WN-62, time was running out for the remnants of the German garrison, including Corporal Franz Gockel. Throughout the morning, he and his 7.9-millimeter machine gun had inflicted significant damage upon the American invaders. "Many were lying on the beach killed or wounded," Gockel said. "You could see when the tide rose some would move, crawling up the beach to get out of the water." The Americans responded with heavy fire of their own from rifles, machine guns, mortars, and tank shells. At one point, a shell exploded right in front of Gockel's earth-and-wood-reinforced dugout. "The weapon blew apart in my face. To this day I do not know what caused the explosion or how I survived." Curiously, in the aftermath of this near miss, all was quiet. Down to only a pistol to defend himself, Corporal Gockel crawled out of the dugout. He had not eaten in eighteen hours. Neither had another soldier that Gockel soon encountered. He asked Gockel to go back to the troop bunker at the rear of the strong point and fetch some lunch. Gockel crawled through the tunnels and trenches of WN-62, even as the battle soon resumed around him. On his way to the bunker, he stopped at one of the mortar Tobruks, where he helped the hard-pressed crewmen load and fire their gun. "They were dropping shells on . . . landing craft, or so they hoped."

A heavy pall of thick smoke hung over the area, restricting visibility to only a few yards in any direction. Gockel moved on to the troop bunker. Inside, he found bread, sausages, and milk that he and his comrades had bought the previous evening from a French farmer. He retrieved his pay book, his dog tags, a set of rosary beads, and a medallion from Lourdes given to him by his devoutly Catholic parents. On his way back to his post, Gockel shared some of the food with a pair of displaced machine gunners. After they finished eating, Gockel resumed his trek, but had to halt. "I wanted to go back . . . but the Americans were already there," he recalled. A bullet tore into Gockel's left hand, wounding three of his fingers. "That's a ticket home for you," a soldier who rendered him first aid said enviously. "We have no idea if we will ever get out of this inferno of fire." The wounded Gockel fled WN-62 and made his way back to the German command post at Colleville-sur-Mer, where fighting was now raging between the town's garrison and the leading groups of American soldiers who had made it off the beach. Gockel managed to hop aboard a truck with other wounded men and get to the German rear area.

Another young machine gunner, Private First Class Hein Severloh, was also nearing the end of his capacity to resist. He was aware that many of his comrades around WN-62 had been killed or wounded, or had drifted away, but his perspective was otherwise extremely narrow. All morning and into the early afternoon, he had almost felt like a worker on a production line—shoot, shoot, reload, shoot, spray incoming troops with his machine gun, pick off individuals with his rifle, then wait out lulls with a quick smoke, a snack, or a hurried conversation. For Severloh, there was nothing personal in the killing, just an animal-like struggle for survival. "They sure as hell would be doing it to you if they got the chance," he thought. Peering through the layers of smoke, he caught glimpses of the grim spectacle on the beach some seventy yards below. "There was blood everywhere, screams, dead and dying. The swell of the sea bobbed more bodies onto the beach."

Severloh's right eye was swollen shut from fragments unleashed by a near-miss explosion of a small-caliber shell. He estimated that he had fired nearly twelve thousand rounds from his piping-hot MG-42 machine gun and another four hundred rounds from his rifle. He was resupplied with ammunition by a dark-complexioned senior NCO whom he did not know. After so much shooting, Severloh's ammo stocks were finally dwindling. All that remained were several belts of night ammo, equipped with tracer rounds that would undoubtedly give away his position to American spotters. He fired a burst laced with tracer ammo. Just as he expected, he got a violent response. Three separate times, shells exploded uncomfortably close. The rounds were probably a mixture of tank and naval gun fire. Each explosion spun his gun upward out of his hands and sprayed an uncomfortable mixture of earth and pebbles into his face. He noticed movement to his left, turned in that direction, and saw a column of American soldiers moving carefully over a crest about two hundred fifty meters away (it was probably troops from C Company, 16th Infantry infiltrating off the beach). More shells burst around him. The Americans were clearly overrunning WN-62. Severloh left his position and ran about twenty-five meters to Lieutenant Bernhard Frerking's artillery observation bunker. Inside the small bunker, the thirty-two-year-old artillery observer was still calling in fire missions, but his gun crews were running low on shells. A lieutenant named Grass had been hit in the knee. He stood hobbled alongside Frerking. In another corner of the dank bunker, a terrified sergeant was weeping, moaning that all was lost. Lieutenant Frerking looked at the survivors around him and ordered, "We are withdrawing and abandoning the position."

Severloh retrieved his MG-42 from his post. He found that the hot barrel had sparked a smoldering grass fire. Frerking and his group left the observation bunker and gathered a few other soldiers in one of the trenches. It was time to go. The lieutenant and Severloh exchanged a solemn handshake. "You go next, Hein," Frerking said sadly. "[I]t's your turn. Take care." For the first time since they had met several weeks earlier, the lieutenant had addressed young Severloh with the familiar *"du"* as opposed to the more formal *"Sie."* A sense of melancholic gravity settled over Severloh. "These last seconds of our parting were full of sad misgivings," he later wrote. "A feeling of sympathy, warmth and attachment welled up . . . in me." After this emotional moment of reflection, Severloh leapt from the trench and began running for the rear as bullets spattered around him. The others soon did the same, covering one another as they went. Within minutes of leaving WN-62, the group was scattered by heavy U.S. fire. Frerking took a bullet to the head and was killed instantly. Everyone else was killed except for Severloh and Private First Class Kurt Wernecke, though both were wounded by machine-gun fire. They made it to Colleville-sur-Mer. Severloh was captured early the next morning.

By the time Severloh and his comrades bolted from WN-62, the German strong points in the 1st Division sector were largely neutralized. WN-61 was firmly under American control, in large part due to the heroics of Staff Sergeant Raymond Strojny. WN-62 was almost completely abandoned. The two 75-millimeter guns were both out of commission. The upper gun bunker had absorbed twenty-seven hits from tank and naval gun fire, seven of which had actually entered the embrasure before exploding. The lower gun casemate was hit eighteen times, including seven inside hits. The crews of these guns either had been killed or had retreated. None of the machine guns were still in operation, nor were the mortars. Resistance had collapsed at WN-64 and WN-65. Only WN-60 still resisted to any degree. Quite possibly, among the trenches and gun pits of the various strong points, individ-

THE FIGHT FOR COLLEVILLE

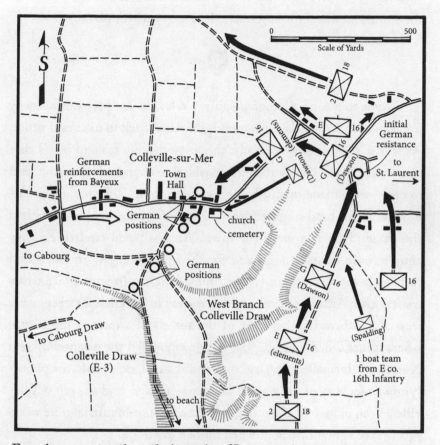

From late morning through the night of June 6–7, the two sides struggled to control this key town astride the main coastal road. Slowly but surely, as the Americans destroyed the beach defenses and advanced inland, they took over much of the town and the many hedgerow-lined fields that surrounded it. Not knowing this, in the early evening several U.S. Navy destroyers shelled the American-controlled portions of Colleville, including the venerable church, and inflicted heavy friendly-fire losses on Captain Dawson's G Company, 16th Infantry.

ual survivors were still a threat to the advancing Americans. But the coastal fortifications in which Field Marshal Rommel had invested such high hopes for repelling the invaders at the waterline had failed in their mission. The fight for Omaha had now shifted inland.[1]

Home to a couple hundred souls, Colleville-sur-Mer was a sleepy seaside farm village whose origins dated back to medieval times. As was so typical of Normandy, the forty-five houses and barns that constituted Colleville—stretching maybe seven hundred yards from end to end—were made of sturdy sand-colored stone. They looked as immovable as the head-high hedgerows and stone walls that honeycombed the maze of fields around the town. An L-shaped twelfth-century church, built upon what passed for the village's high ground, stood timelessly near the town center, immediately adjacent to a narrow coastal road. Anyone who climbed to the top of the church's steeple was treated to a breathtaking view of the sea about a mile to the north, where it met Omaha beach. The village embodied the essence of rural Normandy. It smelled of dairy cows, moist stone, rich earth, the photosynthetic fertility of kelly green hedgerow foliage, and sea salt. Colleville was an old-world place, harking back to a pre-industrial time when subsistence agriculture dominated human existence.

Captain Joe Dawson, striving as ever to lead his men by the highest standard, knew none of this. Nor did he have the time or luxury to appreciate the rise of hypermodernity so inherent in his presence and that of hundreds of other Americans in rustic coastal Normandy. To Dawson, Colleville represented only the locus of the U.S. inland advance, a key objective in the larger mission of establishing a firm beachhead. At the start of this momentous day, he had worried about whether or not his men would respect him enough to follow him in combat. But now, after they had shared the experience of landing at Easy Red beach, ascending the bluffs, and defeating German resistance, those worries were long gone for Captain Dawson. Ever since the first step off the LCVP, he had been at the forefront for his G Company, 16th Infantry. His men respected that, and he could tell. "A calm came over us," he later commented, "a mutual respect began to develop, and it was almost incredible. I felt it in every one of my men." He was right. They had begun to look up to and admire their captain. One of his soldiers never forgot "the pleased look on his face as he urged each man onward." Dawson was proud of the valor and professionalism his men had displayed during the fight to get off the beach. With the captain in the lead, G Company spread out and skirted carefully inland along a dirt road that led to Colleville. At one point, the Americans encountered a Frenchwoman standing under an oak tree. She smiled at Dawson, spread her arms, and said, *"Bienvenue en France!"* He returned the cheerful greeting.

Minutes later, as the company approached the town from the west, it ran into a German bivouac area. "There was some honeysuckle growing on the right of us," Private First Class Carl Atwell recalled. "We didn't know it at the time, but it was full of Germans." Machine-gun, burp-gun. and rifle fire erupted. Soldiers ran in every direction looking for good cover, but it was hard to find. The German machine guns shot low, sweeping bullets along the ground, a technique called grazing fire. "It was just tearing the ground up," Atwell said. "We ran . . . into a deep ditch [with] some stinging nettles about a foot and a half high. I didn't think nothing about the nettles. I hit that ditch." The nettles stung the skin of Atwell and his buddies, but they had no other choice than to hug the sides of the ditch as bullets passed overhead.

Confused fighting ensued. Groups of Americans and Germans traded shots amid the hedgerows, fields, ditches, and trees outside of Colleville. "It was small units firing and falling back that constituted our opposition and was both deadly and time consuming," Dawson said. Behind one hedgerow, Staff Sergeant Joseph Pilck and a group of soldiers caught a glimpse of Germans just beyond the hedgerow, displacing and shooting as they ran. Pilck told his BAR man, Nicholas Naganashe, a Native American soldier from Michigan, to open fire, but he did not respond. "I reached over and touched him on his head and found my hand filled with blood," Pilck later said. Naganashe was dead. Pilck turned to the other men and said, "Let's get the hell out of here."

It took the company more than two hours to subdue German resistance outside Colleville. Not until early afternoon were Dawson's people in position on the western edges of the town itself. By that time, the remnants of other 2nd Battalion formations—often prompted by Colonel Taylor's vigorous orders to get off the beach—had infiltrated inland and were joining the fight for the town, its environs, and the coastal road. Commanders simply corralled anyone they could, at times even people from different companies, and dispensed simple orders to get going. Captain Ed Wozenski, the commander of E Company, had spent the entire morning on the beach dodging heavy enemy fire and gathering anyone he could from his decimated outfit. "I remember distinctly taking my trench knife and pressing it in people's backs to see if they were alive," he said. One by one, he gently poked the point of the trench knife into the backs of prone men. If they moved, he would tell them to get up and follow him. If they did not, he kept going on the assumption that they were dead. It soon dawned on him, though, that some of the men who did not budge were very much alive. "I didn't realize that terror could be so great that . . . a live man could not turn around to see who was sticking a knife into him." He assembled about a dozen soldiers. Under cover of the dense smoke unleashed by burning tanks, burning landing craft, gunpowder, and grass fires, they moved westward to the E-1 draw. As they climbed the bluff, Wozenski happened to catch sight of a yellow flare off in the distance on the right-hand side. The captain knew that all of his section leaders and sergeants carried flares to signal they had made it off the beach, so he decided to head in the direction where he had seen the flare.

His instincts were correct. Within a few minutes, he came face-to-face with Tech Sergeant Phil Streczyk, the intrepid NCO whose boat section (under the command of Lieutenant John Spalding) had taken WN-64. When the New Jersey native caught sight of his captain, a wide grin spread over his face. Wozenski was equally happy to see his sergeant, a man for whom he had such great respect that he once called him "the greatest unsung hero of World War II." As Wozenski greeted Streczyk, he was stunned to see the sergeant deliberately step on a nearby mine. "What in hell are you doing?' Wozenski asked incredulously.

"Oh, don't let it worry you," Sergeant Streczyk replied. "[I]t didn't go off when I stepped on it going up the bluff."

The mine must have been previously defused by an engineer; or perhaps it was a dud. Regardless, Streczyk was right—it did not detonate. Once Captain Wozenski exhaled and his eyes returned to their sockets, he managed to cobble together a force of a few dozen E Company survivors. "They organized in two platoons and continued to sweep toward Colleville where they went into position on the right of 'G' [Company]," an E Company after-action report said. Major William Washington, the battalion executive officer, directed them to set up defensive positions around the road junctions west of town. Led by Lieutenant Rob Huch, the two skeleton E Company platoons made contact with their buddies from the Spalding-Streczyk group plus a few wayward G Company soldiers. Among them, they had about forty-five men.

Captain John Finke, the commander of F Company, first heard about the open beach exit from a battalion runner. The captain's mobility was limited by a heavily taped sprained ankle. He was getting around with the assistance of a cane—earlier in the morning he had selectively whacked men with that cane to keep them moving from the waterline to the shingle bank. He and his top NCO, First Sergeant Ted Lombarski, managed to shepherd about twenty men westward along the embattled beach and up the bluffs, similar to what Wozenski had done only moments before. Thanks to mines, visibility problems, and the confusion of the movement, the two leaders had trouble keeping their men together in one group. Lombarski dealt with the stragglers. Finke kept going and made contact with his battalion commander, Lieutenant Colonel Herbert Hicks, who had set up a hasty command post just in from the bluffs, in the lee of a hedgerow and a clump of trees, along a trail junction. Hicks was sitting on the ground, poring over a large map he had spread out in the dirt. Around him, dozens of soldiers were busily working. Some were stringing communication wire; some manned radios; others were digging foxholes, running messages for Hicks, or just sitting in place, resting. The area was under intermittent machine-gun, rifle and mortar fire, so the mood was tense.

Hicks greeted Finke. "We're under fire here and I want you to outpost our CP."

"I want to go on up to Colleville," Finke replied.

Hicks persisted that he wanted Finke's men to guard the battalion CP. Finke was a plainspoken man, a soldier's soldier who spoke bluntly to subordinates and superiors alike. "You've got to be kidding," he replied. "My job is to fight my men, not to protect the battalion."

Finke gestured at the men all around them and suggested they guard the CP. Hicks shook his head. "They're all valuable specialists. We can't waste 'em that way."

Finke refused to back down. "I'm going to look around here for you, sir, but I refuse to post [guard] your battalion headquarters when you've got plenty of people to protect yourself—that's your mission, not mine. My mission is to get up to Colleville."

"I gave you an order," Hicks replied.

Finke said, "I'll look around here and see what there is, and I'll tell you, but I'm not gonna sit around here with your battalion headquarters." Knowing the importance of the regiment's mission to push inland, Finke was confident that Colonel Taylor would back him up if

Lieutenant Colonel Hicks ever chose to court-martial him. Finke later commented, "He had more men than any rifle company . . . had left at that time except G Company."

Hicks was undoubtedly less than pleased with his subordinate's impertinence, but there was little else he could say. Finke gathered a group of his men and set off along the hedgerows in an effort to find the harassing machine gun. He chose Private William Funkhouser and another soldier to take the lead as first scouts. After a short time, Funkhouser and the other soldier passed through a hedgerow opening and into a field. German machine guns opened up, pinning them down. "I hit the ground," Funkhouser later said. "I couldn't see anything. I started crawling forward." The enemy fire got heavier and more accurate. A stitch of bullets splattered the dirt just ahead of him. Terrified, he rolled away, losing his rifle in the process, and took cover in a ditch. Back at the hedgerow, Finke and the others laid down fire to support Funkhouser and the other scout. A German mortar crew found the range of Finke's group and unloosed an accurate barrage. The mortar shells burst in a deadly staccato rhythm—boom, boom, boom. One of the shells exploded right next to the captain, so close that he thought he had set off a booby trap. "I got two fragments," Finke later said. "Two soldiers on my right flank got two fragments that went in the other direction." Finke was badly wounded, with a compound fracture of his right elbow and a broken tibia bone in the right leg—all this in addition to the original ankle sprain. The group managed to move him and the other wounded men back in the direction of the battalion CP (Funkhouser and the other scout were left behind, but escaped to safety on their own).

Finke was conscious, but in pain and losing blood. His face was pale and sweaty, the pallor often associated with shock. First Sergeant Lombarski and several men, including medics, gathered around and tended to him. Staff Sergeant Don Wilson had just fought his way off the beach with Private First Class Robert "Tex" Grigsby, a man who was, in Wilson's estimation, "one of those rawboned, 'weathered beyond his years' Westerners, twice sergeant, twice busted, but a hell of a 'field soldier.'" By pure chance, Wilson and Grigsby came upon Lombarski, Finke, and the others. The captain looked at Wilson and asked, "How many people have you brought off the beach with you?"

"Just me and Tex," Wilson replied.

"Go back down and bring up the others," Finke ordered.

"There aren't any others, sir, and the beach is still under heavy fire."

The captain did not seem convinced. First Sergeant Lombarski caught Wilson's eye and shook his head, a quick gesture that said not to worry about it. With Finke's wounding, all the officers of F Company were now casualties. As the medics evacuated Finke, he turned to Lombarski and said, "Sergeant, take over the company." Before the medics could take him away, he stopped them, thought for a moment, and then said, "Sergeant Lombarski, don't forget to court martial Delaney." The soldier in question, Private Clarence Delaney, was a cook who, just before the invasion, had written a letter to his girlfriend with some not-so-subtle hints about where and when the great amphibious assault would take place. "It was amazing that the captain still had this on the mind after having been wounded twice," his admiring radioman, Tech 5 James Thomson, later said. Finke was evacuated to the beach. As it turned out, part of his F Company stayed in place guarding the eastern flank of the battalion CP, while some individuals made their way inland toward Colleville.[2]

At the same time when the Americans were pressing for control of the town, German reinforcements from the 2nd Battalion, 915th Grenadier Regiment, 352nd Infantry Division arrived in the Omaha beach area. Their main mission was to consolidate control of Colleville, push the Americans back to Omaha beach, and retake WN-62. Many of these reserves had journeyed by bicycle from assembly points located some twenty-four miles to the south. Though they were hardly fresh, groups of them began to counterattack and put pressure on the 1st

Division penetrations, including the 2nd Battalion at Colleville. Throughout the afternoon, the two sides struggled for control of the town and the coastal road. Firefights raged among the hedgerows, fields, and country lanes. In an orchard astride a junction, the Spalding-Huch group clashed with the newcomers. "We . . . set up our defensive position to the west of Colleville," Spalding said. "We selected a position where no digging was necessary, often using drainage ditches." A line of hedgerows provided some cover and concealment. Huch had the most seniority, so he was in overall command.

German machine-gun and rifle fire erupted from somewhere beyond the hedgerows. Private Vincent DiGaetano, the flamethrower man of Spalding's boat section, had long since used up his weapon's fuel and discarded the empty tank. He was sharing a rifle with Private Fred Reese. DiGaetano heard movement, peered over the hedgerow, and saw German soldiers on the move. He turned to Reese, "Hey, Elmo, I see something!" Reese handed him the rifle. DiGaetano took aim, prepared to fire, but before he could squeeze the trigger, a blast of German machine-gun fire splintered the rifle and destroyed it. An instant later, a potato masher grenade arced over the hedgerow and exploded next to DiGaetano. Hundreds of small wood splinters and some metal shrapnel tore into him. "It wasn't like ours where the whole thing blows apart, fragmentation, you know," DiGaetano later said. "If it was ours, I would have been blown to bits." Most of the splinters did little damage, but one of them gashed into his upper thigh and blood trickled down his leg. Private Jesse Hamilton, a medic who had latched onto the group in the course of the day, crawled over to him and told him to head back to the beach where doctors could attend to him. But DiGaetano, having been through the hell of the beach assault, had no desire to return to that awful place. Hamilton told him to drop his trousers and he would see if he could remove the fragment with a knife. To keep from crying out in pain, DiGaetano bit down on a stick as Hamilton fished the fragment from his rear end.

Along the hedgerow the other soldiers alternated between firing retaliatory bursts and razzing their wounded buddy.

"Diggy got hit in the butt," several said with derision.

"It was too big for the Germans to miss," another wisecracked.

DiGaetano shook his head and thought, "Very funny, guys."

Moments later, the laughing stopped. At just the wrong moment, Sergeant Fred Bisco lifted his head for a quick look through the hedgerow. A stream of German machine-gun and small-arms fire hit him dead on. "He caught it in the face," Private First Class Walter Bieder remembered. "He had half his face blown away." Bisco's dead body fell to the ground. In a rage, the others pointed their weapons through, around, and over the foliage and fired back.

On the left flank, a G Company runner, probably sent by Captain Dawson, was working his way toward them through a neighboring field. An enemy machine gun opened up. The runner (possibly Private First Class Marion Tubbs) fell down in a heap. "After he fell," Lieutenant Spalding told an Army combat historian a few months later, "they fired at least one hundred rounds of machine-gun ammunition into him. It was terrible. But we do the same thing when we want to stop a runner from taking information." Spalding never knew what message the runner had intended to impart.

He and the others remained immobilized by the German presence, huddling against the hedgerow. "You had to lay flat right up against the hedgerow or you got nailed," Bieder said.

Beyond their line of vision, about a quarter mile to the east, Captain Dawson's first section warily approached the first buildings of Colleville, with Dawson himself in the lead. As they approached the church, they began to take sniper fire from the steeple. The church was surrounded by a neck-high stone wall. The steeple, stretching nearly five stories high, dominated the whole structure. Private First Class Carl Atwell was trailing behind his buddy, Private First Class John Hastings, when he heard the sniper open up from the steeple. "He shot right down on Hastings," Atwell said. "If I had been about three steps up, the Germans would have gotten both of us. Hastings twirled around and I tried to catch him. [He] ran around the corner of the building and fell." He lay against a wall, sheltered from the sniper's field of fire. When Atwell got to Hastings, he was bleeding badly and clearly in serious trouble. Atwell called for a medic, but it took several minutes for one to arrive. By then, it was too late. Hastings was in his death throes. "I want my momma," he kept repeating over and over. With a final death rattle, he perished. His lifeblood stained the old-world gravel of Colleville into a rusty, forlorn shade of red. Atwell struggled to keep his emotions in check.

At the same time, Captain Dawson, a sergeant and a rifleman (probably Private First Class Riley Willis of Alabama), managed to make it past the wall, get through a small courtyard, and arrive at the front door of the church, right in the shadow of the steeple. In addition to the sniper in the steeple, Dawson figured, the Germans must have an artillery observer in such a perfect spot. The captain and the other two men burst inside the church and immediately came under small-arms fire. The racket of the gunfire was earsplitting in such a confined space, and with stone walls, no less. Somehow, the Germans missed in their initial volley. The three Americans kept moving through the vestibule and into the sanctuary, where they battled with the Germans face-to-face. The American rifleman was killed. "He was shot by the observer from the tower," Dawson explained and then added euphemistically, "I turned and we secured the tower by eliminating him. The sergeant shot the other two Germans." The death of the rifleman and the killing at such close range of what must have been a German artillery observation team was undoubtedly a searing experience (years later he cryptically described it as "a little encounter"). But, for now, Dawson and the sergeant had no time to dwell on such matters. With the church secured, they left. "Just as I ran out of the church, a German shot at me," Dawson said. "Fortunately, I turned, recognized him and fired back, but not before he had fired another shot." The captain was carrying a carbine. The German bullet ripped through the five-pound rifle. "The bullet from this second shot came through the stock of the carbine and shattered it. One portion of the bullet went through my kneecap and the other portion went through . . . the fleshy part of my right leg which somewhat incapacitated me but I didn't think anything of it at the time." The larger bullet fragment lodged in his knee, causing it to swell up, eventually to twice its size. He made it across the street to a farmhouse with an enclosed courtyard where much of the company was in position. In spite of his wounds, he remained in command.

As reinforcements arrived from both sides, confused fighting continued to rage around Colleville. German commanders still hoped to recapture the town and push all the way to WN-62, but their efforts made little headway. "A heavy counterattack developed on all sides of the entire Company at this time, but was beaten off successfully with nine enemy killed in the town," G Company's after-action report stated. The report also claimed that the company took eight prisoners. Quite probably the German counterattack would have swept G Company from the town, and the remnants of E and F from its environs (including the hard-pressed Spalding-Huch group) if not for the timely arrival of the 2nd Battalion, 18th Infantry, fresh from negotiating its path through the mined bluffs above Easy Red. By following sunken roads and hedge lines, soldiers from this battalion made their way to the western edges of Colleville. "Germans had most of the gates and breaks in hedgerows zeroed in with rifles and machine guns and several of our men were lost as we advanced," one of the unit's post-battle reports said. "The ground was perfectly flat and cut up by thick hedgerows into small fields and orchards, we found . . . enemy in front of us but a large number behind us, between our position and Colleville. There were constant small skirmishes with small units."

There was very little coordination or command and control on either side, just a confused jumble of bloody encounters. In a preview of the hedgerow-dominated struggle that would soon unfold in D-Day's aftermath, commanders had difficulty controlling all but the most basic squad-sized groups. Visibility was limited, as was mobility. The stone houses of the town, and their surrounding barns, walls, and courtyards, limited the field of vision even more. Armor might have made a difference, but neither side had any on hand. Thus the fighting boiled relentlessly from hedgerow to hedgerow, lane to lane, wall to wall, stone building to stone building. It was hardly fertile ground for the sort of mobile counterattack to the beach envisioned by the Germans. As the afternoon hours bled away, so did the troops' momentum, lost among the maze of buildings and hedgerows. Time was their enemy; the counterattack required rapid movement and lightning execution to reach the beach. Instead, the confusion of the stalemate at Colleville favored the steadily reinforcing Americans. Minute by minute, hour by hour, the Germans were losing control of the ancient village.[3]

1

Several thousand yards to the east, just outside the seaside village of Le Grand Hameau, Sergeant Burton Davis and three other men from L Company, 16th Infantry were cautiously moving along a narrow dirt road. Burton's orders were to cut this road, assess its viability as a route of advance for the company, and scout for any evidence of a German presence in the village. Davis stopped to talk with a French civilian. As he and his men clustered around the civilian they noticed someone walking toward them. Glancing up, they saw immediately that the approaching person was a German. One of the patrol members raised his rifle and shot the enemy soldier. Within an instant, liquor-tinged German cries erupted all around them—the effect of the Teutonic voices drunkenly taunting them from somewhere beyond the

BEYOND WN-60

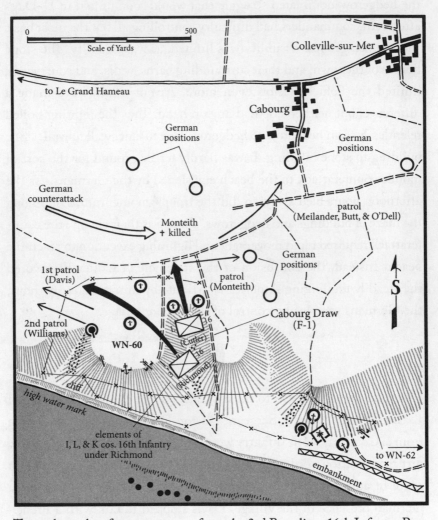

Throughout the afternoon, troops from the 3rd Battalion, 16th Infantry Regiment overwhelmed or bypassed German positions in and around WN-60. The Americans then patrolled east and west, setting up defended perimeters, thus securing the eastern flank of the entire Omaha beach invasion area. Lieutenant Monteith was killed while thwarting a German counterattack designed to regain control of that flank. This, in tandem with his courage leading troops up the draw, earned him the Medal of Honor.

surrounding hedgerows was surreal. "Sgt. Davis could hear them laughing and giving commands in English in the hedgerows," an Army historian later wrote after interviewing Davis and his comrades.

On the heels of the taunts came machine-pistol fire. Davis and the three other men beat a hasty retreat back to L Company's command post a few hundred yards to the west at a small fork in the road and reported what they had seen to Lieutenant Robert Cutler, who had taken command of the company after Captain John Armellino was wounded on the beach. As much as half the company had made it off the beach, up the F-1 draw and past or through WN-60. Cutler had deployed them by boat sections into a perimeter amid the hedgerows around the fork. Even as he sent Davis to the east (or left) in the direction of Le Grand Hameau, he sent another reconnaissance patrol to the west or right of the fork toward the small village of Cabourg. This group, consisting of Private First Class Lawrence Meilander, along with Privates Victor O'Dell and William Butt, advanced along a sunken lane that afforded some nice cover and concealment. When they reached Cabourg, they saw that it was only a small place—maybe ten houses situated along the coastal road, and honeycombed by hedgerows. Warily, the three Americans approached the first houses. A shot rang out from one of the buildings, and a bullet tore into Butt. Meilander and O'Dell crouched over him and administered first aid. As they were absorbed in this task, a group of German soldiers (numbering fifty-two, according to divisional records) emerged from the hedgerows, surrounded them, and took them prisoner.

As Cutler digested Sergeant Davis's report and wondered what had become of the Meilander patrol in Cabourg, a German counterattack slammed into the company's eastern flank. The attackers were supported by accurate mortar and machine-gun fire. Lieutenant Jimmie Monteith's section bore the brunt of the assault. Monteith, the college dropout with the fun-loving, disarming personality, had led his men off the beach under heavy fire that morning by enlisting the assistance of two Sherman tanks. The fighting had been so difficult that, at one point, the young Virginian had breezily asserted to one of his sergeants, "Man—one thing is for sure—this ain't our day." Since then, after ascending the draw and making it to the fork in the road, he had deployed his soldiers in a perimeter along several hedgerows just to the east of the company command post. Monteith's men were taking fire from nearly every direction, creating the impression among many of them that they were surrounded. Indeed several of the men were hit. "In that sector the enemy was not fighting from fixed positions but was moving around in the hedgerows and setting up automatic weapons," Private First Class Aaron Jones recalled. "In this manner a fairly large group started an attack on the position and set up machine guns on the flanks and rear. The Germans yelled at us to surrender because we were surrounded."

The purpose of the German attack was to push the Americans off their hard-won perch at the crest of the F-1 draw. With this accomplished they could reinforce whatever survivors remained at WN-60 and then unleash a deadly witches' brew of enfilading fire against the crowded masses of invaders along the entire expanse of Fox Green and Easy Red (in essence picking up where they had left off earlier that morning). It is highly unlikely that Monteith and his troops realized that such a troubling outcome could hang in the balance; they just knew they must hold. In response to the surrender entreaties, Monteith got up, moved in the direction of the voices, and fired a rifle grenade at one of the enemy machine-gun positions. "He stood in full view at 40 yards, and the first shot fell short," Sergeant Hugh Martin recalled. "The full fire of the gun was turned on him, but he held his position and fired the second grenade to knock out the position."

The crackling of small-arms fire slackened somewhat. Monteith trotted back and asked his platoon sergeant, Tech Sergeant John Worozbyt, for a status report on the platoon. Six men were wounded. Ammo was holding steady. Like any effective lieutenant and platoon sergeant,

Monteith and Worozbyt had developed a strong relationship based upon mutual respect and trust. Lieutenant Monteith noticed that his sergeant's hands were drenched with blood. "He expressed great concern for my safety and the safety of my men," Worozbyt later said. "Lt. Monteith, thinking it was my wound, cautioned me to be careful, and to see that the men were safe." Actually, the blood was from a casualty Worozbyt had treated moments earlier, but he never forgot the lieutenant's genuine affection and concern for his welfare.

They began to take more machine-gun fire. The bullets spattered against the foliage and the muddy ground. Lieutenant Monteith organized a squad of riflemen to lay down some cover fire while he again worked his way toward one of the machine guns. The throaty cough of several M1 Garands rose from the American-held hedgerow while Monteith carried out his lonely counterattack. "Under cover of the fire he sneaked up on the gun and threw hand grenades, which knocked out the position," Private Jones said. With this accomplished, Monteith crossed a two-hundred-yard stretch of open field and launched rifle grenades at another machine-gun position somewhere beyond the hedgerow. "He either killed the crew or forced them to abandon the gun," Jones asserted.

Back at the main hedgerow position, where Jones and the others were trading shots with the Germans, enemy rifle fire intensified. Monteith turned and noticed this. He started across the open field, no doubt with the intention of helping his men deal with this new threat (some thought he was going back for the tanks). In one terrible instant, an accurate burst of machine-gun fire cut him down. He fell dead from multiple bullet wounds. The charismatic, good-natured Virginian who had found his maturity and identity as a small-unit leader in the Army was gone forever. Though saddened by the death of their lieutenant, the survivors fought on under the leadership of Tech Sergeant Worozbyt and repulsed the enemy attack. Unit records claim that they inflicted thirteen casualties on the enemy force. For his leadership and valor in this action and earlier on D-Day, Monteith received a posthumous Medal of Honor. Several factors explain his dramatic success as a platoon leader: his personal initiative, his commitment to the welfare of his soldiers, his thoughtfulness, and his willingness to risk his own life to accomplish the mission—and he paid the ultimate price for that proficiency. Weeks after D-Day, upon receiving the terrible news of Jimmie's death, his older brother, Bob, who was serving as a naval officer, wrote sadly to their grief-shattered mother, "I think I know how you're feeling now. I've lost only a brother who was one of the finest and dearest people in the world, while you've lost a son who you've helped to grow into such a grand person—my heart nearly breaks for you."

Thanks to the efforts of Monteith, Worozbyt, and company, the German counterattack failed utterly and, with it, the last slender enemy hope of pinning the Americans back onto the beach itself. From the head of the F-1 draw and for several miles inland, there were now no continuous lines as such, just pockets of territory under the loose control of one side or the other. Captain Kimball Richmond, the universally respected I Company CO who was acting as a de facto battalion commander, knew he must expand the fledgling American perimeter above the bluffs. Impressed with the importance of linking up with the British invaders of Gold beach to the east, Richmond's main priority was to push in that direction and take Le Grand Hameau. He sent a combat patrol under Lieutenant John Williams along the dirt road (and this on the heels of yet another reconnaissance by Sergeant Davis's group).

Without question, the failure of the German counterattack diminished their ability to halt the American drive for the town. The Williams patrol made it there with no problem. "Lt. Williams outposted the main road with five rifleman and a light machine gun," the battalion after-action report noted. "After this had been done, a German scout car approached the town and was halted. Of its two occupants, one was taken prisoner and the other killed as he tried to escape." The team also captured two staff cars and another scout car in which they found "valuable papers, maps and a complete radio set." Richmond followed up this successful lodgment by cobbling together a combined force of 104 men from the three rifle companies, 79 of whom hailed from L Company. They reached Le Grand Hameau, set up defensive positions around the buildings, and continued patrolling. The capture of this little village was undramatic and anticlimactic, but it represented something very important. Not only had the 1st Division neutralized all the strong points along the division's landing beaches—though it is possible that some defenders of WN-60 were still holding out—thus opening the way up the bluffs and inland. More than that, the soldiers who had made it off the beach were steadily establishing a firm lodgment in Normandy. The ultimate meaning of this was that time had run out for the Germans to destroy the invasion at the waterline. From here on out, they were doomed to a defensive struggle to contain the expanding American presence inland from the beaches. In that sense, the battle had already transformed from an amphibious invasion to secure a coastal landing into the forthcoming campaign to liberate the entirety of France.[4]

Chapter 8

SUPPORT

Although success depended heavily on the infantrymen, especially those who had managed to make their way off the beach and inland, Omaha was still an exercise in combined arms. Thousands of sailors, aviators, and soldiers had jobs to do in support of the infantry. Fighter pilots roamed the skies beyond the beach, strafing enemy vehicles and soldiers, restricting the capacity of German commanders to reinforce their hard-pressed garrisons at the coast. The ships of the bombardment force continued to pound targets at will. Tankers who were fortunate enough to make it ashore and survive for any length of time added their own lethal shells to the staggering ensemble of fire-power. Along the beach, men with a dizzying array of military occupational specialties attempted to do their jobs as the day unfolded (to a great extent this was what led to the overcrowding that so concerned General Wyman). There were signalmen, wire teams, photographers, staff officers, ordnance teams, reconnaissance teams, military policemen, truck drivers, antiaircraft crewmen, mechanics, clerks, chemical mortar crewmen, civil affairs specialists, antitank crewmen, beached sailors and coastguardsmen from wrecked landing craft, sailors from the naval beach battalions, advance parties from joint assault signal companies whose job was to communicate with the bombardment ships, and liaison teams from the 1st Division's artillery battalions.

The artillery units had only minimal impact on D-Day, though the commanders expended rather substantial shipping, cargo, and logistical support to get them ashore. Brigadier General Clift Andrus's division artillery after-action report explained, "By late evening Division Artillery Headquarters Battery were complete and had assumed control of all artillery ashore. Elements of the 7th, 32nd and 62nd FA Bns [Field Artillery Battalions] were on shore and in position. The 7th FA BN was the only unit to fire during this period" after landing. The battalion lost half of its guns in the water and fired a grand total of twenty rounds on D-Day. The 62nd Armored Field Artillery Battalion, equipped with eighteen self-propelled guns, shot another 377 shells, of questionable accuracy and purpose, while the crews were still aboard their respective landing craft. Two of the guns were lost at sea. Crewmen could not land the rest until nightfall.

To some extent this overkill of patronage was necessary. The invasion, after all, required huge amounts of shipping, aerial transport, technological know-how, and matériel. Force O, the naval flotilla at Omaha beach, was staggering in its size and complexity—34,000 troops, 3,300 vehicles aboard nearly 200 landing craft and troopships supported by 2 battleships, 3 cruisers, 12 destroyers, 105 smaller bombardment ships, 33 minesweepers, and 585 service vessels. And this was just one of the landing forces at one of the Allied beaches. At a lower level, Colonel Taylor's 16th Infantry alone had 919 vehicles and was carried aboard 3 troopships, 6 LSTs, 53 LCTs, and 5 LCIs. In the view of one Army historian, the task of the Navy and other supporters was to "convey the ground forces to the area for assault on a hostile and defended shore, assist their landings by gunfire support, protect their lines of communication against enemy surface and underwater attack, and insure the flow of supplies for an indefinite period of future operations." Naturally, once ashore, all of these men and machines could not sustain themselves without a major logistical effort. This was, of course, especially true for the enormous, and decisive, campaign in northern Europe that was to follow the invasion. For this purpose, the Allies had stockpiled some 2.5 million tons of supplies in England, and, to defeat Germany, they would need every last bean, bullet, and jerry can of gasoline.

Regarding support for the invasion, though, the ultimate question is this: *What was actually needed for D-Day itself?* The answer is not that much. If one indicator of this was that the troops at Omaha beach landed with way too much equipment and supplies on their persons, then another was the glut of counterproductive vehicles and support troops present on the beach throughout the day. This made Omaha even more dangerous than it otherwise might have been. "There were many burning vehicles along the beach sending showers of projectiles from exploding ammunition and fragments of metal as mines and demolition materials exploded," an after-action report from the 6th Naval Beach Battalion said. As the report so vividly indicated, most of the vehicles simply served as juicy targets for German artillerymen and pillbox gunners; the majority of the support troops spent the day pinned down or wandering the beach in search of their fractured outfits or fighting as extemporaneous infantrymen. "Too many service troops were landed in the early waves," Major Edmund "Paddy" Driscoll, commander of the 1st Battalion, 16th Infantry wrote in an after-action critique. "This condition caused a crowded beach and increased casualties proportionately." Lieutenant Colonel Chuck Horner, commander of the regiment's 3rd Battalion, could not have agreed more. "Confusion was caused on the beach by the landing of nonfighting units before the beach was able to absorb them. This jamming of the beach hindered the operation of the infantry units in accomplishing their mission and caused extravagant loss of life and waste of equipment."

The bottom line was that all these specialists were not needed this early in the proceedings. In sending them ashore so soon at Omaha, the planners were thinking like logisticians, not assault commanders. As Horner succinctly put it, "[B]attles are not fought on time schedules or according to a timed plan." At Omaha beach on D-Day, all that really mattered, especially in the face of such determined resistance, was getting ashore and staying ashore. The sinews of war could take care of themselves in the days and weeks to follow. Until that time, many of the supporters were just in the way.

The artillery battalions serve as a representative example. What was the point of landing them on the first day? Given the formidable terrain at Omaha, the challenge of landing the heavily laden artillery batteries, the fire direction center equipment, and the like in such a constricted area, finding good shooting locations, sending out observers, and establishing the necessary communications was nearly an impossible mission to accomplish, even if the invaders had faced less resistance. Moreover, there was really no need for the artillery on the first day, not when the fleet could offer such a broad array of withering fire support. To be sure, Army-Navy liaison work and ship-to-shore communications were spotty on June 6. "Army and Navy cooperation must be close cooperation," Lieutenant Colonel Horner wrote in a perceptive critique a few weeks after D-Day, "commanders of both Army and Navy units working together physically until the last man and vehicle has landed from the unit. This was not done; and in four years of amphibious work I have never seen it done." As Horner indicated, this need not have been the case. The planners would have been far better served to address these solvable problems rather than spend so much time and energy on beaching artillery units that, given the sea and weather conditions, were difficult to land safely and were unlikely to have much impact on invasion day.[1]

The two supporting groups that undoubtedly played the most important role, and thus justified their extensive presence at Omaha, were engineers and medics, though even they had trouble focusing on their assigned duties amid the desperate fighting. The Gap Assault Teams, of course, functioned as the vanguard for the extensive engineering effort at Omaha beach, as did advance elements of the Big Red One's 1st Engineer Battalion. "The mission . . . was to clear minefields and other obstacles encountered, to open two exits from the beach, to prepare two vehicle transit areas, and to assist in establishing defensive positions," the 1st Engineers' after-action report stated a few weeks after the invasion.

Actually, this concise statement summed up the mission for nearly all of the engineers on the 1st Division portion of the beach. Generals Gerow and Huebner considered the engineers' assignment to be so important that they assigned a distinct combat engineer battalion to support each Big Red One regiment. The 37th Engineer Combat Battalion was attached to the 16th Infantry; the 348th Engineer Combat Battalion was with the 18th Infantry; and the 336th Engineer Combat Battalion supported the 26th Infantry. In addition, the generals supported the division with the 20th Engineer Combat Battalion and the 6th Naval Beach Battalion. With the exception of the 1st and 20th Engineers, all of these units were part of the recently formed 5th Engineer Special Brigade. The engineers' primary purpose was to construct roads through the narrow beach exits to facilitate inland movement of the vast host of troops and vehicles landing on D-Day and the days to follow. To do this, they also needed to clear the beach for the huge unloading operations necessary to support the inland push through Normandy and beyond.

Throughout the day, beginning with the 37th at 0700 and followed by the other units whenever and wherever they could manage to make it into the beach, these engineers did their best to engage in construction while in the midst of tremendous destruction. The first step was to sweep the beach of all impediments. In many instances, they made common cause with surviving members of the Gap Assault Teams to blow up or clear barbed wire and obstacles. By evening they had cleared and marked thirteen gaps and removed about 35 percent of the obstacles.

Mines were a constant problem. "The beach was so heavily mined, booby trapped, tank trapped with wire entanglements . . . that those of us who came in only 3 hours after the invasion began could pick out a safe trail thru the mine fields [only] by stepping over many of our buddies that had just fallen," Captain John Butler of the 37th later wrote. According to the after-action report of one platoon from the 336th, the soldiers salvaged six mine detectors along the beach and subsequently unearthed a dizzying variety of antitank mines, some of which the Germans had captured from the French Army in 1940. "Some mines were buried so deep so as to avoid detection, causing damage later to a road grader and a weapons carrier. They blew up beneath the pressure of oncoming tanks. Unaware that many anti-personnel mines and schu mines littered this place, many walked over it with unconcern." In one spot, as Private Fred Achterberg crawled on his belly, bayonet in hand, probing gently for mines, the soldier next to him, a thirty-nine-year-old draftee named Walsh, touched off a Schu mine. "There was a loud explosion and flame, gravel and darkness slammed me to the ground," Achterberg recalled. He was okay, but one of Walsh's feet was blown off. Elsewhere, another group probed for hours in a field marked with one of the ubiquitous *Achtung Minen!* signs the Germans had placed all over the bluffs and the beach area. The engineers found nothing except scrap metal and fragments sown at random, for the express purpose of wasting their time and energy in a futile search for mines.

For the "zappers," as the mine-clearance teams were often called, the work of finding and disarming the mines was exacting, the sort of labor that caused sweat to trickle down a man's back and his hands to shake. One mistake, no matter how small, could mean death or dismemberment. "The explosion of a good size mine is terrific," one engineer recalled. "Great quantities of smoke and earth blow skyward." According to the history of A Company, 37th Engineers, mine-detector crews began working their way up the E-1 road "openly exposing them-selves to the well directed artillery fire, and in clear view of the enemy direct fire from the high ground in the rear of the beach." The preferred method of clearing was to get down on hands and knees and probe with a bayonet or trench knife. Some of the engineers did their work with mine detectors, and that entailed standing up or, at best, crouching. Fortunately, many of the mines were planted near the surface and were not especially difficult to spot and disarm. When the mine crews swept an area, they laid down long strips of white cloth tape to mark the safe spots. They used miles of tape on D-Day.

The trouble for the engineers was that there were so many mines to deal with. Moreover, the engineers were often under such heavy fire that it was hard for them to focus completely on their job. In many instances, they fought as infantrymen or were pinned down uselessly for hours under heavy fire. Every minute absorbed in such survival mode came at the expense of the vital jobs of road building and beach clearing. The end result was delays, and lots of them. These delays were a source of immense frustration for commanders, particularly at the company level and below, since they were the ones most responsible for bringing order out of the pandemonium around them.

The commander of A Company, 37th Engineers was Captain Louis Drnovich, a man who had once played football for the University of California–Berkeley Golden Bears. Private First Class John Zmudzin-ski, who functioned as an informal scout for the captain shortly after they landed, thought of him as "a very brave man," and for good reason. Under heavy fire, Captain Drnovich moved around on foot, directing tank fire and guiding vessels into the best possible landing spots. "On one occasion, he personally rescued from drowning, two men who had become trapped in a wrecked Naval craft at the water's edge," a medal citation later said.

Near the E-1 draw, Drnovich and many others in his company got pinned down by accurate and devastating artillery fire. He eventually grew so impatient that he decided to take matters into his own hands. "[He] told me that our only chance for survival was to eliminate the direct artillery fire which was decimating us," Lieutenant James McCain said. Captain Drnovich told McCain to continue with the unit mission while he dealt with the shell fire. Drnovich apparently believed that the fire came from an 88-millimeter piece just over the bluffs. This was an incorrect assumption, since the Germans only had two 88-millimeter guns at Omaha and they were located in concrete casemates at either flank. The one on the eastern flank, at WN-61, was already out of action by the time A Company landed. The other one was at the Vierville draw, in the 29th Division sector. Nor did the Germans have any artillery situated just over the bluffs.

Brandishing an M1 carbine, plus a few grenades, the former college football player stood, and in the recollection of Lieutenant Robert Ross, the captain "cracked and charged off single handed." He disappeared from sight, somewhere beyond the shingle bank. For hours no one heard from him or saw him. He remained missing for the rest of D-Day. The next day, Lieutenant McCain found his dead body. Lieutenant Ross later called the captain's actions "a fine, if badly conceived reaction, to the apparently useless and endless sacrifice of his boys on the beach." Drnovich's willingness to personally face great danger to save his men was of course laudable; his valor and sense of honor were beyond question. However, in combat, there is such a thing as counterproductive bravery. By charging off alone after an unseen and elusive artillery piece that, in any event, was probably located miles away, Drnovich actually put his men and his mission in greater peril. His absence and lack of communication led to more confusion and more delay, not to mention greater pressure on his platoon leaders, who had to fill the leadership void he had created. As the day wore on, his troops could not help but wonder at his whereabouts and then search for him. Suffice it to say, none of this did the company any good. Drnovich's job was not to engage in a one-man, poorly armed artillery-hunting expedition—it was to clear the beach and build a road. If the artillery fire was making that impossible, and inflicting serious losses, then it would have made much more sense to send out a squad-sized combat patrol to deal with it, even if he led the patrol himself, or better yet, he could simply have moved his people out of the kill zone as best he could. Courage, especially of the kind that leads to the supreme sacrifice, should always have a productive purpose. Unfortunately, his was just the opposite.

The engineers also suffered from a paucity of vehicles and equipment, mainly due to the difficulty of landing such items safely at Omaha beach. Tank dozers and D7 armored bulldozers were especially useful for obstacle clearance and road building; they were impervious to antipersonnel mines and could probably survive a Teller mine blast as well. Their armor offered protection from bullets and fragments, too. Thus they were at a premium. No one knew this better than Ensign Joseph Vaghi, a naval beach master or traffic cop from the 6th Naval Beach Battalion. He spotted an empty dozer about twenty yards from the waterline and was concerned that either the rising tide would engulf it or the Germans would easily destroy such a stationary, and valuable, target. Moreover, he had always wanted to drive one of the things. With hardly a thought, the twenty-three-year-old officer hopped aboard the dozer, started it up, and began driving up the beach, away from the waterline. He had covered no more than ten or fifteen feet when one of his men ran up to the vehicle and waved at him to stop so that he could pass along a message from Vaghi's boss, Commander Eugene Carusi, the CO of the battalion. Carusi wanted him off the bulldozer immediately. "You are more valuable as a beach master than as a bulldozer operator," Carusi conveyed in no uncertain terms. Chagrined, but chuckling to himself, Vaghi dismounted and returned to the job of organizing the beach. "I always wanted to operate a bulldozer but this day I was denied the opportunity," Vaghi noted ruefully years later.

Because of the crowded conditions on the beach, the mobility of the bulldozers was limited. The drivers had to proceed very carefully lest they run over obstacles or wounded soldiers, who were often distressingly difficult to distinguish from the dead. Privates Vinton Dove and William Shoemaker of C Company, 37th Engineers took turns piloting one such armored bulldozer. While one drove, the other functioned as a dismounted guide. Under heavy artillery, mortar and small-arms fire, they retrieved several swamped tanks, halftracks and other vehicles from the water. Then, with Dove in the driver's seat, they headed straight for the shingle bank and, according to the company history, "filled in the huge anti-tank ditch that was preventing vehicles from moving inland along E-1. When the ditch had been completely filled, and vehicles were crossing their fill, they returned to the beach to remove tank obstacles." For their valor, both men received the Distinguished Service Cross. In conjunction with a dozer from B Company and others from a mislanded company of the 149th Engineer Combat Battalion, they built a wide enough lane to accommodate the movement of many vehicles up the E-1 draw.

At least one dozer operator who contributed to this vital mission was not so fortunate as Dove and Shoemaker. While Private First Class Jay Adams watched in horror, German artillery zeroed in on a dozer driven by one of his buddies. "He heard a shell coming in, and . . . jumped off, and the shell came in underneath his dozer and blew the bottom out," Adams said. In addition to blowing up the bulldozer, the shell detonated a trailer full of demolitions explosives he had been towing. "The only thing left [of him] was a short piece of the tongue."

Scheduled to land by 1300, the 336th Engineer Combat Battalion had the important task of turning the dirt trails of Exit F-1, at the eastern flank of Omaha beach, into a major road suitable for heavy-vehicle traffic. Without this road, Lieutenant Colonel Horner's 3rd Battalion, 16th Infantry could expect little tank support and no resupply trucks. The absence of such a road would also hinder the 1st Division's ability to link up with the British beachheads to the east. The 336th's orders called for the troops to complete this job by 1830 hours "sufficiently to pass 120 vehicles per hour." Instead, the troops landed late, at about 1500 hours, at Dog Green in the 29th Division sector, on the extreme western flank of Omaha beach, some four thousand yards away from their objective. In a long, ragged column, the troops arduously moved east, across the hellish expanse of the beach. They negotiated their way past wrecked and burning vehicles, as well as dead, dying, and wounded men, and briefly interloped in many intimate small-unit firefights. A D7 bulldozer, towing a trailer full of demolition explosives, followed the column and, though the two vehicles drew a great deal of fire, somehow neither was hit. Many of the men, such as Private Vincent Schlotterbeck, were lugging onerous equipment loads. "I had a mine detector which weighed about sixty pounds," he wrote in a letter to friends. "It was bulky and cumbersome to carry so [I] had to stop occasionally for a minute's rest." In addition to mine detectors, others lugged, in the recollection of one soldier, "bazookas and rockets, hand grenades, rifle grenades, mine marking sets, [and] 30 calibre machine guns." The unit even had a .50-caliber machine gun and some airborne demolition packs.

Upon reaching Easy Red beach, the column made it across the E-1 draw fairly easily. At the E-3 draw, though, they came under such intensive machine-gun and artillery fire that only two men could cross at a time. Not everyone made it. Sergeant Earl Metz was taking shelter behind a tree trunk (probably a felled obstacle) when he heard a shell scream in and explode nearby. "My corporal, Ted Wojtczak was ten feet away on my left," Metz said. "[The] shell . . . took the top of his head off," killing him instantly. Another explosion cost the life of Staff Sergeant Edwin Nenadal of the battalion's intelligence section. Elsewhere, a soldier from the operations section was hugging the sand, trying to present the smallest possible target. When he glanced up he saw "medics working in blood. [Private] Meryl Smith from A Co. was behind me. I heard some noise and looked around. His fingers were gone and there was blood running in the sand. Someone called a medic. He came running up. He wasn't from our detachment. He was on his knees bending over Smith when he was hit by shrapnel. When I looked up again he was bubbling out of a jawless face." About half the men had made it across E-3 when a German shell scored a direct hit on a bulldozer from the 348th near the shingle bank. In the recollection of one post-battle report, the stricken dozer "began to burn, sending up clouds of smoke which covered the gap. Under this cover, the remainder of the men dashed safely across."

It was 1700 hours before the first men finally reached Fox Green beach at the F-1 draw. As the men arrived, they immediately set to work clearing any remaining mines and carving out the road. "It was apparent that the grades of the proposed F-1 road had been miscalculated in the plan," one officer later wrote, "and it was decided to use the route that had been originally selected for a return road to the beach." The proposed road was actually nothing more than a narrow trail, totally unsuitable for vehicles. In essence, the engineers had to build a new road from scratch along the gentlest grade up the draw that they could find. The area was still under artillery and sniper fire. Under the protective snouts of two Sherman tanks, the zappers began climbing the draw, followed by the bulldozer. After the taxing odyssey of crossing the beach, the men were nearing exhaustion, but they pressed on nonetheless. "We were tired, damned tired, and it was the most difficult climb I have ever made," Private Schlotterbeck wrote.

Ever so slowly, they cleared a path for the dozer, which then pushed aside barbed wire, trees, and brush and leveled the ground. In its wake, engineers wielded shovels, picks, and axes. They smoothed the ground and put the finishing touches on the new route. "Working constantly under fire, the crews managed to clear a road about ½ mile to a point where it connected with the existing road," the 336th's D-Day after-action report said. Meanwhile, back on the beach, Major Robert Hunter, the battalion executive officer, commandeered a tank dozer whose leaderless crew was looking for some direction. "I asked them if they could help clear the beach of mined obstacles," Hunter later wrote. "They worked industriously on Fox Red beach . . . till dark in spite of some small arms fire and . . . artillery shots each time the tank stopped to drag the obstacles out of the way." The tank dozer also filled in an antitank ditch. By 2000, Fox Red and Fox Green were largely free of mines and the new F-1 road was ready for tanks, a remarkable achievement under the circumstances. Many of the zappers then began to clear mines from inland fields where commanders planned to set up water stations, medical collecting points, and supply dumps.

The engineers more than justified their presence at the 1st Division side of Omaha throughout D-Day. In addition to the construction of the F-1 road, by nightfall they were hard at work building exit roads at the E-1 and E-3 draws. Moreover, they identified and neutralized thousands of mincs, saving countless lives and limbs. They filled in antitank ditches, cleared all manner of impediments, and, in general, contributed substantially to the all-important effort to get off the beach and inland. In many instances, they assisted or fought alongside infantrymen or used their demolitions to clear enemy fortifications and trenches. Without them, the casualty numbers at Omaha would have been much, much worse.[2]

The assault troops of the 1st Division, and their many partners from the other combat branches, were all taught one overarching concept: the job comes first; all else is secondary. What this meant, as much as anything else, was that soldiers were not supposed to stop and help the wounded. There would be plenty of medics to do that, or so the thinking went. In reality, the medics were nearly overwhelmed by the high volume of casualties and the chaotic conditions. They carried no weapons. Theoretically, they were protected by the Geneva Convention, but this hardly mattered. In the haze, the smoke, and the tumult of the battle, a German soldier who was shooting at a landing craft or a clump of soldiers in a draw could hardly distinguish between armed and un-armed men, even though most of the medics wore armbands and hel-mets adorned with large Red Cross symbols. The job of caregivers and healers demanded an inspiring blend of admirable qualities: courage, forbearance, a calm demeanor, skilled hands, and, more than anything else, a self-sacrificial concern for their fellow soldiers. The medics' pur-pose was to sustain life in a world of death; by the very nature of their task, the welfare of others came first. Their casualty rates often rivaled those of riflemen. Their job was to go to the most dangerous places—where men had just been violently impacted by modern weapons—forget about their natural fear, put aside any feelings of rage against the enemy, stifle revulsion or squeamishness at the sight of horrible wounds, and think only of saving lives. "The medics had the roughest job," Private First Class John Zmudzinski opined, "because they had to try to patch up the wounded instead of looking out for their own safety." If a rifleman or a machine gunner cowered in fear instead of fighting, the lives of his comrades might well be endangered, but this was usually an abstract concept. For medics, there was no such ambiguity. If a medic gave in to cowardice and was unable to function, people would die, probably right in front of him. He had no choice but to act. Min-utes mattered, seconds even. The decisions he made, the actions he took, were suffused with unalterable significance.

At Omaha, the 1st Division was supported by several echelons of medical units that landed throughout the day. Like any infantry divi-sion, the Big Red One had its own medics. Each regiment contained a Medical Detachment with a headquarters section and three battalion sections consisting, in total, of just over 120 soldiers, including ten officers, most of whom were medical doctors or dentists. The enlisted men functioned primarily as litter bearers, clerks, technicians, drivers, and, most commonly, aidmen. In combat, the sections were often organized into aid stations, one for each battalion, each aid station commanded by the ranking surgeon. Many of the aidmen were parceled out among the various companies of the regiment, usually three medics per company. Their job was the toughest of any in the Medical Corps, yet few held a rank above buck sergeant. They lived and died with the combat soldiers. Invariably nicknamed "Doc," first aid was their trade—quick patchwork, relief of pain, and evacuation to the rear, if at all possible. They were the on-the-spot lifesavers, and the good ones were held in the highest possible esteem by the infantrymen.

At the division level, there was a medical battalion. In the Big Red One, this was the 1st Medical Battalion, whose primary mission was to treat and evacuate casualties. This battalion was designed to collect the wounded, stabilize them, and move them on to more permanent facilities to the rear. The 1st Medical Battalion contained four companies, lettered A through D, plus of course a Headquarters Company. Companies A through C were the collecting outfits. In addition to retrieving casualties and treating their wounds, their job was to evacuate them to the division clearing station, supervised and run by D Company, an outfit generally known as the clearing company. The 1st contained about 450 soldiers, including thirty-five commissioned officers, the majority of whom were physicians or dentists. In addition to the usual complement of aidmen, technicians, and clerks, many of the enlisted men were litter bearers, who physically moved wounded men on stretchers. This was a backbreaking, arduous process that siphoned off tremendous amounts of manpower since it often took four men just to carry one casualty (not to mention the fact that it was dangerous, too). The regimental medical detachments and the 1st Medical Battalion were highly mobile organizations equipped with dozens of jeeps, trucks, and ambulances. They were designed for mechanized ground warfare, not amphibious invasions; their vehicles were useless, in the way or, in most cases, simply absent on Omaha beach.

On D-Day, the Big Red One was also supported by attached units that more or less duplicated the function of the division's own medics. The 6th Naval Beach Battalion contained medical sections of its own. Each one of the engineer battalions did as well, though they generally numbered only about twelve to twenty soldiers. And each Gap Assault Team had a medic. The 61st Medical Battalion, which included additional collecting companies as well as special surgical teams from the 3rd Auxiliary Surgical Group, provided yet more medical support. In the main, their landings were as haphazard as those of their 1st Division medical brethren.

All of these medical units were formed around basic principles of linear warfare with the assumption of distinct front lines—find a casualty, treat him, remove him from danger, and transport him to a secure rear area. At Omaha Beach, this was impossible. There was no rear area; evacuation, throughout much of the day, was only a pipe dream. Wounded men who lay anywhere near the waterline were in real danger of drowning as the tide rose. In the recollection of Lieutenant Herbert Goldberg of the 16th Infantry Regiment's Medical Detachment, the medics were "pulling wounded from the surf, dressing their wounds and placing them in the best available cover." The bedlam and danger were such that doctors and aidmen were fortunate to find any secure spot to treat wounded men. One historian aptly wrote: "The situation was so bad that the evacuation of the wounded was toward the enemy." In the confusion, quite a few got pinned down or separated from their units. In many instances, medics lost important equipment such as litters, blood plasma, morphine syrettes, and first aid kits, before they ever even landed. They took to searching the men they treated for badly needed supplies. "From them they took first aid kits containing pain-alleviating morphine, sulfas and bandages," one doctor recalled. "They salvaged blankets which floated up with the tide." Another doctor, Lieutenant (j.g.) Paul Koren, said, "We had to. The beach looked like a neighborhood junkyard with burned-out tanks and landing craft piled all over it. Only there were bodies too and the wounded."[3]

A more difficult, traumatic, and adverse environment in which to function is scarcely imaginable. And yet all along Omaha beach, medics quite often and quite literally held the power of life and death in their bloodstained hands. For nearly everyone else on the beach, the main struggle was against the Germans; for the medics the fight was against death itself. Nowhere was this more true than between the surf and the shingle, where death stalked stricken men like the heartless Grim Reaper. The medics routinely swept through this kill zone, retrieving, at great personal peril, wounded soldiers, and then fought to the limits of human endurance to keep them alive. "The wounded lay with eyes glazed by shock and pain," correspondent Don Whitehead wrote. "The medics worked over them staunching the flow of blood from wounds, easing pain with hypodermics, giving encouragement. The medics had no thought for themselves, or if they did gave no visible indication of it." Corpsman Richard Borden was typical of so many along the beach. "Mostly we worked singly among the wounded and paired or begged help of a passerby from our unit or any other to get our patients moved to the scant protection of the dune." Far too many were beyond help. "There were people with half their face gone," Private Thomas Tolmie, of the 16th Infantry Regiment's Medical Detachment, later said. "You couldn't do much for them."

Private First Class Charles Shay, a nineteen-year-old medic attached to F Company, 16th Infantry, saw several floundering casualties and immediately rushed to their aid. He was a Penobscot Indian from Maine with a strong heritage of patriotism, sacrifice, and military service. Indeed, all three of his brothers were serving in the armed forces. As was true of so many medics, he knew that if he did not act, others would die. "Many of them were doomed to drown if nobody came to their help," he later wrote. "I have no idea how many wounded I helped that day." The number must have been substantial. He dragged water-logged men to the shingle bank, toward the Germans instead of away from them, standard fare for the medics at Omaha. He bandaged bloody wounds, applied splints to broken bones, tied tourniquets to staunch heavy bleeding, and gave plenty of morphine shots to pain-crazed soldiers. "It was difficult for me to witness so much carnage and not be affected emotionally," he said. "It was necessary for me to close my mind to what I was experiencing in order for me to be effective at doing what I had been trained for."

Shay was fortunate. Somehow he did not get hit. Others were not so lucky. At one point, he came upon a fellow medic, Private Edward Morozewicz, who also had been trying to move wounded men from the onrushing tide. Shay immediately recognized that his comrade had received a bad belly wound. "I knew that he was slowly dying," Shay said. "He was conscious enough to know who I was, and we greeted each other. I bandaged his wounds as best I could and administered a shot of morphine to relieve his pain. I knew there was no help for him. I said goodbye to him and we parted—forever." Not far from where Shay was operating, Sergeant Barton Davis saw "a medic rush out to help a wounded man in who was limping and staggering. A machine-gun burst cut them both down, slammed them is the word!! Then kept hitting them again and again. They both died instantly. That medic took an awful chance. He knew the fire was extremely heavy but never hesitated an instant." Another medic, Staff Sergeant Mark Infinger, came uncomfortably close to ending up like the man Barton had seen. Infinger and a buddy were walking along the beach, treating wounded men, when they found themselves in the crosshairs of unseen German guns. "There was all kinds of noise and life around us," Infinger wrote. "[T]hen the enemy starting shelling us with artillery. I dived behind some driftwood on the beach and when I got back up after the shelling there wasn't a sound or anything alive or moving as far as I could see."

All he saw around him was lifeless, dismembered bodies. For Infinger, the silence of the dead was truly awful. Elsewhere, Captain Johan Dahlen, a chaplain who, simply by the nature of his job, often worked alongside the medics, never forgot the sight of "a young navy 1st aid man sitting quietly giving plasma to a wounded man, seemingly oblivious of all the activity going on all around him as well as the enemy shelling."

The aidmen were in a state of perpetual crisis, dealing with an overwhelming number of casualties, many of whom were suffering from a multiplicity of terrible wounds. Danger and death lurked everywhere, lives hung in the balance, and difficult—indeed life-changing—decisions became routine. Tech 3 (a rank equivalent to a staff sergeant) Bernard Friedenberg, a member of the 16th Infantry Regiment's Medical Detachment, came upon a man whose leg was gone from the knee down. Friedenberg sprinkled the raw wound with sulfa powder, designed to ward off infection, and bandaged it as best he could. He extracted a morphine syrette from his aid kit, plunged the tiny needle into the man's thigh, gave him a couple of sulfa pills, and helped him wash them down with a swig of water from a canteen. As Friedenberg treated the maimed soldier, he heard many desperate cries for medical help from nearby wounded men. "I could see explosions from mortar and artillery shells and puffs of sand where bullets were hitting the beach all around me," he said. "I moved on to the next casualty and the next and the next. It seemed endless. I don't remember being frightened. I was too busy to think about being scared."

Friedenberg responded to a cry for help from a young soldier with a gaping, sucking chest wound. "The wound was not in a place where the bleeding could be controlled with a tourniquet," he said. "It was arterial bleeding, blood just spurting out. As he would breathe, the air would blow out of his chest." The twenty-one-year-old medic knew that the man would die if he did not get the bleeding under control. He placed a large compress over the wound and applied pressure. Tech 3

Friedenberg instinctively understood that the man's only chance for survival depended upon the application of constant pressure until someone could operate on him in a real medical facility. This might take hours and, of course, there were no such facilities at Omaha beach. Friedenberg could hear the cries of others who needed his immediate attention. He pondered what to do. If he left the man with the chest wound, he would surely die. If he stayed with him, then others might die. Which men would perish? Which would live? Which family would be altered forever? Which parents would never see their son again? Which child would grow up without a father? The answers to these terrible questions rested upon Friedenberg's shoulders. "Who should live and who should die is not a decision a twenty one year old boy should have to make," he wrote sadly. "It is a decision only God should make but where was God? I don't think He was on Omaha beach that morning." Instead, young Friedenberg alone had to make this momentous decision and he had to do it in a matter of seconds, with little opportunity for reflection. He chose the many over the few. He gave the man with the chest wound a shot of morphine and moved on to help the others. "For more than fifty years I have wondered if I made the right decision and I know I shall never stop feeling guilty." In fact, he suffered from post–traumatic stress disorder for decades (an all too common affliction for guilt-ridden combat medics).

In some cases, the decisions affected limb rather than life. At Fox Green, when Captain John Armellino, the commander of L Company, 16th Infantry, got hit in the leg, the fragments severed one of his arteries. A harried medic applied a tourniquet, sprinkled sulfa powder, and bandaged the leg. "You could hardly walk the beach without stepping on the body of a dead or wounded soldier," Armellino recalled. The treatment stabilized the captain's condition, but it could not, and did not, stop the bleeding altogether. For that, he needed immediate evacuation or else he would lose the leg. Instead, he and many of his wounded men waited all day on the perilous beach, a delay Armellino could ill afford. At night, when a landing craft finally did arrive to evacuate them, Private James Jordan offered to carry Armellino to the boat and place him aboard, but the captain was too good a leader to think of himself first. "He refused and told me to go," Jordan wrote, "I always felt if he let me take him, he would have had immediate medical attention and possibly his leg." As Jordan indicated, the captain lost his leg.

With no time for niceties, the medics were confined to treating men quickly and gathering them, as best they could, in some semblance of a secure spot. Major Charles Tegtmeyer, surgeon of the 16th Infantry, established a crude aid station in a hollow about twenty-five yards away from the regimental command post, just below the crest of the plateau overlooking Exit E-1. Tegtmeyer sent his aidmen and stretcher teams to retrieve wounded men strewn about the area and haul them to this collecting point. Some of the injured men were stuck in minefields. Tech 3 Friedenberg, having moved beyond the beach, came upon several such stranded men and quickly went to their rescue. "Using my trench knife to probe for mines I crawled into the mine field and carried several men out one after another." There was still one more man and he was panicked, crying for help. Friedenberg crawled back into the minefield. When he reached the wounded soldier, the man rolled over and reached for Tech 3 Friedenberg. As he did so, he tripped a Bouncing Betty mine. Friedenberg heard the distinctive "pop" as the mine left the ground. He hugged the ground. "The . . . explosion was deafening and was only a few feet over my head," Friedenberg later wrote. "The shrapnel passed over me and I wasn't wounded but the poor soldier I was going for was actually torn apart. I had blood and pieces of him spattered all over me." Later, when Friedenberg teamed up with Tech 5 Earle Bailey to retrieve yet another wounded soldier who was stranded in a minefield, Major Tegtmeyer would not let his medics go until engineers swept the field. "Eight mines had to be removed before they reached the man," Tegtmeyer wrote. Both Friedenberg and Bailey received Silver Stars.

Dr. Tegtmeyer sent out word that all wounded were to be collected in his little improvised treatment center. "The Battalion [Medical] Sections were instructed to bring their wounded to the Regimental Aid Station as it was unwise to take them to the beach, which was under intense mortar and artillery fire," Lieutenant Goldberg wrote in a history of the detachment. "Only the 1st and 2nd Battalions brought their wounded to the Regimental Aid Station, the 3rd Battalion section being too far to the [east]."

All day long the casualties trickled in. Eventually, there were about eighty patients at the aid station, including Major Dave McGovern, the regimental air liaison officer, who had broken a couple of ribs, and Captain John Finke, the CO of F Company, who had a compound fracture of his right arm, a broken right tibia, and a badly sprained ankle. The busy Tegtmeyer treated them and many more. One of the worst casualties had a bad chest wound. Tegtmeyer examined him and realized that he needed an immediate blood plasma transfusion. The doctor had trouble getting the vital fluid to flow properly into the man's veins (undoubtedly the difficult conditions had much to do with this problem). Tegtmeyer tried and discarded two defective bottles. "A third worked and we were able to get the stuff into him," he recalled. "A few minutes later, his pulse improved and he felt better." Captain John Settineri, the 1st Battalion surgeon, treated another soldier who had taken a bullet to the chest, in the vicinity of his heart. "[The bullet] had nicked the edges of two little notebooks he carried in his left breast pocket." Doctor Settineri examined the man and found that the bullet had punctured the skin of his chest and exited directly out of his back. "His condition was amazingly good. Heart action normal. He had not spit up any blood. The bullet had ricocheted around a rib without injury to vital organs."

Tegtmeyer, Settineri, and the other medical men stabilized such wounded soldiers by liberally applying fresh bandages, administering plenty of fluids, and keeping them as comfortable as possible with blankets and morphine. The medics even dug foxholes and slit trenches for the wounded men. This was fortunate because Tegtmeyer's aid station and the other smaller collecting points sprinkled around the beach area were under a steady drumbeat of shell fire. Tegtmeyer was conversing with Colonel Taylor and Captain Lincoln Fish, commander of the Antitank Company, when one of the shells exploded nearby. Fish sat down, exclaimed, "I'm hit," and clutched his abdomen. Dr. Tegtmeyer opened Fish's jacket and shirt and took a look. "On his abdomen was a large swollen circular weal—a fragment had hit a can of cheese in his pocket." Tegtmeyer had no sooner breathed a sigh of relief than he heard the cries of several more wounded men who needed his help. "In the midst of the wounded I found my dental technician Cpl. [Leroy] Kisker crumpled in a heap, blood pouring from the side of his neck. A fragment had cut him thru the trapezius muscle. The impact of the fragment had been like a rabbit punch and the boy was completely helpless. We dressed the wound rapidly and helped him to his slit trench."

In hopes of protecting their charges—and themselves—from the dangers of enemy fire, medics from the 61st Medical Battalion established a crude collecting point in a pair of makeshift tents near Exit E-3 (probably alongside the pillbox that had housed the 88-millimeter gun). The medics collected and treated the wounded men wherever there was room—most likely even inside the pillbox. "Here the attached surgical teams gave expert emergency medical care and casualties were sheltered from artillery fire," the unit's annual report related. "This station sheltered at least 50 seriously wounded men." Discarded dressings, helmets, boots, and bits of clothing intermixed with stacks of German shells and personal items left behind by the enemy soldiers. Wounded men lay on blankets or litters or simply wherever there was room. Private Clayton "Ray" Voight, a BAR man from E Company, 16th Infantry, who had taken a bullet in the hand during the first moments of the invasion, went inside the pillbox for treatment, but he could hardly stand what he saw and smelled. The air reeked of burned powder, burned flesh, sweat, and the coppery smell of spilled blood. Wounded men moaned and screamed in pain. A badly wounded tank crewman was so heavily wrapped in bandages that, to Voight, he looked like a mummy. "It was the worst thing that ever happened to me, being in there," Voight later said. "The people in there were hysterical. There were people with arms off, and it was just too much to imagine." Unable to stand it any longer, Voight left the pillbox, only to come upon a dead body lying unceremoniously near the entrance. The grisly sight filled him with anger. He turned away in disgust.[4]

Under the conditions prevalent throughout D-Day on Omaha beach, it was almost impossible for doctors to perform any substantial surgery. The medical units of the 5th Engineer Special Brigade, in particular the 3rd Auxiliary Surgical Group, were created to do just that. In essence, the eight-man surgical teams of the 3rd were supposed to function as all-purpose forward field hospitals; again, though, the incorrect assumption of the planners was that these medical personnel would do their work on a reasonably secure beachhead. They were not truly prepared to operate in the middle of a running battle without proper equipment, instruments, lighting, and shelter. "With nothing but morphine, plasma, and dressings, how could they hope to do the job they were supposed to do?" Clifford Graves, the unit's historian, wrote. "How could they treat patients with peritonitis, with fractured femurs, with deep chest wounds? Was this what they had been practicing for these many months? It all seemed utterly futile, frustrating, and fantastic."

In fact, the discombobulation of these surgical teams led to some hard feelings against them on the part of the 1st Division commanders and medics. Lieutenant Colonel Chuck Horner, commander of the 3rd

Battalion, 16th Infantry Regiment, claimed in a scathing, exaggerated post-invasion critique that "their work was nil on D-Day. I personally observed thirty doctors digging foxholes on the beach at about 3 p.m . . . when hundreds of men were dying on the beach from lack of medical care or else drowning because there was no one other than fighting troops to move them from the incoming tide. The excuse offered by these so called practitioners of medicine and surgery was that they had no equipment. These doctors were carrying their blanket rolls, but not one medical kit. At least, if they did have them none used them in time to save hundreds of lives." Major Tegtmeyer welcomed one group to his aid station only to form the opinion that "they . . . were useless. They were without equipment of any kind, no litters and their men would not act as litter bearers nor would their commanding officer order them to." Tegtmeyer claimed that they "were only interested in a place of shelter from enemy fire. I told them to dig themselves foxholes further to the left, get in them and stay out of the way."

These were understandable, cogent criticisms, but not entirely fair. The men whom Horner witnessed digging foxholes were almost certainly not all doctors (it is debatable whether there were even thirty physicians together at any one time among all the medical units operating in the 1st Division sector). Most likely many of the diggers were technicians whose orders were to prepare positions of safety from which to treat wounded men. The implication that their dereliction cost hundreds of lives is hyperbole. To be sure, the team with whom Tegtmeyer dealt should have assisted him in any way possible. It hardly mattered that they would have been outside their element since surgery was their expertise, not first aid or movement of wounded men. However, Horner was incorrect in his assertion that non-divisional medics did nothing on D-Day. In fact, they established two aid stations at the apex of the E-1 and E-3 draws and cared for many wounded men on the beach amid substantial danger. The aidmen of Captain Prentiss Kinney's

A Company, 61st Medical Battalion, for instance, operated from afternoon through the evening on the beach, saving anyone they could. "Casualties were collected in small groups of 6, 8 and 10 and placed on the beach for removing to Hospital ships in the channel," he later wrote. Private Mark Altman, a member of the 61st, plunged into the sea and personally saved two wounded men from drowning. For this act of bravery, he received a Bronze Star. Doctors from the 3rd Auxiliary Surgical Group cared for many of the wounded in and around the pillbox aid station at Exit E-3. "In the semi-darkness, confusion became confounded," the unit history stated. "Prostrate forms were everywhere. Dead and dying lay next to those who might still live. To reach a litter in a far corner required sharp eyes, steady feet, and a strong stomach. The task of creating order was superhuman." For fear of drawing enemy fire, doctors draped blankets over themselves and their patients while they administered transfusions and performed makeshift surgery using only the crude illumination of a penlight shakily held by an orderly.

The real threat to the lives of the wounded came not from any sort of failure on the part of the medics, but from their inability to get them out of harm's way. The fact that wounded men were often moved forward, in the direction of the enemy, said it all—for most of the day, there was really nowhere to avoid danger with any certainty. If wounded men could not get in-depth medical care on the beach (and they almost never could), then it was truly vital for them to be evacuated to ships offshore where they could get the care they so badly needed. The faster this happened, the better. The longer a seriously wounded man lay untreated on the beach or the bluffs, the better chance that he would die. All day long, men waited in vain for evacuation. At times, this prompted tense encounters between medics or combat soldiers and boat crewmen whose orders prohibited them from evacuating casualties. In many instances, medics struggled mightily under fire to manhandle wounded men to a nearby landing craft, only to watch dumbfounded as the craft deliberately pulled away rather than receive the casualties. The soldiers tended to interpret the exodus of sailors and coastguardsmen as stemming from a lack of courage on their part. One company commander wrote that "a few more seconds of endangering their own lives would have saved the lives of many others."

In reality, though, the boat crewmen were just following explicit and unyielding orders. "My first impulse was to get some of the wounded," LCVP coxswain Joseph McCann later said, "but this was against all orders and we were constantly reminded of this by the control boats." Like those of nearly every other coxswain, his instructions were to turn around, get more troops or vehicles, and land them, all according to an unyielding timetable. In response, some medics, like Tech 3 Friedenberg, simply took matters into their own hands. He treated a man with a belly wound who he knew would not survive if he did not get prompt medical attention aboard a ship. Friedenberg saw a Higgins boat land on the beach and unload its troops. When the coxswain wasn't looking, he dragged the wounded soldier to the boat and threw him aboard. The coxswain turned his head and shouted to Friedenberg that he was not to bring back any casualties. "Okay, Mac, throw him overboard!" Friedenberg shouted defiantly. Of course, some of the landing craft crews, such as Ensign F. E. Boyer's LCVP group from the *Empire Anvil*, did pick up and even treat wounded men. "There were many casualties on the beach," his boat report said, "so under Mr. Boyer's direction his boat crews carried stretchers and administered what first aid they could. There was a noticeable lack of medical aid." Boyer's actions were the exception (as the final sentence indicated). Most of the crewmen followed their orders to the letter. The wounded were left ashore to wait and cling to life as best they could.

Here was yet another conceptual failure of the Omaha beach landing. The planners had earmarked so many landing craft for extraneous units—such as the aforementioned artillery batteries—that it created something of a void in medical evacuations. The rigid landing timetable did no good, either. Given the desperate circumstances prevalent on Omaha beach, medical evacuations would of course have been problematic regardless, but these misplaced planning priorities made a bad situation significantly worse. Some of the shipping used to land unneeded trucking companies and artillery batteries could have been better employed to transport wounded men from the beach to the comparative security of the ships offshore. "During the first twelve hours of a beach assault, all medical emphasis should be placed on Evacuation," Dr. Tegtmeyer adeptly commented. There is no way to tell how many lives were lost due to the paucity of amphibious medical evacuation craft, but the number was substantial (nearly every doctor or medic could relate a tale of a patient or patients lost for lack of any way to get them off the beach). Given the laudable commitment of the World War II U.S. armed forces to provide excellent medical care to servicemen, this failure of concept, planning, and sheer humanitarianism is rather stunning. It happened for the same reason the troops went ashore with such heavy loads—because planners and commanders, especially at corps level, were too preoccupied with logistics and timetables, at the expense of practicalities.

Not until well into the evening hours were the medics able to evacuate casualties in any appreciable numbers. The beach was still under intermittent artillery fire. Wounded men were hauled aboard Higgins boats, DUKWs, or other small craft and ferried several thousand yards offshore either to troopships like the USS *Henrico* or, even more commonly, to LSTs. "Oftentimes the LST's and smaller seacraft would merge, and casualties either walked on to the decks or were carried there on litters," historian Deborah Bonanni wrote in a comprehensive study of medics in the Normandy invasion. Often the sailors used ropes and pulleys to hoist stretcher-bound wounded men from landing craft to the decks of ships or LSTs. Private Steve Kellman, who had taken fragments in the leg at Fox Green beach, ended up on an operating table aboard an LST. "A doctor was there, and they cut my clothing off me and cleaned me up the best they could," he later said. "The doctor immediately went to work on the shrapnel wound in my leg, and after about an hour's work I was taken below and put into a sailor's bunk." He caught a couple hours of sleep until a sailor woke him, gave him something to eat, and shaved him. The man did such a nice job with the razor that Kellman asked if he was a barber in civilian life. The sailor replied that he was not a barber but had learned to shave people while working with his undertaker uncle to prepare bodies for viewing. "This was a rather ironic note to this whole episode," Kellman said, "and I laughed about it when he told it to me."

As the wounded started to arrive in large numbers, the doctors and corpsmen toiled desperately to save lives. "They worked for hours amputating arms and legs, removing shrapnel, patching bullet wounds, and trying to calm down some men that were completely out of their minds," Seaman Ferris Burke, a crewman on LST-285, recalled. The scenes of horror that unfolded aboard the various ships almost defied belief—blood, gore, desperation, anguish, sheer human trauma. "The wounds were terrible," Pharmacist's Mate Roger Shoemaker, a corpsman aboard the USS *Henrico*, recalled. "One man lay quietly on a litter smoking a cigarette, with five machine-gun wounds in his chest. Another had one of his buttocks shot off, exposing six inches of the huge sciatic nerve. We worked throughout the day and into the night. We saved many. One we were unable to save was a German prisoner who died from internal bleeding."

Aboard LST-288, Pharmacist's Mate Joseph Carlo was awash in the sights of "bandaged bodies, plaster envelopped [*sic*] limbs, sightless eyes, warped minds, and some from whom the breath of life had been taken away. We worked for hours trying to save mangled, tortured bodies. Some had lost an arm or a leg; some had severe head wounds, charring flash burns, mutilating shrapnel cuts; others were emotionally shocked by their experiences with violence and death and were in a depressed state." One of those mentally and emotionally traumatized men merely sat on the deck, trembling and smoking, his youthful brown eyes staring in shock at nothing and everything. "At the sight of fire—even a match to light a cigarette—he threw himself upon the cold steel deck, trying to dig a hole to hide in, even with his bruised, torn fingers," Carlo said. The soldier's screams were like those of a wounded animal. "His soul, his mind, his spirit had been crushed by 'man's inhumanity to man.'"

Carlo and the other medics worked as gently and efficiently as they could on the herd of wounded men. They gingerly wiped dirt, sand, oil, and grease from burned and torn skin; they gave tetanus shots; they sprinkled sulfa powder on cuts; they gave out pills and made sure the men swallowed them; they administered more morphine shots than they could ever count. At one point, Carlo, another corpsman, and a physician worked feverishly to save the life of a soldier who had lost both of his legs, "exposing two gory, jagged stumps, which I hurriedly wrapped with reams of gauze bandage to arrest the flow of blood." The other corpsman lay next to the maimed man and, with a needle in the arm, gave him a direct blood transfusion. This was all to no avail. The soldier died on their table. "In this dimly lighted damp cavern-like 'hospital', crowded, littered with blood soaked men, our little medical group fought death; and everywhere there was the pungent smell of rotten gangrene, fuel oil, sand, sweat, human-smells of uncontrolled urine and feces, ether, vomit." Aboard the ships and onshore, scores of other medics did the same.

For the Big Red One, Omaha beach was costly beyond the ability of any words to convey. But, without the vital support of the engineers and the medics, it would have been immeasurably worse and much more dearly won.[5]

Chapter 9

BEACHHEAD

Shadows were beginning to chase light away from the gullies, bluffs, and draws of bloody Omaha beach. As late afternoon gave way to early evening, the growl of tank engines could be heard over the cascade of receding tides, the steady din of shell bursts, and the hollering of distinctly American voices. For many of those GIs who were deeply anxious over the possibility—even expectation—of a German panzer counterattack, the sound of armor was not especially welcome. But they need not have worried. The tanks were friendly Shermans from B Company, 745th Tank Battalion. Thanks to the heavy surf and the obstacles, their landing at Fox Green was hardly smooth, but they incurred no losses from enemy opposition or other causes. This revealed something about the nature of the battle as evening approached. Whereas any tank attempting to land on the 1st Division beaches earlier in the day was lucky to survive for more than a few minutes, armor could now land more or less unmolested. With the invasion no longer

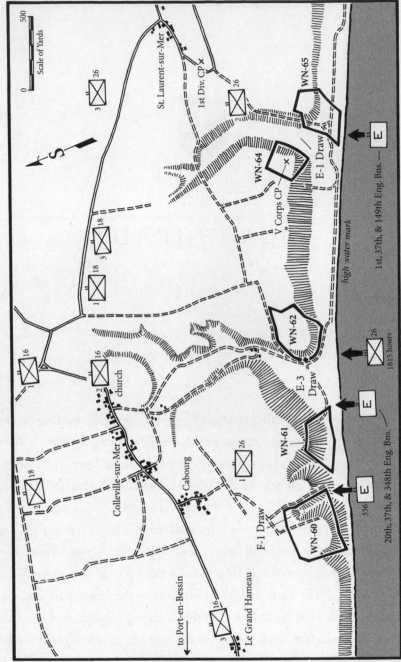

The 1st Infantry Division's nascent beachhead on the evening of June 6–7, 1944. There were no true front lines as such, just perimeters held by one side or the other. Throughout the night, engineers labored to clear mines and build roads in the newly captured draws while small groups of soldiers patrolled and sometimes clashed in violent, but largely anonymous small unit actions. The price of victory was steep: The Big Red One and its attached units suffered more than fifteen hundred casualties on that longest day.

in doubt, and a tenuous beachhead established, the main issue was no longer survivability but mobility. "We had more problems . . . with bodies laying around on the shoreline," Tech 5 Eddie Ireland, driver of a tank named Betty, later recalled. No driver had any desire to crush the remains of dead Americans under their tank's treads (though it probably did happen). In hopes of avoiding this, foot soldiers carefully moved the bodies of their dead comrades aside and waved the tanks through. A column of tanks from B Company followed in the wake of laboring parties from the 336th Engineer Combat Battalion while they built the exit road at F-1.

By no means was this a safe or smooth process. When the engineers finished their work, the tanks slipped past them and, with assistance from members of the 3rd Battalion, 16th Infantry Regiment's Intelligence and Reconnaissance section, continued their ascent up the draw on the new road. One of the Shermans detonated a mine, blowing a tread off and disabling the tank. Another tank veered off the road and ran into a mine. "This delayed the following tanks at least an hour until the road was cleared around the two tanks," the 336th's history said. The advance resumed, albeit with the loss of yet another Sherman to a mine. Once atop the bluff, the survivors took up station and, in the recollection of one engineer, "fired their 75s [main guns] all night long." To the west, at the E-1 draw, a handful of other B Company tanks joined with the few Shermans from the 741st Tank Battalion that had made it through the day's fighting. Together they provided fire support for the troops who were fighting in and around Colleville.

Along a line of hedgerows a few hundred yards southwest of Colleville, the Spalding-Huch group—about forty-five men in all—was involved in sporadic close-quarters fighting, and they were running low on ammunition. Several of the men were down to one remaining clip. Spalding himself had only six rounds left for his carbine. Because German fire seemed to be coming from every direction, some members of this group formed the impression that they were surrounded. A few of them briefly contemplated, and discarded, the notion of surrendering. Huch and Spalding huddled with the other leaders, Lieutenant Jim Krucas and Tech Sergeants Phil Streczyk and Calvin Ellis, to figure out their next move. They decided on a fighting withdrawal in the direction of the beach, where they assumed they would encounter friendly units. Since Huch had seniority and thus overall command, he felt it was his duty to lead the group out. "It's only in combat where you realize at all just how much responsibility an officer has," he wrote to his parents a few weeks later. "Success is measured not in what you say or how you look, but in what you do, how you did it, and was [*sic*] the lives it cost worth it. What I'm trying to say is that out here one really *feels* his responsibility."

Under cover of watchful BAR men, and with Huch in the lead, the soldiers crawled along a ditch, initially in the direction of Colleville and then the beach itself. "We kept ten yard intervals between men going back and there wasn't a shot fired at us," Private First Class Walter Bieder said. He and the others were pleasantly surprised at the lack of opposition, since the Germans seemed to be all around them. The staggered column of prone Americans reached a road (probably the coastal route that connected Colleville and Saint-Laurent). One by one, the men took turns running across the road and then resumed their creeping odyssey in another ditch. "As we crawled along, we passed a German machine gun with two dead Germans and one live German," Lieutenant Spalding later wrote. "Without saying a word we exchanged the German's life for our own safety." When it was Spalding's turn to warily crawl past the enemy soldier, he noticed a distinct twinkle in the man's eyes.

At last, after an exhausting journey through the ditch, the embattled group made contact with men from C Company, 16th Infantry and, after that, with Captain Wozenski and the tattered remnants of his E Company, 16th Infantry, the Big Red One unit that had absorbed the worst losses of any on this terrible day. Wozenski was a true leader of men who cared deeply for his soldiers. The sight of Huch, Spalding, and the other survivors brought home to the captain the high price his company had paid. Tears filled his eyes. "Where are my men?" he cried rhetorically. "Where are my men?"

Lieutenant Spalding, the former sportswriter from Kentucky, was emotionally and physically wrung out from his many brushes with death and the grave responsibility of caring for the members of his boat section. Yet he had no chance to rest. "We took up a defensive position five hundred to seven hundred yards from our original positions . . . closer to Colleville," he said. "We were still in the hedgerows and astride enemy avenues of approach. We had been in almost constant contact with the enemy since we hit the beach." They were supported by machine guns from H Company. As Spalding supervised, some men catnapped while others kept watch. Fortunately, their section of the line remained quiet for the time being. Among the thirty-two members of the Spalding-Streczyk boat section who had hit the beach shortly after H-Hour, two were dead and eight had been wounded. Those who made it through the day's ordeal without a scratch came to think of this as something of a miracle. "No man had a right to come out alive," Spalding later commented. Seven of the men, including Spalding and Streczyk, received the Distinguished Service Cross for their actions on D-Day.[1]

In Colleville, fighting still raged among the sturdy stone barns, walls, and houses. Captain Joe Dawson and his soldiers controlled the western buildings; the remaining Germans were situated along the eastern edges of town, and then as far east as tiny Cabourg a few hundred meters away. In the steeple of the church, Lieutenant John Shelby and his mortar observation team from H Company, 16th Infantry were scanning the area for targets. From the seaward side of the steeple, they heard the telltale shriek of an incoming shell. The projectile smashed against the steeple's facade. Shelby and the other soldiers knew exactly what this meant—the Navy was bombarding Colleville church! They quickly descended the narrow steps out of the steeple, left the church, and took cover. Beginning at 1815 hours and continuing on and off for the next hour and a half, at least three, possibly even four, U.S. Navy destroyers hurled five-inch shells at Colleville. They especially focused their fire on the church and its steeple since it provided such an ideal observation point. "It is believed that this church was being used as an observation post for mortar fire, since the beach at this time was apparently being bombarded apparently from inland," Commander George Palmer, skipper of the USS *Harding*, wrote in the ship's war diary. According to Palmer, his ship fired 133 rounds. The USS *Emmons* and the USS *Baldwin* collectively added at least 66 more. The war diary of the USS *Thompson* claims that, from 1812 to 1822 hours, the ship fired 23 rounds "at church concealed in gulley behind 'Easy Red' beach." The fact that the destroyers were aiming at the church meant that their fire was bound for American, not German, positions.

The ships had no communication with Captain Dawson and G Company. In fact, the naval shore fire control party that was attached to the company had all become casualties and their radios were inoperable (pointing out, once again, the fragile, almost afterthought nature of communications between the ground combat units and their supporting ships for the invasion). As a result, the destroyer crewmen were operating under the erroneous assumption that the Colleville church was still in German hands. The effect of their misguided bombardment was devastating. Each shell weighed fifty-five pounds and was capable of caving in a roof, smashing a hole in a wall, and killing or wounding anyone within many meters in any direction. "It leveled the town," Captain Dawson said. "[A]bsolutely leveled it." The church steeple was pulverized; stony debris collapsed into the nave and the churchyard. Many other buildings were reduced to rubble. Men took cover in ditches, foxholes, and barns. Still the shells kept screaming in and exploding. Unable to communicate with the ships, Dawson frantically ordered his men to shoot flares and pop yellow and orange smoke in hopes that observers aboard the ships would realize they were shooting at friendly troops. Still the bombardment continued. One shell exploded about fifteen feet away from Captain Dawson and Lieutenant Eugene Day, his weapons platoon leader. The two officers somehow did not get hit, but fragments severed the heel of a nearby rifleman. "When that happens, you say a prayer whether you're religious or not," Day later commented. Staff Sergeant Joseph Pilck and a buddy had taken cover in the church from enemy sniper fire only moments before the barrage began. Although shells pummeled the steeple above, they remained unscathed. At one point, Pilck peered through what remained of a window and saw "two American soldiers killed and some wounded in the church yard."

A pall of milky-colored masonry dust combined with the smoke and haze of battle to produce a sensation of cloudiness. Cordite fumes from the naval shells were "so intense that all of 'G,' including the aid men attending the wounded, had to carry on in gas masks," the soldiers said in a post-combat interview with an Army historian. As the shelling ebbed and flowed, the casualties mounted. Men were killed by fragments or concussion, wounded by flying masonry or shrapnel, concussed into a stupor. Finally, at around 1930 hours, a livid Dawson succeeded in conveying a cease-fire message through 2nd Battalion headquarters and on to the destroyers. The proud Texan, who was so preoccupied with pushing himself to perfection, could neither forgive nor forget what he considered to be an inexcusable error on the part of the Navy. "I was angered by it," he said, "angered beyond all measure because I thought it was totally disgraceful. And I was quite bitter about it. That was the worst tragedy that befell us on D-Day, with the exception of losing the men from the hit on my boat." Major William Washington, the battalion executive officer, was equally disgusted with the needless and avoidable loss of life to friendly fire. More than that, he was angry at the loss of a prime observation post for the division's eventual push inland, deeper into Normandy. "I actually thought it was pathetic that we captured a church steeple . . . only to have it shot down by the U.S. Navy."

Casualty estimates from the incident varied. Major Washington put the number of killed and wounded at fifteen; company records indicated that eighteen men had been hit. Tech 5 Lawrence Krumanocker, the company clerk, contended that the shelling killed eight men and wounded another thirteen (if true, this meant that, among the thirteen G Company men killed on D-Day, eight lost their lives from the Navy's fire). Dawson even claimed decades later that the friendly fire had inflicted sixty-four casualties on his company. Regardless of the actual number, there is no question that the mishap caused major losses, crippled morale, and severely hindered the company's ability to take the rest of Colleville on D-Day. As a result, an uneasy stalemate prevailed in the town that night, albeit one in which the American presence in the area grew steadily stronger and the German steadily weaker. Not until the early-morning hours of the next day did G Company secure the town for good. According to Dawson, the final and perhaps most bitter irony of this tragedy was that "POW's taken by 'G' the next day said they had not lost a man during the shelling."[2]

Even as the deadly five-inch shells rained down on Colleville, more troops were landing on Fox Green and Easy Red, just in time to reinforce the 1st Division beachhead. All day long, the soldiers of the 26th Infantry Regiment had remained aboard their ships as a floating reserve, shrouded in apprehensive ignorance about the events unfolding on Omaha beach. Sallying forth primarily from LCIs and LCVPs, the regiment hit the beach at second low tide, between 1803 and 1930 hours. Seasickness was rampant. One soldier vomited so much into a barf bag that he splashed the back of the man in front of him. "Use the goddamn bag," the aggrieved man growled. "Blow it out your ass," the vomiter replied. "[T]he goddamned bag is full."

Like their predecessors in the other regiments, many of the troops found themselves dumped in head-high water, pulled down by the weight of heavy loads, struggling just to make it ashore. "It seemed like a hundred yards to the beach and, weighed down by the full field pack, rifle, gas mask, and bed roll, it was very difficult to move in that much water," Staff Sergeant Mel Rush recalled. Lieutenant Colonel Derrill Daniel, a former entomologist turned commander of the regiment's 2nd Battalion, was pleased to see that "most simply walked on toward shore without losing their equipment—they obviously wanted to be on *land.*"

Once on the beach, they soon witnessed the terrible carnage from the day's fighting, a disquieting and traumatic experience for most. "It was quite a sobering experience for an 18 year old, which I was, to see so many dead still sloshing around in the water like so many logs," Private First Class Charles Toole later wrote. The ramp of Captain Frank Dulligan's LCVP lowered right onto a pair of corpses lying at the waterline. "A sickening feeling," he later remarked. Sergeant Rush was horrified by the sight of "destroyed tanks, half tracks, jeeps and other equipment strewn all along the shore. One picture I can't forget was the sight of a burned out half track with a soldier at the wheel, burned to a crisp." Fires still raged, and noxious smoke poured from many of the destroyed vehicles. Dismembered bodies lay seemingly everywhere. Private Kenneth Romanski came upon a dead body whirling along with the pounding of the surf. "As the waves came in the body would roll. And . . . on the body was his leg, which was holding on by a chunk of meat about the size of your wrist. The body would roll and then the leg would roll. Then the leg would roll back and then the body would roll back. I mean, that was just something I won't forget."

Nor was the beach safe. Enemy artillery shells continued to stream in with terrifying frequency and accuracy (some soldiers even reported enemy machine-gun and small-arms fire, a possible indication that Germans were still alive and fighting from the fortifications of WN-60). As a group of officers congregated to organize the movement off the beach, a bevy of shells roared in and burst among them. Lieutenant John Simons, the intelligence officer of the 2nd Battalion, and Lieutenant William Hume, the executive officer of D Company, were killed. Several others were wounded, including Captain John Kelly, the commander of F Company who took shrapnel in the legs. "I . . . remember absolutely no sense of pain," he said. "My first sensation was the cool breeze on the flesh which had been exposed by the slicing action of the shell fragment." Fragments also ripped into Captain Robert Bridges, the commander of D Company. Bridges called out for Lieutenant Hume, only to hear from another officer that Hume was dead. Medics arrived and loaded the wounded captain onto a stretcher. "While being carried to a concrete dugout [possibly the pillbox aid station], that area was heavily shelled, at times coming so close that the six men carrying the litter set it down (they never failed to set it down gently) and lay down on each side."

The shells took out some of the company-level leadership, but did not otherwise hinder the 26th's movement off the beach. In the twilight and the gathering darkness, columns of soldiers carefully snaked their way inland along the narrow paths cleared earlier in the day by engineers and marked by white tape. They kept going, around, past, and through the shaky positions of the decimated 16th Infantry. In one typical instance, Tech 5 James Thomson, an exhausted radioman from F Company, 16th Infantry Regiment who had been fighting since H-Hour, was awakened by the sound of men tromping past him. "Who is it?" he called out.

"The 26th Infantry Regiment," came a reply in the night.

"Good luck!" he called out and immediately drifted back to sleep.

At times it was difficult amid the continuous shelling, the close presence of mines, and the darkness for the 26th's officers and sergeants to keep their units together. In one incident, Private Warren Coffman, a soldier in C Company, had to go back to the beach all alone to retrieve two entire platoons that were hunkered down ineffectually, waiting for orders. "I don't think Captain [Allan] Ferry ever knew that the third and fourth platoons had lost contact and were left on the beach, or that I had to go back to find them," he later wrote. The regiment's original mission was to push for Bayeux, but given the day's events, this was no longer remotely possible. Instead, Colonel John Seitz, the regimental commander, spread his battalions out to consolidate a perimeter of sorts for the division. The 1st Battalion headed east (to the left from the landing beach) to reinforce Captain Kimball Richmond's makeshift force at Le Grand Hameau where he had, according to one company history, "set up a strong defense in the outskirts and put outposts into town." The 2nd and 3rd Battalions went in the other direction. The former deployed just west of the E-1 draw, not all that far from Saint-Laurent. The latter pushed across the Colleville–Saint-Laurent road and settled in several hundred yards southwest of Saint-Laurent. Together the two battalions held the entire western flank of the 1st Division sector and constituted the border with the 29th Division. The Big Red One now controlled the three key beach exits, most of the coastal road, most of Colleville, and an amorphous perimeter stretching from Exit E-1 in the west to Le Grand Hameau in the east.[3]

The safe arrival of the 26th, in tandem with tanks of the 745th, signaled the consolidation of the Big Red One's beachhead as well as the coming push south from the beaches that would soon follow D-Day. The surviving invaders—often tired to the bone—dug brow-deep foxholes in the moist brown earth. Some of the Americans began the digging process by detonating little blocks of TNT. The muffled cries of "Fire in the hole!" could be heard, followed by the abrupt barking of controlled blasts and, in the recollection of one soldier, "a shower of loose earth flying through the air." The Germans no longer had any real chance of foiling the invasion as Rommel had envisioned. On that first night, along the expanse of the 1st Division's hard-won beachhead, there were not really front lines so much as small-unit perimeters, roaming patrols, and areas under the predominant influence of one side or the other.

The sun finally set at 2207 hours, ending the long Norman day. With the darkness came the chill of the dewy evening. A steady sea breeze, stymied only by the hedgerows and hillocks, swept in from the shore. Shivering soldiers, most of whom were still clammy from the landing, wished only for blankets or coffee. "I have never been so cold and miserable in all my life," one captain wrote a few weeks later in a letter to a fellow officer. The beach itself was glowing from the fires of burning vehicles and the flashes of naval gunfire. The Germans sortied several planes to bomb the beachhead. Tracer rounds arced upward in fiery ropes as the Navy responded with a titanic barrage of antiaircraft shells and bullets. Their glowing lines crisscrossed and stabbed through the night with almost geometric precision. "Orange, white, red tracers and exploding shells streamed towards the darkened sky," Corporal Dick Biehl of B Company, 26th Infantry recalled. "Small pieces of metal, particles of exploding shells, fell on our helmets, making a sort of clattering noise." The shooting eventually petered out, with little damage done on either side, though the Navy did claim to have shot down two aircraft.

1

Farther inland, skirmishes routinely broke out as the two sides bumped into each other in the darkness. "All during the night the . . . Germans sneaked up to the hedgerows, poked their 'burp' guns over the top and fired bursts into our area," Lieutenant John Downing of the 18th Infantry wrote. "Sometimes they were seen by the outposts and fired upon, but they were fairly well concealed by the darkness." Captain Allan Ferry's company clashed with another group of German soldiers in a field near Cabourg. "I lost one messenger and the majority of a whole rifle squad to two Germans on patrol who ambushed us among the hedgerows," Ferry said. The Germans stepped through a hedgerow opening, unleashed a stream of bullets and then ducked behind the hedgerow. One of the platoon sergeants took a pair of soldiers, worked his way around the Germans and pitched grenades at them until their shooting ceased. Later, the company caught a group of enemy soldiers in the middle of a field, and showed no mercy on them. "Somebody shot up a flare and they threw their guns down and hollered, 'Kamerad' but the men didn't hold their fire," Sergeant Jack Gray said. The Americans killed them all. In some cases, the two sides came into close proximity without fighting. In one foxhole, Private First Class Harold Saylor was disassembling and cleaning his rifle (a task he had learned to do blindfolded in training) when, on the other side of a nearby hedgerow, he heard "some soldiers talking in German, and I motioned to my buddy to keep quiet so they wouldn't find us." As the two frightened Americans listened, the German voices grew fainter until they were gone.

Patrols from both sides prowled in the night. Their usual mission was to pinpoint the enemy's location or establish contact with friendly units. Many of the German "patrols" were actually just small groups of survivors trying to escape the beach area. In most instances the patrols returned without making any contact with the enemy. When they did, the firefights were generally brief and inconclusive. Sergeant Bill Wills, an engineer NCO, sent out one such patrol into the inky black night. Ten minutes later he heard shooting. "It lasted about five minutes and then all was quiet. The patrol then returned with no one wounded. They had run into a German patrol, and they were on one side of the hedgerow and the enemy on the other. Both kept shooting but neither side seemed to be hit."

Another by-product of the patrolling, and the day's fighting, was the taking of prisoners, usually in two and threes rather than en masse.

Captain Fred Gercke, the commander of a POW interrogation or IPW team in the 16th Infantry, claimed to have processed 120 prisoners by the end of D-Day. "They all talk freely," he wrote in a letter to a colleague a few weeks later. "Have had to shut some of them up for talking too much. The officers I had (highest rank Captain), also talked fairly freely when engaged in conversation, but did not respond so well to direct questioning. All were very polite and cooperative, have had none of the so called 'arrogant' type. I adopt a fairly stern, matter of fact attitude in most of my interrogations and seem to be getting excellent results. Sometimes, if warranted, I fall into a more easy-going conversational tone of voice, which also has got me good results. Have had very few occasions to shout at any of our prisoners." Through such interrogations as these, American commanders discovered the unwelcome presence of the German Army's 352nd Infantry Division.

In Cabourg that evening, Private First Class Lawrence Meilander, a German-speaking GI whose parents were Luxembourger immigrants, scored the biggest POW haul at the Omaha beachhead. Meilander and two other soldiers, Privates Victor O'Dell and William Butt, had been captured earlier in the day as they approached the little hamlet (Butt had been wounded by a bullet). Because Meilander's father knew little English, the son could speak German and understood something of German culture. As Meilander interacted with his captors, he came to understand that they were halfhearted rear guard types with little inclination to take on the growing American presence in the area. In the course of the night, he persuaded them that their situation was hopeless. If they did not surrender, they would be annihilated by waves of U.S. reinforcements. The sales pitch worked. A total of fifty-two Germans agreed to surrender. With his two fellow American soldiers in tow, Meilander led the Germans out of Cabourg until they finally reached the forward positions of the 2nd Battalion, 18th Infantry a few hundred yards to the south.

All around the 1st Division's perimeter beachhead at the close of that momentous day, the Big Red One soldiers—survivors now of the Normandy invasion's worst killing ground—settled in for the night and the long campaign ahead. Some lay in foxholes, some in captured slit trenches, others in hedgerow ditches. The lucky ones took shelter in buildings or captured pillboxes. Others were still on the beach, still huddling near the shingle bank or lying wounded on stretchers, waiting for evacuation. Their moods varied by the individual. Staff Sergeant John Ellery was elated to have survived what he thought of as a great adventure. "It had been the greatest experience of my life. I felt ten feet tall. No matter what happened, I had made it off the beach." Staff Sergeant Harley Reynolds, who had led one of the first groups off the beach, had then become separated from his unit in the darkness. He spent the night among strangers, feeling slightly lonely. Much to his chagrin, he later learned "I had spent the night within shouting distance of my co. [company] just south of Colleville." Private First Class John Bistrica, a rifleman in C Company, 16th Infantry, found it hard to turn his mind off. He sat in his foxhole replaying the day's events, wondering how he had survived. "I wish I could have kept a record of everything," he later commented. Most struggled with bone-weary exhaustion of the sort that often ensues from life-threatening adrenaline rushes. "I can't ever remember being as exhausted as I was that night," Private First Class Howard Johnson, a bazookaman, later wrote. "The emotional drain was worse than the physical exertion." Staff Sergeant Donald Wilson, whose unit, F Company of the 16th Infantry, had been nearly destroyed, was so tired from the ordeal that he could hardly think straight. He and several other men found a ditch, ate some rations, and then fell fast asleep. "The next thing I knew the sun was well up," he said. Several soldiers were standing over Wilson and his cohorts, nudging their bodies to see if they were dead. "This is as close as I've come to knowing how Lazarus felt."

The beachhead was now secure enough for General Huebner to at last come ashore after a long day of frustrated bystanding aboard ship.

At 1900 hours he and his staff landed on Easy Red beach (General Gerow, the V Corps commander, arrived an hour and a half later). Huebner and his party immediately joined General Wyman at the E-1 draw, where he had established the division's advance command post. As Wyman briefed Huebner on the division's status, Colonel Stanhope Mason, the chief of staff, made preparations for setting up a more permanent command post. Fearing enemy air raids on the beach, the colonel chose an orchard about a thousand yards inland, just a few hundred yards east of Saint-Laurent. With Mason attending to a myriad of necessary details—arranging for communication wires and radio coverage, supervising the movements of all headquarters soldiers, and the like—they eventually made their way inland up the E-1 draw. "It was a matter of trying to stumble through cold weather in wet clothing and, at the same time, do all I could to get some order out of the chaos," Mason later wrote. It took several hours, but they reached the orchard and set up the headquarters. "It was difficult to tell whether Danger Forward [the nickname for the division command post] was in or behind the front line," correspondent Don Whitehead wrote. "All night rifles and burp-guns crackled around headquarters."

Huebner would not have had it any other way. In his view, a commander had to be near the action to truly understand what was happening, control his soldiers, and make good decisions. As the hours passed, and the general talked with more soldiers, he developed a full understanding of just how bitter the struggle had been for his men on D-Day and how well they had performed. "Battles are won by small units and we had those small units on the beach," he later reflected. Colonel Mason was equally pleased. "All in all, we had accomplished the mission! We had a beachhead firmly established, no doubt about it."

Somehow, even though General Huebner had not been directly alongside his soldiers during their greatest hours of peril, he could feel that something had changed in his relationship with the proud, headstrong men of the Big Red One. As he looked into their eyes and conversed with them, he sensed a deepening feeling of mutual respect and confidence. The old soldier, the "Coach," the man who had experienced more hours of combat service than he could ever count, was profoundly impressed with the resourcefulness of his men and their inner toughness. That night, at Colonel Taylor's behest, his personnel officer, Captain Bill Friedman, reported to the general. "Colonel Taylor sends his respects," Friedman said. The young captain updated Huebner on the status of the bloodied 16th Infantry. The regiment had suffered nearly a thousand casualties, a one-third loss rate, but it had made it off the beach and it was still fighting.

General Huebner was deeply moved. Tears welled up in his eyes and he could hardly speak. "You did it," he managed to utter with admiration in his voice. "[Y]ou did it!"[4]

Chapter 10

MEANING

The waves thumped against the sand and rocks, nature's easy, relentless, timeless rhythm, heedless now of humanity's bloody epoch, though nature had been damaged too. Dead fish littered the shoreline and floated in jagged clumps on the foamy, briny waves. The squishy corpses of jellyfish, the size of a man's hand, floated on the water or lay draped on wet sand. "In the center of each of them was a green design exactly like a four-leafed clover," one observer wrote with a tinge of bitter irony. Along the draws and the bluffs, the shredded remains of dead Norman rabbits, their maroon blood caked in gobs and slashes against brown fur, lay where they had been killed by mines, fragments, and even bullets. Shell holes gouged the whole area like some sort of grotesque chicken pox inflicted upon nature. Trees were uprooted or splintered. The smoky remnants of grass fires still smoldered uneasily. In far too many places, the pebbly beach was still coated with the incongruous forms of weather-beaten obstacles. A dog, separated from his master, wandered around searching for him among hordes of busy, hustling, indifferent soldiers.

From Easy Red to Fox Red, the beach-scape was imprinted with the tragedy of war's waste and destruction. "The harsh light of day brought back into view the terrible scene of destruction," Private George "Jeff" Boocks, an engineer who surveyed the carnage the day after the invasion, wrote. "The dead, some twisted in oddly grotesque positions, still lay as they had fallen. Fire-blackened remains of tanks, and battered hulls of landing craft were ugly reminders of the battle that had raged." Bulldozers rumbled slowly to and fro, clearing obstacles; the drivers peered intently ahead, constantly leery of mines.

Like Boocks, others were drawn to the terrible scene of the battle's aftermath, almost as if they must bear witness for history. As Lieutenant Richard Oliphant, a naval observer from the USS *Ancon*, walked the beach, he carefully stepped around corpses and paused, in almost guilty fashion, to study them intently. "One came upon them rather too suddenly and wanted to stare hard but there was that feeling that staring was rude. There was [*sic*] enough wrecked bodies to see all you wanted without staring. The bodies were just there and that was all." Shifting his gaze, he was taken aback by the staggering amount of discarded matériel stretching as far as he could see. "Strewn at the high water level from one end of the beach to the other were packs and knapsacks, water-logged and bursting open, their contents covering the rocks at the back of the beach. Pictures of GIs, laughing, with their arms about their girls. Large art, frames of imitation leather with girls' heads, lay laughing out in the midst of sand. Cigarettes and pathetic little toilet articles strewn everywhere. Drowned trucks littered the sand. Jerry prisoners kept coming in. One could see no hatred on either side. Just silence, mostly, and curiosity." The Americans enlisted the help of these prisoners to retrieve and bury the dead.

Not far from where Oliphant strode the traumatized sands, Ernie Pyle, the soulful war correspondent who had already earned great fame for his moving depictions of average soldiers, was also drifting around, almost in a daze at the tragedy of it all. "It was a lovely day for strolling along the seashore," he wrote sarcastically. "Men were sleeping on the sand, some of them sleeping forever. Men were floating in the water, but they didn't know they were in the water, for they were dead. For a mile out from the beach there were scores of tanks and trucks and boats that were not visible, for they were at the bottom of the water— swamped by overloading or hit by shells, or sunk by mines. On the beach itself, high and dry, were all sorts of wrecked vehicles. There were tanks that had only just made the beach before being knocked out. There were jeeps that had burned to a dull gray. There were big derricks on caterpillar treads that didn't quite make it. But there was . . . more human litter. There were socks and shoe polish, sewing kits, diaries, Bibles, hand grenades. There were the latest letters from home. There were toothbrushes and razors, and snapshots of families back home staring up at you from the sand. There were pocketbooks, metal mirrors, extra trousers, and bloody, abandoned shoes. There were broken-handled shovels, and portable radios smashed almost beyond recognition, and mine detectors twisted and ruined." Pyle even found a discarded tennis racket. He wrote movingly that this and all the other items were "gear that would never be needed again by those who fought and died to give us our entrance into Europe."

To the Big Red One, the cost of the hard-earned, close-run victory at Omaha beach was substantial. For the 1st Division, D-Day was the bloodiest day of a long and bloody war. "The outfit did alright in N. Africa and Sicily," Lieutenant Rob Huch wrote to his parents a week after the invasion, "but the vets still around never experienced anything quite like this affair." According to one official source, the division suffered 1,346 casualties on D-Day, including 971 in the 16th Infantry, the unit that had borne the brunt of the worst fighting. However, a careful check of the division's morning reports indicates a slightly lower, though no less sobering, total of 1,174 casualties, 820 of which were suffered by the 16th (though it should be noted that the morning reports did omit the names of some of the casualties). According to these reports, the division lost 184 killed in action, 713 wounded in action, and 277 missing in action, some of whom were dead but simply unaccounted for. Some of the wounded subsequently died. The 16th lost one-third of its manpower—165 killed, 384 wounded, and 271 missing. Captain Wozenski's E Company suffered 40 dead, 37 wounded, and 40 missing; in Captain Finke's F Company the numbers were 26 killed, 39 wounded, and 34 missing. These tallies do not include the serious losses incurred by the units that fought alongside the Big Red One on D-Day: the Gap Assault Teams, the 741st and 745th Tank Battalions, the antiaircraft crewmen, mislanded 29th Division soldiers, the 6th Naval Beach Battalion, the Navy and Coast Guard landing craft crewmen, the combat engineer battalions, the medics, and the naval shore fire control parties. Collectively, they probably lost somewhere in the neighborhood of 500 men.[1]

The cost of taking Omaha beach went beyond just these awful casualty numbers. Nearly every Big Red One survivor wondered how and why he had lived through such a nightmarish bloodbath. It is fair to say that every man who participated in the invasion was marked by the experience in some way, large or small, regardless of how his life unfolded in the days and years following the invasion. "With D-Day in Normandy as a ten," John Ellery said, "I haven't had an adventure that rated more than a two since." The memory of the dead and maimed remained with them forever after. "We had a lot of sad memories . . . especially for those guys who can't walk any more, had their legs blown off, those that will never be able to do anything any more," Albert Smith, who was a young captain on D-Day, later reflected. He went on to a long Army career, became a major general and even served as assistant division commander of the Big Red One in Vietnam. Ed Wozenski, who had been so emotionally devastated by the destruction of his E Company, nonetheless enjoyed a successful postwar Army career, retiring as a brigadier general. George Taylor's inspirational leadership at Omaha beach earned him the Distinguished Service Cross and a promotion to brigadier general. He became assistant division commander of both the 4th and the 1st Infantry Divisions. He retired from the Army in 1946, suffered a stroke fourteen years later, and died in 1969 after years of debilitation. John Ellery earned a Ph.D. after the war and eventually became vice chancellor of the University of Wisconsin–Stevens Point. He also retired as a colonel in the Wisconsin Army National Guard. Joe Dawson commanded his beloved G Company for five more months after D-Day through many more battles, until he was emotionally and physically in tatters. He was sent home, retrained as an officer in the Office of Strategic Services, and served the rest of the war in that new job. After the war, he parlayed his excellence as a geologist into a lucrative career in the oil business as the owner of Dawson Oil. He enjoyed a marriage that lasted half a century, raised two daughters, and died in 1998.

Happiness and stability eluded many others. Carlton Barrett, the diminutive reconnaissance soldier who earned the Medal of Honor for his extraordinary courage on D-Day, struggled, like many other recipients of that hallowed award, through a troubled postwar life. After a stint with the Veterans Administration, he went back into the Army. He was restless and uneasy, though. He fathered three children, one of whom died shortly after birth, but he ended up divorced from his wife and estranged from his family for decades. Only shortly before his death in 1986 did they reunite with him.

Phil Streczyk's valor on D-Day arguably equaled or even exceeded Barrett's and that of the division's two other Medal of Honor recipients, Jimmie Monteith and Joe Pinder, though such estimations are subjective and perhaps even a bit presumptuous from the safe distance of many decades later. Even so, Wozenski once wrote of the courageous New Jersey native, "If [he] did not earn a Congressional Medal of Honor, no one did." Regardless of medals (and the twenty-five-year-old sergeant did end up as one of the most decorated NCOs of the World War II Army), it is safe to say that no single individual contributed more to the 1st Division's success on D-Day than Streczyk did. He had fought with the 16th Infantry since North Africa, and he continued to fight after D-Day, through Normandy, through the Mons pocket, Aachen, and then into the brutal Hürtgen Forest, leading by example every step of the way. In all, he logged 440 days of frontline combat duty and survived many near misses and wounds. In one instance, a pistol bullet hit him in the base of the neck, yet he refused medical evacuation. Somehow the wound healed, but it left a deep scar. His son Stanley, as a toddler years later, thought of it as a strange hole in his father, and he often poked his little finger into it. Yet the months of unrelenting combat were too much even for a man of Streczyk's unusual savvy and bravery. He reached a breaking point in the Hürtgen Forest. Under an intense bombardment, he shook uncontrollably and babbled incoherently, to the point where he could no longer function. Sergeant Curt Colwell and several other men held him down until he could be evacuated from the front lines with combat fatigue. It was a grim reminder that even the best and bravest soldiers have limits to what they can endure. His case of combat fatigue was bad enough that he was evacuated to a convalescent hospital in the United States. He missed his men (perhaps he felt guilty that he was no longer with them). "The best platoon a man ever had," he told a hometown journalist in 1945, during his convalescence. Streczyk was subsequently discharged from the Army and became a builder in Florida. He married Sophie Karanewsky and they had four children together. But he could not leave the war, and D-Day, behind. Streczyk was in persistent pain from his physical wounds; his emotional wounds might have been even worse. At night he was tormented with traumatic battle dreams. In 1957, after years of emotional and physical pain that only he could begin to understand, he took his own life.

Streczyk's lieutenant, John Spalding, the former sportswriter from

Owensboro, Kentucky, was also forever altered by D-Day and the war. Initially, after surviving so many close calls on D-Day, he thought he was invulnerable. But as the weeks and months of combat wore on, and casualties piled up, an inner fear began to consume him to the point that only his job as an officer kept him from refusing to fight. In the words of a later medical evaluator, Spalding "started to worry, apprehensive that he would make poor decisions which would be costly to his men." The worry threatened to destroy him. He was wounded near Aachen on September 27, 1944, and did not return to the platoon until January, during the Battle of the Bulge. The terrible winter fighting broke him. Racked with fever, anxiety, and depression, he was evacuated with combat fatigue and eventually transferred back to the States. He had terrible war-related nightmares. His confidence was shot. He was irritable, nervous, and depressed. He had begun to hate guns and feared even to be around them. He was plagued by feelings of guilt over the death and wounding of his men and what he felt was his inadequacy in leading them. "I didn't have any unusual experiences," he told a reporter during a brief home leave in 1945, when he was about to be discharged from the Army, "I didn't do a thing. My men did it all. Don't give me the credit." Otherwise, Spalding refused to talk with much specificity about his D-Day experiences. He left the Army, returned home to Owensboro to a war hero's welcome, and went to work in the men's clothing and furnishing section at a local department store (where he had been employed part-time before he entered the Army).

The emotional turmoil stemming from the war could not have been good for his marriage. He and his wife, Perdetta, with whom he had a son, divorced shortly after the war. He did not stay single for long. On October 31, 1946, he married Mary Christine Love. The couple had one daughter and two sons. Spalding was elected to the Kentucky state legislature in 1947 and served two terms. At the department store, he was promoted to manager of men's clothing and furnishings. With a good job, a family, and the deep respect of his local community, Spalding's life seemed back on track. One of his friends happily recalled whiling away many hours conversing with John about politics and baseball. "It just seemed to me I could talk to him and never get tired of him. We were never without conversation." But it was all seemingly too good to be true. On the evening of November 6, 1959, in an incident still shrouded under some level of mystery, Mary Christine shot Spalding with a brand-new .22-caliber rifle. The bullet entered his left side just below his ribs and tore his aorta. He bled to death on the bedroom floor of their modest one-story home. The children lay sound asleep in another bedroom. Mary Christine admitted to the police that the couple had argued the night before, but, apparently in shock or denial, she said, "Something happened. I don't know what it was." Although the county coroner ruled the death a homicide and Mary Christine was charged with murder, she did not go to prison. Instead, she was committed to a mental institution until, several years later, the state decided she posed no further threat and released her. She died in 1991 at age sixty-seven. Spalding was forty-four years old at the time of his death.[2]

1

Thus, every Big Red One soldier who was at Omaha beach paid for that valuable soil in one fashion or another—some with their lives, some with physical wounds, some with the loss of legs, arms, eyes, or the infliction of some other disability, some with their mental or emotional well-being, many simply with the survivor's guilt that comes from living while close comrades did not. Many, like Dawson, searched for meaning in the midst of such unspeakable tragedy. "This war has been unbelievably personal," he wrote to his family a few weeks after D-Day. "What little satisfaction gained from it has been the belief that it all was worthwhile, and that this was shared by all our loved ones and those who represent our nation in society and government alike." Though the victory at Omaha beach was staggering in its cost, Dawson and the thousands of other survivors could take solace in the fact that it was among the most significant of World War II. Don Whitehead succinctly wrote that it "turned the key that unlocked the door to victory in Europe."

Certainly the odds favored the Americans at Omaha beach since they enjoyed the advantage of numbers, control of the sea, and control of the air. Even so, total disaster was a real possibility, especially during the morning hours of June 6. If the soldiers of the Big Red One and their partners in the 29th Division had failed, the Allied position in Normandy would have been severely hindered. The Germans would have been free to split their forces and focus on eliminating widely separate beachheads in the British and Canadian sectors to the east and the American enclave at Utah beach to the west on the Cotentin Peninsula. This would have afforded the Germans significant freedom of movement and good lines of communication through Saint-Lô and other crossroads towns just inland from Omaha beach. Quite possibly, the enemy could have made use of the high ground at Pointe du Hoc and Pointe de la Percée to unleash long-range artillery against the two separate Allied beachheads. Most likely, it would have taken the Allies months to join the two, if ever at all. Their supply situation would have been greatly complicated by the loss of Omaha, since it was the intended site of a Mulberry artificial harbor and, much more significantly, the best-positioned unloading spot for huge quantities of vehicles, equipment, and soldiers. In the political sense, a defeat at Omaha would have sent shock waves throughout the Axis and Allied worlds. It would have been the first time the Germans had foiled a major Allied invasion attempt—Dieppe was more of a raid than an invasion—and it would have strengthened Hitler's diplomatic position in Europe. It also would have afforded him leverage in his constant struggle with his generals. The loss of Omaha beach probably would have been devastating for resistance movements around Europe, not to mention the deleterious effect on morale among Allied POWs and Hitler's victims who were incarcerated in his vast network of concentration camps. The Churchill and Roosevelt governments inevitably would have been weakened, particularly the latter, since 1944 was an election year. Given the American propensity for post-catastrophe political recrimination and accountability, it is not difficult to envision an Omaha beach disaster investigation led by anti–New Dealers. Truly, Omaha was the nexus of the Normandy invasion. The loss of it would have been equivalent to a body without a torso or a building without a foundation. In recognition of the crucial importance of success at Omaha beach, the Army awarded presidential unit citations to the 16th and 18th Infantry Regiments, as well as the 1st Engineer Combat Battalion.

So the obvious significance of the victory, and its terrible cost, leads to one ultimate question: why did the 1st Infantry Division succeed at Omaha beach? The unit's veterans have generally ascribed their success to the unique excellence of their division and its long prior combat experience of the sort that led Eisenhower to once refer to the Big Red One as his own Praetorian Guard. They pointed to their winning record from the Mediterranean and their unique pride as members of the Big Red One. "When we landed, the 1st Infantry Division was like the Green Bay Packers when they were on a winning streak," Alan Ferry, a company commander, later wrote. "[W]e couldn't lose." The veterans of the 16th, who paid the highest price, took the most pride in their organization's accomplishments. Sam Fuller, a member of the 16th who went on to a brilliant Hollywood career as a writer, producer, and director of many films, including his own capstone labor of love, *The Big Red One*, once wrote: "A lot of copy has been written about D-Day and a lot more will be written, but take it from a dogface who was there—any other outnumbered infantry regiment would have been completely wiped out at Omaha beach." Bill Friedman, the regimental personnel officer, fully recognized the contributions of everyone on the beach that day, but afforded the supreme accolades to his own outfit. "I give unstinting credit to the raw courage and gallantry of the 115th and 116th

Infantry Regiments of the 29th Division; to each and every gunner on the warships that covered our advance; to the coxswains who carried us ashore; to the Rangers of legendary strength and tenacity; and to the thousands of soldiers, sailors and airmen of all ranks and nationalities and skills who made our lodgement in Normandy possible. But, as I see it, it was the beautiful, wild, to-hell-with-you 16th that did it at Omaha. Its soldiers walked through the minefields, took out German fortifications and seized the bluffs."

The explanation runs much deeper than understandable unit pride. Experience was certainly an important factor. The 1st Division's staff officers, company commanders, and NCOs were used to planning invasions, and they knew what to do once they hit the beach. It was no accident that many of those who received the highest awards for valor were experienced soldiers, men like Charles Tegtmeyer, Kimball Richmond, Raymond Strojny, Taylor, Streczyk, and Jimmie Monteith, all of whom were used to leading in combat. The value of experience went only so far, though. If it is true that a soldier can stand only so much combat, then it is also true that he will eventually grow unwilling to take chances, or he at least will become overly cautious. Often a new man is more valuable in combat simply because he is fresh enough—and perhaps ignorant enough—to take major risks. In general, if the replacements could survive the first few minutes on Omaha beach, they fought as well as the veterans. Moreover, the all-new 29th Division performed well at Omaha beach and contributed equally to the victory, though it did suffer heavier losses among its initial assault elements.

Though General Huebner's invasion planning was hardly perfect, he succeeded in training his division to a winning standard. This paid major dividends on D-Day. His soldiers knew their weapons (quite a few even field-stripped and cleaned them while under intense fire). The men were physically fit. They understood the importance of supporting firepower at the small-unit level. They all knew to get off the beach as quickly as they could. Their morale was high, though the veterans among them certainly resented their leading role in yet another dangerous mission. They knew how to keep fighting when they were separated from their leaders. They knew how to work with supporting tanks and engineers. They were trained to adapt quickly to unforeseen circumstances—witness the quick thinking of Pinder to save much of his regiment's communications equipment or the willingness of Monteith to personally lead tanks over extremely forbidding terrain or Lawrence Meilander sweet-talking his German captors into surrendering.

Their pre-invasion supporting fire failed. Their pre-invasion intelligence information was distressingly incomplete. They were carrying too much equipment. Not all of them knew how to swim. Most were landed in the wrong spot, under trying circumstances. The survivors nonetheless figured out how to deal with all this adversity, at least well enough to avoid disaster and accomplish the mission of establishing a beachhead. "Only someone who was actually there can tell you how close we came to getting pushed off that beach," Bernard Friedenberg, the courageous medic, later wrote. "Combat teams were formed on the spot and they went to work."

In the main, they respected their leaders and expected them to perform to a high standard. The relationship between Joe Dawson and his G Company soldiers is a prime example of this. He was determined to prove himself to them. They, in turn, looked to him as a source of know-how and leadership. "The reward has been in their looks of confidence in me," he wrote reverently in a letter home. "That has paid me the highest tribute life has ever given me." The division's boat sections were designed to provide good leadership and significant firepower within the smallest elements on the beach. The Spalding-Streczyk boat section demonstrated how well this could work. To be sure, few sections remained so intact and so effective, but the profusion of machine guns, pole charges, Bangalore torpedoes, bazookas, mortars, and small-unit leaders at Fox Green and Easy Red had the effect of motivating action among many little groups up and down the beach. Sergeants

Harley Reynolds and Raymond Strojny serve as good examples of the larger whole. Reynolds, through the force of his competence and personality, led an intact group through the wire and overwhelmed important fortifications. Strojny employed a discarded, damaged bazooka, and willingly put himself at great personal peril to destroy the deadly 50-millimeter gun at WN-61. Within the division, there were enough individuals like these men—usually at the NCO or platoon leader level—who knew what had to be done and were ready to do it. For the 1st Division, Omaha beach was a junior leader's fight. Among senior officers, only General Wyman and Colonel Taylor had any real impact on D-Day. The day belonged to the Streczyks, the Spaldings, the Richmonds, and the Monteiths. In football parlance, senior officers designed the playbook. The small-unit individual leaders, from private first class to captain, improvised on the playbook and made it work in real life.

But there was more in play than just these important factors. More than anything else, the human factor was paramount. Whether Huebner was responsible for it or not, the 1st Infantry Division possessed a culture of personal accountability at the basic human level. The greatest motivation to fight and accomplish objectives for the American soldier in World War II was the man to his right and to his left, and this was definitely true at Omaha beach. The soldiers of the Big Red One were willing to sacrifice themselves and risk death, not just for their cause, not just for the pride of their unit, but, in the end, for one another. "The fact that the success of the invasion might restore the vote . . . or unfetter the local press . . . wasn't going to inspire any infantryman to dash up the beach and tear concrete pillboxes apart with his bare hands," John Downing, who led soldiers as a young lieutenant on D-Day, later wrote. "We were in a position where as infantrymen we had an unpleasant and unhealthy task to perform. Each man had a family or intimate friends at home and he had his friends in his company. He would conduct himself so as to win the respect and approbation of these and certainly would do his utmost not to disgrace himself in their eyes. If his efforts furthered certain ideals at a more elevated plane, that was a gratuitous effect and not the prime driving force. Later, if you survive, it is pleasant to sit back with the feeling of a job well done and muse about principles of social significance, in which to clothe your past activities. At the moment of action your principles are primitive."

The personal relationships to which Downing alluded, in turn, produced courage within those who were in a state of shock, frightened out of their wits, or simply confused about what to do next. It usually manifested itself in little things that became significant—underaged Joe Argenzio taking out a machine-gun nest with grenades, Curt Colwell risking his own life to blow a hole in the barbed wire at Easy Red, William Russell, with blood pouring down his face, urging his men to get out of the water and keep moving, Monteith endangering his own life to personally fight off a German counterattack so that his platoon sergeant, John Worozbyt, and the other members of their boat section would not have to, and, maybe most of all, medics like Charles Tegtmeyer, Charles Shay, and Bernard Friedenberg braving the most dangerous spots to save their stricken friends. "Summing it all up," Major Carl Plitt, the operations officer of the 16th Infantry, aptly wrote in a critique twenty-four days after D-Day, "the plan for Operation 'NEPTUNE' was a good one but it didn't work! It was the individual courage and heroism of the American Soldier that won the Beaches EASY RED and FOX GREEN on 6 June 1944."[3]

1

Not far from Colleville, on the bluffs overlooking Easy Red and Fox Green, where Joe Dawson, John Spalding, Phil Streczyk, and thousands of others once exited Omaha beach, there is now a beautiful, yet melancholy place. Lovingly maintained by the American

Battle Monuments Commission, the Normandy American Cemetery stretches for 172 pristine acres. It contains a wall for the missing, a reflecting pool, a chapel, a memorial, a bronze sculpture dedicated to American youth, a visitor center, an overlook, and most significantly, 9,387 white crosses and Stars of David, marking the spots where American servicemen and four servicewomen are buried. Scattered throughout the vast cemetery are the graves of 88 Big Red One soldiers who were killed on D-Day; there are 10 more 1st Infantry Division names listed on the wall of the missing. Lieutenant Colonel John Mathews, the West Pointer who was killed before his feet could ever touch French soil, is buried here. So is Lieutenant Edmund Duckworth, who left behind a young English widow, and Captain Frank Fitch, who was killed by mines along the edges of the beach, and Private First Class John Hastings, felled by a sniper in Colleville, and Sergeant Lou Ramundo, the first man killed in Spalding's section, and Sergeant Joseph Zukowski, who barely made it to the waterline, and Private Edward Morozewicz, the medic who lost his life while trying to save others, and Private First Class Homer Richard, the French Canadian BAR man who was drafted into the U.S. Army and died as an American. Jimmie Monteith is also buried here; the words on his cross are emblazoned in gold to honor his status as a Medal of Honor recipient. These men and so many others like them are forever young. Their hallowed graves represent a certain timelessness, an enduring monument to their division and what it accomplished on D-Day. Every one of their 1st Division comrades left behind something of himself at Omaha beach; these 98 men left behind everything. In a larger sense, they represent the World War II generation and its moment of truth and trial; so many decades ago, a generation nearly gone but never really entirely, momentous events still real in our consciousness, still relevant, still with us in modern memory. And may that always be so.

ACKNOWLEDGMENTS

There are many people to thank. In fact, as an author, I almost wish I could develop a credit page, similar to the end of a movie. Instead, this will have to suffice. I could never have written *The Dead and Those About to Die* without the support and assistance of a great many talented, dedicated people. The final product—and any errors—are of course my responsibility, but my shortcomings need not take away from the accomplishments of these individuals.

The military archivists at the National Archives in College Park, Maryland, were helpful and patient in guiding my research during my long visit. I would especially like to thank Rick Peuser for going above and beyond the call of duty to assist me. The staff at the American Folklife Center, Library of Congress did a fine job of making several veterans' memoirs and interview transcripts available to me. At the National Personnel Records Center in my hometown of St. Louis, I had the opportunity to pore over the relevant 1st Infantry Division morning reports for the D-Day time period, thanks to the assistance of Donna

Noelkin and Wanda Williams. These morning reports contain a treasure trove of information, including casualties, promotions, demotions, sicknesses, and narratives of unit actions on D-Day. At the Eisenhower Library in Abilene, Kansas, archivists Herb Pankratz and Kevin Bailey efficiently made much fascinating material, including the letters of Lieutenant Rob Huch, available to me. The U.S. Army Military History Institute in Carlisle, Pennsylvania, is one of the most remarkable military archives in the world. I would like to thank the director, Dr. Conrad Crane, along with the staff historians at the reference and research room for their professionalism and their incredible knowledge of Army history. I am especially grateful to Jessica Sheets and Guy Nasuti for their expertise and friendship. My old friend Cynthia Tinker at the Center for the Study of War and Society at the University of Tennessee was kind enough to make several relevant oral histories from their amazing collection available to me. A few years ago, while researching a previous book called *September Hope: The American Side of a Bridge Too Far*, I had the welcome opportunity to spend a couple of weeks delving into the Cornelius Ryan Collection at Ohio University. I came away deeply impressed with the richness of the material Ryan gathered for his various books—veterans' questionnaires, correspondence, memoirs, photographs, interview transcripts, and the like. So I was quite excited to return to Ohio University for an in-depth look at portions of the *Longest Day* material that were relevant to the 1st Division. Once again, Doug McCabe, the knowledgeable curator of the collection, was extremely helpful. This book is much the richer for Doug's expertise and my access to these fascinating sources gathered decades ago by the great Ryan and his assistant Frances Ward.

A special and heartfelt thank-you goes to my friends at the Cantigny First Division Museum in Wheaton, Illinois, who were kind enough to award me a fellowship to pay for some of the considerable research costs. In fact, the original idea for the book germinated during a conversation with Paul Herbert, the museum's director, whose passion for the history of the Big Red One knows no bounds. Without Paul's wisdom and continued support in more ways than I can count, this book would not exist. The museum's McCormick Research Center is the lodestone for any study involving the Big Red One. Eric Gillespie, the director, warmly welcomed me during my research visit and made sure I had complete access to whatever I needed. Andrew Woods, the center's research historian, is truly the guru of Big Red One history. Not only is he the keeper of the archives, but he has a wizard-like knowledge of practically every aspect of the division's history, especially Omaha beach. I had the pleasure of working closely with him during my visit to the McCormick Research Center and then subsequently when he patiently endeavored to answer my many questions. He has been a perfect sounding board and a kindred spirit in the study of the 1st Division on D-Day. Thank you, Andrew!

Beyond the archives, so many other people gave generously of their time and expertise to make sure I stayed on the proper course. Colonel Steve Clay, historian of the 16th Infantry Regiment, put me in touch with veterans of the regiment and shared a wealth of knowledge derived from his well-researched history of the 16th. Flint Whitlock, author of the only other book focusing primarily on the 1st Division at Omaha beach, skillfully fielded my many questions and, in general, welcomed me to the topic with great collegiality (an attitude that is not always prevalent among historians). The same was true for Joe Balkoski, another leading author of the Normandy invasion. In the course of the research and writing of *The Dead and Those About to Die*, I had the valuable opportunity to correspond and speak with Joe about many aspects of the topic, and this book is much the better for his contributions. My earnest hope is that I have been able to build upon the strong foundation that these two fine historians have established. Steve Zaloga, another esteemed historian, was kind enough to send me an advance copy of his book *The Devil's Garden: Rommel's Desperate Defense of Omaha Beach on D-Day*. Steve's work enhanced my understanding of the

German defenses at Omaha beach and also the important role of U.S. armor on D-Day. Patrick Lewis gave me a copy of *Into the Bucket with the 197th Anti-Aircraft (SP) Battalion*, a self-published history of his father's World War II unit. The book advanced my understanding of the fight for the vital Exit E-1. Professor Simon Trew, deputy head of the Department of War Studies, Royal Military Academy at Sandhurst, and a true D-Day savant, brought many key aspects of the 1st Division fighting to my attention and pointed me toward many excellent sources. Thank you, Simon. I would like to thank David Allender for taking the time and trouble to post his fascinating work on the John Spalding–Phil Streczyk boat section at his Web site, www.warchronicle .com, and thus make this valuable information easily accessible to other historians. Jim Erickson, a reporter for a St. Louis–area newspaper, functioned as my informal research assistant. He traveled to Spalding's hometown in Kentucky and accessed a great deal of interesting and new information, most of it courtesy of Tina Gerteisen, Spalding's granddaughter. My deepest thanks to both Jim and Tina. Also, I would like to thank Stanley Streczyk and the entire Streczyk family for providing me with personal information about their loved one, the legendary Sergeant Phil Streczyk. Theresa Furey did the same for her father, who was a young soldier in the 18th Infantry on D-Day. Other family members of Big Red One soldiers—too numerous to mention, really—provided much-appreciated support and guidance.

Jordan Edelstein, grandson of Captain Anthony Prahl, commander of H Company, 16th Infantry Regiment, was helpful through many stages of this book. Over the course of several years, Jordan has gathered much fascinating material on H Company and the 16th as a whole, and much of it can be accessed at his Web site, www.thefightingfirst.webs .com. He was always available to answer questions and to help in any way I asked. Thanks, Jordan. John Brueck, the guiding force behind Normandy Drop Zone Tours, went out of his way to put me in touch with fellow historians during my visit to Normandy. My good buddy and fellow Army historian Kevin Hymel was kind enough to make an interesting article about the experiences of a Big Red One soldier on D-Day available to me. Marty Morgan, one of the world's leading battlefield guides and an accomplished historian of the modern U.S. military, provided me with several welcome and time-saving tips. My good friend Robert von Maier, the brilliant editor of *Global War Studies*, the leading journal in World War II history, acted as a wonderful sounding board during this project and put me in touch with several fellow scholars. Another good friend, Paul Clifford, forwarded me much useful information on Omaha beach. Alan Amelinckx, director of visitor services at the Normandy American Cemetery, and an Iraq War veteran, gave generously of his time and considerable expertise, and in general was a wonderful host during my visit.

I would like to issue a special word of thanks to two individuals whose help was of paramount importance. Paul Woodage, a Normandy-based battlefield historian whose knowledge borders on voluminous, was kind enough to get together with me during my visit to the region, guide me to some key First Division spots, and discuss the relevant history in great depth. Needless to say, this made for a better book. Moreover, Paul did all this at a time of great sadness and loss in his personal life, and I will always be grateful to him for his generosity and comradeship. Pierre-Louis Gosselin, the founder, director, and curator of the Big Red One Museum in Colleville-sur-Mer, has dedicated his life to studying the history of the 1st Division. He has gathered an impressive blend of artifacts, photographs, personal accounts, and documents. Much of this priceless information is stored in lovingly maintained binders at the museum. Over the years, he has forged relationships or close friendships with countless veterans. He knows the Big Red One battle areas in Normandy firsthand, through years of on-site study and documentation. Pierre warmly welcomed me to his museum and, in the course of many conversations, genially shared his in-depth knowledge with me. He saved me from many errors and acted as a kindred spirit of sorts. My hope is that this book will advance his efforts and further our mutual goal of promoting a better understanding of 1st Division history. My heartiest thank-you to Pierre and his family.

Missouri University of Science and Technology, where I am privileged to "work" as a professor of history, provided some welcome financial support to offset travel and research costs. My colleagues in the Department of History and Political Science are always a source of guidance and support: Diana Ahmad, Mike Bruening, Petra DeWitt, Shannon Fogg, Patrick Huber, Tseggai Isaac, Michael Meagher, Jeff Schramm, Kate Sheppard, and of course our distinguished emeriti, Russ Buhite, Wayne Bledsoe, Lawrence Christensen, Harry Eisenman, Don Oster, Jack Ridley, and Lance Williams, as well as Robin Collier, an incredible secretary and good friend. I am especially grateful to our dedicated and energetic chair, Larry Gragg, a true friend and mentor.

Rick Britton, my old friend, the master cartographer, once again worked his magic, producing vivid, accurate maps. This book, like so many previous ones, is greatly enriched by his talent. The same is true for Brent Howard, an editor without peer, whose knowledge of both my field and his make for a formidable intellect. I would like to thank Brent for his belief in me and my work. I have said the same thing before about Ted Chichak, my agent, but it bears repeating. Thank you, Ted!

I am blessed with so many friends who have helped, whether they realize it or not, to sustain me during the writing of this book: Sean Roarty, Mike Chopp, Richard Lanni, Dick Hyde, Stu Hartzell, Thad O'Donnell, Pat O'Donnell, Don Patton, Joe Carcagno, Ron Kurtz, Doug Kuberski, Dave Cohen, Steve Kutheis, Steve Loher, Mark Williams, John Villier, Tom Fleming, Steve Vincent, Skeeter and Gretchen Cowell, Biggy Unruh, Bob Kaemmerlen, and Norm Richards.

The source of my greatest support is, of course, family. In a formal sense, Ruth and Nelson Woody are my in-laws, but they are really like another set of parents. I can never repay them for all their hospitality and love, but I can say that Nelson's taste in choosing a favorite baseball team is truly impeccable. My great appreciation to Nancy, Charlie, Doug, Tonya, the boys, David, Angee, and the girls for putting up with me. I am grateful to Mike and Nancy, my two elder siblings—much older, really!—for the many ways they have supported me and helped me over the years. Mike shares my love of sports, and second-guessing managers and coaches. Nancy and her husband, John, are surprisingly enthusiastic about letting me do the dishes when I eat at their house and for that I'm grateful. My nieces, Kelly and Erin, and my nephew, Michael, are a constant source of humor, affection, and entertainment. All I can say to Kelly is "Go Mizzou!" To Erin, I say "Go Tulsa!" To Michael, I say "Go Rockets!" My parents, Michael and Mary Jane, have made everything good in my life possible. I learned a long time ago that I can never be worthy of everything they have done for me, so I just try to let them know how much I appreciate them and all they have taught me. My final and most special word of thanks goes to my soul mate and wife, Nancy, without whom I'd be nowhere and nothing. Like me, she lived and died with this book each day throughout the long research and writing process. She also tolerated my long absences, in addition to tromping with me through remote parts of the Omaha beach area and serving as an unofficial photographer. As always, a mere thank-you is inadequate, but the limitation of language confines me to that simple expression . . .

John C. McManus
St. Louis, MO

SELECTED BIBLIOGRAPHY

ARCHIVES AND MANUSCRIPT COLLECTIONS

Abilene, KS. Dwight D. Eisenhower Library (EL).

Athens, OH. Cornelius Ryan Bridge Too Far Collection, Mahn Center for Archives and Special Collections, Alden Library, Ohio University.

Carlisle, PA. United States Army Military History Institute (USAMHI).

College Park, MD. National Archives and Records Administration (II).

Columbia, MO. State Historical Society of Missouri Research Center, University of Missouri–Columbia.

Knoxville, TN. University of Tennessee Special Collections Library, Repository of the Center for the Study of War and Society.

Lexington, VA. John A. Adams '71 Center for Military History and Strategic Analysis (Adams Center), Virginia Military Institute.

New Orleans, LA. National World War II Museum.

St. Louis, MO. National Personnel Records Center.

Washington, D.C. Library of Congress, Veterans History Project (LOC).

Wheaton, IL. McCormick Research Center, First Infantry Division Museum (MRC).

BOOKS

Ambrose, Stephen. *D-Day, June 6, 1944: The Climactic Battle of World War II.* New York: Simon & Schuster, 1994.

Astor, Gerald. *June 6, 1944: Voices of D-Day*. New York: Dell, 1994.

——. *Terrible Terry Allen: Combat General of World War II—The Life of an American Soldier*. Novato, CA: Presidio Press, 2004.

Atkinson, Rick. *Day of Battle: The War in Sicily and Italy, 1943–1944*. New York: Henry Holt and Company, 2007.

Badsey, Stephen and Bean, Tim. *Battle Zone Normandy, Omaha Beach*. Gloucestershire, UK: Sutton Publishing, 2004.

Balkoski, Joseph. *Omaha Beach: D-Day, June 6, 1944*. Mechanicsburg, PA: Stackpole Books, 2004.

Baumer, Robert and Reardon, Mark. *American Iliad: The 18th Infantry Regiment in World War II*. Bedford, PA: Aberjona Press, 2004.

Beevor, Antony. *D-Day: The Battle for Normandy*. New York: Penguin Books, 2010.

Bernages, Georges. *Omaha Beach*. Bayeux: Heimdal, 2002.

Bradley, Omar. *A Soldier's Story*. New York: Henry Holt and Company, 1951.

Cantigny First Division Foundation. *Blue Spaders: The 26th Infantry Regiment, 1917–1967*. Wheaton, IL: Cantigny Military History Series, 1996.

Capa, Robert. *Slightly Out of Focus*. New York: Henry Holt and Company, 1947.

Carrell, Paul. *Invasion! They're Coming!* New York: Bantam, 1984.

Clay, Steven. *Blood and Sacrifice: The History of the 16th Infantry Regiment from the Civil War Through the Gulf War*. Wheaton, IL: Cantigny Military History Series, 2001.

D'Este, Carlo. *Decision in Normandy*. Old Saybrook, CT: Konecky and Konecky, 1984.

Fane, Francis and Moore, Don. *The Naked Warriors*. New York: Appleton-Century-Crofts, 1956.

Fowler, Will. *D-Day: The First 24 Hours*. Miami, FL: Lewis International, 2003.

Fuller, Samuel. *A Third Face: My Tale of Writing, Fighting, and Filmmaking*. New York: Alfred A. Knopf, 2002.

Gawne, Jonathan. *Spearheading D-Day: American Special Units in Normandy*. Paris: Histoire and Collections, 1998.

Grossman, Dave and Christensen, Loren. *On Combat: The Psychology and Physiology of Deadly Conflict in War and in Peace*. Portland, OR: PPCT Research Publications, 2007.

Harrison, Gordon. *The United States Army in World War II: Cross Channel Attack*. Washington, D.C.: U.S. Army Center of Military History, 1993.

Historical Division, U.S. War Department. *Omaha Beachhead, 6 June–13 June, 1944*. Washington, D.C., 1945.

Isby, David, ed. *Fighting the Invasion: The German Army at D-Day*. London, UK: Greenhill Books, 2000.

Johnson, Franklyn. *One More Hill*. New York: Bantam, 1983.

Kaufmann, J. E. and Kaufmann, H. W. *Fortress Third Reich: German Fortifications and Defense Systems in World War II*. New York: DaCapo Press, 2003.

Kilvert-Jones, Tim. *Omaha Beach: V Corps' Battle for the Normandy Beachhead*. South Yorkshire, UK: Leo Cooper, 1999.

Kingseed, Cole, ed. *From Omaha Beach to Dawson's Ridge: The Combat Journal of Captain Joe Dawson*. Annapolis, MD: Naval Institute Press, 2005.

Kirkland, William. *Destroyers at Normandy: Naval Gunfire Support at Omaha Beach*. Washington, D.C.: Historical Foundation Publications, 1994.

Knickerbocker, H. R. et al. *Danger Forward: History of the First Division, 1941–1945*. Nashville, TN: Battery Press, 1947.

Lewis, Adrian. *Omaha Beach: A Flawed Victory*. Chapel Hill, NC: University of North Carolina Press, 2001.

Lypka, Pete. *A Soldier Remembers: A Memoir of Service in the 1st Infantry Division, 1941–1945*. Chicago, IL: Cantigny First Division Foundation, 2007.

McManus, John C. *The Deadly Brotherhood: The American Combat Soldier in World War II*. New York: Ballantine Books, 2003.

———. *The Americans at D-Day: The American Experience at the Normandy Invasion*. New York: Forge, 2004.

———. *The Americans at Normandy: The Summer of 1944—The American War from the Normandy Beaches to Falaise*. New York: Forge, 2004.

———. *Grunts: Inside the American Combat Experience, World War II Through Iraq*. New York: NAL Caliber, 2010.

Milano, Vince and Conner, Bruce. *Normandiefront: D-Day to Saint-Lô Through German Eyes*. Gloucestershire, UK: Spellmont, 2012.

Morison, Samuel Eliot. *History of United States Naval Operations in World War II: The Invasion of France and Germany*. Boston: Little, Brown, 1957.

Nelson, James. *The Remains of Company D: A Story of the Great War*. New York: St. Martin's Press, 2009.

Pyle, Ernie. *Brave Men*. New York: Grosset & Dunlap Publishers, 1945.

Ramsey, Winston, ed. *D-Day Then and Now*. Volumes I and II. London, UK: Church House, 1995.

Ryan, Cornelius. *The Longest Day*. New York: Touchstone, 1994.

Severloh, Hein. *WN62: A German Soldier's Memories of the Defence of Omaha Beach Normandy, June 6, 1944*. Garbsen, Germany: H.E.K. Creativ Verlag, 2011.

Still, Paul, ed. *Assault on Normandy: First-Person Accounts from the Sea Services*. Annapolis, MD: Naval Institute Press, 1994.

Towne, Allen. *Doctor Danger Forward: A World War II Memoir of a Combat Medical Aidman, First Infantry Division*. Jefferson, NC: McFarland & Company, Inc., Publishers, 2000.

Wheeler, James Scott. *The Big Red One: America's Legendary 1st Infantry Division from World War I to Desert Storm*. Lawrence, KS: University Press of Kansas, 2007.

Whitlock, Flint. *The Fighting First: The Untold Story of the Big Red One on D-Day*. Boulder, CO: Westview Press, 2004.

Zaloga, Steven. *D-Day Fortifications in Normandy*. Oxford, UK: Osprey, 2005.

——. *U.S. Amphibious Tanks of World War II*. New York: Osprey, 2012.

ENDNOTES

FOREWORD

1   Omar Bradley, "'Thank God for the First Division': General Bradley Remembers D-Day," *Worcester Telegram*, June 5, 1964.

2   Colonel George Taylor, "Observations on an Infantry Regiment in Combat," September 24, 1943, George Taylor Papers, Box 3, Folder 11 at the McCormick Research Center, First Infantry Division Museum, Wheaton, IL (MRC). In this wide-ranging, thoughtful treatise on modern combat, Taylor wrote that "in a landing operation, there are two classes of men that may be found on the beach: those who are already dead, and those who are about to die."

PROLOGUE: SHOCK

1   Dave Grossman and Loren Christensen, *On Combat: The Psychology and Physiology of Deadly Conflict in War and in Peace* (Portland, OR: PPCT Research Publications, 2007), pp. 30–55.

2   16th Infantry Regiment, "History of the Invasion of France," Record Group 407, Entry 427, Box 5231, Folder 18; 16th Infantry Regiment, Medical Detachment, History, Record Group 407, Entry 427, Box 5247, Folder 23; 3rd Battalion, 16th Infantry Regiment, After Action Report (AAR), Record Group 407, Entry 427, Box 5247, Folder

25, all at National Archives, College Park, MD; E Company, 16th Infantry Regiment, Morning Report, June 6, 1944; F Company, 16th Infantry Regiment, Morning Report, June 6, 1944, both at National Personnel Records Center, St. Louis, MO; F Company, 16th Infantry Regiment, Unit Roster, 16th Infantry Regiment Association Collection, Unit Roster File; Clayton "Ray" Voight, oral history, Eisenhower Center Collection, Box 2; Charles Shay, speech, November 2011; unpublished memoir, no pagination; notes from interview with Andrew Woods, no date, all at MRC; E Company, 16th Infantry Regiment, AAR by Captain Edward Wozenski; Rob Huch, letter to family, June 26, 1944, both in William Huch Collection, World War II Participants and Contemporaries Papers, Dwight D. Eisenhower Library (EL), Abilene, KS; Frank King, oral history interview, October 25, 2005, Frank King Collection, #37809; Clarence Cox, unpublished memoir, pp. 3–4, Clarence Cox Collection, #3740, both at American Folklife Center, Library of Congress (LOC), Washington, D.C.; Benjamin Telinda, questionnaire, Box 12, Folder 46; Paul McCormick, questionnaire, Box 12, Folder 8, both in Cornelius Ryan Longest Day Collection, Mahn Center for Archives and Special Collection (Mahn Center), Alden Library, Ohio University, Athens, OH; William Funkhouser, interview with Jesse Burnett, October 1, 2006, Military Oral History Collection, John A. Adams '71 Center for Military History and Strategic Analysis (Adams Center), Virginia Military Institute, Lexington, VA; Edward Wozenski, oral history interview, 1972, Imperial War Museum Collection (IWM), London, England, copy of transcript in author's possession; E Company, F Company, H Company, L Company, 16th Infantry Regiment, combat interviews; Lieutenant John Spalding, combat interview with Master Sergeant Forrest Pogue and Staff Sergeant J. M. Topete, February 9, 1945, all in combat interview #1 (hereafter referred to as CI-1), copy of the entire collection in author's possession. The interviews can also be found in Record Group 407, Entry 427A, Box 19023, Folder 1 at the National Archives; Laurent Lefebvre, *They Were on Omaha Beach*, self-published, 2003, pp. 133–34, 165–66.

3   Major Carl Plitt, Comments and Criticism of Operations Fox, Fabius I and Neptune, June 30, 1944, Record Group 407, Entry 427, Box 5244, Folder 6; Major Edmund Driscoll, Lieutenant Colonel Herbert Hicks, and Captain Lincoln Fish, Comments and Criticism of Operation Neptune, June 29–30, 1944, Record Group 407, Entry 427, Box 5244, Folder 8; 16th Infantry Regiment, AAR; 3rd Battalion, 16th Infantry Regiment, AAR, all at National Archives; 16th Infantry Regiment, Field Order #5, May 15 and 16, 1944, George

Taylor Papers, Box 2, Folder 6; F and L Companies, 16th Infantry Regiment, Unit Rosters, Fred Hall, unpublished memoir, pp. 17–18, all at MRC; E Company, 16th Infantry AAR by Wozenski, EL; Fred Hall, oral history; John MacPhee, oral history, both in Dwight D. Eisenhower Center (EC) collection, National World War II Museum, New Orleans, LA; William Joseph, questionnaire, Box 11, Folder 46; Edward Wozenski, questionnaire, Box 12, Folder 55, both in Ryan Collection, Mahn Center; Wozenski, oral history, IWM; E Company, F Company, H Company, L Company, 16th Infantry Regiment, combat interviews, CI-1; Major Edwin Elder, "The Operations of the 3rd Battalion, 16th Infantry (1st Infantry Division) in the Assault Landing and Establishment of the Beachhead on Omaha Beach Near Colleville, France, 6–10 June 1944, Personal Experience of a Battalion Operations Officer," pp. 14–15; Vincent Michael McKinney, interview with Aaron Elson, February 5, 1999, located at www.tankbooks.com; Jonathan Gawne, *Spearheading D-Day: American Special Units in Normandy* (Paris: Histoire and Collections, 1998), p. 100; Paul Carrell, *Invasion! They're Coming!* (New York: Bantam, 1984), pp. 73–77; Georges Bernages, *Omaha Beach* (Bayeux: Heimdal, 2002), pp. 76–80. I discussed the American tendency to overestimate firepower and technology in two other World War II invasions, Guam and Peleliu, in *Grunts: Inside the American Combat Experience, World War II Through Iraq* (New York: NAL Caliber, 2010). For the best specific discussion of the failure of the Omaha beach bombardment and the mistakes in planning, see Adrian Lewis, *Omaha Beach: A Flawed Victory* (Chapel Hill, NC: University of North Carolina Press, 2001). The idea that the beach might be cratered was just a soldier's rumor. General Bradley explicitly instructed the Air Force to avoid any cratering on the beach because he feared this would greatly impede the movement of vehicles, supplies, and equipment inland. This, of course, made the aviator's job that much more hopeless.

CHAPTER 1: BACKGROUND

1   16th Infantry Regiment, Historical Report, November 1943, Record Group 407, Entry 427, Box 5232, Folder 8; 16th Infantry Regiment, "History of the Invasion of France," both at National Archives; Stanhope Mason, unpublished memoir, pp. 8–19, Stanhope Mason Papers, Box 7, Folder 25; John Downing, unpublished memoir, p. 233, John Downing Collection, Box 1; Voight, oral history, all at MRC; Steve Kellman, oral history, EC and listed at www.military.com; Cole Kingseed, ed., *From Omaha Beach to Dawson's Ridge: The Com-*

bat Journal of Captain Joe Dawson (Annapolis, MD: Naval Institute Press, 2005), pp. 121–22; Omar Bradley, *A Soldier's Story* (New York: Henry Holt and Company, 1951), pp. 236–37. Stanhope Mason related the story about the division patch and Lieutenant Colonel Jimmy Wright. Elsewhere in his memoir, General Bradley made the erroneous claim that the 1st was the only amphibious-combat-experienced infantry division available in England. The 9th Infantry Division, which had made the North Africa landing, was also available, but was earmarked for the assault on Utah beach.

2   Stanhope Mason, unpublished memoir, general citation from background discussion of Allen; Downing, unpublished memoir, pp. 227–28, both at MRC; Charles Murphy, interview with Dr. Charles W. Johnson, April 13, 1993, Center for the Study of War and Society, University of Tennessee, Knoxville, Tennessee (CSWS); Major R. J. Rogers, "A Study of Leadership in the First Infantry Division During World War II: Terry de la Mesa Allen and Clarence Ralph Huebner" (master's thesis, U.S. Army Command and General Staff College, 1965), pp. 2–5, 85–87, located at USAMHI; Colonel Bryce Denno, "Allen and Huebner: Contrast in Command," *Army*, June 1984, pp. 62–68; Samuel Fuller, *A Third Face: My Tale of Writing, Fighting, and Filmmaking* (New York: Alfred A. Knopf, 2002), p. 135; Franklyn Johnson, *One More Hill* (New York: Bantam, 1983), pp. 76–77; Robert Baumer with Mark Reardon, *American Iliad: The 18th Infantry Regiment in World War II* (Bedford, PA: Aberjona Press, 2004), pp. 134–36, 163–67; Rick Atkinson, *Day of Battle: The War in Sicily and Italy, 1943–1944* (New York: Henry Holt and Company, 2007), pp. 159–60; Kingseed, *Omaha to Dawson's Ridge*, pp. 64–65, 105–7; Bradley, *Soldier's Story*, pp. 110, 154–57. For an in-depth look at Allen's life, see Gerald Astor, *Terrible Terry Allen: Combat General of World War II—The Life of an American Soldier* (Novato, CA: Presidio Press, 2004).

3   Clarence Huebner, biographical sketch, Record Group 407, Entry 427, Box 5027, Folder 5, National Archives; Clarence Huebner, biographical sketch, Chester Hansen Papers, Series II, Box 9, Folder 19; Joe Dawson, interview with Robert Rowe, July 28, 1989, Robert Rowe Papers, Box 1, Folder 23; Rogers, "Study of Leadership," pp. 53–58, 63, all at USAMHI; Joe Dawson, interview with John Votaw, April 16, 1991, G Company, 16th Infantry Material; Stanhope Mason, reminiscences, pp. 1–2; George Pickett, notes from interview with Andrew Woods, February 28, 2002, all at MRC; Arthur Chaitt, "Clarence R. Huebner, Lieutenant General USA Retired, 1888–1972," *Bridgehead Sentinel*, Spring 1973, pp. 1–10, 22; Denno, "Allen

and Huebner," pp. 62–65, 68; H. R. Knickerbocker et al., *Danger Forward: History of the First Division, 1941–1945* (Nashville, TN: Battery Press, 1947), pp. 205–6; Baumer and Reardon, *American Iliad*, pp. 165–67; Bradley, *Soldier's Story*, pp. 156–57. For an excellent look at Huebner's experiences as a combat commander with the 1st Infantry Division in World War I, see James Nelson, *The Remains of Company D: A Story of the Great War* (New York: St. Martin's Press, 2009).

4   Major General Clarence Huebner, notes on commander's conference, August 23, 1943, Stanhope Mason Papers, Box 1, Folder 8; Daniel Lyons, oral history, June 17, 1994; Mason, reminiscences, pp. 54–56, all at MRC; Rogers, "Study of Leadership," pp. 59–67, USAMHI; Chaitt, "Clarence R. Huebner," pp. 7–16, 20–21; Denno, "Allen and Huebner," pp. 69–70; Johnson, *One More Hill*, pp. 114–15; Baumer and Reardon, *American Iliad*, pp. 168–69.

5   18th Infantry Regiment, Historical Reports, December 1943, January 1944, February 1944, Record Group 407, Entry 427, Box 5254, Folders 5, 6, and 7; 16th Infantry Regiment, Historical Reports, December 1943, January 1944, February 1944, March 1944, Record Group 407, Entry 427, Box 5232, Folder 8; "History of the Invasion of France," all at National Archives; 1st Infantry Division, training program, April 1944, Stanhope Mason Papers, Box 7, Folder 26; Taylor, "Observations on an Infantry Regiment in Combat," both at MRC; Frank Beetle, interview with Dr. Macklin Burg, University of Washington, January 15, 1988, located www.military.com; Wozenski interview, IWM; Lieutenant John Baumgartner et al., *16th Infantry Regiment: 1861–1946*, self-published, 1999 reproduction of 1945 version, p. 68.

6   16th Infantry Regiment, Historical Reports, February 1944, March 1944, April 1944, Record Group 407, Entry 427, Box 5232, Folders 8 and 9; 18th Infantry Regiment, Historical Report, February 1944, all at National Archives; Charles Ryan, oral history, Eisenhower Center oral history transcripts, Box 2; Hall, unpublished memoir, p. 15, both at MRC; F. L. Mutter, oral history, EC; Edward Steeg, unpublished memoir, pp. 53–54, Edward Steeg Collection #3775; Howard Johnson, unpublished memoir, no pagination, Howard Johnson Collection #47635, both at LOC; Harley Reynolds, unpublished memoir, pp. 4–5, copy in author's possession; Wozenski interview, IWM; McKinney interview, www.tankbooks.com; Baumgartner et al., *16th Infantry Regiment*, p. 69; Gawne, *Spearheading D-Day*, pp. 84–90. The division participated in dry-run invasions known as Operations Fox and Fabius.

7   Major General Clarence Huebner, diary, Stanhope Mason Papers, Box 7, Folder 13; Chaitt, "Clarence, R. Huebner," pp. 12–13, both in MRC. Private First Class Melvin Hughes, a military policeman, was on guard duty at Huebner's quarters the evening of Roosevelt's visit. He saluted Roosevelt and briefly conversed with him before he met with Huebner. In an interview conducted decades later with Doug Klein, Hughes expressed the opinion that at the time Roosevelt was tipsy, probably from knocking back a few drinks earlier with Quentin and his fiancée. A transcript of this June 9, 1990, interview can be found at the MRC.

8   1st Infantry Division, Special Services Division, Report on Activities, January–April, 1944, Record Group 407, Entry 427, Box 5173, Folder 10, National Archives; William Faust, unpublished memoir, pp. 93–100, World War II Survey Material, Survey #1826, USAMHI; Johnson, unpublished memoir, no pagination, LOC; Rafael Uffner, unpublished memoir, pp. 362–68, Rafael Uffner Collection, Box 1; Charles Dye, oral history, Box 11, Folder 23; Downing, unpublished memoir, pp. 265–66, all at MRC; Baumgartner et al., *16th Infantry Regiment*, p. 69; Lieutenant John Spalding, letter to LeRoy Spalding, May 20, 1944, excerpts made available to the author by Tina Gerteisen; Demetrius "Pete" Lypka, *A Soldier Remembers: A Memoir of Service in the 1st Infantry Division, 1941–1945* (Chicago: Cantigny First Division Foundation, 2007), pp. 124–26. I would like to thank Jim Erickson for interviewing Lieutenant John Spalding's granddaughter Tina Gerteisen and working with her to make Spalding's personal letters and other firsthand material available to me.

9   SHAEF, information on underwater obstacles, April–June 1944, Record Group 331, Entry 12, Box 13, Folder 2; SHAEF, G2 "Martian" Reports, March 15, 1944 #87; April 12, 1944 #91; May 24, 1944 #97, all in Record Group 331, Entry 13, Box 34; SHAEF, G2 Neptune-Argus Report, May 10, 1944, #13, Record Group 331, Box 36; First Army, G2 Estimate of Situation, May 11, 1944, Record Group 407, Entry 427, Box 19305, Folder 590, Pre-Invasion Planning Files; Colonel Benjamin "Monk" Dickson, Memo regarding underwater obstacles, April 24, 1944, Record Group 407, Entry 427, Box 19309, Folder 630, Pre-Invasion Planning Files; V Corps, Information on beach obstacles, May 17, 1944, Record Group 338, Entry 142875E, Box 13, Folder 7, V Corps G3 Training and Operations Records; V Corps, G2 Estimate of Enemy Situation, April 1, 1944, Record Group 407, Entry 427, Box 19316, Folder 687, Pre-Invasion Planning Files; V Corps, G2 Estimate of Enemy Situation, May 15, 1944, Record Group 407, Entry 427, Box 19313, Folder 663,

Pre-Invasion Planning Files; Major General Leonard Gerow, Clearing of wire obstacles by air bombing, February 9, 1944, and Breaching beach obstacles, April 29, 1944, both in Record Group 407, Entry 427, Box 19312, Folder 647, Pre-Invasion Planning Files; 1st Infantry Division, G2 Estimate of Enemy Situation, April 6, 1944, Record Group 407, Entry 427, Box 19310, Folder 632, Pre-Invasion Planning Files; Lieutenant Colonel Fritz Ziegelmann, "352nd Infantry Division, 5 December 1943 Through 7 June 1944," Record Group 549, Foreign Military Studies, B-432 and B-433; Admiral Friedrich Ruge, "Rommel and the Atlantic Wall," Record Group 549, Foreign Military Studies, A-982, all at National Archives; Engineer Provisional Brigade, Operation Report Neptune, Omaha Beach, 26 February–26 June, 1944, located at USAMHI; Field Marshal Erwin Rommel, diary, April 23, 1944; Field Marshal Erwin Rommel, memo, April 22, 1944, both in Box 27, Folder 8, Ryan Collection, Mahn Center; Lewis, *Omaha Beach: A Flawed Victory*, pp. 201–4. A duplicate copy of the V Corps G2 Estimate of Enemy Situation from May 15, 1944, is also available at Record Group 338, Entry 142875E, Box 13, Folder 1, V Corps G3 Training and Operations Records, National Archives.

10   Report on demonstration of various weapons against obstacles to landing operations, Fort Pierce, FL, February 8–12, 1944; V Corps, Underwater obstacles breaching plan; Rear Admiral John Hall, Breaching of underwater obstacles, all in Record Group 407, Entry 427, Box 19312, Folder 647, Pre-Invasion Planning Files; General Omar Bradley, Overlord planning conference, December 21, 1943, Record Group 407, Entry 427, Box 19245, Folder 209, Pre-Invasion Planning Files; First Army, Directive for Engineers and NCDU's, Record Group 407, Entry 427, Box 19306, Folder 601, Pre-Invasion Planning Files; Brigadier General William Kean, Memo to General Bradley regarding underwater obstacles, April 20, 1944, Record Group 407, Entry 427, Box 19309, Folder 630, Pre-Invasion Planning Files; Colonel R. K. McDonough and Colonel John Hill, Notes from conference with Rear Admiral John Hall regarding underwater obstacles, March 29, 1944, Record Group 407, Entry 427, Box 19314, Folder 679, Pre-Invasion Planning Files; Gerow, clearing of wire obstacles by air bombing; 1st Infantry Division, Special Engineer Task Force Plan, May 22, 1944, Record Group 407, Entry 427, Box 19310, Folder 633, Pre-Invasion Planning Files; Lieutenant Commander Joseph Gibbons, oral history, September 27, 1944, Record Group 38, Entry P-11, Box 10, U.S. Navy Oral Histories, all at National Archives; Engineer Provisional Brigade, Post-invasion comments on underwater obstacles, Robert Rowe Papers, Box 7,

Folder 22; Operation Report Neptune, Omaha Beach, both at US-AMHI; Milton Jewett, interview with Cornelius Ryan, June 5, 1958, Box 18, Folder 14, Ryan Collection, Mahn Center; Georges Bernage, *Omaha Beach* (Bayeux, France: Heimdal, 2002), pp. 25–26, 60–61; Gawne, *Spearheading D-Day*, pp. 126–41; Lewis, *Omaha Beach: A Flawed Victory*, pp. 197–209; Bradley, *Soldier's Story*, pp. 244, 260–61.

11   V Corps, Intelligence Operations, Record Group 407, Entry 427, Box 2872, Folder 6; 1st Infantry Division, G2 Maps of Colleville and St. Laurent, March 29, 1944, Record Group 407, Entry 427, Box 5005, Folder 1; 26th Infantry Regiment, Field Order, May 19, 1944, Record Group 407, Entry 427, Box 5267, Folder 3; SHAEF, G2 Martian Report, March 15, 1944; First Army, G2 Estimate of Enemy Situation, May 11, 1944; V Corps, G2 Estimate of Enemy Situation, May 15, 1944; 1st Infantry Division, G2 Estimate of Enemy Situation, April 6, 1944; Ziegelmann, "352nd Infantry Division," all at National Archives; Robin Pearce, *Marshalling Camps of the 1st Infantry Division, World War II*, Ph.D. dissertation, Robin Pearce Collection, Box 1; 16th Infantry Regiment, S2 Estimate of Enemy Situation and Order of Battle, May 16, 1944, George Taylor Papers, Box 2, Folder 6, both at MRC; Lieutenant General Max Pemsel, Chief of Staff, Seventh Army (German), interview notes, no date, no identification of interviewer, Box 27, Folder 3, Ryan Collection, Mahn Center; Baumgartner et al., *16th Infantry Regiment*, pp. 68–69; Stephen Badsey and Tim Bean, *Battle Zone Normandy: Omaha Beach* (Gloucestershire, UK: Sutton Publishing, 2004), pp. 30–34; Tim Kilvert-Jones, *Omaha Beach: V Corps' Battle for the Normandy Beachhead* (South Yorkshire, UK: Leo Cooper, 1999), pp. 58–61; Johnson, *One More Hill*, pp. 133–34; Lewis, *Omaha Beach: A Flawed Victory*, pp. 279–82; Bradley, *Soldier's Story*, pp. 271–72. Bradley wrote that immediately before boarding the ship for Normandy, his intelligence officer, Colonel Benjamin "Monk" Dickson, found out that troops from the 352nd had been moved from Saint-Lô to the beaches "for a defense exercise." Dickson forwarded this information to V Corps and the 1st Division but, with the assault units sealed aboard their ships, it was apparently far too late to inform them of this crucial intelligence. Because Bradley repeats the fallacy of the random 352nd Infantry Division defense exercise, I am skeptical of his claim. If Dickson truly had uncovered accurate, fresh information on the whereabouts of the 352nd before the invasion, he would have known that portions of the division had moved to the Normandy coast well before June. In fairness to Bradley, perhaps he, like so many other Americans, simply heard the anti-invasion exercise

myth in the years following D-Day and unconsciously repeated it in his memoir.

CHAPTER 2: INTENTIONS

1   1st Infantry Division, Plans and Orders, Record Group 407, Entry 427, Box 5005, Folder 7; 1st Infantry Division, Tactical Study of Terrain, March 25, 1944, Record Group 407, Entry 427, Box 19310, Folder 632, Pre-Invasion Planning Files; 16th Infantry Regiment, Summary of regimental situation on D-Day, Record Group 407, Entry 427, Box 5238, Folder 3; Ziegelmann, "352nd Infantry Division," all at National Archives; 1st Infantry Division, Martian Defense Legend of Omaha Beach, May 16, 1944, and 16th Infantry Regiment, Tactical Study of Terrain, May 16, 1944, both in the George Taylor Papers, Box 2, Folder 6; 352nd Infantry Division at Omaha Beach, Easy Red File, all at MRC; Historical Division, U.S. War Department, *Omaha Beachhead, 6 June–13 June, 1944* (Washington, D.C.: War Department, 1945), pp. 11–27; Steven Zaloga, *D-Day Fortifications in Normandy* (Oxford, UK: Osprey, 2005), pp. 12–29, 33, 42–48; J. E. Kaufmann and H. W. Kaufmann, *Fortress Third Reich: German Fortifications and Defense Systems in World War II* (New York: DaCapo Press, 2003), p. 313; Balkoski, *Omaha Beach*, pp. 130–32; Pierre-Louis Gosselin, Director and Curator, Big Red One Museum, Colleville-sur-Mer, conversations with author, July 2013; Paul Woodage, battlefield historian, conversations with author, July 2013; personal survey of WN-60 through WN-65 battle sites, multiple years but primarily July 2013. Gosselin founded the only Normandy museum devoted to the Big Red One, and his expertise is both voluminous and impressive; Woodage is another leading expert and battlefield historian who also lives in Normandy. Regarding the German order of battle, historians have never determined with absolute precision the number of German defenders at Omaha beach as a whole, much less the 1st Infantry Division sector. My estimate is based on the blend of sources listed above and is my own subjective opinion.

2   1st Infantry Division, Landing Diagram, Annex #6 to Field Order #5, April 12, 1944, Record Group 338, Entry A142875E, Box 12, Folder 2, V Corps G3 Training and Operations Records; G3 Report on Operations, June 1944, Record Group 407, Entry 427, Box 5104, Folder 12; Ship and Craft Allotment, March 15, 1944, Record Group 407, Entry 427, Box 19311, Folder 636, Pre-Invasion Planning Files; Major William Duncan, Results of training, tests, and tactical opera-

tions on DD tanks at Slapton Sands, England, April 30, 1944, Record Group 407, Entry 427, Box 19313, Folder 659, Pre-Invasion Planning Files; Plans and Orders; Special Engineer Task Force Plan; 16th Infantry Regiment, "History of the Invasion," all at National Archives; 1st Infantry Division, tank employment plan, D-Day Display Documents File; 16th Infantry Regiment, Plans, Landing Tables, Landing Diagram, all in George Taylor Papers, Box 2, Folder 6, at MRC; Assault Force O, Landing Plan, May 20, 1944, Robert Rowe Papers, Box 9, Folder 16; Major William Lord, Assistant G3, 1st Infantry Division, questionnaire, World War II Survey #1, both at USAMHI; Knickerbocker et al., *Danger Forward*, pp. 208–9; Historical Division, *Omaha Beachhead*, pp. 28–34; Lewis, *Omaha Beach: A Flawed Victory*, pp. 282–301. The plans were far more detailed than what I have discussed. In fact, historians have devoted long chapters and even entire books to the topic (Lewis's volume is the best example). For the sake of brevity and clarity, and since so much is already known about the plans, I have limited my discussion to a summary, based upon what I feel are the best primary sources. On D-Day, the 29th Infantry Division landing teams were technically under the command of General Huebner and the 1st Infantry Division, making him a de facto corps commander for a few hours. In my opinion, this administrative setup had little bearing on the conduct and course of the actual battle, so I have chosen simply to mention it here rather than cover it in depth.

CHAPTER 3: H-HOUR

1 Lieutenant Dean Rockwell, Evaluation of DD LCT Operations, April 30, 1944, Record Group 407, Entry 427, Box 19313, Folder 659, Pre-Invasion Planning Files; 741st Tank Battalion, AAR, June 1944, Record Group 407, Entry 427, Box 13053, Folder 4; 741st Tank Battalion, Unit Journal, June 6, 1944, Record Group 407, Entry 427, Box 13503, Folder 1; 741st Tank Battalion, Field Order #1, May 21, 1944, Record Group 407, Entry 427, Box 13053, Folders 4 and 5; Duncan, Results of training, tests, and tactical operations on DD tanks, etc., all at National Archives; 741st Tank Battalion, unpublished history, p. A14, Sarah Katz file; Andrew Woods, e-mail with general info, both at MRC; 741st Tank Battalion, LCT assignments and landing spots, Robert Rowe Papers, Box 27, Folder 7; A and B Companies, 741st Tank Battalion, boat assignments, Robert Rowe Papers, Box 12, Folder 3; Assault Force O, Action Report on DD tanks, July 14, 1944; Reports from LCT commanders to Lieutenant Dean Rockwell on the launching of DD tanks, summer 1944,

both items in Robert Rowe Papers, Box 13, Folder 1; Millard Case, interview with Robert Rowe, July 18, 1987, Robert Rowe Papers, Box 8, Folder 11; Ralph Woodward, interview with Robert Rowe, July 17, 1987, Robert Rowe Papers, Box 8, Folder 13, all at USAMHI; Robert Skaggs, questionnaire, Box 12, Folder 38, Ryan Collection, Mahn Center; P. L. Fitts, oral history, EC; Alan Weiner, "The First Wave," *American Heritage*, May/June 1987, pp. 136–38; Steve Zaloga, "The Great D-Day Myth," *World War II*, June/July 2008, pp. 40–46; Historical Division, *Omaha Beachhead*, p. 42; Gawne, *Spearheading D-Day*, pp. 158–60; Balkoski, *Omaha Beach*, pp. 100-104. Background information on Captain Thornton can be found at www .thecitadelmemorialeurope.wordpress.com. He was KIA on September 14, 1944, at the Siegfried Line. Some records, such as a 16th Infantry lessons learned report, authored by Major Carl Plitt, the S3 (Record Group 407, Entry 427, Box 5244, Folder 6, National Archives), claim that six DD tanks made it to the beach. I believe this is an error. In my view, the 741st sources are the best and most accurate on this issue for the obvious reason that they were in the best position to know.

2 3rd Battalion, 16th Infantry Regiment, AAR, Record Group 407, Entry 427, Box 5247, Folder 25; I Company, 16th Infantry Regiment, Company History, Record Group 407, Entry 427, Box 5249, Folder 9; D-Day AAR, Record Group 407, Entry 427, Box 5250, Folder 7; K Company, 16th Infantry Regiment, Company History, Record Group 407, Entry 427, Box 5249, Folder 10; D-Day AAR, Record Group 407, Entry 427, Box 5250, Folder 8; L Company, 16th Infantry Regiment, Company History, Record Group 407, Entry 427, Box 5249, Folder 11; D-Day AAR, Record Group 407, Entry 427, Box 5250, Folder 14, all at National Archives; HMS *Empire Anvil*, AAR and Record of Events; Ronald Featherstone and George Mawer, questionnaires, all in Robert Rowe Papers, Box 10, Folder 21 at USAMHI (Featherstone and Mawer were both Royal Navy LCA crewmen who shuttled the 3rd Battalion to the shore); Albert Mominee, oral history, EC; I Company, 16th Infantry Regiment, Morning Report, June 6, 1944; K Company, 16th Infantry Regiment, Morning Report, June 6, 1944; L Company, 16th Infantry Regiment, Morning Report, June 6, 1944, all at National Personnel Records Center; Elder, "Operations of the 3rd Battalion, 16th Infantry," pp. 13–15. Copies of the company histories and AARs can also be found in the Normandy Box at MRC.

3 Lieutenant Colonel Fritz Ziegelmann, operations officer's log, June 6, 1944, Record Group 549, Foreign Military Studies, B-388; Zie-

gelmann, "352nd Infantry Division," both at National Archives; German soldiers at WN-62; 352nd Infantry Division at Omaha Beach, both in Easy Red File, MRC; Franz Gockel, unpublished memoir, no pagination, Robert Rowe Papers, Box 16, Folder 14, US-AMHI; Hannah Cleaver, "Franz Gockel," *The Observer*, May 8, 2004; Hein Severloh, *WN62: A German Soldier's Memories of the Defence of Omaha Beach Normandy, June 6, 1944* (Garbsen, Germany: H.E.K. Creativ Verlag, 2011), pp. 52–56; Carrell, *Invasion! They're Coming!* pp. 73–76; Bernages, *Omaha Beach*, pp. 78–79, 99–100; Gosselin conversations. The Internet contains some good information on the German defenders of Omaha beach. See, for example, www.scalemodeler.co.za for a nice layout of WN-59.

4 USS *Henrico*, Action Report, June 26, 1944, Record Group 38, Entry UD351, Box 1027, Folder 1; USS *Henrico*, Deck Log, June 6, 1944, Record Group 24, Box 4265, Folder 2; E Company, 16th Infantry, History, Record Group 407, Entry 427, Box 5249, Folder 7; F Company, 16th Infantry, History, Record Group 407, Entry 427, Box 5249, Folder 8; 16th Infantry Regiment, Unit Journal, June 6, 1944, Record Group 407, Entry 427, Box 5328, Folder 12; 16th Infantry Regiment, "History of the Invasion of France," all at National Archives; E Company, 16th Infantry, AAR, EL; Wozenski, McCormick questionnaires, Ryan Collection, Mahn Center; Wozenski, oral history, IWM; Voight, oral history, MRC; E Company, F Company, 16th Infantry, Morning Reports, June 6, 1944, National Personnel Records Center; E Company, F Company, 16th Infantry, combat interviews, CI-1; Samuel Eliot Morison, *History of United States Naval Operations in World War II: The Invasion of France and Germany, 1944–1945* (Boston: Little, Brown, 1957), pp. 137–38; Balkoski, *Omaha Beach*, pp. 134–35; personal survey of boat section landing spots, July 2013. The *Henrico*'s action report claimed that "the beach was easily identified and all boats landed on the proper beaches." To my knowledge, there are no surviving accounts from any of the LCVP crewmen.

5 16th Infantry Regiment, "History of the Invasion of France"; F Company, 16th Infantry, History, both at National Archives; John Finke, interview with Robert Rose, April 2, 1989, Robert Rowe Papers, Box 1, Folder 25; Andrew Nesevitch, interview with Robert Rowe, August 22, 1988, Robert Rowe Papers, Box 2, Folder 3; Edward Zukowski, interview with Robert Rowe, June 21, 1989, Robert Rowe Papers, Box 2, Folder 6; Information on disposition of men from F Company, 16th Infantry Regiment, Robert Rowe Papers, Box 27, Folder 1, all at USAMHI; John Finke interviews with John

Votaw and Eric Gillespie, August 9, 1989, and August 29, 1991; F Company, 16th Infantry, Unit Roster, 16th Infantry Regiment Association Collection, Unit Roster file, both at MRC; John Finke, oral history, IWM; Thomson, oral history, EC; F Company, 16th Infantry, combat interview, CI-1; F Company, 16th Infantry, Morning Report, June 6, 1944, National Personnel Records Center; Lefebvre, *They Were on Omaha Beach*, pp. 133–34; Donna Littlejohn, "UCLA's WWII Casualties Tracked Through Research Project," *Daily Breeze*, March 28, 2013; "May They Never Be Forgotten," *Hooah: Newsletter of the UCLA Department of Military Science*, Fall 2007, p. 7; personal survey of boat section landing spots, July 2013. This article includes a list of UCLA students who have been killed in America's wars. Aaron Dennstedt is on this list. On August 10, 1946, Dennstedt's heartbroken mother wrote a letter to the Army's historical division urging them to thoroughly tell the story of the 1st Infantry Division's battle at Omaha beach. "Of course you folks are the ones who know what is entitled to a place in the final history or record . . . while I am just another proud mother of an only son. And if it is not included I will try to understand." She enclosed a copy of Lieutenant Dennstedt's posthumous Silver Star citation. The letter and citation can be found at Record Group 319, Entry 72, Box 1, Folder 4, Records of the Army Staff Historical Division, Army Forces in Action, Omaha Beachhead, National Archives.

6   16th Infantry Regiment, "History of the Invasion of France"; E Company, 16th Infantry, History, both at National Archives; E Company, 16th Infantry, AAR; Huch letter, June 26, 1944, both at EL; Earl Chellis, interview with Robert Rowe, June 18, 1989, Robert Rowe Papers, Box 1, Folder 22, USAMHI; Wozenski, McCormick, Telinda questionnaires, Ryan Collection, Mahn Center; Wozenski, oral history, IWM; E Company, 16th Infantry, combat interview, CI-1; E Company, 16th Infantry, Morning Report, June 6, 1944, National Personnel Records Center; David Allender, www .warchronicle.com; Allender self-published much of the information he gathered for this excellent site in a book-of-the-month club selection entitled *Until the Victory Is Won: The Story of One Group of Heroes from D-Day to the End*, 2001; personal survey of boat section landing spots, July 2013.

7   16th Infantry Regiment, "History of the Invasion of France"; E Company, 16th Infantry, History; Ziegelmann, "352nd Infantry Division" and operations officer log, June 6, 1944, all at National Archives; E Company, 16th Infantry, AAR, EL; Stanley Dzierga, interview with Robert Rowe, June 21, 1989, Robert Rowe Papers,

Box 1, Folder 24; Gockel, unpublished memoir, both at USAMHI; Hein Severloh, personal account, Easy Red file, MRC; John Spalding, questionnaire, Distinguished Service Cross Citation, Box 12, Folder 40, Ryan Collection, Mahn Center; E Company, 16th Infantry, combat interview; Spalding, combat interview, CI-1; E Company, 16th Infantry, Morning Report, June 6, 1944, National Personnel Records Center; John Spalding, letter to family, June 15, 1944, letter to mother, June 28, 1944, excerpts in author's possession courtesy of Tina Gerteisen and Jim Erickson; Glenn Hodges, "Owensboro's War Hero," *Owensboro Messenger-Inquirer*, June 27, 1999, p. 3E; Cleaver, "Franz Gockel"; Steven Zaloga, *The Devil's Garden: Rommel's Desperate Defense of Omaha Beach on D-Day*, p. 58, advance manuscript copy in author's possession courtesy of Steven Zaloga; several fascinating interviews and historical research on the Spalding section are located at David Allender's www.warchronicle.com; Severloh, *WN62*, pp. 58–65; Bernages, *Omaha Beach*, pp. 99–101, 138; Carrell, *Invasion! They're Coming!* pp. 76–77; Gosselin conversations; personal survey of Spalding section landing site and route off Easy Red beach, July 2013. Before his death in 2006, Severloh conducted a dizzying array of interviews for scores of media outlets and documentaries. While taking these sources into consideration, I have chosen to focus primarily upon his written accounts, since they tend toward an especially high level of thoughtfulness, circumspection, and accuracy. Ramundo is listed as a PFC in the 1945 combat interview, but his cross at the American cemetery in Normandy lists him as a sergeant, so I have elected to refer to him by the higher rank.

8   Assault Force O, CTF 124, Action Report, July 27, 1944, Record Group 319, Entry 72, Box 1, Folder 7; Harrison Marble, letter to Army Historical Division, August 12, 1946, Record Group 319, Box 1, Folder 4, both in Records of the Army Historical Division, Army Forces in Action, Omaha Beachhead, National Archives; Lieutenant Colonel John O'Neill, Special Engineer Task Force, Report, Robert Rowe Papers, Box 16, Folder 7; Engineers at Omaha Beach, Robert Rowe Papers, Box 16, Folder 8; Naval Combat Demolition Units, AAR, June 18, 1944, Robert Rowe Papers, Box 10, Folder 6; Engineer Provisional Brigade, Operation Report Neptune and post-invasion comments on underwater obstacles, all at USAMHI; Harrison Marble, questionnaire, Box 18, Folder 27, Ryan Collection, Mahn Center; David Snoke, letter to parents, June 6, 1945, Folder #2809, Collection #68, World War II Letters, State Historical Society of Missouri Research Center, Columbia, MO; HQ Company, A Company, C Company, 299th Engineer Combat Battalion, Morning Report, June 6, 1944, National Personnel Records Center; U.S. Army Center for

Military History, *The Normandy Invasion: The Technical Services in Overlord*, pp. 319–23, located at www.history.army.mil/html/reference/Normandy; www.299thcombatengineers.com; Francis Fane and Don Moore, *The Naked Warriors* (New York: Appleton-Century-Crofts, 1956), pp. 57–63; Balkoski, *Omaha Beach*, pp. 147–50; Gawne @dsmfgFTP!, *Spearheading D-Day*, pp. 131–42; personal survey of Gap Assault Team landing sites, July 2013.

9   Assault Force O, Action Report; Gibbons, oral history, both at National Archives; O'Neill report; Engineers at Omaha Beach; Naval Combat Demolition Units, AAR; Engineer Provisional Brigade, Operation Report Neptune and post-invasion comments on underwater obstacles, all at USAMHI; Barton Davis, questionnaire, Box 17, Folder 47; Joseph Gibbons, notes from NCDU action report, Box 14, Folder 35; Gerald Burt, questionnaire, Box 17, Folder 39; Milton Jewett, notes from interview with Cornelius Ryan, June 5, 1958, Box 18, Folder 14, all in Ryan Collection, Mahn Center; John Talton, unpublished memoir, pp. 11–15; Carroll Guidry, oral history, both in EC; Chuck Hurlbut, interview with Aaron Elson, September 26, 1998, located at www.tankbooks.com; Michael Accordino, recollections posted at www.299thcombatengineers.com; the Web site also has a list of battalion soldiers who were killed on D-Day; CMH, *Technical Services at Overlord*, pp. 322–26; Fane and Moore, *Naked Warriors*, pp. 62–66; Balkoski, *Omaha Beach*, pp. 147–51; Gawne, *Spearheading D-Day*, pp. 135–38. The Gap Assault Teams crossed the Channel in LCTs, along with the tank dozers that supported them. The ride was rough in the choppy seas. Three of the LCTs swamped or broke down. This resulted in loss of equipment along with much seasickness and misery. In spite of this, all of the teams succeeded in transferring, in the dark, to their bucking LCMs.

10   Overlord Planning Conference, December 21, 1943, Record Group 407, Entry 427, Box 19245, Folder 209, Pre-Invasion Planning Files; A Company, 741st Tank Battalion, crew reports on D-Day, Record Group 407, Entry 427, Box 13503, Folder 1; 741st Tank Battalion, AAR; Unit Journal, June 6, 1944, all at National Archives; Jack Boardman, interview with Robert Rowe, July 18, 1987, Robert Rowe Papers, Box 8, Folder 10; LCT assignment and landing spots, both at USAMHI; Woods e-mail; 741st Tank Battalion, unpublished history, pp. 24–28, both at MRC; Edward Sledge, questionnaire, Box 12, Folder 39, Ryan Collection, Mahn Center; Zaloga, "The Great D-Day Myth," pp. 45–47; Zaloga, *D-Day Fortifications in Normandy*, pp. 43–45; Gawne, *Spearheading D-Day*, pp. 163–66; the best Web site on the 741st is www.taximan.info; personal survey of tank land-

ing sites, July 2013. Decades after the war, Hein Severloh, the German machine gunner at WN-62, met and befriended a former American tank gunner he called "Jack Borman." According to Severloh, this American veteran believed he destroyed one of the antitank guns at WN-62, killing or wounding several Germans, and was racked with guilt for the damage he had done. Severloh assured him there were no hard feelings, and this seemed to comfort the man somewhat. I believe Boardman and "Borman" are the same person.

11   16th Infantry Regiment, "History of the Invasion of France"; 3rd Battalion, 16th Infantry Regiment, AAR; I Company, 16th Infantry Regiment, Company History and AAR; K Company, 16th Infantry Regiment, Company History and AAR; L Company, 16th Infantry Regiment, all at National Archives; Lee Hamlett, interview with Robert Rowe, May 25, 1987, Robert Rowe Papers, Box 1, Folder 27, USAMHI; K and L Companies, 16th Infantry Regiment, Unit Rosters, 16th Infantry Regiment Association Collection, Unit Roster File; 1st Infantry Division, Public Information Office, press release on return of D-Day veterans to Omaha beach, circa 1954, Stanhope Mason Papers, Box 4, Folder 1; Steve Kellman, oral history, Eisenhower Center oral history transcripts, Box 1, all at MRC; Leo Stumbaugh, questionnaire, Box 12, Folder 43, Ryan Collection, Mahn Center; Roger Brugger, oral history, EC; L Company, 16th Infantry, combat interview, CI-1; E Company, 116th Infantry Regiment, combat interview, CI-81; I Company, 16th Infantry, Morning Report, June 6, 1944; K Company, 16th Infantry, Morning Report, June 6, 1944; L Company, 16th Infantry, Morning Report, June 6, 1944, all at National Personnel Records Center; Captain John Armellino, personal account, posted at www.americandday.org; McKinney interview, www.tankbooks.com; Staff Sergeant Vincent Mike McKinney, letter to mother, June 6, 1945, copy in author's possession courtesy of Barbara McKinney; Elder, "Operations of the 3rd Battalion, 16th Infantry," pp. 14–17; Lefebvre, *They Were on Omaha Beach*, pp. 135–36; Balkoski, *Omaha Beach*, pp. 132–34; Gosselin, Woodage conversations, July 2013; personal survey of boat section landing sites, several years, but especially July 2013.

CHAPTER 4: SURVIVORS

1   37th Engineer Combat Battalion, History, Record Group 407, Entry 427, Box 15038, Folder 5; 16th Infantry Regiment, "History of the Invasion of France," both at National Archives; G Company, 16th Infantry, unit rosters, 16th Infantry Regiment Association, Unit

Roster file and G Company, 16th Infantry Regiment material; Joe Dawson, letter to mother, May 30, 1944, and letter to family, June 16, 1944, 16th Infantry Regiment Association Collection, Box 191, Folder 2; Joe Dawson, interview with Andrew Woods, August 25 and 26, 1998, G Company, 16th Infantry Material; Joe Dawson, Al Smith, Bill Washington, Chuck Horner, group interview with Andy Rooney, CBS News, April 29, 1984, G Company, 16th Infantry Material; Joseph Pilck, oral history, Eisenhower Center oral history transcripts, Box 1; Dawson interview with Votaw, all at MRC; Spalding questionnaire, Ryan Collection, Mahn Center; Joe Dawson, oral history; Frank Mutter, oral history, Carl Atwell, oral history, all at EC; Joseph Pilck, questionnaire, WWII Survey #55; Lawrence Krumanocker, letter to Joanna McDonald, no date, Joanna McDonald Papers, Box 3, Folder 1; Dawson, interview with Rowe, all at USAMHI; E Company, 16th Infantry Regiment, combat interview; Spalding combat interview; G Company, 16th Infantry, combat interview all in CI-1; E Company, 16th Infantry, Morning Report, June 6, 1944; G Company, 16th Infantry, Morning Report, both at National Personnel Records Center; Spalding, letter to mother, June 28, 1944; Andrew Woods, "Dawson's Draw," *Bridgehead Sentinel*, Fall 1998, pp. 2–3; www.warchronicle.com; Kingseed, *Omaha Beach to Dawson's Ridge*, pp. xix–xx, xxvii–xxviii; Balkoski, *Omaha Beach*, pp. 167–68, 205; Gosselin conversations; personal survey of battle site, July 2013. In various interviews over the years, Dawson said that, in addition to Baldridge, a soldier named "Sergeant Cleff" accompanied him inland. According to G Company's rosters, there was no one by that name in the unit. There was a PFC William Cuff, and he was on Dawson's boat, so perhaps that is who he meant. However, all of the contemporary records mention only Baldridge and no one else as accompanying Captain Dawson, so my account reflects this. Also, Dawson in several interviews given decades after the war indicated that he encountered Spalding *on the way up* the bluff and asked him to provide cover fire while he attacked the enemy machine-gun nest. But Spalding made no mention of this seemingly significant occurrence in his combat interview with Forrest Pogue, conducted in early 1945, nor in any of his postwar accounts. None of Spalding's men mentioned this, either. Moreover, *none* of the wartime G Company records (including the combat interview conducted in August 1944 at a time when memory was likely to be strongest) mentions that Dawson contacted Spalding on the way up. This would seem to be an important item to omit in these kinds of official records, and from both the G and E Company perspectives. For this reason, and after discussing this issue in some depth with Pierre-Louis Gosselin, I believe that Dawson was mistaken in his postwar recollections about the sequence of events as he ascended the bluff. He actually met up with Spalding *after* he destroyed the machine-gun position with the two grenades. My narrative reflects this interpretation of the facts.

2   T/5 John Joseph Pinder, Medal of Honor file, Record Group 338, Box 24, First Army Awards Case Files; Private Carlton Barrett, Medal of Honor file, Record Group 338, Box 2, First Army Awards Case Files; 16th Infantry Regiment, Intelligence and Reconnaissance Platoon, history, Record Group 407, Entry 427, Box 5241, Folder 7; Headquarters Company, 16th Infantry Regiment, history, Record Group 407, Entry 427, Box 5247, Folder 13; 16th Infantry Regiment, "History of the Invasion of France"; Unit Journal, June 6, 1944, all at National Archives; Biographical information on Lieutenant Colonel John H. Mathews, John Mathews file and D-Day display documents file; Sam Fuller, "Recollections of D-Day," Normandy Heroes File; T/5 John "Joe" Pinder, biographical information, museum correspondence and information, 16th Infantry Regiment, Intelligence and Reconnaissance Platoon, diary, June 6, 1944, all in Joe Pinder File (much of the file contains correspondence among the MRC staff centering around what sort of radio Pinder was hauling—the original documents are quite explicit that it was an SCR-284); Thomas McCann, interview with Andrew Woods, March 7, 2003, Carlton Barrett file, all sources at MRC; Raymond Briel, questionnaire, Box 11, Folder 15; John Carroll, questionnaire, Box 11, Folder 16; Carlton Barrett, questionnaire, Box 11, Folder 10, all in Ryan Collection, Mahn Center; Lieutenant Colonel John Mathews, biographical information, Chester Hansen Papers, Series II, Box 9, Folder 19; John Carroll, questionnaire, WWII Survey #1258 and Robert Rowe Papers, Box 29, Folder 5; Thomas McCann, survey, WWII Survey #7753, all at USAMHI; Headquarters and Headquarters Company, 16th Infantry, combat interview, CI-1; Headquarters and Headquarters Company, 16th Infantry, Morning Report, June 6, 1944, National Personnel Records Center; Thomas Allen, "Savior at Omaha Beach," *Military History*, June/July 2009, p. 19; George Tanber, "D-Day Victim's Daughter Recalls 'Reunion' Journey," *Toledo Blade*, November 11, 1998; Dick Thompson, "Baseball's Greatest Hero, Joe Pinder," *The Baseball Research Journal*, no date, pp. 3–10; Gerald Astor, *June 6, 1944: The Voices of D-Day* (New York: Dell, 1994), pp. 239–40. Pinder's career stats can be accessed at www.baseball reference.com. McCann claimed that after D-Day while recuperating in the hospital from his wounds, Barrett wrote a scathing letter to a sergeant in the I&R platoon in which he criticized either Lieu-

tenant Foley or Lieutenant Fitzpatrick (or perhaps both). The sergeant would not let Foley read it for fear of jeopardizing the young private's chances of getting the Medal of Honor. Foley's testimony was indeed crucial to Barrett receiving the award. Barrett, like many other Medal of Honor recipients, had a troubled postwar life. For a time he worked for the VA. Then he went back into the Army. He married in the late 1940s and fathered three children, one of whom died a few minutes after birth. Barrett got divorced in 1960 and ended up estranged from his family, out of contact for decades. According to McCann, one of Barrett's daughters finally tracked him down, with the help of the VA, in the 1980s at a private hospital. She had him transferred to a VA hospital where he had a leg amputated. He remarried his wife in 1985 and died the next year.

3   USS *Samuel Chase*, Action Report, June 26, 1944, Record Group 38, Entry UD351, Box 1393, Folder 18; Deck Log, June 6, 1944, Record Group 24, Box 7870, Folder 3; Headquarters Company, 16th Infantry Regiment, Company History, Record Group 407, Entry 427, Box 5249, Folder 2; B Company, 16th Infantry, Company History, Record Group 407, Entry 427, Box 5241, Folder 7; C Company, 16th Infantry, Company History, Record Group 407, Entry 427, Box 5249, Folder 6; D Company, 16th Infantry, Company History, Record Group 407, Entry 427, Box 5250, Folder 16; 16th Infantry Regiment, "History of the Invasion of France," all at National Archives; 16th Infantry Regiment, Landing Tables, May 15, 1944; Harley Reynolds, thoughts on members of B Company, 16th Infantry Regiment Association Collection, Box 394, Folder 9; Harley Reynolds, oral history, February 7, 1994, 16th Infantry Regiment Association Collection, Box 394, Folder 11; Charles Thomas, oral history, Eisenhower Center oral history transcripts, Box 2; Albert Smith, interview with John Votaw for the BBC, December 4, 1993, all at MRC; Arthur Schintzel, interview with Cadet William Doyle, October 22, 2006, Adams Center, VMI; John Weaver, letter to Joanna McDonald, no date, Joanna McDonald Papers, Box 3, Folder 1, USAMHI; John Ellery, oral history; Harold Saylor, oral history, both at EC; Niles Knauss, questionnaire, Box 12, Folder 1; James Pence, questionnaire, Box 12, Folder 22; John Ellery, questionnaire, letter to Frances Ward, May 28, 1958, Box 11, Folder 31; LeRoy Herman, questionnaire, Box 11, Folder 38, all in Ryan Collection, Mahn Center; A Company, 16th Infantry, Morning Report, June 6, 1944; B Company, 16th Infantry, Morning Report, June 6, 1944; C Company, 16th Infantry, Morning Report, June 6, 1944, all at National Personnel Records Center; 1st Battalion, 16th Infantry, combat interview; A Company, 16th Infantry, combat interview; B

Company, 16th Infantry, combat interview, C Company, 16th Infantry; D Company, 16th Infantry, combat interview, all in CI-1; Scott T. Price, *The U.S. Coast Guard at Normandy*, located at www.uscg.mil; Reynolds, unpublished memoir, pp. 9–13, copy in author's possession; Robert Capa, *Slightly Out of Focus* (New York: Henry Holt and Company, 1947), pp. 145–47; Balkoski, *Omaha Beach*, p. 205; Gosselin conversations; personal survey of 1st Battalion boat section landing sites, July 2013. According to D Company's records, the unit landed at least an hour after the rifle companies.

4   Lieutenant Colonel Lionel Smith, Distinguished Service Medal recommendation, Record Group 407, Entry 427, Box 15038, Folder 5; 37th Engineer Combat Battalion, S2 Lessons Learned on German Mines, Record Group 407, Entry 427, Box 15042, Folder 6; 37th Engineer Combat Battalion, History; 16th Infantry Regiment, "History of the Invasion of France," all at National Archives; Reynolds' thoughts, oral history; Thomas, oral history, all at MRC; Frank Chesney, oral history; Edward Foley, oral history, Saylor, oral history, all at EC; William Dillon, unpublished memoir, pp. 10–11, WWII Survey #2034, USAMHI; Frank Ciarpelli, questionnaire, Box 11, Folder 19; Knauss, Pence, Herman questionnaires, all in Ryan Collection, Mahn Center; Headquarters Company, 37th Engineer Combat Battalion, Morning Report, June 6, 1944; B Company, 37th Engineer Combat Battalion, Morning Report, June 6, 1944; A Company, B Company, C Company, 16th Infantry Morning Reports, June 6, 1944, National Personnel Records Center; A Company, B Company, C Company, 16th Infantry, combat interviews, CI-1; Reynolds, unpublished memoir, pp. 16–17, copy in author's possession; Lieutenant Colonel Jack Mason, "The Story of Albert Papi," *Army*, June 2004, pp. 48–49. I thank my friend Kevin Hymel for making a copy of this article available to me.

5   16th Infantry Regiment, "History of the Invasion of France," National Archives; Reynolds' thoughts, oral history; Smith interview, all at MRC; Buddy Mazzara, oral history; Ellery, oral history, both at EC; Ellery, questionnaire, letter to Ward; Spalding, questionnaire, both in Ryan Collection, Mahn Center; A Company, B Company, C Company, E Company, 16th Infantry Morning Reports, June 6, 1944, National Personnel Records Center; A Company, B Company, C Company, E Company, 16th Infantry, combat interviews; Spalding combat interview, CI-1; Spalding, letter to mother, June 28, 1944, copy in author's possession; Reynolds, unpublished memoir, pp. 16–20, copy in author's possession; Buddy Mazzara, "I Remember D-Day," *Old Bethpage Tribune*, June 5–11, 1980; Bruce

Buck interview, July 3, 2001, and other firsthand material is located at www.warchronicle.com; Astor, *Voices of D-Day*, pp. 233–34; Bernages, *Omaha Beach*, pp. 42–49; Gosselin conversations; personal survey of Ruquet Valley, July 2013. I would like to thank Pierre-Louis Gosselin for identifying the WN-64 bunker cleared by Mazzarra, Erben, and company, as well as for chronicling the Spalding-Streczyk group's small-unit fight for the strong point.

6   Ziegelmann, operations officer's log, June 6, 1944; 16th Infantry Regiment, "History of the Invasion of France," both at National Archives; Hall, unpublished memoir, p. 18, MRC; Hall, oral history, Thomson, oral history, EC; Raymond Strojny, questionnaire, Distinguished Service Cross Citation, Box 12, Folder 41; Henry Krzyzanowski, questionnaire, Box 12, Folder 4, both in Ryan Collection, Mahn Center; Nesevitch, Zukowski interviews, USAMHI; Theo Aufort, oral history, EC; Raymond Strojny, personal information circa 1945, copy in author's possession, courtesy of Paul Woodage; E Company, 116th Infantry, combat interview, CI-81; F Company, 16th Infantry, combat interview, CI-1; F Company, 16th Infantry, Morning Report, June 6, 1944, National Personnel Records Center; Zaloga, *The Devil's Garden*, p. 59; Bernages, *Omaha Beach*, pp. 32–34; Fred Hall, personal conversations with author, May–June 2004; Hall and I were part of a sixty-year anniversary tour of Normandy; Woodage conversations; personal survey of WN-61, multiple years but especially July 2013. According to the German records, WN-61 was "in enemy hands" by 0903 on D-Day morning.

7   Lieutenant Jimmie Monteith, Medal of Honor file, Record Group 338, Box 21, First Army Awards Case Files; USS *Doyle*, War Diary, June 6, 1944, Record Group 38, Box 808, Folder 1; 16th Infantry Regiment, "History of the Invasion of France"; Unit Journal, June 6, 1944; L Company, 16th Infantry, Company history, D-Day AAR, all at National Archives; Jimmie Monteith, personal documents, Jimmie Montieth File; Albert Smith, interview with Major Ed Aymor, February 28, 1993, Eisenhower Center material; L Company, 16th Infantry, Unit Roster, all at MRC; Steve Kellman, oral history, EC; John Worozbyt, questionnaire, Box 12, Folder 54, Ryan Collection, Mahn Center; L Company, 16th Infantry, Combat interview, CI-1; L Company, 16th Infantry, Morning Report, June 6, 1944, National Personnel Records Center; Armellino, personal account, www.americandday.org; McKinney interview, www.tankbooks.com; McKinney, letter to mother; Clara Cox, "Jimmie Monteith: An American Hero," *Virginia Tech Magazine*, Summer 2009; Lefebvre, *They Were on Omaha Beach*, pp. 166–67; Zaloga, *The Devil's Garden*, pp. 40–43, 61–62; Balkoski,

Omaha Beach, pp. 207–9; Whitlock, *Fighting First*, pp. 151–52; Bernages, *Omaha Beach*, pp. 27–32; Gosselin conversations; Woodage conversations; personal survey of 3rd Battalion beach exit site, July 2013. Sergeant Wells and Private Jones both received the Distinguished Service Cross for their bravery. I would like to thank Jordan Edelstein for his help in identifying Lieutenant John Williams, the leader of the third section.

8   USS *Doyle*, Action Report, Record Group 38, Entry UD351, Box 952, Folder 26; Deck Log, June 6, 1944, Record Group 24, Box 2851, Folder 2; War Diary, June 6, 1944; 16th Infantry Regiment, "History of the Invasion of France"; 3rd Battalion, 16th Infantry, AAR; I, K, L, M Companies, 16th Infantry, D-Day AARs and company histories; Ziegelmann, operations officer's log, June 6, 1944, all at National Archives; Andrew Woods, research project on WN-60 for Professor Simon Trew, June 13, 2009; Captain Kimball Richmond, Distinguished Service Cross Citation, G Company, 16th Infantry Material; Medical Detachment, I, L, K, M, and Headquarters Company, 3rd Battalion, unit rosters all at MRC; Karl Wolf, questionnaire, letter to Frances Ward, April 16, 1958, Box 12, Folder 52; Salvatore Albanese, questionnaire, Box 11, Folder 3; Michael Kurtz, questionnaire, letter to Frances Ward, June 22, 1958, Box 12, Folder 5, all in Ryan Collection, Mahn Center; "Kimball Russ Richmond: World War II Infantry Company Commander," compiled by F. James Richmond, Albums 1 and 2, World War II Participants and Contemporaries Collection, EL; a copy of this fascinating tribute can also be found in World War II Survey #7208, USAMHI; Joseph Argenzio, interview with Cadet Corey Bachman, October 20, 2006, Adams Center, VMI; Ben Franklin, interview with Kurt Piehler, John Romeiser, and Braum Denton, November 19, 2004, CSWS; Mominee, Brugger oral histories, EC; L Company, 16th Infantry, combat interview, CI-1; I, K, L, M, Headquarters Company, 3rd Battalion, 16th Infantry, Morning Reports, June 6, 1944, all at National Personnel Records Center; Chip Reid, "Sacrifice and Victory Provide Solace to Slain Soldier's Son," *Danbury* (CT) *News-Times*, May 30, 2004; James Gunter, "Normandy Revisited: 20 Years Later," *Stars and Stripes*, June 6, 1964; Zaloga, *The Devil's Garden*, pp. 58–60; Balkoski, *Omaha Beach*, pp. 208–10; Gosselin conversations; personal survey of 3rd Battalion beach exit site, July 2013. The traditional view of most D-Day historians, based on 16th Infantry sources, is that WN-60 fell into American hands by 0900. However, my colleague Professor Simon Trew of the Department of War Studies, Royal Military Academy, Sandhurst, believes that WN-60 did not come under American control until late on D-Day. He bases his ar-

gument primarily on Lieutenant Colonel Ziegelmann's operations officer log, which indicates that the strong point was still in communication with the 352nd Infantry Division's headquarters for much of the day. I believe there is merit in both points of view and my narrative reflects that. The strong point probably was *neutralized* in terms of firing on the beach, by midmorning. However, given the tendency of the assaulting Americans to clash with Germans in the trench lines at the western edges of the strong point and then press inland, it seems very plausible that parts of the diminished WN-60 remained under German control until the afternoon. Professor Trew was kind enough to articulate his point of view on this and many other D-Day topics in an April 19, 2012, e-mail to the author.

CHAPTER 5: BRASS

1   George Taylor, Distinguished Service Cross Citation and supporting documents, Record Group 338, Entry A1 591, Box 33, First Army Awards Case Files; 16th Infantry Regiment, "History of the Invasion of France"; Medical Detachment, 16th Infantry, History; 741st Tank Battalion, AAR, all at National Archives; Charles Tegtmeyer, unpublished memoir, pp. 3–8, Charles Shay folder; Fuller, "Recollections of D-Day"; Jack Thompson, interview with John Votaw, September 14, 1989; "Sixth Naval Beach Battalion: Operation Rescue Report," 1998, contains unit records, plus firsthand accounts from Borden and several other men; Taylor, "Observations on an Infantry Regiment in Combat," all at MRC; Colonel George Taylor, biographical information, Chester Hansen Papers, Series II, Box 9, Folder 19; Chellis interview, both at USAMHI; Charles Tegtmeyer, questionnaire, Box 12, Folder 45; Father Lawrence Deery, letter to Frances Ward, no date, Box 11, Folder 28; Bill Friedman, questionnaire, Box 11, Folder 35; Thomas Merendino, questionnaire, Box 12, Folder 10; Kenneth Quinn, Box 12, Folder 27; Lieutenant Colonel Robert Skaggs, Distinguished Service Citation; Briel questionnaire; Ciarpelli questionnaire, all in Ryan Collection, Mahn Center; Warren Rulien, oral history; John Bistrica, oral history; Saylor oral history; Richard Lindo, oral history, all at EC; Demetrius "Pete" Lypka, interview with Cadet David Williams, October 21, 2006, Adams Center, VMI; 16th Infantry Regiment and Headquarters, 16th Infantry, combat interviews, CI-1; 16th Infantry Regiment and Headquarters Company, 16th Infantry, Morning Reports, June 6, 1944, National Personnel Records Center; Patrick Lewis, *In the Bucket with the 197th Anti-Aircraft (SP) Battalion*, self-published, 2007, pp. 106–7; Lypka, *A Soldier Remembers*, pp. 121–22; Fuller, *A Third Face*, pp.

128, 163–65; Knickerbocker et al., *Danger Forward*, pp. 208–9; Gosselin conversations; personal survey of Taylor landing site, July 2013. There is some question as to how Fuller and others could have known about the actions of the Spalding-Streczyk group so early on D-Day. However, members of the group had filtered back to the beach with prisoners and wounds, so they could easily have related their experiences. Taylor's words have become legendary in the history of D-Day and, even more specifically, the 1st Infantry Division. So much so that many division veterans who did not see Taylor have mentioned his inspirational words prominently in their writings and their discussions of Omaha beach. To these men, the phrase seems to capture the spirit of the division perfectly. In my narrative I utilized only sources from veterans who directly observed and heard Taylor. The movie *The Longest Day* incorrectly portrayed Brigadier General Norman "Dutch" Cota, assistant division commander of the 29th Infantry Division, as uttering the famous words. This is, in my opinion, a real travesty.

2 1st Infantry Division, G3 Journal, June 6, 1944, Record Group 407, Entry 427, Box 5123, Folder 1; G3 Report on Operations, June 1944, Record Group 407, Entry 427, Box 5104, Folder 13; Brigadier General Willard Wyman, biographical sketch, Record Group 407, Entry 427, Box 5027, Folder 5; Cannon Company, 16th Infantry, company history, Record Group 407, Entry 427, Box 5247, Folder 19; Kenneth Emond, letter to Army Historical Division, August 26, 1946, Record Group 319, Entry 72, Box 1, Folder 4, Records of the Army Historical Division, Army Forces in Action, Omaha Beachhead (Emond was the company clerk of Cannon Company); 16th Infantry Regiment, "History of the Invasion of France," all at National Archives; Brigadier General Willard Wyman, biographical information, Chester Hansen Papers, Series II, Box 9, Folder 19; *PC-553*, Deck Log, June 6, 1944, Robert Rowe Papers, Box 11, Folder 15, both at USAMHI; Cannon Company, 16th Infantry, Unit Roster, 16th Infantry Regiment Association Collection, Unit Roster File, MRC; Robert Riekse, questionnaire, correspondence with Frances Ward, 1958–1959, Box 12, Folder 29, Ryan Collection, Mahn Center; Ernest Carrere, unpublished memoir, p. 22; William Otlowski, oral history, both at EC; Cannon Company, 16th Infantry, combat interview, CI-1; Cannon Company, 16th Infantry, Morning Report, June 6, 1944, National Personnel Records Center; Marion Softky, "Tasting the Real Old West: Willard Wyman Talks About His Novel, 'High Country,' at Kepler's, *Almanac News*, September 6, 2006; Knickerbocker et al., *Danger Forward*, pp. 211–13. General Wyman's son Willard became an educator and novelist. In

this interview, he mentioned his mother's emotional struggle during the summer of 1944.

3   1st Medical Battalion, AAR, May–June 1944, Record Group 407, Entry 427, Box 5278, Folder 3; 1st Infantry Division, G3 Journal, June 6, 1944; G3 Report on Operations; 16th Infantry Regiment, "History of the Invasion of France," all at National Archives; 6th Naval Beach Battalion, "Operation Rescue Report"; McCormick Research Center staff correspondence and information on whether an LCI landed at 0630 near the E3 draw; Severloh, personal account, all at MRC; LCI (L) Flotilla 10, Action Report, July 1, 1944; Rear Admiral M. H. Imlay, letter to Frances Ward, May 11, 1958, Box 14, Folder 38; 1st Infantry Division, D-Day messages, Box 11, Folder 2; Riekse questionnaire, all in Ryan Collection, Mahn Center; A Company, 1st Medical Battalion, combat interview, CI-1; A Company, 1st Medical Battalion, Morning Report, June 6, 1944, National Personnel Records Center, the morning report for Headquarters, Division Artillery claims that ninety men from the outfit were aboard LCI-85, but the report listed no casualties or any further elaboration; Herbert Goodick, personal account, at www.witnesstowar .org; information on the 6th Naval Beach Battalion is at www.6th beachbattalion.org; LCI-85 Action Report, June 24, 1944; Seaman First Class Gene Oxley, recommendation for Silver Star, July 14, 1944, both at www.uscg.mil; Lieutenant (j.g.) Arthur Farrar, "LCI's are Veterans Now," *Alumni Association Bulletin, U.S. Coast Guard Academy*, December 1944; Coit Hendley, "D-Day: A Special Report," *Washington Times*, June 6, 1984; Lefebvre, *They Were on Omaha Beach*, pp. 196–97; Severloh, *WN62*, pp. 58–60; Knickerbocker et al., *Danger Forward*, pp. 212–14. Riekse was badly wounded in the hip on D-Day and had to be evacuated. Severloh, the German machine gunner, maintained that an LCI was the first ship to land on D-Day morning. However, there is no way that could be true. I believe he was simply a couple hours off in his estimate of the time when the LCIs began to land. I also think there is a very good chance he fired at LCI-85 since it landed almost under the nose of his position in WN-62.

4   V Corps, G3 Journal, June 6, 1944, Record Group 407, Entry 427, Box 2955, Folder 3; 1st Infantry Division, G3 Journal, June 6, 1944, and G3 Report on Operations (at 1031, Huebner radioed Wyman that "the 18th Infantry is landing as planned; use where needed"); Paul Bystrak, personal account in Blythe Finke, "Old Buddies Tell All," no pagination; Huebner diary, June 6, 1944; Mason, unpublished memoir, pp. 41–44; Mason, oral history, all at MRC; Major

Chester Hansen, diary, June 6, 1944, Chester Hansen Papers, Series II, Box 4, Folder 9 (Late in the morning on D-Day, General Bradley sent his aide Hansen into Omaha beach to apprise him on the situation); Kenneth Lord, questionnaire, Box 12, Folder 6; Ben Talley, unpublished memoir, D-Day messages, interview with Frances Ward, June 6, 1958, Box 19, Folder 3, all in Ryan Collection, Mahn Center; Brigadier General Ben Talley, personal bio, at www.arlingtoncemetery.net; Bruce Jacobs, "D-Day Diary: How It Was Ten Years Ago on Omaha Beach," *Saga*, no date; Arthur Chaitt, "D-Day Twenty Years Later," *Bridgehead Sentinel*, Summer 1964, pp. 1–3; Chaitt, "Clarence R. Huebner, Lieutenant General USA Retired, 1888–1972," *Bridgehead Sentinel*, p. 13; Bradley, *A Soldier's Story*, pp. 270–74. As I mentioned in endnote #2 of Chapter 2, General Huebner on D-Day had operational control over both the 1st and the 29th Infantry Divisions. This meant he was also receiving information from and about the 29th Division side of Omaha beach. Indeed, at almost the same time he sent in the 18th Infantry, he also authorized the landing of the 29th Division's 115th Infantry Regiment on the western side of Easy Red. For the sake of clarity and brevity, and since the focus of this book is on the 1st Division, I have confined my discussion to Huebner's efforts to lead and control his own division. Colonel Mason and Major Kenneth Lord, an assistant operations officer, both claimed that Huebner left the *Ancon* at around midday and landed on Omaha beach at about 1700 (presumably after spending five hours bobbing around the water in a small craft!). However, the naval and divisional records prove beyond any doubt that Huebner did not leave the *Ancon* until at least 1700.

CHAPTER 6: REINFORCEMENTS

1   18th Infantry Regiment, Landing Diagram, Record Group 407, Entry 427, Box 19310, Folder 635, Pre-Invasion Planning Files; 18th Infantry Regiment, Unit History, June 1944, Record Group 407, Entry 427, Box 5254, Folder 8; 18th Infantry Regiment, S1 Journal, June 6, 1944, Record Group 407, Entry 427, Box 5256, Folder 5; 2nd Battalion, 18th Infantry Regiment, Field Order #2, May 20, 1944, Record Group 407, Entry 427, Box 5265, Folder 12; 2nd Battalion, 18th Infantry Regiment, AAR, June 1944, Record Group 407, Entry 427, Box 5265, Folder 10; USS *Anne Arundel*, Action Report, June 14, 1944, Record Group 38, Entry UD351, Box 809, Folder 21; War Diary, June 6, 1944, Record Group 38, Box 569, Folder 3; Deck Log, June 6, 1944, Record Group 24, Box 361, Folder 7, all at National Archives; History of the 18th Infantry Regiment, Stanhope Mason

Papers, Box 7, Folder 1; 18th Infantry Regiment, Landing Tables, George Taylor Papers, Box 2, Folder 4; Richard Conley, oral history, Eisenhower Center oral histories transcripts, Box 1, all at MRC; Richard Lindo, oral history, EC; Richard Conley, questionnaire, letter to Frances Ward, April 9, 1958, Box 11, Folder 21, Ryan Collection, Mahn Center; Headquarters Company, 2nd Battalion, 18th Infantry, Morning Report, June 6, 1944; E Company, 18th Infantry, Morning Report, June 6, 1944; F Company, 18th Infantry, Morning Report, June 6, 1944, G Company, 18th Infantry, Morning Report, June 6, 1944; H Company, 18th Infantry, Morning Report, June 6, 1944, all at National Personnel Records Center; Whitlock, *Fighting First*, pp. 189–90; Balkoski, *Omaha Beach*, pp. 251–53; Baumer and Reardon, *American Iliad*, pp. 189–91.

2   197th Antiaircraft Battalion (SP), History, Record Group 407, Entry 427, Box 13761, Folder 4; AAR, June 1944, Record Group 407, Entry 427, Box 13761, Folder 7; USS *Frankford*, Action Report, June 24, 1944, Record Group 38, UD351, Box 989, Folder 3; Deck Log, June 6, 1944, Record Group 24, Box 3467, Folder 6; 18th Infantry Regiment, Unit History, June 1944; S1 Journal, June 6, 1944; 741st Tank Battalion, AAR, report on crew experiences; Unit Journal, June 6, 1944, all at National Archives; Colonel Stanhope Mason, letter to Rear Admiral John Hall, July 8, 1944, Stanhope Mason Papers, Box 7, Folder 3; Edward Robinson, tour guide, correspondence on what neutralized the pillbox at WN-65, both at MRC; Hyman Haas, oral history; Everett Schultheis, oral history; Alan Anderson, oral history; Wallace Gibbs, oral history, all at EC; Headquarters Battery, 467th Antiaircraft Battalion (SP), Morning Report, June 6, 1944; A Battery, 467th Antiaircraft Battalion (SP), Morning Report, June 6, 1944; B Battery, 467th Antiaircraft Battalion (SP), Morning Report, June 6, 1944; C Battery, 467th Antiaircraft Battalion (SP), Morning Report, June 6, 1944; D Battery, 467th Antiaircraft Battalion (SP), Morning Report, June 6, 1944, all at National Personnel Records Center; more primary-source 467th records can be accessed at www.antiaircraft.org; James Knight, "The DD That Saved the Day," *Proceedings of the Naval Institute*, August 1989, pp. 124–26; Lewis, *In the Bucket*, pp. 114–18; Balkoski, *Omaha Beach*, pp. 254–55; Baumer and Reardon, *American Iliad*, pp. 191–93; Bernages, *Omaha Beach*, pp. 46–47; Badsey and Bean, *Omaha Beach*, pp. 162–63; Historical Division, *Omaha Beachhead*, pp. 83–85; Morison, *Invasion of France and Germany*, pp. 143–45; Gosselin conversations; Woodage conversations; personal survey of WN-65 pillbox and battle site, multiple years but especially July 2013. The contentious pillbox at WN-65 is still in place today and can be seen

by any visitor to Omaha beach. Controversy still rages among historians and veterans as to who or what truly neutralized the pillbox on D-Day morning. The traditional view, espoused by most D-Day scholars including Morison, the official naval historian, is that the USS *Frankford* scored the knockout blow. More recently, the veterans of both the 467th and the 197th have claimed credit. The 467th even placed a plaque over the aperture. Some veterans, like Sponheimer, believe that their unit wrecked the pillbox and that the other outfit made no contribution. Edward Robinson, a ballistics expert and Normandy tour guide, believes, on the basis of pockmarks visible along the face of the pillbox, that, the halftracks destroyed the emplacement. My view is that, given the nature of combat and the chaotic situation on the beach that morning, there is almost no chance that one group or weapon exclusively neutralized the pillbox. The concrete is clearly pockmarked by .50-caliber bullets and probably 37-millimeter shells, as Robinson indicated, but it is also torn away by heavier shells, too, no doubt from the *Frankford* and maybe the tanks as well. Moreover, different groups of German soldiers almost certainly migrated in and out of the pillbox throughout the morning until forced out or coaxed into surrender by American fire, including a direct assault by several soldiers. Thus, my narrative reflects this consideration of the primary-source evidence from 1944 and from personal observation of the pillbox's remnants decades later.

3   LCI-93, Action Report, June 19, 1944, Record Group 38, Entry UD351, Box 1102, Folder 21; LCI-487, Deck Log, June 6, 1944, Record Group 24, Box 1198, Folder 5; LCI-489, Action Report, June 20, 1944, Record Group 38, Entry UD351, Box 1114, Folder 19; Deck Log, June 6, 1944, Record Group 24, Box 1200, Folder 2; LCI-497, Action Report, June 23, 1944, Record Group 39, Entry UD351, Box 1114, Folder 27; 1st Battalion, 18th Infantry Regiment, AAR, June 1944, Record Group 407, Entry 427, Box 5265, Folder 11; 2nd Battalion, 18th Infantry Regiment, AAR; 18th Infantry Regiment, S1 Journal, June 6, 1944, all at National Archives; John France, information on LCIs and K Company, 18th Infantry on D-Day, Roland Ehlers LCI file; Ryan, oral history; History of the 18th Infantry Regiment; Downing, unpublished memoir, p. 291, all at MRC; LCI (L) Flotilla 10, Action Report, July 1, 1944, Box 14, Folder 38; Dale Boyd, questionnaire, Box 11, Folder 14; Donald Parker, questionnaire, Box 12, Folder 21, all at Ryan Collection, Mahn Center; Elmer Seech, oral history; Dean Weissert, oral history; Ralph Burnett, oral history, all at EC; Johnson, unpublished memoir, no pagination; Steeg, unpublished memoir, p. 66, both at

LOC; 1st, 2nd, and 3rd Battalion, 18th Infantry Regiment, all company morning reports, June 6, 1944, all at National Personnel Records Center; John France, "LCI-93, LCI-487, Normandy," at www .usslci.com; Baumer and Reardon, *American Iliad*, pp. 196–97.

4   18th Infantry Regiment, Unit History, June 1944; 1st and 2nd Battalions, 18th Infantry, AAR; Lewis Smith, oral history, Eisenhower Center oral history transcripts, Box 2; Downing, unpublished memoir, pp. 295–99; History of the 18th Infantry Regiment, all at MRC; George Duguay, letter to Frances Ward, July 15, 1958, Box 35, Folder 3; Hyrum Shumway, questionnaire, Box 12, Folder 37; Teno Roncalio, questionnaire, Box 12, Folder 30; Conley, questionnaire, letter; Parker, questionnaire, all at Ryan Collection, Mahn Center; Frank Murray, oral history; Seech, Conley oral histories, all at EC; Johnson, unpublished memoir, no pagination, LOC; James Joseph Furey, interview with Mary Katherine Wilkerson, November 13, 2008, copy of transcript provided to me by Theresa Furey; Headquarters Company, 2nd Battalion, 18th Infantry, Morning Report, June 6, 1944; I Company, 18th Infantry, Morning Report, June 6, 1944; L Company, 18th Infantry, Morning Report, June 6, 1944, all at National Personnel Records Center; Baumer and Bean, *American Iliad*, pp. 197–202; Badsey and Bean, *Omaha Beach*, pp. 77–80; Gosselin conversations; personal survey of Exit E-1 site, July 2013.

CHAPTER 7: INLAND

1   Ziegelmann, operations officer's log, June 6, 1944; Ziegelmann, "352nd Infantry Division," both at National Archives; Severloh, personal account, MRC; Gockel, unpublished memoir, USAMHI; Werner Pluskat interview, no date, no identification of interviewer, Box 27, Folder 4, Ryan Collection, Mahn Center; www .omahabeach.vierville.free.fr English translation version; Cleaver, "Franz Gockel"; Zaloga, *The Devil's Garden*, pp. 59–63; Vince Milano and Bruce Conner, *Normandiefront: D-Day to Saint-Lô Through German Eyes* (Gloucestershire, UK: Spellmont, 2012), pp. 101–7, 122–25; David Isby, ed., *Fighting the Invasion: The German Army at D-Day* (London, UK: Greenhill Books, 2000), pp. 214–17; Bernages, *Omaha Beach*, pp. 138–39, 144–45; Severloh, *WN62*, pp. 70–77; Carrell, *Invasion! They're Coming!* pp. 83–86; Zaloga, *D-Day Fortifications in Normandy*, pp. 45–50; conversation with Hans Hooker, Superintendent, Normandy American Cemetery, July 2013; Gosselin conversations; personal survey, WN-62, multiple years but especially July 2013. Major Werner Pluskat, commander of a Ger-

man artillery battalion at Omaha beach, expressed frustration with ammunition shortages on D-Day. Commanders had stored surplus ammunition several miles inland and then found it extremely difficult to move the ammunition to the beaches because of Allied fighter attacks; Pluskat's resupply apparently was destroyed in this fashion. He also stated in an interview for Cornelius Ryan that division command forbade him from using his battery at Port-en-Bessin. According to him, it never even fired on D-Day. His anger and frustration over this were quite evident. Long after the war, Franz Gockel found the grave of Siegfried Kuska and several of his other WN-62 comrades at La Cambe, the site of the German cemetery in Normandy. Several days after D-Day, Severloh, in the POW compound, encountered Adolf Schiller, one of the defenders of WN-61. Schiller claimed that he had held out in his position until the evening of June 7 and then had hidden for another night in an abandoned Sherman tank just below WN-62. When he emerged from the Sherman on June 8, he was captured.

2 1st Infantry Division, detailed map of Colleville-sur-Mer, Record Group 407, Entry 427, Box 5005, Folder 1; 16th Infantry Regiment, "History of the Invasion of France"; 2nd Battalion, 16th Infantry, AAR; E and F Companies, 16th Infantry, Company Histories; 16th Infantry Regiment, Unit Journal, June 6, 1944, all at National Archives; F and G Companies, 16th Infantry, Unit Rosters; G Company, 16th Infantry, boat section roster; Dawson interview with Votaw; interview with Woods; interview with Rooney and CBS; Pilck, oral history; Finke, interview with Votaw; interview with Gillespie, all at MRC; Finke, interview with Rowe; Dawson, interview with Rowe, both at USAMHI; Dawson, oral history; Mutter, oral history; Atwell, oral history, all at EC; Wozenski questionnaire, at Ryan Collection, Mahn Center; Wozenski interview, IWM; Funkhouser interview, VMI; E, F, G, and H Companies, 16th Infantry, Combat interviews, CI-1; E, F, G, and H Companies, Morning Reports, June 6, 1944, National Personnel Records Center; Woods, "Captain Joe Dawson," *Bridgehead Sentinel*; Lefebvre, *They Were at Omaha Beach*, pp. 197, 220–21; Gosselin conversations; personal survey of G Company route of advance and Colleville-sur-Mer, July 2013.

3 Ziegelmann, operations officer's log, June 6, 1944; "Ziegelmann, "352nd Infantry Division"; 16th Infantry Regiment, "History of the Invasion of France"; E and F Companies, 16th Infantry, Company Histories; 2nd Battalion, 18th Infantry, AAR; 1st Infantry Division map of Colleville, all at National Archives; F and G Companies, 16th Infantry, Unit Rosters; G Company, boat section roster; Dawson in-

terview with Votaw; interview with Woods; interview with Rooney and CBS; History of the 18th Infantry Regiment, all at MRC; Atwell, oral history; Dawson, oral history, both at EC; Spalding questionnaire, at Ryan Collection, Mahn Center; Walter Bieder interview, July 2, 2008; Buck interview, DiGaetano interview, all at www .warchronicle.com; E, F, G and H Companies, 16th Infantry, combat interviews, CI-1; E, F, G, and H Companies, Morning Reports, June 6, 1944, National Personnel Records Center; Zaloga, *The Devil's Garden*, pp. 61–64; Woods, "Captain Joe Dawson," *Bridgehead Sentinel*; Balkoski, *Omaha Beach*, pp. 284–87; Woodage conversations; Gosselin conversations; personal survey of Colleville-sur-Mer, including the church, July 2013. Soldiers from the 1st Battalion, 16th Infantry also participated in the Colleville battle. As they filtered inland, they protected the right flank, west of town, not far from the Spalding-Huch group and 2nd Battalion, 18th Infantry. On D-Day, PFC Marion Tubbs functioned as a runner to battalion headquarters and a guide for wire parties and received a posthumous Silver Star for his actions. Because of this, I believe he was the runner who was killed while trying to make contact with the Spalding-Huch group.

4 1st Infantry Division, map of Colleville-sur-Mer and Le Grand Hameau; 16th Infantry Regiment, "History of the Invasion of France"; 16th Infantry Regiment, Unit Journal, June 6, 1944; 3rd Battalion, 16th Infantry, AAR; I, K, L Companies, 16th Infantry Regiment, Company Histories; Lieutenant Jimmie Monteith, Medal of Honor file, all at National Archives; I, L, and K Companies, 16th Infantry Regiment, Unit Rosters; Jimmie Monteith File; Captain Kimball Richmond, Distinguished Service Cross Citation, all at MRC; Worozbyt questionnaire, Ryan Collection, Mahn Center; L Company, 16th Infantry, combat interview, CI-1; I, K, L, M Companies, 16th Infantry, Morning Reports, June 6, 1944, National Personnel Records Center; Elder, "Operations of the 3rd Battalion, 16th Infantry," pp. 18–20; Cox, "Jimmie Monteith: An American Hero"; Balkoski, *Omaha Beach*, pp. 289–94; Woodage conversations; Gosselin conversations; personal survey of battle site and spot of Monteith's death, July 2013.

Chapter 8: Support

1 1st Infantry Division, G4 AAR, June 1944, Record Group 407, Entry 427, Box 5166, Folder 11; 1st Infantry Division, Civil Affairs, AAR, June 1944, Record Group 407, Entry 427, Box 5172, Folder 4; 1st Infantry Division, Artillery, AAR, June 1944, Record Group

407, Entry 427, Box 5174, Folder 6; 7th Field Artillery Battalion, AAR, June 1944, Record Group 407, Entry 427, Box 5210, Folder 12; Unit Journal, June 6, 1944, Box 5210, Folder 18; 32nd Field Artillery Battalion, AAR, June 1944, Record Group 407, Entry 427, Box 5212, Folder 4; Assault Force O, Action Report; Major Edmund Driscoll and Lieutenant Colonel Chuck Horner, Comments and Criticisms on Operation Neptune, all at National Archives; 1st Infantry Division, Landing Tables; 16th Infantry Regiment, Landing Tables, both in George Taylor Papers, Box 2, Folder 4; 1st Infantry Division, G4 diary, June 6, 1944; 6th Naval Beach Battalion, Unit Citation, February 12, 1945, 6th Naval Beach Battalion File, all at MRC; Historical Division, *Omaha Beachhead*, pp. 2, 36.

2   1st Engineer Combat Battalion, AAR, June 1944; Unit Journal, June 6, 1944, Record Group 407, Entry 427, Box 5205, Folders 1 and 14; 20th Engineer Combat Battalion, AAR, June 1944, Unit Journal, June 6, 1944, Record Group 407, Entry 427, Box 15022, Folder 7; 37th Engineer Combat Battalion, AAR, May–July 1944, Record Group 407, Entry 427, Box 15038, Folder 5; S2 Journal, June 6, 1944, Folder 10; 37th Engineer Combat Battalion, History and Company Histories; 336th Engineer Combat Battalion, Field Order #9, May 8, 1944, Record Group 407, Entry 427, Box 15217, Folder 6; 336th Engineer Combat Battalion, History, Record Group 407, Entry 427, Box 15216, Folder 8; 348th Engineer Combat Battalion, History, Record Group 407, Entry 427, Box 15220, Folder 14; Unit Journal, June 6, 1944, Folder 7, all at National Archives; "Sixth Naval Beach Battalion: Operation Rescue Report, Unit Citation"; Joseph Vaghi, unpublished memoir, p. 6, both in 6th Naval Beach Battalion File, MRC; 5th Engineer Special Brigade, History, Robert Rowe Papers, Box 16, Folder 6; Engineer Provisional Brigade, Operation Report Neptune, both at USAMHI; John Butler, questionnaire, Box 17, Folder 40; James McCain, questionnaire, letter to Frances Ward, April 9, 1958, Box 18, Folder 29; Robert Ross, questionnaire, Box 18, Folder 52; John Zmudzinski, questionnaire, Box 19, Folder 18, all in Ryan Collection, Mahn Center; Jay Adams, interview with Tom Swope, July 5, 2001, Jay Adams Collection, #AFC/2001/001/151, LOC; John Zmudzinski, oral history; Vincent Schlotterbeck, letter to Friends, May 22, 1945, both at EC; Headquarters Company, A Company, B Company, C Company, 37th Engineer Combat Battalion, Morning Reports, June 6, 1944; A Company, B Company, C Company, 336th Engineer Combat Battalion, Morning Reports, June 6, 1944; B Company, C Company, 348th Engineer Combat Battalion, Morning Reports, June 6, 1944,

all at National Personnel Records Center; California Golden Bears, History, p. 178, All Time Football Lettermen, at www.cstv.com; Keith Bryan, *Pack Up and Move: A Pictorial History of the 348th Engineer Combat Battalion* (self-published, 1946), pp. 38–41; David Venditta, "From D-Day to the Elbe River," *Morning Call*, March 17, 2003; *The Corps of Engineers: The War Against Germany*, pp. 326–331, located at www.history.army.mil; Gawne, *Spearheading D-Day*, pp. 236–57; Historical Division, *Omaha Beachhead*, pp. 103–8. At Omaha beach, there were two engineer special brigades, the 5th and the 6th. In general, the 5th was on the 1st Division side of the beach, the 6th at the 29th Division side. Both brigades were part of the Engineer Provisional Brigade under Brigadier General William Hoge. Louis Drnovich was a member of the 1934 Cal Bears football team. He received a posthumous Silver Star for his bravery at Omaha beach.

3   1st Medical Battalion, AAR, May–June 1944, Record Group 407, Entry 427, Box 5278, Folder 3; Medical Detachment, 16th Infantry Regiment, History, Record Group 407, Entry 427, Box 5247, Folder 23; 16th Infantry Regiment, "History of the Invasion of France," all at National Archives; "Sixth Naval Beach Battalion: Operation Rescue Report, Unit Citation," MRC; Engineer Provisional Brigade Report, Operation Neptune; Deborah Bonanni, "United States Army Medical Support During the Invasion of Normandy, 6–9 June, 1944," Hood College, 1976, pp. 54–59, both at USAMHI; Zmudzinski questionnaire, Ryan Collection, Mahn Center; 61st Medical Battalion, Annual Report, 1944, located at www.history.amedd.army. mil; *The Medical Department: Medical Services in the European Theater*, pp. 208–10, located at www.history.army.mil; Clifford Graves, *Front Line Surgeons: A History of the 3rd Auxiliary Surgical Group*, self-published, 1950, pp. 127–31, copy in author's possession; Stephen Ambrose, *D-Day, June 6, 1944: The Climactic Battle of World War II* (New York: Simon & Schuster, 1994), p. 474.

4   1st Medical Battalion, AAR; Medical Detachment, 16th Infantry Regiment, History; 16th Infantry Regiment, "History of the Invasion of France"; 16th Infantry Regiment, Unit Journal, June 6, 1944, all at National Archives; Medical Detachment, 16th Infantry Regiment, Unit Roster, Unit Roster File, 16th Infantry Regiment Association Collection; Shay speech, November 2011; unpublished memoir, no pagination; notes from interview with Andrew Woods, no date; Andrew Woods, notes on medics on D-Day, "Sixth Naval Beach Battalion: Operation Rescue Report, Unit Citation"; Tegtmeyer, unpublished memoir, pp. 8–12; Voight, oral history, all at

MRC; Bernard Friedenberg, unpublished memoir, no pagination, Bernard Friedenberg Collection, AFC/2001/001/38871; Thomas Tolmie, interview with Christin Seifert, August 2007; Thomas Tolmie Collection, AFC/2001/001/76657, both at LOC; Engineer Provisional Brigade Report, Operation Neptune; Finke interview, both at USAMHI; Mark Infinger, questionnaire, Box 18, Folder 11; Johan Dahlen, questionnaire, Box 11, Folder 26; James Jordan, questionnaire, Box 11, Folder 45; John Settineri, questionnaire, Box 12, Folder 33; Tegtmeyer questionnaire; Davis questionnaire, all in Ryan Collection, Mahn Center; A Company, 1st Medical Battalion, combat interview; Medical Detachment, 16th Infantry Regiment, combat interview, both in CI-1; Medical Detachment, 16th Infantry Regiment, Morning Report, June 6, 1944; A, B, C, and D Companies, 1st Medical Battalion, Morning Report, June 6, 1944, all at National Personnel Records Center; Jack Brooks, interview with the author, March 11, 2012; Armellino personal account, www.americandday.org; 61st Medical Battalion, annual report 1944, www.history.amedd.army.mil; Jennifer Walsh, "WWII Medic, Prisoner of War Shares Experiences with Medical Community," September 10, 2009, at www.army.mil; Joshua Rhett Miller, "World War II Medic Still Haunted by 'the Boy on the Beach,'" June 6, 2012, www.foxnews.com; Knickerbocker et al., *Danger Forward*, p. 214; Balkoski, *Omaha Beach*, pp. 330–31; Woodage conversations; Gosselin conversations; personal survey of battle site, July 2013. Tegtmeyer in his memoir referred to Herbert Goldberg as his first sergeant. However, Goldberg wrote the detachment's history a few weeks after D-Day and signed the report as a lieutenant. Bernard Friedenberg has recently self-published his memoir under the title *Of Being Numerous: World War II as I Saw It*. Brooks was an officer in the supply section and a good friend of Finke's who visited with him while the wounded Finke waited for evacuation.

5   USS *Dorothea Dix*, Action Report, June 14, 1944, Record Group 38, Entry UD351, Box 951, Folder 19; Deck Log, June 6, 1944, Record Group 24, Box 2817, Folder 1; USS *Henrico*, Deck Log, June 6, 1944; 1st Medical Battalion, AAR; Medical Detachment, 16th Infantry Regiment, History; 16th Infantry Regiment, "History of the Invasion of France"; 16th Infantry Regiment, Unit Journal, June 6, 1944; Lieutenant Colonel Herbert Hicks, Lieutenant Colonel Charles Horner, and Captain Lincoln Fish, Comments and Criticism of Operation Neptune, all at National Archives; HMS *Empire Anvil*, AAR and Record of Events; Bonanni, "Medical Support During the Normandy Invasion," pp. 59–63, 69–72, both at USAMHI; Tegtmeyer, unpublished memoir, pp. 11–13; Friedenberg, unpublished memoir,

LOC; Prentiss Kinney, questionnaire, letter to Frances Ward, May 29, 1958, Box 18, Folder 22; Joseph Carlo, questionnaire, letters to Frances Ward and Cornelius Ryan, April 23, 1958, and May 23, 1958, Box 15, Folder 5, all in Ryan Collection, Mahn Center; Joseph McCann, oral history; Ferris Burke, oral history; both at EC; Kellman, oral history, www.military.com; A Company, 1st Medical Battalion, combat interview; Medical Detachment, 16th Infantry Regiment, both at CI-1; 61st Medical Battalion, annual report, 1944, www.history.amedd.army.mil; *Medical Services in the European Theater*, pp. 212–18; Ferris Burke's daughter posted a nice tribute to him at www.fairview.ws; Graves, "Front Line Surgeons," pp. 157–58, 161–62, 164–65; Roger Shoemaker as told to Bill Cannon, "Lasting Impressions of the Longest Day," *World War II*, June 2004, pp. 42–47; Balkoski, *Omaha Beach*, pp. 331–32; Woodage conversations. Captain Emerald Ralston's A Company, 1st Medical Battalion was badly decimated aboard the ill-fated LCI-85. Even so, he and about a dozen of his men managed to land on D-Day evening and link up with Major Tegtemeyer's aid station.

CHAPTER 9: BEACHHEAD

1   745th Tank Battalion, AAR, June 1944; Unit Journal, June 6, 1944, both in Record Group 407, Entry 427, Box 13509, Folder 1; 741st Tank Battalion, AAR, June 1944; Unit Journal, June 6, 1944; E Company, 16th Infantry, History; 16th Infantry Regiment, "History of the Invasion of France"; 336th Engineer Combat Battalion, History, all at National Archives; 745th Tank Battalion, History, pp. 41–43; Eddie Ireland, unpublished memoir, p. 304; Eddie Ireland, oral history; Eddie Ireland, overview of experiences on D-Day; James Krukas, interview with Andrew Woods, no date, Eisenhower Center Oral History Transcripts, Box 1, all at MRC; Spalding questionnaire, Ryan Collection, Mahn Center; Lieutenant Rob Huch, letter to folks, June 29, 1944, EL; E Company, 16th Infantry, combat interview; Spalding, combat interview, both in CI-1; B Company, 745th Tank Battalion, Morning Report, June 6, 1944; E Company, 16th Infantry, Morning Report, June 6, 1944, both in National Personnel Records Center; John Spalding, Medical Report, Wakeman Convalescent Hospital, circa May 1945; Bieder, DiGaetano interviews, all at www.warchronicle.com; Gosselin conversations.

2   USS *Baldwin*, Action Report, June 16, 1944, Record Group 38, Entry UD351, Box 826, Folder 26; Deck Log, June 6, 1944, Record Group 24, Box 695, Folder 4; USS *Emmons*, Action Report, June 22,

1944, Record Group 38, Entry UD351, Box 964, Folder 6; Deck Log, June 6, 1944, Record Group 24, Box 3114, Folder 6; USS *Thompson*, War Diary, June 6, 1944, Record Group 38, Entry UD351, Box 1473, Folder 9; Deck Log, June 6, 1944, Record Group 24, Box 8971, Folder 6; 16th Infantry Regiment, "History of the Invasion of France," all at National Archives; G Company, boat section roster; Dawson interview with Votaw; interview with Woods; interview with Rooney and CBS; Krukas interview; Pilck, oral history, all at MRC; Dawson, oral history, EC; Krumanocker letter, USAMHI; William Washington, questionnaire, letter to Cornelius Ryan, September 2, 1958, Box 12, Folder 50, Ryan Collection, Mahn Center; G Company, 16th Infantry, combat interview, CI-1; G Company, 16th Infantry, Morning Report, June 6, 1944, National Personnel Records Center; USS *Harding*, Action Report, located at www.oo cities.org; Woods, "Dawson's Draw," *Bridgehead Sentinel*; William Kirkland, *Destroyers at Normandy: Naval Gunfire Support at Omaha Beach* (Washington, D.C.: Naval Historical Foundation Publication, 1994), pp. 60–61; Balkoski, *Omaha Beach*, pp. 288–89; Kingseed, *From Omaha Beach to Dawson's Ridge*, pp. 151–52; Gosselin conversations; personal survey of Colleville-sur-Mer, July 2013. I would like to thank Pierre-Louis Gosselin for showing me the location of the G Company positions and pointing out which buildings were hit by the naval fire. The records of the USS *Thompson* are rather confusing. The war diary chronicles the shelling of a church "behind Easy Red" beach, which certainly would indicate the Colleville church. However, a subsequent entry says that the ship then shifted its fire to a building next to the Vierville church, in the 29th Division sector. The Navy's official history, *The Invasion of France and Germany*, authored by the otherwise peerless Samuel Eliot Morison, completely whitewashes the friendly-fire incident at Colleville. On page 146, Morison claims that the shelling wrecked the church steeple and only slightly wounded one French civilian, who was then treated in an American hospital in England.

3 26th Infantry Regiment, AAR, June 1944; Unit Journal, June 6, 1944, both in Record Group 407, Entry 427, Box 5267, Folder 3; Robert Bridges, letter to Army History Division, May 30, 1949, Record Group 319, Entry 72, Box 1, Folder 4, Records of the Army Staff Historical Division, Armed Forces in Action, Omaha Beachhead; 1st Infantry Division, G3 Report; G3 Journal, June 6, 1944; L Company, 16th Infantry, History, all at National Archives; 1st Battalion, 26th Infantry Regiment, History; Warren Coffman, speech for 26th Infantry Regiment Reunion, both in John Gorman Papers,

Box 1; Frank Murdock, interview with John Votaw and Paul Gorman, October 23, 1995, all at MRC; Mel Rush, oral history; Kenneth Romanski, oral history; Thomson, oral history, all at EC; Frank Dulligan, questionnaire, Box 11, Folder 29; Derrill Daniel, questionnaire, Box 11, Folder 27; John Kelly, questionnaire, Box 11, Folder 48; 26th Infantry Regiment, all company morning reports, A through M, including Headquarters, June 6, 1944, all at National Personnel Records Center; Lieutenant Colonel Derrill Daniel, "Landings at Oran, Gela and Omaha Beaches (An Infantry Battalion Commander's Observations)," 1950, p. 27, located at USAMHI; Littlejohn, "UCLA's WWII Casualties," *Daily Breeze*; "May They Never Be Forgotten," *Hooah: Newsletter of the UCLA Department of Military Science*, Fall 2007, p. 6; Warren Coffman, *I Never Intended to Be a Soldier*, self-published, 1999, pp. 60–63; Lefebvre, *They Were on Omaha Beach*, pp. 243–46; Cantigny First Division Foundation, *Blue Spaders: The 26th Infantry Regiment, 1917–1967* (Wheaton, IL: Cantigny Military History Series, 1996), pp. 54–55. Murdock was commander of the 1st Battalion, 26th Infantry. Lieutenant John R. Simons was an alumnus of UCLA, class of 1942. He was one of two UCLA alumni to lose his life on D-Day with the 1st Division. The other was Aaron Dennstedt.

4   USS *Ancon*, Action Report, June 21, 1944, Record Group 38, Entry UD351, Box 808, Folder 3; Deck Log, June 6, 1944, Record Group 24, Box 334, Folder 3; V Corps, G3 Journal, June 6, 1944; 1st Infantry Division, Plans and Orders; G3 Report; G3 Journal, June 6, 1944; *PC-553*, Deck Log; 3rd Battalion, 16th Infantry, AAR; I and L Company Histories; 16th Infantry Regiment, "History of the Invasion of France," all at National Archives; Huebner diary, June 6, 1944; Mason, unpublished memoir, pp. 43–48; "History of the 18th Infantry Regiment"; Downing, unpublished memoir, p. 303; 1st Battalion, 26th Infantry, History, all at MRC; Lieutenant Colonel Robert Pratt, Assistant G3, V Corps, diary, June 6, 1944, V Corps Survey Material, Survey #1391; *PC-553*, Deck Log, June 6, 1944, Robert Rowe Papers, Box 11, Folder 15; Rogers, "Study of Leadership," pp. 68–69, all at USAMHI; Jack Gray, oral history; Saylor, Ellery, Bistrica oral histories, all at EC; Steeg, unpublished memoir, p. 67; Johnson, unpublished memoir, no pagination, both at LOC; Captain Fred Gercke, commander, IPW Team #24, letter to Major Stremlau, June 27, 1944, located in CI-1; C Company, 26th Infantry, Morning Report, June 6, 1944, National Personnel Records Center; Elder, "Operations of the 3rd Battalion, 16th Infantry," pp. 16–20; Chaitt, "D-Day Twenty Years Later," *Bridgehead Sentinel*, Summer

1964, pp. 1–4; Reynolds, unpublished memoir, pp. 21–22; Thomas Meilander, guest book post, November 20, 2003, at www.americandday.org; Omaha Beach tide and sun chart, June 6, 1944, provided to the author by Jordan Edelstein; Coffman, *I Never Intended to Be a Soldier*, pp. 63–64; Lefebvre, *They Were on Omaha Beach*, p. 248; Paul Stillwell, ed., *Assault on Normandy: First-Person Accounts from the Sea Services* (Annapolis, MD: Naval Institute Press, 1994), p. 67; Astor, *Voices of D-Day*, pp. 342–44; Cantigny First Division Foundation, *Blue Spaders*, pp. 54–55; Historical Division, *Omaha Beachhead*, pp. 106–9; Balkoski, *Omaha Beach*, pp. 317–19; Morison, *Invasion of France and Germany*, p. 156; Knickerbocker et al., *Danger Forward*, p. 216; Kilvert-Jones, *Omaha Beach*, pp. 168–70; Gosselin conversations. The action reports and deck logs of the *Ancon* and the *PC-553* document Huebner's movements off the ships and to the beach. The division records pinpoint when he landed.

CHAPTER 10: MEANING

1   1st Infantry Division, G1 AAR, daily casualties, journal, June 6, 1944, Record Group 407, Entry 427, Box 5010, Folder 15; 16th Infantry Regiment, casualty reports, June 6–8, 1944, Record Group 407, Entry 427, Box 5243, Folder 5; Lieutenant Richard Oliphant, oral history, July 10, 1944, Record Group 38, Entry P-11, Box 21, U.S. Navy World War II Oral Histories, all at National Archives; Lieutenant Rob Huch to parents, June 14, 1944, EL; History of the 1st Infantry Division, Stanhope Mason Papers, Box 7, Folder 1; Unit Citation, both at MRC; George "Jeff" Boocks, unpublished memoir, p. 6, MS1892, Box 2, Folder 13, CSWS; 1st Infantry Division, all unit Morning Reports, June 6–10, 1944, National Personnel Records Center; Ernie Pyle, *Brave Men* (New York: Grosset & Dunlap Publishers, 1945), pp. 250–51; Historical Division, *Omaha Beachhead*, pp. 108–10; Balkoski, *Omaha Beach*, pp. 350–52. My personal analysis is based on a study of the division's morning reports, a source I believe is the best available to quantify the actual losses. Still, it is quite possible, even probable, that the reports underestimated the overall casualty numbers, though they differed from the G1 estimate by only seven fewer casualties.

2   Smith, interview with Votaw; McCann, interview with Woods, both at MRC; McCann questionnaire, USAMHI; Wozenski questionnaire, Ryan Collection, Mahn Center; Wozenski interview, IWM; Ellery, oral history, EC; details on Taylor's postwar life can be found

at www.firstdivisionmuseum.org; DiGaetano interview, Spalding Medical Report, Spalding, Streczyk personal profiles at www .warchronicle.com; the marriage of Phil Streczk to Sophie Karanewsky is corroborated in the 2002 obituary of one of their daughters at www.recordonline.com; Daviess County, Kentucky, John Spalding Death Certificate, November 9, 1959; John Spalding personal and family information, all in author's possession courtesy of Jim Erickson and Tina Gerteisen; "No Place Like Old United States, Much Decorated Sergeant Says," no date, no author, copy in author's possession; "First Owensboran to Receive Distinguished Service Cross Home on 30-Day Sick Leave," no author, *Owensboro Messenger-Inquirer*, May 27, 1945; "Mrs. John M. Spalding, 36, is Charged with Killing Husband: World War II Hero Shot to Death in Home," no author, *Owensboro Messenger-Inquirer*, November 7, 1959; Glenn Hodges, "Owensboro's War Hero: Lt. John Martin Spalding's Actions on and after D-Day Brought Honor to Him and His Company"; Glenn Hodges, "Spalding Received Distinguished Service Cross from Eisenhower," both in *Owensboro Messenger-Inquirer*, June 27, 1999; Greg Kocher, "Owensboro Man Praised in Book about D-Day Invasion," *Owensboro Messenger-Inquirer*, no date; Stanley Streczyk, conversation with the author, June 13, 2013; Ron Streczyk, conversation with the author, July 20, 2013; Kingseed, *From Omaha Beach to Dawson's Ridge*, pp. 241–46. Stanley Streczyk told me that his father did not get along well with Spalding or think highly of him. In the absence of other firsthand corroboration, I decided to omit that from the main text. Stanley's younger brother, Ron, related a story his mother had told him about his father. After D-Day, during the Normandy fighting, one of Tech Sergeant Streczyk's men was severely wounded in a firefight. The stricken soldier's jaw was gone and he begged for death. The sergeant obliged and put him out of his misery. Later he felt guilty about it. As with the story of friction with Spalding, I have elected to leave this detail out of the main text for lack of corroboration. If true, perhaps it explains some of Streczyk's postwar struggles.

3   Plitt, Lessons Learned, June 30, 1944, National Archives; Captain Joe Dawson, letter to family, June 30, 1944, 16th Infantry Regiment Association Collection, Box 191, Folder 2; Fuller, "Recollections of D-Day"; Downing, unpublished memoir, p. 289, all at MRC; Friedenberg, unpublished memoir, no pagination, LOC; John C. McManus, *The Deadly Brotherhood: The American Combat Soldier in World War II* (New York: Ballantine Books, 2003); Knickerbocker et al., *Danger Forward*, p. 217; Cantigny First Division Foundation, *Blue*

Spaders, p. 55; Kilvert-Jones, *Omaha Beach*, pp. 6–7. Eisenhower made his Praetorian Guard remark on July 2, 1944, when he decorated twenty-two 1st Division men with the Distinguished Service Cross. The recipients included Wyman, Taylor, Hicks, Tegtmeyer, Richmond, Dawson, Merendino, Spalding, Colwell, Strojny, Streczyk, and Gallagher.

PAGE ONE
Major General Clarence Huebner (McCormick Research Center)
Brigadier General Willard Wyman (McCormick Research Center)

PAGE TWO
Colonel George Taylor (McCormick Research Center)
Captains Kimball Richmond, John Finke, and Edward Wozenski
(McCormick Research Center)

PAGE THREE
C Company, 16th Infantry Regiment, landing at Easy Red beach
(National Archives)
Boat section heading toward Easy Red beach (National Archives)

PAGE FOUR
Easy Red beach about an hour after the first landings (National Archives)
Medic moves along the cliffs at Fox Green beach (National Archives)

PAGE FIVE
Soldiers pinned down at waterline (Photograph by Robert Capa, Courtesy
of Magnum Photos)
Easy Red beach and ridgeline (Photograph by Robert Capa, Courtesy of
Magnum Photos)

PAGE SIX
Looking west on Fox Green beach (McCormick Research Center)
Heavy machine gun team moving along the cliffside (McCormick Research
Center)
Dead soldiers at Fox Green beach (McCormick Research Center)

PAGE SEVEN
Shingle bank, looking east (Cornelius Ryan Collection, Ohio University)
Shingle bank, looking west (Cornelius Ryan Collection, Ohio University)

PAGE EIGHT
Soldiers huddling under cliffs (McCormick Research Center)
Modern-day view of cliffs (Nancy McManus)
Aftermath at Easy Red beach (McCormick Research Center)

PAGE NINE
Flooded antitank ditch (McCormick Research Center)

Diagram of German obstacles (McCormick Research Center)
Aerial view of Omaha beach on D-Day (National Archives)

PAGE TEN
Lieutenant Jimmie Monteith (National Archives)
T/5 John "Joe" Pinder (National Archives)
Private Joe Argenzio (Paul Woodage)
Sergeant Fred Bisco (www.warchronicle.com)

PAGE ELEVEN
Lieutenant John Spalding (McCormick Research Center)
Spalding after the war (www.warchronicle.com)
Tech Sergeant Phil Streczyk (www.warchronicle.com)

PAGE TWELVE
E-1 exit overlooking Easy Red beach (McCormick Research Center)
Path through the minefields (www.warchronicle.com)
Remnants of the church at Colleville-sur-Mer (National Archives)

PAGE THIRTEEN
After the battle (McCormick Research Center)
88-millimeter gun casemate at WN-61 (Nancy McManus)

PAGE FOURTEEN
Eisenhower and Bradley decorating 1st Infantry Division soldiers
(McCormick Research Center)
Private Carlton Barrett receiving Medal of Honor (National Archives)

PAGE FIFTEEN
Pillbox at WN-65 today (Nancy McManus)
Rebuilt church at Colleville-sur-Mer (Nancy McManus)
Farm complex across from Colleville-sur-Mer (Nancy McManus)

PAGE SIXTEEN
View today from Easy Red beach (Nancy McManus)
Easy Red beach, from the perspective of WN-62 (Nancy McManus)
Panoramic view of Omaha beach (Nancy McManus)

INDEX

Courtesy of the author

JOHN C. MCMANUS earned a PhD in American and Military History from the University of Tennessee, where he served as Assistant Director of the Center for the Study of War and Society and was a Normandy Scholar. As a leading authority on the Normandy invasion, he holds a Cantigny First Division Museum Fellowship. He is currently a full professor of U.S. Military History at Missouri University of Science and Technology, where he teaches a variety of courses, including one on World War II and another on the Modern American Combat Experience. He also serves as the official historian for the United States Army's Seventh Infantry Regiment.

CONNECT ONLINE

johncmcmanus.com